DATE DUE

OC 17 '02			
NOV 13 2002			

THE ENCYCLOPEDIA OF Figure Skating

The author and Facts On File, Inc.
would like to acknowledge the World Figure Skating Museum & Hall of Fame
in Colorado Springs, Colorado for its invaluable contributions to this encyclopedia.
Both Beth Davis, the museum's curator, and Karen Cover, a dedicated volunteer,
have generously shared their time and expertise, for which we sincerely thank them.

R

THE ENCYCLOPEDIA OF

Figure Skating

John Malone

Facts On File, Inc.

The Encyclopedia of Figure Skating

Facts On File, Inc.
11 Penn Plaza
New York NY 10001

Library of Congress Cataloging-in-Publication Data

Malone, John Williams
The encyclopedia of figure skating / by John Malone.
p. cm.
ISBN 0-8160-3226-2 (hardcover : alk. paper). — ISBN 0-8160-3796-5
(pb. : alk. paper)
1. Skating—Encyclopedias. I. Title.
GV849.M34 1998
796.91'2'03—dc21 97-46360

Text design by Cathy Rincon
Cover design by Semadar Megged
Illustration on page 170 by Dale Williams

Printed in the United States of America

MP FOF 10 9 8 7 6 5 4 3 2
(pb) 10 9 8 7 6 5 4 3

This book is printed on acid-free paper.

Contents

This book is dedicated

to the memory of

Maribel Vinson Owen

and her daughters

Maribel and Laurence Owen

Introduction

My first memorable encounter with figure skating came in 1947, when I was eight years old. It came with a trip from Andover, Massachusetts, 25 miles north of Boston where I grew up, to see the Ice Capades at Boston Garden. The stars of the show, as had been the case for several years and would continue for another decade, were the 1942 United States Men's Champion, Bobby Specht, and Donna Atwood, who had been Pairs Champion with Eugene Turner in 1941. I was excited by the lavish production numbers and laughed at the clowns on ice, but it was the skating itself that hooked me from the start.

The following year, I read everything I could find in newspapers and magazines about the renewed Winter Olympics taking place in St. Moritz, Switzerland, where America's Dick Button and Canada's Barbara Ann Scott took the individual Gold Medals. Later, I saw them both skate in person, as I would dozens of other Olympic, World and United States champions in the decades to come. A lifelong passion for the sport had been born.

In 1951, a new artificial (but outdoor) skating rink was built by Phillips Academy Andover, where my father taught American history, and although it was principally used for hockey, it was decided to offer figure skating lessons one night a week to faculty, townspeople and their children. The teacher engaged was one of the great figures in the history of the sport, Maribel Vinson Owen, who had been Ladies' Champion of the United States nine times and Pairs Champion six times with two different partners. She had never managed to beat Sonja Henie for the World or Olympic Gold Medal, although there were those who thought she should have, but she had won World Silver and Bronze Medals and Olympic Bronze from the 1932 Games at Lake Placid, New York.

Although I had been skating all my life on hockey skates, I was already too old to start figure skating seriously and took only ice dance lessons from Maribel. But my sister Heath, four years younger, was seriously involved and eventually became the New England Juvenile Champion before deciding, to Maribel's dismay, that she didn't have the dedication to shoot for the top. But as a result of the years my sister did take lessons, I found myself hanging around rinks in Boston and other Massachusetts cities, and I got to know many future American champions in the process.

I also became very close to Maribel and her two daughters, Maribel Jr. (whom everybody called Little Maribel even after she grew taller than her mother) and little Laurence, whom I watched develop into one of the most beautiful free-skaters I have ever seen. I also spent a lot of time talking to Maribel's mother, Mrs. Vinson, who had been at rinkside (or on the ice as a casual skater) for nearly a half-century and who had wonderful stories to tell about the great skaters of the past. I sometimes spent a night or two at Maribel's home in Winchester, Massachusetts, took Little Maribel to my senior prom at Andover and saw a lot of the family even after my sister stopped taking lessons.

I was a senior at Harvard when the plane carrying the entire United States World Figure Skating Team crashed at Brussels, Belgium in 1961. I knew almost every skater and coach killed in that crash, but it was the loss of Maribel and her daughters that was most devastating. Just days earlier, Laurence had become U.S. Ladies' Champion at 16—the youngest winner since her mother in 1928—and Little Maribel had won the Pairs Championship with her partner Dudley Richards, to whom she had recently become engaged.

The death of Maribel and her daughters affected me deeply, but the love of figure skating they had nurtured in me continued unabated. Looking back over nearly 50 years of thrilling moments, there are so many great skaters and extraordinary performances to cherish that it is difficult to single out the peak experiences. But there are some who left a special mark. In 1956, Hayes Alan Jenkins, Ronnie Robertson and David Jenkins finished first, second and third at both the Olympics and World Championships, and an injured Tenley Albright, whom Maribel coached, still managed to become America's first woman to win an Olympic Gold Medal in figure skating, while Carol Heiss took the Silver.

I recall with special pleasure the perfection of England's John Curry in the 1976 Olympics and World Championships and the 1988 duel between the two Brians, Boitano of the United States and Orser of Canada. As an American, I was thrilled by the Olympic victories of Peggy Fleming, Dorothy Hamill, Scott Hamilton and Kristi Yamaguchi, but in Pairs and Ice Dancing I have to admit a special regard for two foreign couples, the Soviet Union's Ludmila and Oleg Protopopov in Pairs, and Great Britain's Jayne Torvill and Christopher Dean in Ice Dancing; both couples achieved sheer poetry in motion.

Yet some of the most memorable performances I have witnessed have not brought Gold Medals. The endless pluck with which the enchanting Janet Lynn sought an ever-elusive World Championship or the Olympic Silver Medal performance of Paul Wylie in 1992, when he finally conquered his nerves and lived up to his talents, offer their own unique rewards. There are times when skaters one has watched for years simply give the best performances of their lives without winning any medal at all that give us memories to cherish.

This encyclopedia, obviously, was for me a labor of love. It is a reference book first and foremost, of course, packed with the kind of information such a book requires. But I hope that fans of the sport, new and old, will find reading it a pleasure as well. All the skaters whose names appear in it are medalists, but it should be said that I also have the deepest respect for those who never won a major competition but nevertheless gave great joy to those of us watching them strive for the best that was in them.

NOTE: Because this is the first full-scale biographical encyclopedia of figure skating, there were serious difficulties in ascertaining the death dates, and sometimes even the birth dates, of some earlier or lesser-known skaters. The author and publisher welcome any information that readers can provide concerning such dates (or other factual material) and will try to include such data in future editions.

A

ACKLES, MARGIE *(b. 1939) U.S. Ice Dance Champion with Charles Phillips (b. 1938).*

Margie Ackles and Charles Phillips won the Silver Medal in Ice Dancing at the U.S. Championships in 1959 behind repeat champions Andrée Anderson Jacoby and her husband, Donald Jacoby. They finished 4th at that year's World Championships; the Jacobys became Silver Medalists. In 1960, Ackles and Phillips succeeded the Jacobys as U.S. Champions and again came in 4th at the World's. Having achieved their main goal of becoming U.S. Gold Medalists, they retired from amateur competition.

ADAIR, DONALD *See* ROCA, RENEE.

AHRENS, JANETTE *(b. 1923) U.S. medalist both in Pairs and as a solo skater.*

Janette Ahrens' first U.S. medal came in Pairs when she took the Silver Medal with partner Robert Upgren (b. 1922) in 1942, behind Doris Schubach and Walter Noffke. The same order of finish occurred in 1943, but that year Ahrens also took the Bronze Medal in the Ladies' competition behind Gretchen Merrill and Dorothy Goos. When Robert Upgren retired, Ahrens teamed up with Arthur Preusch to win a third Pairs Silver Medal in 1944, again placing 2nd to Schubach and Noffke.

Ahrens then concentrated on solo skating and won the Silver Medal behind Gretchen Merrill in 1945, 1946 and 1947. In 1947, as World Championship competition resumed, she finished 6th.

ALBRIGHT, TENLEY *(b. 1935) U.S., World and Olympic Champion.*

At the age of nine, Tenley Albright got her first pair of real figure skates. Although she was soon spotted at the Skating Club of Boston by Maribel Vinson Owen, nine-time U.S. Champion between the late 1920s and the late 1930s, Albright had no interest in skating seriously, disdaining the school figures she would eventually become so good at. In 1946, she contracted nonparalytic polio and was in the hospital for several weeks. Her doctors and her father, Hollis Albright, a Boston surgeon, urged her to do more skating to strengthen her weakened muscles. Her back and shoulders had been particularly affected; in overcoming that disability she developed the most erect carriage of perhaps any figure skater, which gave her skating a special elegance.

She won her first Senior U.S. Championship medal, the Silver, behind Sonya Klopfer in 1951 and then took 6th place at the World Championships. In 1952, Albright became U.S. Champion and gained the Silver Medal at the Olympics in Oslo, Norway. She was unable to skate at the World's that year because of an injury but became

Olympic Gold Medalist Tenley Albright was the epitome of grace.
(Courtesy World Figure Skating Museum)

World Champion the following year, narrowly beating Gundi Busch of East Germany. In 1954, Busch turned the tables, took the Gold and then retired. Albright now had to contend with fellow American Carol Heiss, who came in 2nd at the U.S. Championships in 1953–55 and took the Silver at the World's behind Albright in 1955.

Carol Heiss had a more outgoing personality than Albright and often smiled broadly while performing her free-skating program. Albright's coach Maribel Owen had always been frustrated by Tenley's reserve: Skaters from that period remember Owen standing at the side of the rink during practice sessions bellowing, "Smile," at the top of her lungs. In the long run it worked: Albright smiled, it was said, simply to get her coach to shut up.

The year 1958 would bring three confrontations between Tenley Albright and Carol Heiss: the Olympics, the World's and finally the U.S. Championships. The skating world believed that the two Americans would finish 1st and 2nd at all three competitions, but there was insecurity as to the order. Most skaters were rooting for Albright to crown her career with an Olympic Gold Medal.

While practicing for the Olympics at Cortina d'Ampezzo, Italy, Albright hit a bump in the ice of the outdoor arena, tripped and opened a two-inch gash in her calf with her own skate. It was front-page news in Boston, and her father immediately flew to Italy to oversee his daughter's recovery. The major question was how much the injury might affect her performance.

Slim and willowy, Tenley Albright had a loveliness on the ice that seemed almost fragile, but she also had a great deal of grit and focus. Aside from her skating, she was a pre-med honor student at Radcliffe. During the Olympic competition, she as usual took first place in the school figures. In those days a single axel was the most difficult jump women did. (The first double axel in competition was performed only five years earlier by Dick Button.) Could Albright land her axel securely on her injured leg? She could and did and had no difficulty with the trademark stag jump that photographers always asked her to perform for the camera. As always, her extremely musical and flowing program was marked by the extraordinary grace that caused more than one period skating expert to proclaim that she did for skating what Pavlova did for ballet.

But the battle for the Gold was not over. Carol Heiss skated with her usual strength and verve and received slightly higher marks in the free-skating, which counted 40 percent against 60 percent for the school figures. The judges awarded the Olympic Gold Medal to Albright and the Silver to Heiss.

At the World Championships at Garmisch, East Germany, Albright's leg still hurt, and there was no doubt some psychological letdown after winning the Olympics. At Garmisch, Heiss prevailed, narrowly gaining the first of her five successive World Championships. Albright immediately embraced her warmly—and then beat Heiss again at the U.S. Championships in Philadelphia to take her fifth successive U.S. title.

Albright skated professionally on a limited basis so that she could repay her father the $50,000 he had spent on her skating career—a sum that would cover only a couple of years' expenses today. She earned her medical degree at Harvard and is today a distinguished Boston surgeon, just as her father had been.

Tenley Albright was the first American woman to win either an Olympic or a World Gold Medal in skating. Although the technical difficulties of her free-skating programs were second to none in her day, they pale behind the herculean feats that women skaters now perform. Nevertheless, numerous skating experts who have watched the sport of figure skating for 50 years or more comment that while there have been greater women skaters, there was never anyone whom it was more of a pleasure to watch moving across the ice.

ALLEN, LISA-MARIE *(b. 1958) U.S. medalist.*

As Linda Fratianne won her second U.S. Championship in 1978, Lisa-Marie Allen became the Silver Medalist and repeated as runner-up to Fratianne for the next two years. Allen was 7th at the World Championships in 1978, 6th in 1979 and 7th again in 1980; she finished best at the 1980 Olympics in Lake Placid, New York, coming in 5th.

ALLEN, SCOTT *(b. 1946) U.S. Champion.*

In the aftermath of the Brussels airplane crash of 1961 that killed the entire U.S. World Figure Skating Team, many predicted that it might be a decade before U.S. skaters would again challenge for World and Olympic medals, a far too pessimistic estimate. Scotty Allen, the first to prove it, became the U.S. Junior Champion in 1961 at age 15. Moving up to the senior ranks in 1962, he took the U.S. Silver Medal behind the older Monty Hoyt and repeated in that position the following year behind Thomas Litz, another older skater, finishing 8th and 5th at the World Championships in those two years.

Topping both Litz and Hoyt, Allen became U.S. Champion in 1964 and won an Olympic Bronze Medal in Innsbruck, Austria only three years after the Brussels crash had killed the great American hopes Bradley Lord and Gregory Kelley. At the 1964 World's he placed 4th, but the following year, despite losing his U.S. Championship to Gary Visconti, he gave his best competitive performance ever to take the World Silver Medal, while Visconti placed 6th in a bad outing. Regaining his national title in 1966, Allen was 4th at the World's, while Visconti took the Bronze Medal. In 1967, his final year of amateur skating, Allen won the U.S. Silver Medal again and took 5th at the World Championships. Although his amateur career was less successful at the end, the Olympic Bronze he won in 1964 remained a special achievement in terms of lifting the overall morale of U.S. figure skaters.

ALTWEGG, JEANNETTE *(b. 1930) British Olympic Gold Medalist.*

Jeannette Altwegg was such a fine athlete that in her mid-teens she had to make a choice between the two sports at which she excelled, tennis and figure skating. She realized that either sport would demand her undivided attention if she was to become a champion. After narrowly losing the Junior finals at Wimbledon in 1946, Altwegg decided to concentrate on skating. The following year, she became the British Ladies Champion. Altwegg's coach, Swiss taskmaster Jacques Gerschwiler, began to teach in London in the 1930s; he cultivated Altwegg's superlative school figures, which then counted for 60 percent in competition, until they were more than enough to compensate for a relative weakness in free-skating.

Altwegg took Olympic Bronze in 1948 and the World Bronze in 1949, the Silver in 1950 and both the European and World Gold Medals in 1951. At the 1952 Olympics in Oslo, Norway, she beat out

America's Tenley Albright and France's Jaqueline du Bief, both better free-skaters, for the Gold Medal. There had been only one British woman to capture Olympic Gold before her—Madge Syers in 1908—and there has been none since.

AMATEUR STANDING

Although the importance of amateur standing was stated in the rules established by the International Skating Union at the end of the 19th century, it was largely taken for granted until the 1930s, when British-stage ice shows began to proliferate and Shipstad and Johnson's Ice Follies appeared in America in 1936. That year, three-time Olympic Gold Medalist from Norway Sonja Henie turned professional and was soon making movies. With the performance of skating routines now a business, the question of amateur standing became much more central.

For the next several decades, the rules were simple: If you were paid for performing a skating routine, you were no longer an amateur and could not compete in national or World Championships or the Olympics. Olympic rules were particularly stringent: When it was discovered after the 1960 Olympics that Silver Medalists in Pairs Marika Kilius and Hans Jurgen Baumler of West Germany had signed an Ice Capades contract just before the games, they were officially stripped of their medals. They said that they had no idea that simply signing a contract would end their amateur status because they had not yet skated professionally. Most records still show them as the Silver Medal winners. No action was taken against them concerning their World Silver Medal the same year.

At that time, expenses could be paid to skaters who appeared in fund-raising exhibitions, but the fees could cover travel, hotel accommodations and meals only. Yet, a difficulty had already become glaringly apparent: The skaters from the Soviet Union and the Eastern-bloc countries were entirely subsidized by the state, while in the Western democracies skaters had to find wealthy patrons to support them if their parents were not rich enough to foot the bills for an increasingly expensive sport.

To compensate for this disparity, national figure-skating organizations began to give grants to financially needy skaters, but the grants were not large enough to take up the slack entirely; other sources often had to be found. In 1981, for instance, the city of Nottingham, England made an official grant to its native-born skaters Jayne Torvill and Christopher Dean to carry them through the 1984 Olympics. In America, young Indiana brother-and-sister Pair Natalie and Wayne Seybold, who won two U.S. Silver and two Bronze Medals, were able to keep on competing only because the small town they came from created a private fund to pay their expenses.

In 1956, the first American woman to win an Olympic Gold Medal in figure skating, Tenley Albright entered Harvard Medical School, but also announced that she had contracted to make limited appearances with the Ice Capades to pay her surgeon father back for the more than $50,000 he had spent on her amateur career. (These days, that amount would cover less than two years of expenses for a top competitor.) A new approach was clearly necessary.

New rules were put in effect following the 1988 Olympics. Because longtime professional basketball players, among others, were now to play in the Olympics, skating officials obviously had a mandate to relax the restrictions on the income of amateur skaters. The officials decided to allow amateur skaters to be paid for some appearances, including television commercials, but the ever-conservative officials were determined to keep a fairly tight rein on such funds: A skater could be paid only for approved appearances—which did not include big-money contracts with shows like the Ice Capades—and the purse strings for such money, as well as commercial endorsements earnings, were still to be controlled by national skating associations. Skaters had to request funds from escrow accounts, and their expenditures were closely monitored. A few skaters, such as Kurt Browning of Canada, already well into his 20s, were given control over their own earnings, but these cases were rare and close monitoring continued.

As some skating officials had predicted from the start, the barn door was now open: Reinstatement for Olympic competition open to former champions who had earned huge sums as professionals was another step toward completely open competition. That few of the former champions did well at the 1994 Olympics was an embarrassment that may serve to curb other pro skaters, but it is clear that the line between amateur and professional is being steadily eroded. In February 1995, for example, the International Skating Union announced that it was considering giving prize money, drawn from the large fees the ISU receives for television rights, to skaters in amateur competitions. That would obviously be the end of amateurism as it has long been understood.

ANDERSON, ANDRÉE

See JACOBY, DONALD.

ANDERSON, JACK AND MARY

(b. 1924, 1926) U.S. Ice Dancers.

In a period largely dominated by older couples, this young brother-and-sister team took the Bronze Medal in Ice Dancing at the 1944 U.S. Championships, the first ever held in Minneapolis, Minnesota.

ANISSINA, MARINA

(b. 1975) French ice dancer, national champion and Olympic Pairs medalist with Gwendel Peizerat (b. 1972).

After placing 10th at the 1994 World Championships, Marina Anissina and Gwendel Peizerat took 2nd place at the French Nationals and moved up to 6th place at the World's the following year. By 1996 they had become French National Champions and took 4th place at the World's. In 1998 Anissina and Peizerat took Olympic Bronze at Nagano, behind Gold Medalists Pasha Grishuk and Evgeny Platov and Silver Medalists Anjelika Krylova and Oleg Ovsiannikov.

ARNOLD, SIDNEY

(b. 1933) U.S. Ice Dance medalist with Franklin Nelson (b. 1933).

In a tight contest, Sidney Arnold and Franklin Nelson took the Bronze Medal in Ice Dancing at the 1956 U.S. Championships behind Joan Zamboni and Roland Junso (Gold) and Carmel and Edward Bodel (Silver). How closely matched these couples were was further demonstrated at that year's World Championships, in which Zamboni/Junso were 4th, the Bodels 6th and Arnold and Nelson 7th.

ARTIFICIAL ICE

Although speed skating flourished on frozen rivers, ponds and canals in Nordic countries from the 17th century on, figure skating did not begin to gain widespread popularity until the invention of artificial ice and covered (if not enclosed) rinks. For one thing, the fundamental variations on the figure eight known as school figures, the crucial element in early figure-skating competitions, required fresh smooth ice to be properly laid down.

Numerous experiments in producing artificial ice began in the 1840s. The first known skating rink was established in New York City in 1870, a specially designed building with tubes on the floor that contained a mixture of ammonia in gaseous form, ether and carbonic acid; when flooded, this mixture generated sufficient cold to freeze the water. But there were flaws in the process and the venture collapsed. Another attempt in Manchester, England in 1876 flopped because it created such an intense, damp cold that it suffused the rink with the equivalent of a London fog. More successful efforts were launched during the next 20 years in England, Germany and France; by the turn of the century, skating rinks became more and more commonplace in Europe and North America.

In time, however, a strange dichotomy between practice and competition skating developed: Almost all skaters trained at indoor rinks; yet World and Olympic competitions were often held outdoors, even though the ice might be artificial. Although the reason for this was couched in terms of noble tradition, the real reason was money: An outdoor rink, especially one that had to accommodate large crowds, was much cheaper to build than an indoor stadium. The results were sometimes ridiculous. Highly trained champion skaters found themselves laying down school figures whose patterns were almost immediately obliterated by falling snow; during the free-skating portion, entrants sometimes had to compete against gale-force winds rather than each other as a sudden gust literally picked up and threw skaters in midjump to the ice.

In 1967, the International Skating Union finally decreed that all future World and Olympic competitions would be held in indoor arenas.

ASH, LUCILLE *See* KOTHMAN, SULLY.

ATWOOD, DONNA *(b. 1932) U.S. Pairs Champion and Ice Capades star.*

At the age of 19, Donna Atwood became U.S. Pairs Champion as the partner of Eugene Turner, who also won the Men's Championship as he had the year before. She was immediately signed by John H. Harris' newly formed Ice Capades. The next year, Bobby Specht, who had taken the Bronze Medal in Pairs in 1941 with Joan Mitchell and had become National Men's Champion in 1942, was also signed by the Ice Capades. For the next 15 years, Atwood and Specht were the stars of the centerpiece story spectacle mounted each year by the company. Each year brought a new centerpiece, based on fairy tales such as Cinderella and Sleeping Beauty or such operettas as Sigmund Romberg's *The Student Prince.* These lavishly produced numbers for the entire company were scaled-down half-hour versions of the kind of full-length "ice ballet" that had been popular for many years as stage extravaganzas at vast theaters in England such as the London Hippodrome.

Donna Atwood was very pretty in a style then popular in Hollywood (she looked like a fluffier Rita Hayworth), and both she and Specht, who had matinee-idol looks himself, were adept at projecting themselves to the back rows of such arenas as New York's Madison Square Garden. Both fine skaters, their Pairs experience made it possible for them to perform a variety of lifts that, while not particularly taxing, gave a good deal of skating authenticity to the romantic characters they portrayed.

In the 1950s, the Ice Capades began to feature such special guests as Olympic Gold Medal winners Dick Button and Tenley Albright, but they appeared only in the largest cities. Across the rest of the country, a visit from the Ice Capades focused on Donna Atwood and Bobby Specht, the exemplars of a kind of professional skater that no longer exists—skating actors who in their way demonstrated a show-biz conviction quite different from the more technically challenging skating performances of a Dorothy Hamill or a Brian Boitano in their occasional forays into story ice ballets.

AXEL

Often called "the king of jumps" because of the height and distance achieved when it is properly executed, the axel is the oldest of the major free-skating jumps. It is named for its inventor, Norwegian speed and stunt skater Axel Paulsen. Paulsen was known as "the fastest human on skates" in the 1870s, but his name is not found in record books because international competition had not yet begun. In the 1880s Paulsen toured Europe giving exhibitions, and it was during this period that he devised the jump that carries his name.

Because Paulsen wore speed skates, which do not have the special characteristics that allow skating on two separate edges, the jump he performed was undoubtedly much cruder than what we recognize as an axel today. An axel is easily identified by a spectator because it is the only jump launched while the performer is skating forward. The skater gathers speed while skating backward but then turns to take off from the forward outside edge of the jumping leg. The leg is bent at the knee as the skater enters the jump but must be fully straightened before takeoff to gain the full thrust from the thigh muscles. The left leg is used for the takeoff, one-and-a-half revolutions are completed in the air and the landing is made on the outside edge of the right skate going backward, with the free left leg pulled through and extended behind the skater.

The axel was a mainstay of the competitive male skater's repertoire from the turn of the century but not commonly attempted by women until the late 1920s. There was always talk about adding an additional revolution in the air to create a double axel, but this was not to become a reality until Dick Button achieved the feat in 1951. The double axel is not quite two times an axel because that would mean landing on a forward edge and distorting the characteristic profile of the jump. Rather, the skater takes off as in doing a single axel from a forward left outside edge, completes two-and-one-half revolutions in the air and lands on the back right outside edge.

It took another quarter-century to achieve a triple axel, which adds one more full revolution in the air with the same forward takeoff and backward landing. Vern Taylor of Canada was the first to perform it in competition at the 1978 World Championships. He never won a World or Olympic medal, but he will always have a place in the *The Guinness Book of Records* for this accomplishment. Many other men soon made the jump part of their programs, and it became a requisite element for any would-be champion. To date, the triple axel has been landed in competition by only two women, Midori Ito of Japan and Tonya Harding of the United States, although neither of them has been able to do it consistently.

B

BABILONIA, TAI *(b. 1960) U.S. and World Pairs Champion with Randy Gardner (b. 1958).*

Tai Babilonia and Randy Gardner, originally brought together when still children because Tai was the only girl shorter than Randy, developed a bond that fueled one of the great American skating partnerships. Becoming National Junior Pair Champions in 1973 when Babilonia was only 13 and Gardner 15, their strength of talent earned them the 1974 U.S. Silver Medal, a rare leap from the Junior ranks to the top echelon of the Senior skating hierarchy. They were 2nd that year and again in 1975 to the very experienced Melissa Militano and Johnny Johns. At first Babilonia and Gardner did not make as great an impact internationally, finishing 10th in both the 1974 and 1975 World Championships.

Winning the national title in 1976 at 16 and 18, the two now began to impress the international judges, placing 5th at both the Olympics and the World's that year. Easily retaining their national title in 1977, they became the first American Pair in five years to win a World medal, taking the Bronze, as JoJo Starbuck and Kenneth Shelley had in 1971 and 1972. The World Champion in 1977 as in 1971–72 was Irina Rodnina of the Soviet Union, who had been winning for nine consecutive years, first with Alexsei Ulanov and now with Alexandr Zaitsev.

By this time, Babilonia and Gardner had carved out a special niche in Pair skating, which British skating expert Howard Bass summed up: "Always exciting and more theatrical than most to watch, they are highly creative and have introduced a number of new sequences which others have failed to match in quality." As great skaters always do, they were extending their discipline's vocabulary, generating new moves that were becoming a benchmark for younger skaters. Of their exemplary technical proficiency, no other pair of the period, not even the masterful Rodnina and Zaitsev, could match their mastery in side-by-side moves; the timing on the jumps and spins they performed separately was always to the split second and they were also the first to perform triple throw jumps. The two were very evenly matched in height, and although Randy Gardner looked very slim, he had become very strong through weight training.

In 1978, in their third year as U.S. Champions, they repeated as World Bronze Medalists. Then in 1979, when Rodnina and Zaitsev, who had married, took a year off, Babilonia and Gardner beat back challenges by the up-and-coming Soviet Pair Marina Cherkosova and Sergei Shakhrai and by Sabine Baess and Tassilo Theirbach of East Germany to become World Champions. They broke a string of 14 Soviet victories in Pairs and became the second U.S. Pair ever to win the World Gold Medal—the sister-and-brother Pair Karol and Peter Kennedy

Tai Babilonia and Randy Gardner during their professional career.
(Courtesy Michael Rosenberg)

had done it 29 years earlier, in 1950. Some said that the absence of Rodnina and Zaitsev gave them their World title, but the judges' marks told a different story: Babilonia and Gardner's scores were slightly higher than the Soviets had achieved the previous year.

One of the great Pair shoot-outs for the Gold Medal was expected with Rodnina and Zaitsev's return for a final competition at the 1980 Olympics in Lake Placid, New York but it was not to be. Randy Gardner injured his groin in the early winter and had to take time off from skating, although he seemed fine as the couple won their fourth U.S. Championship in January. But he may have come back too soon: As the Olympics began, his groin injury worsened. A shot of pain killers right before the Short Program competition only made matters worse: His leg became numb and he fell heavily on his warm-up jumps. With Babilonia weeping and the largely American audience at Lake Placid in shock, the couple was forced to withdraw. Rodnina and Zaitsev took the Gold Medal, the third Olympic victory for Rodnina.

After this grave disappointment, Babilonia and Gardner signed a three-year contract with the Ice Capades. She was haunted by the Olympic debacle, however, taking it harder than he, even though it had been in no way her fault. They kept performing, but by 1988, when they were with Festival on Ice in Las Vegas, Tai Babilonia had become addicted to sleeping pills and alcohol. She quit skating, got the help she needed, was back on the ice with Gardner the next year. As time wore on, Tai Babilonia was able to see, as Randy Gardner always had, that however disappointing the Olympic withdrawal was, they had achieved a kind of success given to only a few and that their triumphs were meant to be celebrated.

BACK FLIP

This spectacular backward somersault is often used in show and exhibition skating but has been disallowed in amateur competition.

The skater must work up considerable speed before turning backward; the takeoff is made from both feet as the skater crouches over the ice and then explodes upward and over, landing again on both feet. The skater is necessarily bent over while landing, but the speed with which an upright position is regained after landing has much to do with the effectiveness of the stunt.

Because it does not make use of the edges of the figure-skate blade, the back flip can also be performed wearing hockey skates. Essentially a gymnastic or circus move, it has a long history in ice shows, where it was usually performed by skating clowns or daredevil, barrel-jumping artists.

At the 1976 World Championships, U.S. Men's Champion Terry Kubicka performed a back flip. The International Skating Union immediately moved to ban it from competition, supposedly because it was too dangerous, but the fact that it did not make use of the skating edges also offended purists. Top skaters still use it in ice-show performances or professional skating competitions, where it is allowed: Former Olympic Gold Medalists Robin Cousins and Scott Hamilton both do it with great effect to the delight of audiences.

The only woman who performs it is French World Silver Medalist Surya Bonaly, who has a gymnastics background. She has been severely reprimanded for using it during competition warm-ups, however, where it could indeed be dangerous, as well as distracting, to other skaters.

BADGER, SHERWIN *(1900–82) U.S. Men's and Pairs Champion and a premier figure in U.S. figure skating's early history.*

Sherwin Badger took his first U.S. figure-skating medal in 1918, the Silver in Pairs with Clara Frothingham. No competition was held in 1919, but Badger came back in 1920 to win the Pairs Silver Medal with a new partner, Edith Rotch. That year he also became the U.S. Men's Champion, a title he retained through 1924. No American men competed in the World Championships until 1928; that year, Badger returned to competitive skating after a four-year absence to form a Pairs team with Beatrix Loughran, the U.S. Ladies' Champion of 1925–27. Given a World Team berth despite their lack of a U.S. title, they finished 5th.

In 1930, Badger and Loughran won the U.S. Pairs Gold Medal and repeated as Champions in 1931 and 1932. Though they won the Bronze Medal at the World Championships in New York in 1930 and at Montreal in 1932, they did not travel to Berlin for the 1931 Championships. However, in 1932 they capped their Pairs career by taking the Silver Medal at the Lake Placid, New York Olympic Games.

Badger was deeply involved in figure skating for the remainder of his life as a judge and as the longtime president of the U.S. Figure Skating Association. In 1976 he was among the first six inductees into the new U.S. Figure Skating Hall of Fame.

BAIER, ERNST *(b. 1905) German World medalist as a solo skater; World and Olympic Champion in Pairs with Maxie Herber (b. 1921).*

Ernst Baier initially came to prominence as a solo skater, taking the 1931 World Championships Men's Bronze Medal in Berlin, his home city. He won the Bronze again in 1932 and then twice took the Silver Medal behind Austria's Karl Schafer, who had been World Champion since 1930 and would continue to dominate the men's division through 1936. Baier concluded his solo career by taking the 1936 Olympic Silver behind Schafer.

But Baier was even more successful as a Pairs skater with partner Maxie Herber, also a strong solo skater although not a World medalist. The couple won the World Bronze in 1934, but Baier was injured in 1935 and did not compete at all. In 1936, however, Baier and Herber reached the top, winning both the Olympic and the World Championships. Skating historians agree that in doing so they raised Pairs skating another notch in terms of technical difficulty and artistic flow. Aided by the fact that Hitler's obsession with "Germany over all" had led to unprecedented funding of German sports programs, they were the first pair for whom symphonic music was especially composed and recorded with a full orchestra, with every note of music tied to their skating moves.

Baier and Herber never talked politics and no one knew whether they were Nazi party members or not, but they were very popular personalities in the skating world. They repeated as World Champions in 1937–39. In 1994, Ernst Baier attended a gala televised skating spectacular in Boston, Massachusetts for many generations of World and Olympic Champions.

BAINBRIDGE, WALTER *See* WARING, LOIS.

BAIUL, OKSANA *(b. 1978) Ukrainian World and Olympic Champion.*

Oksana Baiul blazed into the skating world in 1993 like a comet: Only 15, she stunned both audience and judges at the World Championships with her artistry and technical command. The favorite to win the 1993 World Gold Medal was the previous year's Silver Medalist Nancy Kerrigan of the United States, with strong challenges expected from European Champion Surya Bonaly of France and 1992 World Bronze Medalist Lu Chen of China. Kerrigan self-destructed, missing several jumps, and Baiul clearly outskated Bonaly and Lu Chen to take the Gold.

Petite and fragile looking, Baiul's background won immediate attention from the world press: Her father divorced her mother and disappeared when she was two and, raised by her mother and grandparents, she started to skate very early in preparation for a ballet career. She stuck with the skating. Her grandfather died in 1987, followed by her grandmother in 1988, and in 1991, when Baiul was only 13, her mother died very suddenly of cancer. To make matters worse, her coach went to Canada because of the Soviet Union's collapse and the vast Soviet sports program along with it. Viktor Petrenko's coach, Galina Zmievskaya, took Baiul into her home and began to coach her, while Petrenko himself (who had just married Zmievskaya's elder daughter) helped with expenses. At 15, she became World Champion.

Not everyone was enchanted with Baiul's skating: Olympic Silver Medalist Paul Wylie, even before the 1994 Olympics, said, "She puts Katarina Witt to shame, the way she mugs for the judges. She's just the girl they were looking for." There were other doubters who were less frank than Wylie, and the questions about whether she was quite as good as advertised grew after her victory, by one-tenth of a point, over Kerrigan at the 1994 Olympics. (Paul Wylie is, of course, a close friend of Nancy Kerrigan.) This was one of the most controversial judging decisions in many years, with the difference being provided in the artistic scores by judge Jan Hoffmann, who himself had lost the Olympic Gold by a narrow margin when he was skating for East Germany in 1980.

The crux of the 1994 Olympic debate was that Kerrigan, who had won the short program, skated her long program with no mistakes, while Baiul double-footed the landing of a triple flip. In addition, Kerrigan did two triple jumps in combination with a double jump, and Baiul did not. On the other hand, Baiul had been injured the day before and was skating with pain-killing injections, and she had put in an unexpected double-axel/double-toe-loop combination at the end of her program. The questions abounded: Had the judges found Kerrigan's program too front-loaded, with all the most difficult material in the first two minutes? Was Baiul's balletic artistry simply preferred to Kerrigan's cool elegance? Or was it just that Baiul had more charisma? Everyone had an opinion, with the experts and other competitors weighing in on both sides of the argument. It was a controversy so intense that it is likely to go on for years.

Both Baiul and Kerrigan turned professional, and while skating together on the same 70-city tour in 1995 were noted to get along very well together. Baiul, still only 17, passed up the cutoff date to declare her intention to seek reinstatement as an amateur for the 1998 Olympics, but she said that she hoped the rules would change so that she could compete again. In the meantime, she is a major draw—as is Kerrigan—with audiences on tour.

BARAN, RIA *(b. 1930) World and Olympic Pairs Champion with Paul Falk (b. 1929).*

Ria Baran and Paul Falk of West Germany exploded to the top of Pairs skating in 1951, taking the World Gold from the previous year's winners, Karol and Peter Kennedy of the United States, who won the Silver this time. The couple, who subsequently married, were the first skaters from either West or East Germany to win a World medal in skating since before World War II.

Masterful technicians with an elegant style, Baran and Falk retained their World title in 1952 and as well captured the Gold Medal at the Olympics in Oslo, Norway, edging out the Kennedys in both competitions. They then turned professional. Although Baran and Falk reigned at the top of Pairs skating for too little a time to have any lasting effect on other Pairs, they provided the first sign of how strong the skating programs in the two Germanys would become over the next decade.

BATCHELOR, ERICA *(b. 1934) British World medalist.*

Although Great Britain produced two of the 1930s most important women skaters, Cecilia Colledge and Megan Taylor, as well as postwar World Champion Jeannette Altwegg, its women's division was soon eclipsed by Ice Dance teams, culminating in Torvill and Dean and major male skaters John Curry and Robin Cousins. Erica Batchelor's Bronze Medal at the 1954 World Championships was the last World medal won by a British woman to date, ascribed partly to the strength of British Ice Dancing that attracted the country's most talented women skaters to that discipline rather than solo skating. Erica Batchelor was very popular in her home country and had a successful professional career, but on the world stage she was a secondary figure.

BAUGNIET, PIERRE *See* LANNOY, MICHELINE.

BAUMLER, HANS JURGEN *See* KILLIUS, MARIKA.

BAXTER, SKIPPY *(b. ?) U.S. medalist.*

A free-skater with considerable pizzazz, Skippy Baxter took two U.S. medals in 1940, the Men's Bronze and the Pairs Silver with partner Hedy Stenuf, herself the Women's Silver Medalist that year. Baxter then skated with the newly created Ice Capades throughout the 1940s.

BAXTER, VIRGINIA *(b. 1932) U.S. and World medalist.*

Though not as strong as some women in the school figures, Virginia Baxter, known as Ginny, took the U.S. Bronze Medal for three years running, 1949–51. The first two years she was 7th in the World's both times. She did not skate at the World's in 1951 but came back in 1952 to win the World Bronze at Paris behind the French dazzler Jacqueline du Bief and her own teammate Sonja Klopfer. At that year's Olympics she took 5th place but gave, according to Dick Button in his 1955 autobiography, "one of the finest free skating performances I have ever seen."

BEJSHAK, JOHN *See* O'NEILL, CLAIRE.

BELITA (Stage name of GLADYS LYNNE JEPSON-TURNER) *(b. 1923) British skater who became a stage and movie star.*

Since ice shows appeared in the late 1930s, many young amateur skaters who never won a major medal turned professional to appear in such ice extravaganzas. Often these skaters could not financially afford the very expensive amateur route to the top, or else when school figures were a major competition element, these skaters were not particularly good at such figures although they possessed strong free-skating abilities.

Perhaps the most famous such skater was also the first to go from amateur competition into ice shows: Gladys Lynne Jepson-Turner was on the British Olympic team in 1936. The following year, at 14, taking her stage name *Belita* from a grandfather's Argentine ranch, she turned professional to co-star in *Opera on Ice*, performed on a temporary rink installed on the Royal Opera House, Covent Garden, stage in London. She toured the United States and was an Ice Capades star during its first two seasons, 1940–41. Signed by Hollywood as a rival to Sonja Henie, Belita made such movies as *Ice Capades* (1941) and *Silver Skates* (1943) before branching out into dramatic roles in *The Gangster* (1947) and *The Hunted* (1948). She later danced in the films *Invitation to the Dance* (1957) and *Silk Stockings* (1957).

BELOUSOVA, LUDMILA *See* PROTOPOPOV, OLEG.

BENENSON, EMILY *(b. 1954) U.S. Pairs medalist.*

In 1973, when Emily Benenson teamed with Johnny Johns to win the U.S. Bronze Medal in Pairs, the Gold Medal was won by the sister-and-brother team of Melissa and Mark Militano, who had been four-year Silver Medalists. Having finally won the championship, Mark decided to retire. His younger sister, who wanted to continue, persuaded Johnny Johns to become her new partner, a move that brought two more Gold Medals. Left without a partner, Benenson joined with Jack Courtney (b. 1953), and they took the Pairs Bronze in both 1975 and 1976. Only two U.S. Pairs were eligible for the World and Olympic teams in those years, so Benenson and Courtney were thus excluded from international competition.

BENNETT, MARGARET *(b. 1910)*
U.S. Silver Medalist.

Margaret Bennett was one of five women to place 2nd to the great Maribel Vinson as she amassed her unequaled nine U.S. Gold Medals from 1928 to 1937 (she did not skate in 1934). Bennett took the Silver Medal in 1932 and placed 11th at the Olympics and 12th at World's that year.

BERENS, SUSAN *See* WAGELEIN, ROY.

BERESFORD, ROSEMARY *(b. 1898)*
U.S. Champion.

At the only U.S. Championship to be held between 1915 and 1920, Rosemary Beresford took the Gold Medal, beating Theresa Weld, herself a five-time winner beginning in 1920.

BEREZHNAYA, ELENA *(b. 1977)*
Russian Olympic Pairs medalist with Anton Sikharulidze (b. 1976)

With then partner Oleg Sliakov, Elena Berezhnaya competed for Latvia after the breakup of the Soviet Union until the day in January 1996 when, while practicing side-by-side camel spins, Sliakov accidentally struck her head with his skate. The blade penetrated Berezhnaya's skull, causing a severe head injury that required two surgeries, affected her ability to speak, and partially paralyzed her right side. As soon as she was able to leave the hospital, Anton Sikharulidze, a friend who skated for Russia, took Berezhnaya to St. Petersburg to consult with famed coach Tamara Moskvina. It was unclear whether Berezhnaya would be able to skate again, but with the support of Sikharulidze, her recovery bordered on the miraculous, and within three months she was back on the ice.

Bereshnaya and Sikharulidze seemed to be natural partners, and by March of 1997 they had taken 3rd place in the short program at the World Championship, placing 9th overall. In 1998 after winning 2nd place at the Russian Nationals, they were regarded as strong Olympic contenders, along with fellow Pairs skaters and compatriots Kazakova and Dmitriev. At Nagano they took the Silver Medal behind Kazakova and Dmitriev and ahead of Mandy Woetzel and Ingo Steuer of Germany.

BERGER, ALFRED *See* ENGLEMANN, HELENE.

BERGER, HULDA *(b. 1912) U.S. medalist.*

Hulda Berger took the Bronze Medal at the U.S. Championships in Boston, Massachusetts in 1931 behind Gold Medalist Maribel Vinson and Silver Medalist Edith Secord. The latter two had held those positions for the previous two years.

BERNDT, DOUG *See* BROWN, BARBARA.

BERRY, ROGER *See* DAVENPORT, ALMA.

Theresa Weld Blanchard won a total of 32 U.S. Figure Skating medals.
(Courtesy World Figure Skating Museum)

BESTEMIANOVA, NATALIA *(b. 1961) Soviet World and Olympic Ice Dancing Champion with Andrei Bukin (b. 1957).*

For seven years, 1981–1988, Natalia Bestemianova and Andrei Bukin were medalists at the World Championships and the Winter Olympics. They began with a Bronze Medal in 1981 behind new World Champions Jayne Torvill and Christopher Dean and Soviet colleagues Irina Moiseeva and Andrei Minekov, the former World Champions affectionately known by western skaters as Min and Mo. For the next three years, Bestemianova and Bukin were 2nd to Torvill and Dean at the World Championships, ahead of Min and Mo in 1982 and America's Judy Blumberg and Michael Seibert in 1983 and 1984. They were also the Silver Medalists behind Torvill and Dean at the 1984 Olympics.

Ice Dancing had never seen anything like Torvill and Dean, but once they turned professional, the classical purity of Bestemianova and Bukin came back into focus as they won four successive World Championships and the 1988 Olympics over their Soviet compatriots Marina Klimova and Sergei Ponomarenko. There are many who still consider them the apex of classical Ice Dance style.

BETTS, PETER *See* LITTLEFIELD, YVONNE.

BEWERSDORF, UWE *See* GROSS, MANUELA.

BIELLMANN, DENISE *(b. 1960) Swiss World Champion.*

In the late 1970s and early 1980s, Denise Biellmann often contended for a World medal but never quite attained the level of the United States' Linda Fratianne and East Germany's Anett Poetzsch. Good at school figures and much admired for her balletic free-skating style, Biellmann's jumps frequently gave her trouble. After Fratianne and Poetzsch retired from amateur skating in 1980, however, Biellmann seized the opportunity: Skating with the greatest confidence of her career, she edged 15-year-old Elaine Zayak of the United States to gain the World Gold Medal and then promptly turned professional.

Biellmann had extraordinary physical flexibility and invented a signature spin in which she grasped her left leg and pulled it straight above her head in midrevolution. She performed this maneuver, which could have been ungainly, with such finesse that it flowed easily into her program; inevitably she wowed the audience. The spin, known as a Biellmann, has since been performed by several other women, but none have done it with the grace and ease that its originator brought to it.

BITTERMAN, JOAN *See* HISLOP, BRAD.

BLANCHARD, THERESA WELD

(1896–1978) U.S. Ladies' and Pairs Champion.

The first U.S. Ladies Champion (1914), Theresa Weld Blanchard skated competitively for another 18 years and became the founding editor of *Skating*, the official U.S. Figure Skating Association magazine. Friendly rival of two generations of figure skaters, she eventually became "mother hen" to several more generations.

When the first U.S. Championships were held at New Haven, Connecticut in 1914, Theresa Weld (she would marry in 1920 and become known thereafter as Theresa Weld Blanchard) not only won the first Ladies' title but was also the Silver Medalist in Pairs with Nathaniel Niles, that year's Bronze Medalist in the Men's competition. There were no further competitions until 1918, when she won the Ladies' Silver Medal behind Rosemary Beresford and became Pairs Champion with Niles. There was no competition in 1919. She regained the Ladies' title in 1920 and defended it successfully four more times, through 1924. In 1925 and 1926, Blanchard was the Ladies' Silver Medalist behind Beatrix Loughran and in 1927 took the Bronze behind Loughran and 14-year-old Maribel Vinson. She did not compete in the Ladies' division in any World Championships (Loughran was the first American woman to do so, in 1924; Vinson was the second, in 1928); She did compete, however, as a soloist in three Olympics, taking the Bronze Medal at Antwerp, Belgium in 1920 and placing 4th in 1924 and 10th in 1928, when she was 31 years old.

During the period from 1918 to 1928, she and Nathaniel Niles were U.S. Pairs Champions nine times. They took a Silver Medal in 1928, when Maribel Vinson and Thornton Coolidge took the first of five Pairs Golds. Blanchard and Niles were also 4th at the 1920 Olympics, 6th in 1924 and 9th in 1928. They also competed several times at the World's, placing 7th in 1928, 6th in 1930 and 8th in 1932. She and Niles were great believers in the amateur spirit of participation; there was no chance of their winning medals after the mid-1920s, but they took great delight in simply being there.

Blanchard and Niles also won the Gold Medal in the first U.S. Ice Dance competition in 1914, when only the waltz was contested. Over the years they won five more Gold Medals in Ice Dance, in both the waltz and the fourteen step, as well as five Silver and two Bronze Medals, the last in 1932, 18 years after their first Gold.

As editor of *Skating* for three decades, Theresa Weld Blanchard watched over the careers of successive waves of avid figure skaters, warmly dispensing her encouragement and advice with splendid impartiality. She and Maribel Vinson were the first two women to be elected to the U.S. Figure Skating Hall of Fame in 1976.

BLODGETT, POLLY *(b. 1918) Versatile U.S. medalist.*

Polly Blodgett won her first U.S. medal in 1936 when, skating with Roger Turner, she took the Silver Medal in Pairs. Narrowed concentration on solo skating paid off in 1937 with Blodgett's Silver Medal behind Maribel Vinson's unparalleled ninth Gold in her final competition. In 1938, Blodgett's hopes of becoming U.S. Champion following Vinson's retirement were thwarted by the fast rise of Joan Tozzer, who would stay at the top for three years. Audrey Peppe, who had won the Bronze in 1936, came back to take the Silver, and Polly Blodgett had to settle for the Bronze.

BLUMBERG, JUDY *(b. 1960) U.S. Ice Dance Champion with Michael Seibert (b. 1959).*

Skating fans first noticed Judy Blumberg and Michael Seibert in 1979 when they took the U.S. Bronze Medal in Ice Dancing behind repeat Champions Stacey Smith and John Sumners and Silver Medalists Carol Fox and Richard Dalley. In 1980 they moved up to the Silver Medal behind Smith and Sumners, pushing Fox and Dalley back to the Bronze. Blumberg and Seibert placed 7th at the 1980 Olympics and 6th at the World Championships, in each two places ahead of Smith and Sumners. In 1981, they became U.S. Champions, beating Fox and Dalley and finished 4th at the World Championships when Jayne Torvill and Christopher Dean won their first World Gold. In 1982, Blumberg and Seibert were again U.S. Champions and again 4th in the World's.

Blumberg and Seibert joined the Ice Dancing elite in 1983 when they won the World Bronze behind Torvill and Dean and the Soviet couple Natalia Bestemianova and Andrei Bukin. Winning their fourth U.S. title in 1984, they were considered certain Olympic medalists. No one was expected to seriously challenge Torvill and Dean, of course, but Blumberg and Seibert seemed assured of a Bronze, with the possibility of a Silver. Although always noted for a jazzy American style of Ice Dancing, they decided to try something new for this Olympic year, performing to Rimsky-Korsakov's *Schéhérezade* in a pas de deux that Dick Button described before the Olympics in a *New York Times* article as "breathtaking" and "extraordinary." But what happened to them at the Olympics was a prime example of the power of judges and their ability to sabotage skaters.

Torvill and Dean skated to Ravel's *Bolero* that year, hardly conventional Ice Dance music. Both that choice and the Americans' use of the Rimsky-Korsakov music were approved months beforehand by head Ice Dance referee, former World Champion Ice Dancer Lawrence Demmy of Great Britain. Some judges who, while reluctantly willing to accept the use of *Bolero* because there was an actual Spanish dance of that name, were infuriated by the use of *Schéhérezade*, and although it had been approved, they simply wouldn't accept it. The leader of these judges was Cia Bordogna of Italy, who gave Blumberg and Seibert an extremely low 5.5 for artistic impression. In a defiant interview with *Sports Illustrated* following the competition, she said that *Schéhérezade* broke a rule requiring that music had to be suitable to the dance floor as well as to the ice rink. She was unimpressed by the argument that several ballets had been choreographed to the music—when she said dance floor, she meant ballroom dance floor and defensively insisted that four other judges ducked this issue by marking Blumberg and Seibert down in the compulsory dances to ensure that they would have trouble winning a medal—and they did not win a medal; they came in 4th by a tie-breaking difference of one-tenth of a point in one judge's technical mark. The medalists were Torvill and Dean, Gold; Bestemianova and Bukin, Silver; and another Soviet couple, Marina Klimova and Sergei Ponomarenko, Bronze.

Blumberg and Seibert were initially so angry that they considered retiring from amateur skating; instead, they went on to take their second Bronze Medal at the World Championships (still skating to *Schéhérezade*) and in 1985 were again U.S. Champions and World Bronze Medalists. Subsequent to their successful professional career, Judy Blumberg became a television commentator on the sport and Michael Seibert continued as a choreographer and as codirector of "Discover Stars on Ice."

BOBEK, NICOLE *(b. 1978) U.S. Champion.*

At the time of the 1995 U.S. Figure Skating Championships, 17-year-old Nicole Bobek had a new coach, Richard Callaghan, her eighth in seven years. *The New York Times* skating reporter Jere Longman summed up the situation: "Richard Callaghan had heard all the stories about Nicole Bobek. That she was a free spirit, wild, uncontrollable. Abrasive. Gifted but indifferent to training." On the plus side, she was regarded as extraordinarily musical, could do all the required jumps, at least in practice, and had in her competitive arsenal one of the best spirals anyone had ever seen. But her competitive career was very spotty—she often fell apart and finished behind other skaters with less-apparent talent. Her first U.S. Senior Medal was the 1994 Bronze Medal behind Tonya Harding and Michelle Kwan, a medal won during Nancy Kerrigan's absence from the Nationals because of the knee injury inflicted on her by one of Harding's associates. Bobek was dispatched to the World Championships in 1994 because both Olympic Silver Medalist Kerrigan and a disgraced Harding were not going to be there; Bobek did not quite make the cut into the final group contending for medals.

Having lost weight and apparently dedicated herself to training, Nicole Bobek skated beautifully in Providence, Rhode Island in 1995 to become U.S. Champion over the expected winner, Michelle Kwan, generating talk of a possible World medal, perhaps even the Gold. At the Birmingham, England World Championships, she skated a flawless short program to take the lead, and though in the long program she ran into trouble, Bobek still skated well enough to win the World Bronze behind Lu Chen of China and Surya Bonaly of France.

Bobek was finally established as one of the world's leading women skaters but was unable to capitalize on this standing in 1996: An ankle injury, at first seemingly minor, worsened during a lucrative 16-city tour with a *Nutcracker On Ice* production. By the time she reached the Nationals, the ankle was badly swollen; she withdrew before the long program after skating poorly in the short program. Younger rival Michelle Kwan became not only U.S. Champion but also 1996 World Champion. Bobek vowed to come back in top shape in 1997, setting up the possibility of a rivalry with Kwan to match that of Debi Thomas and Jill Trenary in the run-up to the 1988 Olympics.

BOECKL, WILLY *(1896–1975) Austrian World Champion.*

Willy Boeckl took his first two World medals before World War I: the Silver behind fellow Austrian Fritz Kachler in 1913 and the Bronze behind Gosta Sandahl of Sweden and Kachler in 1914. In 1922, as postwar competition resumed, he took another Bronze behind Sweden's unbeatable Gillis Grafstrom and, again, Kachler. Silver Medalist in 1923 and 1924, he finally gained the World Title in 1925 and retained it through 1928. But when Grafstrom competed at the 1924 and 1928 Olympics, Boeckl had to settle for Silver both times.

He later gave up his structural engineer career to migrate to the United States, where he became a noted teacher at New York's Skating Club.

BODEL, CARMEL WATERBURY AND EDWARD *(b. 1928, 1926) U.S. Ice Dance Champions.*

Husband-and-wife Ice Dance team Carmel Waterbury and Edward Bodel were active in amateur competition for more than a decade, capturing their first U.S. Bronze Medal in 1946; their next Bronze Medal came in 1949, the year of their marriage. In 1951, the Bodels became the U.S. Champions and then again took Bronze Medals in 1952 and 1953. In 1954 and 1955 they won successive U.S. Gold Medals and took the Silver in 1956, their final competition.

Ice Dancing was included in World Championship competition for the first time in 1952, where the Bodels took 4th place. They were 7th at the World's in 1953, gained the Bronze Medal in 1954, were 4th again in 1955 and then fell to 6th and 7th place in 1956 and 1957. They competed during a period in which there were a half-dozen U.S. Ice Dance teams of surprisingly equal accomplishment, with medal placings changing hands year after year.

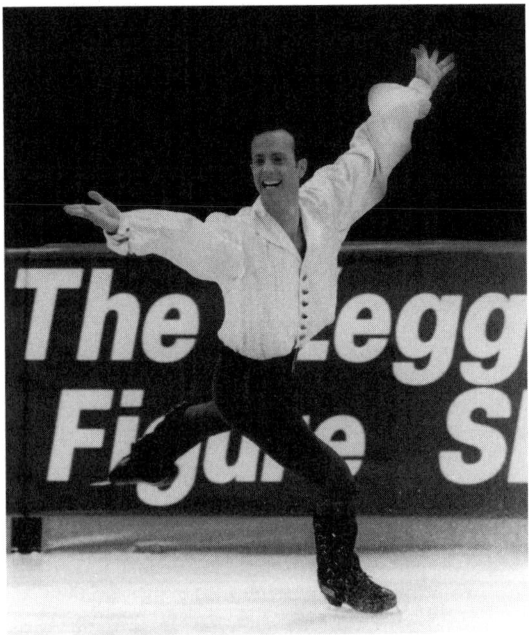

Brian Boitano returned to amateur skating for the 1994 Olympics.
(Courtesy Paul Harvath)

Two other American couples, Carol Peters and Daniel Ryan and Sharon McKenzie and Bert Wright, also took World Bronzes, the former in both 1952 and 1953 and the latter in 1957. However, the Bodels competed over a longer span than any of the others as much for the sheer pleasure of skating as for medal ambitions, they said.

BOHATSCH, MAX *(b. 1893) Austrian Champion and World medalist, 1900–1910.*

Ulrich Salchow of Sweden reigned as World Champion from 1901 to 1911. Max Bohatsch, one of several skaters who challenged his domination, was the World Bronze Medalist at St. Petersburg, Russia and took the Silver in Stockholm, Sweden in 1905 and again in his home city of Vienna, Austria in 1907.

BOITANO, BRIAN *(b. 1963) U.S., World and Olympic Champion.*

Brian Boitano marked himself as a potential successor to U.S. and World Champion Scott Hamilton in 1983 by taking the U.S. Silver Medal in Pittsburgh, Pennsylvania. Already 20, he was, however, no overnight success. A phenomenal jumper from his skating start at the age of eight after having been inspired by a performance of the Ice Follies in San Francisco, Boitano initially rose quickly to become U.S. Junior Champion in 1978, but then he seemed to stall in his development, largely because he impressed judges as being all technique and little artistry. The fight to develop artistic flair and an effective personality on the ice would continue right up to the 1988 Olympics.

In 1984, he was again U.S. Silver Medalist. He had placed 7th at the 1983 World Championships, improved to 6th in 1984 and, even more encouraging, was 5th at the Olympics in Sarajevo, Yugoslavia. Scott Hamilton took the Gold Medal that year. As expected, Boitano became U.S. Champion in 1985 and won the World Bronze Medal behind the Soviet Union's Alexandr Fadeev and Canada's Brian Orser. In 1986, after winning his second U.S. title, Boitano vaulted over Orser and Fadeev to become World Champion as the other two men faltered under pressure.

In 1987 Boitano received a shock: Again U.S. Champion, he lost his World title to Brian Orser, who had won the World Bronze in 1983 and the World Silver every year since, as well as the 1984 Olympic Silver. Orser had finally controlled his nerves to beat Boitano with points to spare. Orser was an electrifying personality on the ice and a master at playing to the audience; by contrast, Boitano appeared dull—neither the audience nor the judges were in his corner. Comments from skating reporters, officials and even judges made it abundantly clear where the problem lay: Boitano skated like a "robot."

When faced with this sort of criticism, a lot of skaters get their backs up and insist on continuing to do things "their way"—but not Boitano. He understood what they were talking about and became determined to do something about it. He had a year to work on his presentation and artistry before the 1988 Olympics in Calgary, Canada.

Boitano was unusual in that he had the same coach from the day he began to take lessons: Linda Leaver was his coach and also his friend. He is godfather of her youngest child. She had taken him all the way to the World Championship, but they agreed that some additional input could be useful and turned to former Canadian Pairs Skating Champion Sandra Bezic, now a successful skating choreographer.

Although even World Champions must practice their triple jumps constantly, that aspect of Boitano's skating was not a worry: He had landed the first triple axel ever performed at the U.S. Championships in 1982 before he even became a medalist. He had also invented a triple-lutz variation, named after him because no one else could do it: the *tano lutz* involved raising one arm above his head as he revolved in the air, a technically extraordinary feat in that it is much more difficult to maintain balance and speed of revolution without both arms being held close to the body. But this jump did not have the kind of effect it should have because it was not integrated into his programs in a way that truly showed it off. That was just one of the things Sandra Bezic helped him accomplish.

That there was something new, something more to Brian Boitano's skating became evident in the short program at the U.S. Championships. He skated to Meyerbeer's *Les Patineurs* ("The Skaters"). The tricky required elements were all flawlessly executed, but it was what happened between them that was different. Boitano was playing a *character*, a cocky youth showing off at the local pond. Toward the middle of the program, he lifted one foot off the ice, ran his fingers along the blade and flicked the ice shavings to one side, a gesture so casual—yet obviously a part of the choreography—that it brought a soft "oooh" from the audience. He also daringly incorporated a few small turns and steps reminiscent of pre–World War I skating style that, combined with spectacular modern moves like the triple axel, seemed to sum up the whole history of figure skating. Many people said afterward that it had been one of the few times they had ever been moved by a short program.

He skated his long program to music composed by Carmine Coppola for the restored version of Abel Gance's epic silent film *Napoleon*. Here again he was a character, a young officer in the French army, wearing a modified Napoleonic uniform with epaulettes. It was a bravura display of technique with an emotional edge: for the first time his signature jump, the tano lutz, carried an emotional punch and brought gasps and huge applause.

His fourth and highest-marked U.S. title in his pocket, Boitano faced the showdown with Brian Orser in Calgary, Canada at the Winter Olympics. The press hyped this clash for months as "The Battle of the Brians," increasing the pressure on both men; fortunately they were good friends and had many similar interests, and one thing they did not talk about when they were together was skating. Despite Boitano's obvious artistic development, the handicappers still gave Orser the edge: He had won the Olympic Silver Medal four years earlier, had steadfastly continued as an amateur in search of the Gold, was the host country favorite and was reigning World Champion.

The first test was the school figures, counting 30 percent and being skated for the last time in international competition. Here Alexandr Fadeev of the Soviet Union finished 1st, Boitano 2nd and Orser 3rd. In the short program, worth 20 percent, Orser skated flawlessly and with great excitement, winning this element. Boitano, also making no mistakes, was nevertheless more cautious than at the U.S. Championships. Fadeev fell apart. Now whichever Brian won the long program would be the Olympic Champion.

Boitano skated first. This time he was not cautious, skating with even greater brio than he had at the U.S. Championships. One perfectly executed maneuver followed another: triple-axel/double-toe-loop combination, utterly level camel spin, a spectacular death-drop spin, a triple-flip/triple-toe-loop combination. "But there was something new here,"

Newsweek reported, "something few among the judges or the crowd had ever seen in him before. He was emoting. A gasp could be heard during his fabulous spread eagle, in which, cutting backward at a harrowing angle, he carved a wide, slow circle on the outside edges of his blades. He never missed a subtlety or a beat." At the end, Boitano raised his fists and shook them with joy, breaking into an enormous smile as his eyes clouded with tears. He had not yet won the Gold Medal, but he had achieved what meant most to him—simply to skate the best long program he ever had. He would say later, "I had been told as a child that no one ever skated their best in an Olympic performance. My dream was to change that, to prove that it didn't have to be that way."

Brian Orser, skating to Shostakovich's *The Bolt*, had his countrymen screaming almost from the start. It was in fact the best long program he ever skated, too. But there was a slight bobble on a triple flip, just enough off for the judges to see it clearly; at the end, apparently tiring, he did a double rather than a planned triple axel. Four judges put Orser first, but five had Boitano marked on their cards, and the Gold Medal was his. Boitano then went on to win the World Championship back from Orser as well, the Canadian seeming less exciting than usual, as though the loss of the Olympic Gold had taken something out of him.

To judge by the two Brians' professional careers, the Olympic judges gave it to the right one. Orser gave many brilliant professional performances, but Boitano did more than that: he continued to develop artistically, continually seeking new depths of feeling and expression. He had also kept his technical edge over the years as no other professional skater ever had, performing his triple jumps with the perfected ease that came from continual hard practice. As a result, he won the World Professional Championship five consecutive times, from 1989 through 1993.

Boitano skated in a number of highly rated television specials. One of them, 1989's *Carmen on Ice*—a project that was Boitano's idea—starred Katarina Witt as Bizet's gypsy, Boitano as Don José and Brian Orser as the toreador Escamillo. All three skaters won Emmy awards for their performances.

Boitano made a great deal of money from his television work and ice show tours, but when the opportunity came for past champions to become reinstated as amateurs to compete in the 1994 Olympics, he was thrilled, especially because he had pushed for this change, and happily gave up the lucrative contracts to prepare for another Olympics. Other skaters, including Witt and 1992 Olympic champion Viktor Petrenko, joined him. Surprisingly, he did not win the U.S. Championship; Scott Davis successfully defended his title. Although Boitano had been fighting an injury and was slightly hampered, he made no excuses. At the Olympics, he fell on his combination jump in the short program and was immediately out of contention for a medal, something that also happened to Petrenko and World Champion Kurt Browning of Canada. "Skating's Old Guard Gives Way to New" was the headline in the *New York Times*. Boitano took it philosophically and went right back to winning professional championships.

BOLTRES, GEORGE *See* PRANTELL, NETTIE.

BONALY, SURYA *(b. 1973) French and European Champion and World medalist.*

Surya Bonaly was born in North Africa (there are conflicting stories about exactly where) and adopted by a French missionary couple. Her mother, who became her chief coach despite having no experience in skating, fed the press many colorful stories about her daughter's background, which were initially accepted but later roundly questioned.

What is definitely known is that Surya's initial athletic training as a gymnast was put to good use, especially in her jumping, when she turned to figure skating. She became French Champion and European Champion in 1990 at the age of 16. By then, school figures were no longer an element of competition, and she was able to rely on her spectacular jumping ability. But Bonaly's technical marks were always much higher than her artistic marks, and the discrepancy between the two has always hurt her in World and Olympic competition, especially because the artistic marks are used as a tie-breaking mechanism in judging. No one disputes her talent as a jumper—she packs her programs with the triple jumps and has performed a quadruple loop numerous times in practice without ever testing it in competition—but many judges and skating commentators have said that although she can land her many jumps cleanly, she does so with a rough style that is far from textbook perfection.

In addition, there has always been much discussion of Bonaly's flat-footed skating style. Dick Button went so far as to say on the air that she "needed to take a couple of years off and learn to skate." By this he meant that she does not use her edges properly when she skates between jumps or, especially, when she is doing footwork sequences. The general public tends to pay minimum attention to footwork sequences unless they are overtly spectacular, but they are a required element in both the short and long programs, and in this regard Bonaly has often lost technical as well as artistic points with the judges. Footwork sequences may be overlooked by the public, but they are of major importance to judges, an element that is often crucial in distinguishing between a Gold and a Silver Medalist.

Because of her dependence on her jumping, Bonaly is in trouble if she misses any of her spectacular moves, as happened in a number of major competitions. Although she won the European Championship five times in succession (even beating a slightly injured Oksana Baiul in 1994 after Baiul had become World Champion), Bonaly was 4th or 5th at the World's and Olympics year after year in the early 1990s, finally breaking through to take the Silver Medal behind Baiul in 1993. In this competition, the favorite, Nancy Kerrigan, fell apart. At the 1994 Olympics, Bonaly's jumps were secure in her short program, but as *The New York Times* reported, she "wobbled on her spirals and hopped along on the ice, her skating not yet completely rid of the gymnastic influence of her youth." She was 3rd after the short program, which was won by Kerrigan with Baiul 2nd. But Bonaly fell, along with many others, during her long program and slipped to 4th, with China's Lu Chen taking the Bronze behind Baiul and Kerrigan.

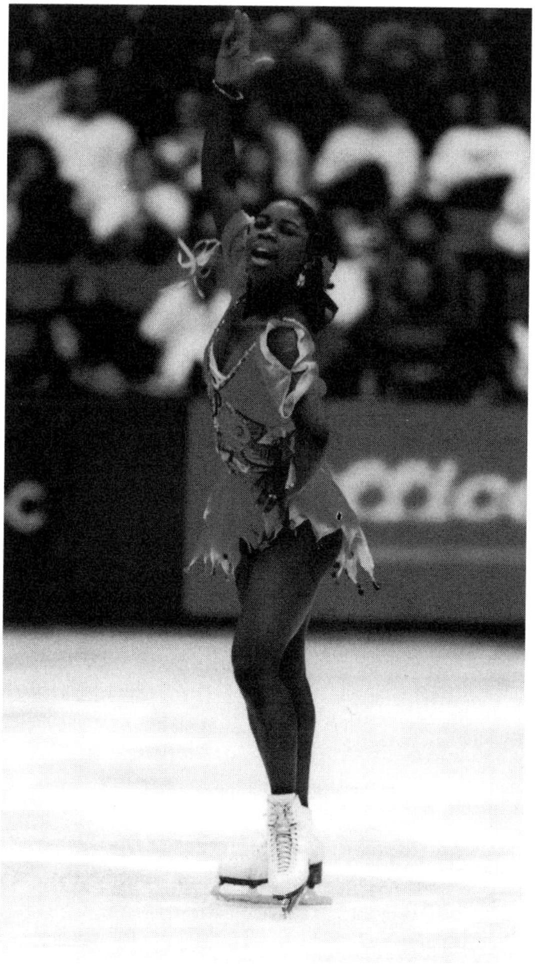

The spectacular jumper Surya Bonaly in 1994.
(Courtesy Paul Harvath)

None of the Olympic women medalists participated in the 1994 World Championships, with Lu Chen and Baiul both recovering from injuries and Kerrigan pleading exhaustion from the three-ring circus caused by the Tonya Harding situation at the Olympics. It seemed that at last Bonaly could claim the World Championship. But she was clearly, if narrowly, outperformed by Japan's Yuka Sato, who was flawless in the competition of her life. Sato received her Gold Medal on the podium, but when it came time to be awarded the Silver, Bonaly first refused to either mount the platform or accept the medal, then took it and was virtually pushed up onto the podium by the presiding official, where she removed the medal from around her neck. This display caused her to be booed by the Japanese audience and brought her a string of caustic headline stories around the world.

In 1995, Bonaly won her fifth European Championship. But at the World's, she botched her triple lutz in the short program and was only 4th going into the finals. Everyone had problems in the long program except China's Lu Chen, who won the Gold Medal. Bonaly initially looked as though she would win only the Bronze, with U.S. Champion Nicole Bobek taking the Silver, but then the U.S. Silver Medalist Michelle Kwan skated so well that when all the numbers were computed, Bonaly took the Silver and Bobek the Bronze. Perhaps trying to repair the damage from the previous year or recognizing that she had never beaten Lu Chen, Bonaly graciously thanked Michelle Kwan for elevating her to the Silver.

After five consecutive victories in the European Championships, Bonaly was upset by the young Russian skater Irina Slutskaya in 1996 and gained only the Silver Medal. Her problems continued at the World Championships in Edmonton, Canada. For the first time since 1993, she was kept off the medal platform, finishing in 5th place. This was in part due to a very shaky performance in the short program, but it also reflected the fact that Slutskaya was performing equally spectacular jumps and doing so with greater finesse. Although Bonaly said she would continue to compete through the 1998 Winter Olympics, she was now faced with a new generation of competitors, and many commentators felt she had missed her chance to reach the top of her sport.

BOTTICELLI, MICHAEL *See* FRANKS, SHERYL.

BOURNE, SHAE-LYNN *(b. 1974)*

Canadian World Ice Dance medalist with Victor Kraatz (b. 1971).

Shae-Lynn Bourne and Victor Kraatz gradually moved up the international Ice Dance ladder, reaching 4th place in 1995. In 1996 on home-country ice in Edmonton, Alberta, they finally made it to the medal platform with performances that matched their zippy audience-pleasing style, augmented by a new level of technical assurance. They were a solid 3rd in both the compulsory and original dance sections, and their Bronze Medal brought Canada its first World medal in Ice Dancing since Tracy Wilson and Robert McCall took the Bronze at the 1988 Winter Olympics and World Championships.

BOWDEN, NORRIS *See* DAFOE, FRANCIS.

BOWMAN CHRISTOPHER *(b. 1968)*

U.S. Champion.

From 1987 through 1992, Christopher Bowman won five U.S. medals and two World medals but never lived up to the expectations that were placed upon him: to become World and Olympic Champion. His first U.S. Senior Men's Medal came with a strong performance that gave him the U.S. Silver Medal behind Brian Boitano in 1987, but then, in a pattern that was to become characteristic, he skated sloppily at the World's and placed 7th. In 1988, he took the U.S. Bronze behind Boitano and Paul Wylie and was a respectable 5th at the World's, but in neither performance did judges rate him nearly as high as they had at the U.S. Championships the year before.

The dashing Chris Bowman in 1988.
(Courtesy Paul Harvath)

When Boitano turned professional, Bowman became galvanized in 1989 to achieve his greatest success, becoming both U.S. Champion and World Silver Medalist behind Canada's Kurt Browning. Still recovering from an injury, he was unable to compete at the 1990 U.S. Championships, but as is customary in such cases involving a reigning World medalist, he was named to the U.S. World team that year anyway and proved himself worthy by taking the Bronze Medal behind Browning and Viktor Petrenko of the Soviet Union. By this time, however, Bowman had become the object of much attention in the tabloid press for his partying ways, and skating professionals were shaking their heads over his flamboyant antics and lackadaisical practice habits.

Much-publicized rifts with coach Frank Carroll surfaced in 1991 when Bowman placed 2nd to Todd Eldredge at the U.S. Championships and 5th at the World Championships. He was still greeted with vast applause by audiences, and teenage girls squealed as they once had at the Beatles. On one occasion, a girl actually fell over the barrier onto the ice trying to present him with flowers. He played to the audience, winking and smiling outrageously at times, and sometimes skated directly up to television cameras to mug into them while performing. Judges did not find these displays nearly as cute as audiences did. Most of the time, Bowman seemed entirely unrepentant, going so far as to describe himself to the press as "Hans Brinker from hell." But he was moved to tears by the breakup with Coach Carroll, suggesting that his usual bravado was to some degree an act.

With a new coach, former World and Olympic medalist Toller Cranston of Canada, he asserted himself to win the U.S. Championship again in 1992. But at both the Olympics and World Championships that year, he seemed ill at ease and placed 4th in both competitions. He then turned professional but did not pursue that career with any real fervor.

BRAAKMAN, GEORGE *(b. 1906) U.S. medalist.*

George Braakman competed in the era just before U.S. skaters began to compete regularly in the World Championships. A sense of his ability can be gauged from the fact that in 1925 he was the U.S. Silver Medalist behind Nathaniel Niles, who at the 1924 Olympics came in 6th. Braakman took the U.S. Bronze Medal in 1927 when Niles was again champion; second place went to Roger Turner, who would go on to take the World Silver in 1930 and 1931. It was not until the 1920s that U.S. figure skating really began to be taken seriously; Braakman holds an honorable place among its early practitioners.

Isabelle Brasseur and Lloyd Eisler performing a one-handed lift.
(Courtesy Michelle Harvath)

BRACKET *See* SCHOOL FIGURES.

BRADSHAW, ROBERT *(b. 1954) U.S. medalist.*

In 1973, Robert Bradshaw took the U.S. Silver Medal at Minneapolis, behind Gordie McKellen, who won the first of three successive U.S. Championships. Bradshaw placed 12th at that year's World Championships. Between 1970 and 1978 there was intense competition among a group of strong free skaters for the national title, but many were weak in figures and none was able to win a World medal.

BRASSEUR, ISABELLE *(b. 1971) Canadian and World Pair Champion with Lloyd Eisler (b. 1964).*

Growing up in the town of St.-Jean-sûr-Richlieu near Montreal, Canada, Isabelle Brasseur began to skate when she was six. She was encouraged to try Pairs skating because she was small, an advantage because of the strenuous lifts the discipline entails. She was only moderately successful. When she was 17, her first partner decided to give up skating; Lloyd Eisler was suggested as a partner. A 24-year-old skater from Ontario, he retired from the sport in 1986 when his third partner, Katherina Matousek, with whom he had won the World Bronze in 1985, was forced to give up competitive skating because of injuries.

Brasseur spoke no English, and Eisler knew very little French, but despite that drawback and their age difference, they formed an immediate rapport. Her style was soft and flowing, his very athletic; instead of producing a discordant clash, these differences proved to be complementary in ways that brought out the best in both of them. They began to skate together in 1987. The following year won the Canadian Bronze Medal and placed a respectable 9th at the 1988 Calgary Olympics. This was rapid progress for a newly formed Pair. By 1990 they had taken the Canadian Silver Medal and then surprised everyone—and showed their true strength—by capturing the World Silver Medal. In 1991, they became Canadian Champions and once again World Silver Medalists.

The World Gold Medalists in 1991 were Natalia Mishkutenok and Artur Dmitriev of the Soviet Union. In 1990, they had been the Bronze winners and had overtaken Brasseur and Eisler in their next meeting. This set up a stirring confrontation for the 1992 Olympics in Albertville, France as the Canadians tried to become the first Pair from their country to win an Olympic Gold Medal since Barbara Wagner and Robert Paul in 1960. The Soviets, who in 1992 would appear under the rubric of the post-communist Commonwealth of Independent States, were a balletic Pair in the traditional Soviet mold, while Brasseur and Eisler were more contemporary and daring. "Technically, both teams are equal. But the styles are like night and day," Eisler commented before the Olympics.

Brasseur and Eisler did have one lift in their repertoire, however, that no other Pair in the world performed: Called a triple lateral twist, it involved Eisler raising Brasseur over his head and throwing her higher into the air, where she made three horizontal revolutions before being caught. The ability to perform this dangerous stunt was as much a tribute to Brasseur as to Eisler. Their coach, Josee Picard, put it in perspective: "The reason they can do all these tricks is not only because Lloyd is so strong, but also because Isabelle is so gutsy. Not many people want to be thrown that high." Audiences watching figure skating don't always realize the extent to which the success of a top Pair depends upon the fearlessness of the woman partner: The courage of the woman determines how daring a couple's routine will be, although she must have absolute trust in her partner.

Brasseur and Eisler did have one technical weakness: their execution of side-by-side double jumps, especially the difficult double axel, which requires two-and-one-half revolutions in the air. Perfectly executed, these jumps should be marked by simultaneous takeoffs, turns and landings. Isabelle Brasseur admitted that these jumps were the one element of the program that made her nervous. Sometimes she did not complete the full number of revolutions or two-footed the landing; when she did it correctly, Eisler, too, might make a mistake. The couple had trouble with the jumps at both the Olympics and the World's in 1992. Their marks suffered accordingly and they could only manage to take the Bronze Medal at both events.

The skating disappointments of 1992 were put in perspective, however, by Isabelle's father's unexpected death in fall 1992. Lloyd had also been close to him, and his death brought them to the realization that skating was not everything. The emotional turmoil they both experienced deepened their rapport on the ice; their new understanding that there were more important things than skating calmed their nerves at competitions. At the 1993 World Championships, they skated the finest performance of their lives and became Champions of the World. Mishkutenok and Dmitriev had turned professional, but observers noted that Brasseur and Eisler had higher marks than the Soviet couple had previously amassed in beating them.

Brasseur and Eisler were initially the clear favorites for the 1994 Olympic Gold Medal but suddenly found they would be competing against both the 1988 and 1992 Russian Gold Medalists, both couples having been granted amateur reinstatement for the 1994 games. Ekaterina Gordeeva and Sergei Grinkov seemed to be particularly dangerous: When they had won in 1988, Gordeeva had been only 16; now husband and wife, she and Grinkov were skating with the pure classical line for which they were noted with a new emotional intensity. Despite several small bobbles by Grinkov in the long program, they won another Gold Medal in 1994 in a controversial decision. Mishkutenok and Dmitriev, skating a more difficult program, were the Silver Medal winners, and Brasseur and Eisler once again took only the Bronze.

All three couples had at least one first-place vote from the judges. As with all the other skating events at the Olympics in Lillehammer, controversy swirled. Lloyd Eisler, always outspoken, added fuel to the debate by stating. "I don't agree they should be back," he said. "Tonight, we're the Gold Medal winners." Isabelle Brasseur always let her partner do most of the talking to the press, but she nodded her head vigorously in agreement at this comment. The couple then prepared to launch their own professional careers.

BREEN, PETER *See* MAYER, RACHEL.

BREWER, ROBERT *(b. 1939) U.S. medalist.*

Skating at the end of a decade in which American men had dominated international figure skating, Robert Brewer placed 4th in the United States in 1957 and 1958 and won the Bronze Medal in 1959 and 1960. Because American men had taken the top three places in both 1955 and 1956 at the World's, four men from the United States were allowed to compete in 1957, and with David Jenkins and Tim Brown taking the Gold and Silver World Medals in 1958, there were again four U.S. representatives in 1959. In these years, Robert Brewer placed 8th, 10th and 11th at the World Championships and 7th at the 1960 Olympics.

BRINKMAN, CHARLES *(b. 1928) U.S. Pairs medalist.*

In 1946 and 1947, Charles Brinkman won the U.S. Bronze Medal in Pairs skating with two different partners: first with Patty Sonnekson (b. 1927) and then with Carolyn Welch (b. 1929). The Gold Medalists in 1946 were Donna J. Pospisil and Jean Pierre Brunet and in 1947 Yvonne Sherman and Robert Swenning. Both years the Silver Medalists were Peter and Karol Kennedy, who would then go on to reign as U.S. Champions for five years. Brinkman did not get to compete at the World's because the U.S. contingent was limited to two couples.

BROCKHOFFT, ELLEN *(b. 1906) German Champion in mid-1920s.*

German Champion from 1923 to 1925, Ellen Brockhofft took the World Silver Medal in 1924–25 behind the great Austrian skater Herma Plank-Szabo. In 1925, Brockhofft's German rival Elisabeth Bockel was right behind her in 3rd place, but they would be the last German women soloists to win World medals until Gundi Busch took the Ladies' Silver Medal in 1953.

BROWN, BARBARA *(b. 1952) U.S. Pairs medalist.*

Partnered with Doug Berndt, Barbara Brown was the U.S. Bronze Medalist in Pairs in 1971 and 1972. This was a considerable accomplishment during a period marked by strong U.S. Pairs competition, led by JoJo Starbuck and Ken Shelley and the sister-brother team of Melissa and Mark Militano. At the World's, Brown and Berndt placed 11th in 1971 and 14th in 1972.

BROWN, MARTHA *(b. 1900) U.S. medalist.*

When Martha Brown won the Silver Medal behind Theresa Weld in 1920, U.S. figure skating was still in its developmental stage. The first competition was held in 1914, but there was no event in 1915–17 or in 1919. Brown, a skater from the conservative old school, made her mark just before a more athletic form of women's skating took hold.

BROWN, TIM *(b. 1936) Major U.S. medalist.*

Tim Brown had the misfortune to compete directly against David Jenkins year after year: From 1957 to 1960, Jenkins was the U.S. Gold Medalist and Brown the Silver Medalist. Brown demonstrated how fine a skater he was in terms of that period, however, by taking the Silver to Jenkins' Gold at successive World Championships in 1957–58, as well as the World Bronze in 1959. Although he was again U.S. Silver Medalist in 1960, male competitors' quality rose internationally with the presence of Canada's Donald Jackson, Czechoslovakia's Carol Divin and France's two Alains, Giletti and Calmat. At the 1960 Olympics, Brown took 5th place and did not skate at the World competition that year.

With Jenkins' retirement, 1961 should have been Tim Brown's year to gain the national title, but his own skills had slipped just as Bradley Lord and Gregory Kelley made forward strides. Brown's winning the Bronze was actually an example of bizarre, ironic fortune, however: Neither Jenkins nor Brown had competed at the previous year's World Championships, and although Lord and Kelley had come in 6th and 9th, respectively, the lack of an American medalist meant that there were only two positions open on the upcoming

1961 World team. Lord and Kelley took those places and were both killed in the Brussels airplane crash that wiped out the entire U.S. World Team in 1961. Brown, left behind, owed his life to his mediocre performance at the Nationals.

Despite never becoming national champion, Tim Brown had a splendid amateur career. Nothing better showed his love for skating and his talent's versatility than his second Men's Silver Medal and his Bronze in Ice Dancing with Susan Sebo in 1958. He took the challenge of entering that separate competition because it was fun.

BROWNING, KURT *(b. 1966)*

Canadian World Champion.

Few skaters have spent more time in the shadow of a champion from the same country as Kurt Browning of Canada. Brian Orser was Champion of Canada from 1981 through 1988, and from 1984 through 1988, Kurt Browning was runner-up. During those years, Browning never captured a World medal: the Soviet Union's Alexandr Fadeev, U.S.'s Brian Boitano and Orser commanded the medal platform in one order or another for three years, and the Soviet Union's Viktor Petrenko took over the Bronze from teammate Fadeev in 1988. But with the retirement of the two Brians after 1988, Kurt Browning was more than ready to take command.

This lithe, elegant skater from Edmonton, Alberta with the powerhouse jumps dominated men's skating for the next three years, becoming both Canadian and World Champion from 1989 to 1991. It seemed a matter of destiny that he would repeat as World Champion and take the Olympic Gold in 1992: Petrenko (World Silver Medalist in both 1990 and 1991), and Americans Christopher Bowman (Silver Medalist in 1989 and Bronze Medalist in 1990) and Todd Eldredge (1991 Bronze winner) were all given to erratic competitive performances. Browning planned to turn professional after an expected Olympic win.

But it was not to be. A back injury forced him off the ice at the beginning of November 1991. For six weeks he was not able to skate at all, and even after he returned to practice, his progress was not rapid enough to enable him to compete in the Canadian Championships, which Elvis Stojko won. As World Champion, Browning was still eligible for the Olympic and World competitions, but many wondered if he was as completely healed as he claimed. It turned out that he was not. At the Olympics, he slipped at crucial moments in the short program and missed several jumps in the long. He ended up in 6th place, while Petrenko took the

Canada's Kurt Browning won his second of five World Championships in 1990.
(Courtesy Paul Harvath)

Gold, the United States' Paul Wylie the Silver and Czechoslovakia's Petr Barna the Bronze.

At the World Championships, Browning pulled himself together, performing almost as spectacularly as he had the year before. But he was still not quite up to standard, and Petrenko skated better than he had at the Olympics (where many observers thought Wylie should have won) to take the Gold Medal. In Wylie's absence, Elvis Stojko took the Bronze—the first time two Canadian skaters had ever shared the podium at the World's.

Browning now faced a major question: Should he turn professional as planned or, with the one-time opportunity afforded by a mere two-year wait for the next Winter Olympics, keep competing as an amateur and go for the Olympic Gold? There were several factors—financial, physical, competitive—that suggested he should turn professional, but his final decision was primarily a matter of pride. He wanted to attain the amateur goal he had set for himself—to be World and Olympic Champion.

All went well in 1993. He was again both Canadian and World Champion, with Stojko 2nd at both competitions, but in winter 1994 Elvis Stojko claimed the Canadian Championship. Browning had not skated badly, but he went to the Olympics without the imprimatur of being national champion. Further, both the 1988 and 1992 Olympic Gold Medalists—Boitano and Petrenko—were reinstated as amateurs, making the competition particularly tough. As it turned out, both Boitano and Petrenko faltered in the short program. But so did Browning, falling on a triple flip, a jump he hadn't missed in years. As he left the ice, he told his coach, "I guess the Olympics just aren't for me:" He was in 12th place after the short program. He skated beautifully to music from *Casablanca* for the long program, but it pulled him up only to 5th place. Not competing at the 1994 World's, Browning instead began his professional career by commentating from the broadcast booth. Always articulate, he did it well.

Kurt Browning's amateur career did not end with the triumph he wanted. But for several years he was unarguably the best male skater in the world, and he will have a special place in figure-skating history for performing the first complete quadruple jump, a four-revolution toe loop, even before he became World Champion, at the 1988 World Championships in Belgrade. Moreover, as his *Casablanca* routine demonstrated at the 1994 Olympics, he matured artistically into a skater capable of acting while skating. There are not too many skaters who can do that, and that ability is likely to give him a significant professional career.

BRUNET, JEAN PIERRE *(1927–46)*

Brilliant young U.S. Pairs Champion killed tragically at age 19.

Son of the great French Pairs skaters Pierre Brunet and Andrée Joly Brunet, Jean Pierre came to the United States with his parents in the mid-1930s. At the age of 17, Jean Pierre, with partner Donna J. Popisil, became U.S. Pairs Champion in 1945 and repeated the following year. He was also competing in the Men's division as a soloist and was on the verge of breaking into the top three. Dashing and very popular, his death in an automobile accident in summer 1946 caused much sadness. It so affected his father that for years he refused to teach male skaters, making an exception only for Donald Jackson of Canada in the late 1950s.

BRUNET, PIERRE *(b. 1902) French*

Pairs innovator was World and Olympic Champion with Andrée Joly (b. 1901), who became his wife.

Spectators and judges at the 1924 Olympics, the first official Winter Games, held at Chamonix, France, were startled by a young French couple named Pierre Brunet and Andrée Joly in the Pairs competition. Performing lifts never before seen and far more side-by-side jumps and spins than any Pair had previously used, they thrilled many but caused several conservative judges to denounce them for what one called circus tricks. They ended up with the Bronze Medal.

France's Andrée and Pierre Brunet revolutionized Pairs Skating in the 1930s.
(Courtesy World Figure Skating Museum)

The following year, the Brunets (now married) were the World Silver Medalists behind Herma Jaross-Szabo, who also won the Ladies' Gold Medal, and her partner Ludwig Wrede, but in 1926 the Brunets themselves became World Champions. Due to Andrée's pregnancy with their first child, Jean Pierre, the Brunets did not compete in 1927. Returning to competition in 1928, they became both World and Olympic Champions, beating Lilly Scholz and Otto Kaiser of Austria in both contests. By now the Brunets' daring new approach was accepted as the standard for excellence, and younger pairs were following their lead, but no couple ever beat them in amateur competition. They were absent in both 1929 and 1931, but when they competed in 1930 and 1932, they won handily, also capturing a second Olympic Gold in 1932.

They emigrated to America in the mid-1930s, where Pierre became one of the most important coaches, guiding many top solo and Pairs skaters, including Canada's Donald Jackson, who won the 1962 World Championship with what is still considered one of the greatest free-skating performances of all time.

BRUNNER, MELITTA *(b. 1907)*

Austrian World and Olympic medalist as a Pair with Ludwig Wrede (1905), as well as World medalist as a solo.

Like her few-years-older countrywoman Herma Jaross-Szabo, Melitta Brunner was a top competitor in both Ladies' and Pairs skating. Always in the top five, Brunner took her only solo medal in 1929, winning the World Bronze behind Norway's unbeatable Sonja Henie and Austrian Fritzi Burger. She had greater success in Pairs, winning not only the 1928 Olympic and World Bronze as the second partner of Ludwig Wrede, (who had been World Champion with Jaross-Szabo) but also the World Silver in 1929 and 1930. With her two medals in 1929, she became one of the handful of skaters to win World medals in two different disciplines in the same year.

BUCK, ANGELIKA AND ERICH

(b. 1950, 1949) Sister-and-brother Ice Dance team from West Germany.

Angelika and Erich Buck won the World Bronze Medal in Ice Dancing in 1970 behind the first Soviet couple to win the Ice Dance Gold Medal, Ludmila Pakhomova and Aleksandr Gorshkov, and Americans Judy Schwomeyer and James Sladky. The next two years the Bucks topped the Americans for the Silver Medal and in 1973 took the Silver again over Hilary Green and Glyn Watts of Great Britain. But neither they nor anyone else could ever beat Pakhomova and Gorshkov, who went on to take the first Olympic Gold Medal in Ice Dance in 1976. But just as the Soviets contributed a new Ice Dance to the standard repertoire—the Tango romantico—in 1974, so did the Bucks a year earlier with the Ravensburger Waltz.

BURGE, WENDY *(b. 1957) Stalwart U.S. medalist who never quite made it to the top.*

In 1975, Wendy Burge was 2nd to Dorothy Hamill at the U.S. Championships and 4th at the World's (Hamill was 2nd). But the up-and-coming Linda Fratianne surged past her into 2nd place in the United States in 1976, while Burge slipped to 5th at the World's and took 6th place at the Olympics in Innsbruck that year. She kept at it another year, again taking the U.S. Bronze, but finished only 8th at the World's and retired from amateur skating.

BURGER, FRITZI *(b. 1910) Austrian Champion and World and Olympic medalist.*

A splendid free skater whose amateur career unfortunately overlapped with that of Norway's Sonja Henie, four-time Austrian champion Fritzi Burger was also challenged on her home ground by Melitta Brunner and Hilde Holovsky; even so, she achieved a very distinguished record: In her first year as Austrian Champion, she succeeded five-time World Champion Herma Jaross-Szabo and placed 2nd to Sonja Henie at the 1928 Olympics in St. Moritz and 3rd at that year's World Championships in London behind Henie and America's Maribel Vinson. In 1929, she took the World Silver but was out of the medal standings in 1930. She took the 1931 World Bronze, while her countrywoman, Hilde Holovsky, gained the Silver Medal behind Henie. In Burger's final competitive year, she finished with a flourish, taking the Silver Medal behind Henie at both the 1932 Olympics in Lake Placid, New York and the World Championships in Montreal.

BURGER, HEINRICH *See* HUBLER, ANNA.

BURKE, PETRA *(b. 1946) Canadian and World Champion.*

Petra Burke, a skater with dash and speed, became Canadian Champion in 1963 and was both the Olympic and World Bronze Medalist the following year, with Skoujke Dijkstra of the Netherlands and Regine Heitzer of Austria taking the Gold and Silver at both competitions. In 1965, after three-time World Champion Dijkstra retired, Petra outskated two-time Silver Medalist Heitzer to become World Champion. Seeking to repeat as champion in 1966, she fell victim to U.S. skater Peggy Fleming (World Champion at the age of 16 and Bronze Medalist the year before) and 18-year-old East Germany's Gabrielle Seyfert (at 18 already winner of three Silver and two Gold Medals). With a second Bronze to her credit, Burke then turned professional.

BUSCH, GUNDI *(b. 1934) West German World Champion.*

In 1953, Gundi Busch became the first German woman to win a World medal since Ellen Brockhofft and Elisabeth Bockel took the Silver and Bronze in 1925. United States Olympic Silver Medalist Tenley Albright took the Gold, but Busch was right behind her in points to take the Silver. The next year, Busch won the European Championship for the second time and eclipsed Albright for the World Gold.

BUTTON, DICK *(b. 1930) U.S., World and Olympic Champion, later television commentator on the sport.*

His first skating teacher told a pudgy 12-year-old Dick Button that "hell would freeze over" before he became a real skater. That 1942 judgment made Button's father angry enough to hire top teacher/coach Gustav Lussi, to instruct his youngest son. Lussi worked primarily out of Lake Placid, New York, site of the 1932 Winter Olympics, and Button was to spend his summers there for the next 10 years. Within a year Lussi had Button in 2nd place in his first competition, the Eastern States Novice title. Next time out, on April 17, 1943, he became the Middle Atlantic Novice Champion and three years later, at the age of 16, U.S. champion.

Swiss-born Lussi was a stickler for discipline but he was also supportive of Button's quest to add inventive and difficult new moves to his repertoire. The first of Button's innovations, the flying camel, was first performed at the 1947 World Championships in Stockholm. Button added a new element to the well-known camel spin by jumping into it. For many years, his version was called the Button Camel.

At the 1947 World Championships Button came in 2nd to Hans Gerschwiler of Switzerland, although the grand old man of figure skating, Ulrich Salchow, told Button he should have won.

Button immediately began to prepare for the coming Olympics, another chance at the World title and the defense of his U.S. title. He and Lussi decided to enter Button first in the European Championships, two weeks before the Olympics. No American had previously contested the European title. If he could win it from Hans Gerschwiler, he would have an edge for the Olympics. Even if he didn't win, his performance would accustom judges to his power-packed free-skating program. The gamble paid off. In Prague, Czechoslovakia he won the European Gold Medal, as did another North American in the Women's competition, Canada's Barbara Ann Scott. From then on, only skaters from European countries would be allowed to compete at this event.

Both Button and Scott then won Olympic Gold Medals at St. Moritz in Gerschwiler's home country. The Swiss skater took the Silver Medal and then retired from amateur skating. Button was still only 18. Although he set his sights on a second Olympic title four years in the future, there was a problem: He had already been accepted by Yale University but would not be allowed to take time off to skate competitively. Yale's rival was willing to let him pursue his amateur skating career provided he kept his grades up, so Button went to Harvard instead.

In 1949, Button became the first figure skater to receive the James E. Sullivan Award, the most prestigious honor in amateur U.S. sports. Awarded annually to "the amateur athlete who, by performance, example, and good influence, did the most to advance the cause of good sportsmanship during the year" and voted by more than 600 sportswriters, the award was important to Button because it signified that figure skating was at last being taken seriously as a major sport in the United States.

During the next three years, Button repeated as U.S. and World Champion each year. In 1948 he was the first skater to perform a double axel, requiring two-and-a-half turns in the air. In 1951 he first

Dick Button at the start of his fabled career, U.S. Champion at 16.

(Courtesy World Figure Skating Museum)

performed a double-loop-combination jump: This last involved taking off on a back outside edge, revolving twice in the air, landing cleanly and then launching into a repeat of the same jump without taking any extra steps. Such double-jump combinations are now a basic part of every world-class skater's repertoire, but at the time the double-loop combination set a new standard; skaters around the world had to scramble to catch up.

In the summer of 1951, Button started to work on a triple loop, requiring three full revolutions in the air. Many coaches and skaters regarded this as an impossible task, and as the summer wore on at Lake Placid, Button began to wonder if they weren't right. Not only was he failing to make the jump, but the effort to do so was badly affecting his other jumps. "When I tried to do a simple axel," he wrote in his autobiography, *Dick Button on Skates*, "I couldn't control my rotation. It was impossible to remain cool, for the harder I tried, the less sense of direction, of rotation, of control was in any jump. . . . Double salchows, axels, double flips, even single flips were 'lost.' But surely no one ever appeared more amusing than I did, wandering around the ice looking for even a solitary double salchow."

The other jumps came back, but the triple loop remained elusive, and he stopped trying to conquer it. Then, shortly before Christmas, practicing at the Boston Skating Club, he decided on the spur of the moment to give it another try, and suddenly he "got" it. It needed a lot more work, but he had the feel of it. He accomplished the jump before an audience for the first time at an exhibition in Vienna just before the 1952 Olympics at Oslo, Norway. Because he had tried it the previous day and fallen, there was so much speculation as to whether he would try it in competition that he felt inordinately pressured: If he attempted the triple loop and fell, it could lead to other mistakes and cost him the Gold Medal.

In Norway he took a strong lead in the competition's school-figures portion. Button then placed the triple loop early in his free-skating program. "I was extraordinarily conscious of the judges, who looked so immobile at rinkside. But this was it. The edge cut the ice and my arms lowered, shoulders turning against the rotation to allow a grip that would follow through. My knees closed as my feet crossed in the air. The wind cut my eyes, and the coldness caused tears to stream down my cheeks. Up! Up! Height was vital. Round and around again in a spin which took only a fraction of a second to complete before it landed on a clean steady back edge. I pulled away breathless, excited and overjoyed, as applause rolled from the faraway stands like the rumbling of a distant pounding sea."

Button won his fifth straight World Championship and his seventh U.S. title in 1952 and that fall entered Harvard Law School. He also turned professional after nine years as an amateur skater, skating a limited schedule of appearances with the Ice Capades at intervals that did not conflict with his studies. After he left amateur figure skating, he wondered aloud if the emphasis on jumping that resulted from his style has been entirely a good thing, if it has perhaps gone too far.

For the last two decades, Button has been a television commentator on the sport. He is revered by most skaters, not least because his commentary has always been as fair as it has been tough. Never hesitating to tell viewers what a skater needs to do to improve, he has nevertheless been kind and supportive off the air. In a 1993 television interview, he was asked whether he thought the general public remembered him as much as a skater as they did as a commentator. He replied, "I don't care if they remember me as a skater or as a commentator. It's just nice to be remembered."

BYRN, YNGVAR *See* SCHOYEN, ALEXIA.

C

CALMAT, ALAIN *(1942) French World Champion.*

The 1960 World Championships proved a banner year for the French team, as young Alain Calmat skated to the Bronze Medal, the sister-and-brother Ice Dancers Christine and Jean Paul Guhel took the Bronze Medal and Men's Champion Alain Giletti grabbed the World Gold from expected winner Donald Jackson of Canada. The following year the World Championships were canceled because of the deaths of the American team in an airplane crash at Brussels, but in 1962, Alain Calmat was again the Bronze Medalist. In 1963 and 1964, Calmat moved up to the Silver Medal behind 1st-place Donald McPherson of Canada and then Manfred Schnelldorfer of West Germany. He was also the 1964 Silver Medalist at the Olympics in Innsbruck, Austria. In 1965 he finally laid claim to the World title, beating the U.S.'s Scott Allen and Canada's Donald Knight.

CAMEL SPIN

The camel spin is one of the most commonly seen moves in free-skating. The skater spins on one foot, with the body and the extended free leg held parallel to the ice, while the back is arched. The arm positions may be varied to give the spin a slightly different look, but the extended leg must not droop and the spin must be performed without any wobble to gain the highest marks. An outgrowth of the ballet position called the arabesque, the camel spin goes far back into figure skating history. But it was given a dramatic new life by Dick Button, who was the first person to jump into the spin. For many years this variation was called the Button Camel, but then came to be known as the flying camel. Brian Boitano later became renowned for the great height he was able to achieve in his jump into a solid landing and an exceptionally fast and well-controlled spin. Among women, Dorothy Hamill developed a new variation that involved bending the lower part of the free leg upward from the knee, a move that came to be known as the Hamill camel.

Camel spins are also often performed, separately but in tandem, by pair skaters. With pairs, judges look closely to see that both skaters revolve at the same rate while performing the camel and that they conclude the spin at the same instant, facing in the same direction. Perfectly controlled side-by-side camel spins can make a crucial difference in the marks for pair skaters.

CAMPBELL, MARY *See* JOHNS, JOHNNY.

CAMPBELL, ROGER *(1943–61) U.S. Ice Dance medalist.*

Roger Campbell took the U.S. Bronze in Ice Dancing in 1960 with Yvonne Littlefield, and the couple placed 8th at that year's World Championships. Splitting with Littlefield, he took the U.S. Silver with new partner Dona Lee Carrier in 1961. Both were killed in an airplane crash at Brussels.

CAMPER, VICKI *(b. 1947) U.S. Ice Dance medalist.*

With partner Eugene Heffron, Vicki Camper surprisingly took a Silver Medal at the U.S. Championships in 1968 and placed 7th at the World's. In a period marked by a large number of accomplished U.S. ice dancers, the couple decided that they were unlikely to better such placements and retired.

CANDELORO, PHILIPPE *(b. 1972) Flamboyant French Champion and World and Olympic medalist.*

The 1994 Winter Olympics men's figure-skating competition was full of surprises, with such "big guns" as Browning, Boitano and Petrenko falling, literally, out of contention and, on the plus side, the showing of French Champion Philippe Candeloro. A skater known for his colorful personality, Candeloro also had a reputation for falling apart in competition—he'd done it at the European Championships shortly before the Olympics, finishing 5th.

The flamboyant Philippe Candeloro skating bare-chested in an exhibition.
(Courtesy Michelle Harvath)

But at the Olympics, his flash and daring was more securely tied to technical control. Skating both his short and long programs to selections from *The Godfather* movies, he created a character on ice. The audience loved him, and the judges put him solidly into 3rd place for the Bronze Medal behind Russia's Aleksi Urmanov and Canada's Elvis Stojko. He repeated his performance at the World Championships in Sapporo, Japan and although his skating was a little sloppier, he once again took the Bronze Medal. At both competitions he skated an exhibition number that had him draped in a billowing U.S. flag shirt, which he then removed to skate bare to the midriff. There was general acknowledgment in the skating world that whether or not he ever becomes World Champion, Philippe Candeloro certainly can count on being a major box-office attraction as a professional down the line.

In 1995, Candeloro was again the World Bronze Medalist behind World Champion Elvis Stojko and, this time, America's Todd Eldredge. Touring in shows almost nonstop during the next year, Candeloro seemed unprepared for competition in 1996, finishing only 5th at the European Championships. At World's he had the most disastrous outing in the short program for any major skater in memory, faltering on every jump and ending up in 16th place, with no hope for a medal no matter how well he skated in the long program. To conservatives in the skating world, this was an object lesson in the dangers of concentrating on show tours rather than the hard basic work necessary to keep an amateur in shape for the rigors of the required elements of the short program.

Never predictable, Candeloro competed at the 1998 Olympics in Nagano and demonstrated that he could still thrill audiences with his flamboyant style while skating well enough to win the Bronze behind Gold Medalist Ilia Kulik of Russia and Silver Medalist Elvis Stojko of Canada.

CARRELL, JOHN *See* DYER, LORNA.

CARRIER, DONA LEE *(1941–61) U.S. Ice Dance medalist killed at Brussels in 1961.*

It is unusual, in a discipline that puts so much emphasis on togetherness, for ice dancers to excel in the first year of a new partnership. But Dona Lee Carrier proved a superb match for partner Roger Campbell, who had won the U.S. Bronze with Yvonne Littlefield in 1960. Carter and Campbell made a splendid showing at the U.S. Championships in 1961, taking the Silver Medal. But their promise was brutally extinguished in an airplane crash at Brussels just days later.

CARRUTHERS, CAITLIN ("KITTY") and PETER *(b. 1962, 1960) Dynamic American Pairs team.*

Adopted brother and sister Peter and Kitty Carruthers had great unison.
(Courtesy Paul Harvath)

Adopted two years apart both at the age of about three months by Charley and Maureen Carruthers of Burlington, Massachusetts, Peter and Kitty began to skate together as a Pair in 1973 when Peter was 13 years old and Kitty was 11. They moved steadily up through the Pairs ranks, taking the U.S. Junior Championship in 1978 and coming in 2nd to Tai Babilonia and Randy Gardner in senior competition in 1980. At the 1980 Olympics at Lake Placid, the last-minute withdrawal of Babilonia and Gardner because of the latter's groin injury left the Carrutherses with the job of upholding U.S. honors, along with U.S. Bronze Medalists Sheryl Franks and Michael Botticelli. The Carrutherses finished a respectable 5th in their first international competition, while Franks and Botticelli came in 7th. At that year's World Championships they placed 7th.

They became U.S. Champions in 1981 and held the title without difficulty through 1984. During these years, the Carrutherses spent much of the year training in Wilmington, Delaware, the home rink of their coach, Ron Ludington, who in 1960 with his then wife Nancy, was the last American to date to win an Olympic Medal in Pairs, the Bronze. Ludington also coached Lea Ann Miller and William Fauver, who were runners-up to the Carrutherses in 1981, 1983 and 1984. While some skaters find it difficult to share a coach with their closest rivals, both couples felt it was good for them, honing their competitive edge.

The Carrutherses were very American Pairs skaters, emphasizing speed, daring and athleticism. Kitty was always willing to try new and dangerous lifts and jumps, so fearless that Ludington once said of her, "Kitty would have made a great ski jumper." That style put them at a disadvantage with some of the European and Soviet-bloc judges who preferred a more balletic approach, but the brother and sister were so so good at what they did that they were also in the medal hunt at World Championships. They finished 5th in 1981, took the Bronze Medal in 1982 and were 4th in 1983.

Going into the Olympic year of 1984, they were at the peak of their form. Kitty fell hard at the U.S. Championships while doing a throw-triple salchow, but she got up and finished strongly, even though she said afterward that she was in a kind of daze from the force of the fall. The 1984 Olympics in Sarajevo, Yugoslavia provided them with a great opportunity. Although their competition included the 1982 World Champions East Germany's Sabine Baess and Tassilo Thierbach, 1983 World Champions USSR's Elena Valova and Oleg Vasiliev and the strong Canadian Pair Barbara Underhill and Paul Martini, Bronze Medalists at the World's the previous year (just edging the Carrutherses), no one Pair had established clear dominance.

The major question in terms of their Olympic program was whether or not to include a quadruple-throw salchow in their performance. They had been able to complete this manuever, which no Pair had ever done in competition, 60 percent of the time in practice, but that left a large margin for failure. It was left up to coach Ron Ludington to make the final decision about whether or not to include the "quad" or stick with the triple; he decided against because the Carrutherses were tied with the younger Soviet couple, Larissa Selezneva and Oleg Makarov, after the short program, with Valova and Vasiliev securely in first place.

Peter and Kitty Carruthers skated the best they ever had on that February night in Sarajevo, and they hugged one another in joy at center ice after completing their program. The score was so close that it was 15 minutes before the results were finally announced. Valova and Vasiliev took the Gold Medal, the Carrutherses the Silver and Selezneva and Makarov the Bronze. It was the first time in 24 years that the U.S. flag had been raised at a Pairs medal ceremony at the Olympics and 32 years since another brother and sister, Karol and Peter Kennedy, had garnered a Silver Medal in Olympic Pairs for the United States. What's more, the Carrutherses were the first Americans to win any medal at the 1984 Winter Olympics.

Afterward, in an article for the *New York Times*, Peter Carruthers wrote, "When you go home from the Olympics with a Silver Medal, it may be difficult to convince people that you went to the Olympics not to win that medal, but to enjoy the experience. But that's the truth." Nevertheless, the medal had made the Carrutherses into real stars, and they signed a multiyear contract with the Ice Capades in late March 1984.

CARTWHEEL LIFT

This lift performed by Pairs skaters requires great strength by the male partner as well as perfect timing. The woman performs a cartwheel above the ice while supported by her partner, the difficulty lying in the fact that she is lifted to one side of her partner, which demands even greater strength than the overhead lifts in which the woman is held directly above her partner's head. Timing is extremely important not only at takeoff but also during the lift because the man must change hand positions several times as the woman swings full circle through the air.

CARZ, SHARON *(b. 1970) U.S. Pairs medalist with Doug Williams (b. 1969).*

Sharon Carz and Doug Williams won the U.S. Bronze in Pairs skating in 1990 behind the teams of Kristi Yamaguchi and Rudy Galindo and Natasha Kuchiki and Todd Sand. Carz and Williams placed 13th at that year's World Championships.

CHACK, MICHAEL *(b. 1971) U.S. medalist.*

The 1993 U.S. Championship Bronze Medalist Michael Chack is a skater who impresses greatly in practice but often falls prey to nerves in competition. He created a jump called the Chack-toe, a triple toe loop performed with the added difficulty of keeping the arms straight down at his sides.

CHALOM, EVE *(b. 1979) U.S. Ice Dancing medalist with Mathew Gates (b. 1985).*

In their first year of senior competition after winning the Junior Championship in 1995, Ice Dancers Eve Chalom and Mathew Gates captured the U.S. Bronze Medal, beating many more-experienced couples. Immediately heralded as the best future hope for U.S. Ice Dancing in many years, their rapid rise was made all the more unusual in that Eve Chalom is 60 percent hearing impaired in both ears, a disability that she feels has led her to develop a special degree of concentration that is very useful in the difficult Ice Dancing compulsories.

CHANGE SIT SPIN

Invented by Swedish skater Gillis Grafstrom, Olympic Gold Medalist in 1920, 1924 and 1928, the change sit spin is an essential free-skating element for both men and women. It involves a spin that is begun on one foot while in an upright position. The skater then drops to a sitting level, with the free leg crossed in front of the other; after several revolutions, the skater rises erect, switches feet and descends again for a second sit spin. Originally called a change foot sit spin, it is also referred to as a sit change sit.

This spin is not too difficult to perform adequately, but those who are really good at it make other skaters look klutzy. At its most ordinary, it can appear somewhat jerky in execution and is often marred by excessively hunched shoulders. Those who have truly mastered the spin give it both a degree of speed and a seamless flow that lifts it to another level. American Ladies' Champion of the late 1970s, Linda Fratianne, was particularly noted for the elegance of her change sit spin, and no one since the U.S.'s Ronnie Robertson in the 1950s has performed it with such dazzling speed as 1993 and 1994 U.S. Men's Champion Scott Davis.

CHEN LU *See under* LU.

CHERKASOVA, MARINA *(b. 1959) Soviet World Champion Pairs skater with Sergei Shakhrai (b. 1958)*

Soviet Pair Cherkasova and Shakhrai were national champions in 1979, a year that Irina Rodnina and her partner/husband Alexandr Zaitsev did not skate following the birth of their son. Cherkasova and Shakrai then took the Silver Medal at that year's World Championship behind U.S.'s Tai Babilonia and Randy Gardner. In 1980, Rodnina and Zaitsev returned for a final year of competition, reclaiming their Soviet title and taking a second Olympic Gold Medal at Lake Placid, New York. Because of a groin injury to Randy Gardner, the Olympics were deprived of the much anticipated showdown between Rodnina/Zaitsev and Babilonia/Gardner, and Cherkasova and Shakhrai were able to add an Olympic Silver Medal to their laurels. Rodnina and Zaitsev retired from amateur competition prior to the World Championships; with Babilonia/Gardner still out, the number two Soviet Pairs team garnered the World Gold Medal in their own final amateur appearance. Cherkasova and Shakhrai were a highly accomplished Pair, but their Silver and Gold Medals were essentially handed to them. There was no question that they were actually the third-best Pair in the World, although at another time they might well have been the unquestioned best.

CHETVERUKHIN, SERGEI *(b. 1950) Soviet World and Olympic medalist.*

Sergei Chetverukhin was the first Soviet male skater to win a World Championship medal, taking the Bronze in 1971. (Two Russians had taken medals long before the rise of the Soviet Union, in 1896 and 1903.) The Soviet skating authorities had long focused on Pairs and Ice Dance couples, and it was only when a larger group of young male skaters began to come along in the 1970s that any emphasis was placed on solo training. In 1972, Chetverukhin took both the Olympic and World Silver Medals and added another World Silver in 1973 before making way for his teammates Sergei Volkov and Vladimir Kovalev. The Gold winner of all the events in which Chetverukhin won medals was Ondrej Nepela of Czechoslovakia.

CHEVALIER, JEANNE *See* SCOTT, NORMAN.

CHIN, TIFFANY *(b. 1968) U.S. Champion.*

At the age of 15, in 1983, Tiffany Chin won the U.S. Bronze Medal and placed 9th at the World

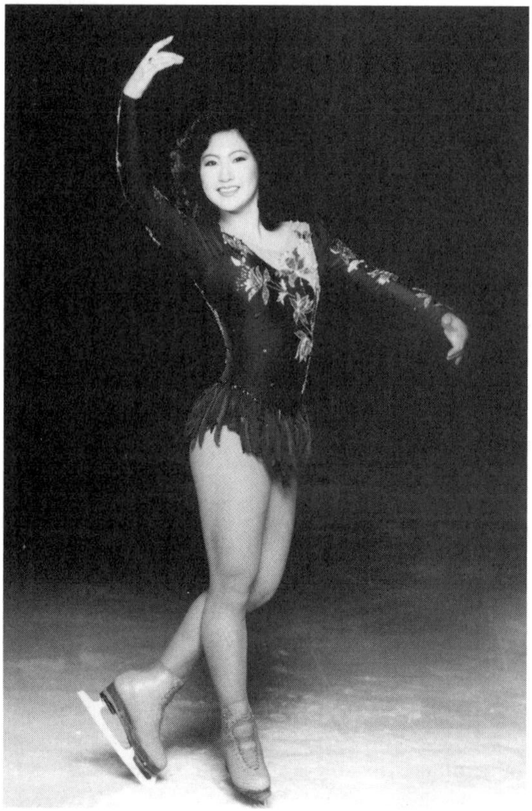

Tiffany Chin is regarded as a particularly elegant skater.
(Courtesy Michael Rosenberg)

Championships. The next year she was the U.S. Silver Medalist, winning both the long and short programs, but held back by her poor showing in school figures, she was unable to beat repeat champion Rosalynn Sumners. At the Olympics, her figures again gave her trouble: she placed 12th after the compulsories, only to rebound with her usual artistic program and four triple jumps to end up in 4th place. An injury kept her out of that year's World Championships, however.

Becoming U.S. Champion in 1985, the 5'1", 90-pound Chin took the Bronze at the World Championships behind East Germany's Katarina Witt and the Soviet Union's Kira Ivanova. In 1986, Debi Thomas and Caryn Kadavy, who had been 2nd and 3rd the previous year, skated past Chin to take the U.S. Gold and Silver. Her Bronze Medal and previous year's showing earned her a trip to the World Championships, where she skated to another Bronze Medal. Chin had always been prone to injuries—a serious stress fracture had knocked her out of skating for a year after she won the U.S. Junior Championship—but now a combination of foot and leg problems knocked her out of competition again. Her mother was pilloried in the press for having pushed her back into practice too soon following various injuries and at one point found herself defending her actions in a lengthy television interview. Tiffany was never able to regain her previous form, and a potential Olympic Gold Medal in 1988, which had always been her aim, was never realized. She currently skates professionally and teaches figure skating in Simi Valley, California.

CHRISTENSON, CHRIS *(b. 1874) U.S. Champion.*

As Sherwin Badger won his fourth straight U.S. Championship in 1923, 48-year-old Chris Christenson took the Silver in a year marked by the absence of the 1918 champion and three-time Silver Medal winner Nathaniel Niles. With the return of Niles the following year, Christenson was pushed back to the Bronze, with Badger again the victor. Christenson did not compete in 1925 as Niles became champion again. Returning in 1926, Christenson won the U.S. Gold Medal over Niles and Ferrier Martin; at 51 he was the oldest U.S. Champion ever. Because no U.S. men competed in the World Championships until 1928, Christenson's international standing cannot be measured.

CLARK, GARY *See* HECKERT, JOANNE.

CLEAN LANDING

Clean landings are a vital consideration for judges in marking the jumps of competitors. If a jump is securely landed on a single edge of one skate, it is considered clean, although there are a number of more subtle considerations that also come into play. The most blatant errors in landing a jump are usually obvious to even a less-than-fully knowledgeable audience. A fall is the worst that can happen, in which case the jump is simply considered as not having been performed. A jump that is landed with two feet is heavily penalized, but if the second foot merely touches the ice for a moment, fewer points are deducted. This kind of touchdown is sometimes so quick that the audience, and even some judges, may miss it. Marks are also lowered if a skater lands on the flat of the blade instead of the edge, although such a landing is likely to cause a fall.

Sometimes a skater will land a jump but, instead of maintaining the backward flow, will quickly turn to skate forward in order to keep from falling. This ungainly move will also mean a small point subtraction. Ideally, a cleanly landed jump involves a poised extension of the free leg behind the skater, maintained long enough to give a sense of grace in the case of a jump performed by itself. When a combination jump is being performed, it is the smoothness of the takeoff into the second jump that is paramount. Some skaters may land many of their jumps cleanly but with a wobbly, inelegant or truncated free leg extension; when this is done repeatedly, the skater will lose points in the artistic marks as well.

Great skaters will always have good extension of the free leg, but even among the major champions, some have been especially noted for this quality. Peggy Fleming's famous grace was due in part to her ability to maintain the free leg extension at the end of jumps. When she was skating at her best, Debi Thomas had extraordinary follow-through at the end of her very high jumps. Among men, both Brian Boitano and Paul Wylie are particularly admired for their ability to carry a clean landing through into a finish that leaves an indelible impression, in which technique and artistry become seamlessly fused.

CLIFF, LESLIE AND VIOLET

(b. 1915, 1917) British brother-and-sister World Bronze Medalists.

In 1936, the favorites to win the Olympic Gold Medal in Pairs were three-time World Champions Emilie Rotter and Laszlo Szollas of Hungary. But to their shock they were able to take only a Bronze Medal, as they had in 1932. The Gold went to Germany's Maxi Herber and Ernst Baier and the Silver to Austria's Ilse and Erich Pausin. Fourth at the Olympics were Leslie and Violet Cliff. The Hungarians were so distraught by what happened to them at the Olympics that they did not compete at the World's; there the Cliffs took the Bronze behind the German and Austrian Olympic medalists. They became the first British Pairs Champions to win a World medal since John Page and Ethel Muckelt in 1924. The Cliffs repeated as Bronze Medalists in 1937, again behind the Germans and Austrians, and then turned professional.

COCKRELL, MARK *(b. 1963) U.S. medalist.*

Mark Cockrell was the Bronze Medalist behind Scott Hamilton and Brian Boitano at the U.S. Championships in 1983 and 1984. At the 1983 World's, he was 14th and moved up to 13th in 1984; he was also 13th at the 1984 Olympics. He skated for one more year, taking the Silver behind

Boitano in 1985 and improved to 8th at the World Championships.

COLE, KING *See* DYER, LORNA.

COLLEDGE, CECILIA. *(b. 1918)*

British World Champion.

Cecilia Colledge was a strong challenger to Sonja Henie in the mid-1930s, but her greatest rivalry was with British teammate Megan Taylor. Taylor was the stronger free skater, although Colledge was hardly deficient in this regard. Colledge is almost universally regarded as the finest practitioner of the school figures who ever competed: Her upper body positions while doing the figures was always exemplary in terms of style, while the tracings she laid down on the ice came close to perfection again and again.

She and Taylor traded the British Gold and Silver Medals back and forth, and one or the other was always the runner-up to Henie during the Norwegian skater's last several competitions. Taylor took the World Silver in 1934, and Colledge won it in 1935; although Colledge won the coveted 1936 Olympic Silver Medal in 1936 at Henie's final Olympics, Taylor came right back and took the World Silver. The following year, with Henie now in Hollywood, Colledge prevailed as World Gold Medalist, with Taylor 2nd, but in 1938, it was Taylor 1st and Colledge 2nd.

Cecilia Colledge then turned professional and starred in many London-stage ice shows. Following World War II, she emigrated to the United States and established herself at the Skating Club of Boston as one of the foremost coaches in the United States during the next three decades.

British World Champion Cecilia Colledge became a famous coach.
(Courtesy World Figure Skating Museum)

COMBINATION JUMP

A sequence of two successive jumps that are performed without taking an extra step is called a combination jump. After landing the first jump, the skater must then take off into the second jump from the same foot he or she landed on, without additional preparation. This means that the initial jump must be landed cleanly and with speed, or the takeoff into the second jump will be compromised.

A combination jump is always included as part of the short program, with the jumps involved announced nearly a year in advance. Combination jumps are also an expected part of the long program, but here the individual skater may choose the jumps to be executed. Many men perform two triple jumps in combination, often a triple axel followed by a triple loop among the top competitors. Most women, even at the highest level, perform a triple jump followed by a double jump, with very few risking a triple-triple combination.

Combination jumps are the great leveler in the short program. There is no commoner way for medal favorites to put themselves out of contention than by missing the required combination jump in the short program because such severe point penalties are assessed. For example, both Kurt Browning and Brian Boitano missed their combinations in the short program at the 1994 Olympics. Browning had

had this experience before, but it had never happened to Boitano, who said afterward that if it had occurred when he was 19, "I probably would have considered suicide."

Combination jumps are now also a required element in Pairs competition; triple jumps are not yet specified as part of the Short Program combination, although a few top Pairs do perform them in the long program. Given the stamina necessary for Pairs lifts, a triple-double combination is still regarded as too severe a test of technical mastery in this discipline, although if more couples perform them, they may be seen as an ultimate way to differentiate between Gold and Silver Medal performances.

COOK, ALICE *See* FAUVER, WILLIAM.

COOK, HOLLY *(b. 1968) U.S. medalist.*

Holly Cook had been considered a potential medalist at the U.S. Championships for several years in the late 1980s, but something always seemed to go wrong. Attractive and dynamic, she was plagued by falls at crucial times in competition. In 1990 she put her problems behind her by taking the U.S. Bronze behind Jill Trenary and Kristi Yamaguchi and then topped that accomplishment by also taking the World Bronze one place ahead of Yamaguchi. It was a fine finish to an amateur career marked by many disappointments but a determination to keep at it.

COSTUMES

The clothing worn by figure skaters has from the beginning been a barometer of both fashion and cultural mores. In the 1890s, as national and international competition was first organized, male skaters wore top hats and tails while the women were draped in skirts to below the ankle and wore the kind of elaborate hat that could easily have a stuffed bird perched atop it. Because it was impossible to perform even a simple jump and keep a top hat on, the clothing of competitors at the early World Championships quickly took a practical turn. Hats remained in vogue, but they were now much more close fitting, with berets and tam-o'-shanters being sported by the men, and much snugger, less decorated hats appearing on the women. The tailcoat was replaced by double-breasted outdoor coats to the waist, and trousers were cut much more closely. Women's skirts remained ankle length well into the 1900s, but the great Madge Syers of Britain, who had had the audacity to enter the Men's competition at the World Championships in 1902, forcing the establishment of a Ladies' competition beginning in 1906, started to wear her skirts cut to midcalf; other women skaters followed suit.

Still, it was not until after World War I that skating attire began to resemble anything like what we see today. Spangled or otherwise glittery costumes for women, with skirts above the knee, became common in the 1930s, and men's jackets were tighter and of lighter material. But even after World War II, costumes for competition remained much more conservative than they did in the ice shows the same skaters joined when they turned professional. The plunging necklines and very short skirts seen in the Ice Follies were frowned upon in competition, and it wasn't until the mid-1960s that costumes in any color but black or white became acceptable for male competitors.

The boundaries were most aggressively pushed by Pairs skaters, whose outfits had become virtually indistinguishable from those worn by professionals in the late 1970s. But even in 1983, Torvill and Dean were advised to change from the electrifying costumes in Day-Glo colors they had worn while winning the British Championships before defending their World title—Ice Dance judges remained, as ever, the most conservative. By the end of the 1980s, however, competition attire had taken on the open glitter of theatrical costuming across the board. Still, there are some restrictions. In his exhibition performance after winning the 1994 Olympic Bronze Medal at Lillehammer, Norway, France's Philippe Candeloro skated naked to the waist. That would still not be acceptable in competition.

In 1996, Jere Longman, the figure-skating reporter for the *New York Times* wrote: "As usual, figure skating's National Championships provided a week of the inspiring, the riveting, the poignant, the outrageous, the revealing, the concealing, the soaring and the plunging. And that was just the costumes." Things had come a long way since the bundled-up beginnings of competitive figure skating a century earlier.

COURTLAND, KAREN *(b. 1970) U.S. Pairs medalist with R. Todd Reynolds (b. 1966).*

Karen Courtland had had several other Pairs partners without achieving medal success when she teamed up with R. Todd Reynolds in 1989. In 1993, the couple were the U.S. Bronze Medalists behind Pairs Calla Urbanski and Rocky Marval and Jenni Meno and R. Todd Sand. They repeated that standing at the U.S. Championships in 1994 and placed 14th at the Olympics in Lillehammer, Norway.

COURTNEY, JACK *See* BENENSON, EMILY.

COUSINS, ROBIN *(b. 1957) British World Silver and Olympic Gold Medalist in 1980.*

The youngest of the three sons of Fred and Jo Cousins, Robin was born in Bristol, England. Introduced to figure skating on a vacation in Bournemouth in the summer of 1965, he took up the sport the following year when the first ice rink was opened in Bristol. By 1972 he had become Britain's Junior Champion. Moving up to the senior ranks, Cousins came in 2nd to John Curry. He excelled at jumping, achieving remarkable height, but this ability took a physical toll, causing cartilage damage to both the ankle and knee of his right leg, on which he landed his jumps. To correct the damage, he underwent surgery, thereby slowing his development.

By 1976, when John Curry took both the World and Olympic titles, Cousins had become one of the top 10 skaters in the world, finishing 10th at the Olympics and 9th at the World Championships. The following year he took first place at the Skate Canada competition and won his first official international medal, a Bronze, in the European Championships. He repeated that placing the following year and gained the World Bronze Medal as well. But these successes also brought home a glaring weakness. At both competitions he won the freeskating, but his imprecise school figures dragged his performance down.

1980 Olympic Champion Robin Cousins performing professionally in 1993.
(Courtesy Paul Harvath)

By 1977, however, he had begun to spend a good part of the year practicing in Colorado Springs; there, the coaching of Carlo Fassi and his wife, Christa, gradually began to show results. By the 1980

Olympic year, he believed he was ready to win. He took his first international Gold at the European Championships and then barely beat out East Germany's Jan Hoffmann for the Gold at the Olympics with a dazzling free-skating routine. He was unable to bring off the hat trick though: his school figures faltered at the World Championships and he placed 2nd to Hoffmann.

But he had his Olympic Gold Medal, and as he turned to the world of professional skating, he continued to develop. Freed from the pressure of school figures, he was able to take his free-skating to a new level of artistic excellence, winning many professional championships and thrilling audiences.

CRAMER, LILIAN *(b. 1902) U.S. medalist.*

At the third National Figure Skating Championships, held in New York in 1920, Lilian Cramer won the Bronze Medal. She took the Silver in 1921 and the Bronze again in 1923. The Gold winner those three times was Theresa Weld Blanchard, who took the Bronze Medal at the 1920 Olympics and finished 4th at the 1924 Olympics. Beatrix Loughran, who bested Cramer for the U.S. Silver Medal in 1923, was the Silver Medalist at the 1924 Olympics. Although Lilian Cramer did not participate either time (Nathaniel Niles was the only other U.S. team member), she was certainly a world-class skater of her era.

CRANSTON, TOLLER *(b. 1952) Individualistic Canadian stylist.*

Competitive figure skating never saw anyone quite like Toller Cranston, and at least so far as the judges were concerned, it didn't know quite what to make of him. Slender and long haired, he was good enough at the school figures to be in regular contention for a medal at the World Championships and Olympics during the early 1970s, and he had no difficulty repeating as Canadian Champion year after year. But his free-skating style was so unusual that it consistently aroused the antagonism of many judges, particularly those from the Eastern bloc. He was not a spectacular jumper, although he could perform all the required jump elements with consistency. What made him stand out was the highly artistic nature of his overall programs, which included many maneuvers and positions that reflected his interest in dance—modern dance even more than ballet. His arms and legs were often bent at curious angles that caused those who did not like his style to speak of him as a "human pretzel." What's more, he skated to unusual, often modern, music and wore elegant but unconventional costumes. It was common for him to receive very high artistic marks from a few judges and absurdly low ones from others. Audiences at competitions often gave him huge ovations and regularly booed the judges for not giving him higher marks. Time and again he finished in 4th or 5th place.

There were many observers who felt that he should have had many more medals—Dick Button among them—but he broke through the judging barrier only twice, taking the World Bronze in 1974 and the Olympic Bronze in 1976. He then turned professional and skated with various shows for a number of years. In recent years he has been a skating coach and choreographer in Canada as well as pursuing a successful second career as a painter.

CURRY, JOHN *(1949–94) Great, innovative British and Olympic Champion.*

Growing up in Manchester, England in a working-class family, John Curry was attracted to the ballet at a very early age, but his father wouldn't hear of his taking dance lessons. Yet because figure skating was classified as a sport, he was finally allowed to take lessons in that discipline starting at age seven. For the majority of skaters, artistry takes the longest time to develop, but for Curry the athletic side of the sport came late. This was not because he had any real problems mastering the jumps but because he didn't think they were particularly interesting.

In 1970, Curry became the British Champion, a title he would retain throughout his amateur career, but he initially made litte impact in international competition, finishing 14th and 9th at the 1971 and 1972 World's and 11th at the 1972 Olympics. A 4th-place finish in both the European and World Championships in 1973 did not satisfy him, and he moved to Colorado to work with Coach Carlo Fassi, who had trained many champion skaters, including Peggy Fleming. The initial results were mixed: In 1974 he won his first international medal, a Bronze at the European Championships but fell to 7th at the World's. By the following year, however, Fassi's intensive concentration on technique began to pay off for Curry with a European Silver Medal and a World Bronze Medal.

The 1976 Olympics at Innsbruck, Austria were unusual in that there was no clear favorite in the men's division. The previous year's World Champion, the Soviet Union's Sergei Volkov, had been supplanted by his countryman, 1975 World Silver Medalist Vladimir Kovalev. Canada's Toller Cranston, despite his eccentric free-skating style, could not be counted out, and there was always East Germany's Jan Hoffmann, the 1974 World Champion, to consider. But it was to be John Curry's Olympics: During the past year, everything had come together for him, resulting in a balance between technical prowess and artistry that resulted in extraordinarily high marks in both judging categories, including several perfect 6.0s. He repeated this standard of excellence to become the 1976 World Champion. Commenting for U.S. television, Dick Button gave Curry his ultimate accolade of "having left the sport different and better than he had found it."

John Curry's impact on figure skating was just beginning, however. He was not interested in the usual professional career; as he later told the *New York Times* dance critic Jennifer Dunning, "I never could see the point of spending 12 years training to go dress up in a Bugs Bunny suit." Instead, he formed his own company and took it not to arenas but to the Broadway stage in *Ice Dancing*, which opened in 1977 and was a hit not only in New York but subsequently in London, Los Angeles and San Francisco. With former U.S. Pairs Champion JoJo Starbuck and a company of skaters willing to perform difficult ensemble work instead of just star turns, the show featured a live orchestra playing works from classical Handel and Impressionist Debussy to contemporary Philip Glass; ice dances were specially created by major dance choreographers such as Peter Martins and Twyla Tharp as well as by Curry himself. One standout was Curry's interpretation of Debussy's *Afternoon of a Faun*, originally danced by Nijinsky.

John Curry then started a school for ice skaters who wanted to follow his precepts, and in 1984 a new company, including Dorothy Hamill, David Santee and JoJo Starbuck, played to sold-out houses at New York's Metropolitan Opera House. A 1985 tour began at Washington's Kennedy Center. But audiences in places other than major cities resisted Curry's innovative approach to skating; they preferred to take the kids to the elaborate arena ice shows with their cartoon spectaculars. In addition, there was new competition from professional championship contests between the latest crop of Olympic and World Champions with judges and prize money.

For a time, Curry turned to acting, appearing on Broadway and on tour in a revival of the musical *Brigadoon*, in which he brought down the house performing the famous "Sword Dance"—without skates. He continued to make occasional skating appearances, but in 1987 he was diagnosed as being HIV positive. He developed full-fledged AIDS in 1991. He went back to live with his widowed mother, Rita, in England and told the world about what had happened to him in an article he wrote that appeared in the *London Daily Mail* in 1992. He died of an AIDS-related heart attack on April 15, 1994. At the time of his death, Dick Button said that Curry had been "the finest and most intelligent all-round skater I've ever seen." Peggy Fleming, interviewed by the *New York Times*, said, "He was a real purist, totally devoted to the art of skating. He also had the technique and athleticism to make that art look effortless. It was a wonderful blend of what skating is about—art and sport. It's a huge loss."

D

Below:
Britain's Frances Dafoe and Norris Bowden, World Pairs Champions in 1954 and 1955.
(Courtesy World Figure Skating Museum)

DAFOE, FRANCIS *(b. 1933) Canadian World Pairs Champion with Norris Bowden (b. 1932).*

Francis Dafoe and Norris Bowden were the first Canadian Pair ever to win the World Championship, as well as the first of three Canadian couples

who would hold the World title within less than a decade. They first came to international prominence at the 1953 World Championships in Davos, Switzerland where they came in 2nd to Jennifer and John Nicks of Great Britain. The following year at Oslo, Norway they took the Gold Medal followed by France's Sylvia and Michel Grandjean and by the Austrian team that would prove to be their eventual nemesis, Elisabeth Schwartz and Kurt Oppelt.

After repeating as World Champions in 1955, with the Austrian couple now right behind them in 2nd place, Dafoe and Bowden went into the Olympics in 1956 as narrow favorites. But Schwartz and Oppelt beat them in a very close contest at Cortina, Italy and then did it again at the World Championships in Garmisch, West Germany. Both couples then turned professional.

DALLEY, RICHARD *See* FOX, CAROL.

DANNE, WOLFGANG *(b. 1946) West German Pairs Champion.*

Partnered with Margot Glockshuber, Danne was West German Champion in Pairs from 1965 to 1968. The couple did not have the excitement of their immediate predecessors, Marika Kilius and Hans Jurgen Baumler, but they were good enough to win the World Silver Medal behind the great Protopopovs in 1967 and a Bronze at the following year's Olympics.

DANZER, EMMERICH *(b. 1944) Austrian World Champion.*

Emmerich Danzer was involved in one of the most astonishing upsets in figure-skating history at the 1968 Olympics at Grenoble, France. Danzer had been World Champion the two succeeding years, with his countryman Wolfgang Schwartz in 2nd place. Danzer was the superior competitor in school figures, indeed a master of them, which always gave him an edge. But at this all-important contest, Danzer developed a case of nerves and botched his school figures badly. Schwartz gave an extraordinary performance in the free-skating and won the Olympic Gold Medal, while Danzer did not even get a medal. But a few weeks later at the World Championships, Danzer came back to take that title for the third consecutive time. Tim Woods of the United States was 2nd at both competitions, while Schwartz was content with his Olympic Gold and did not compete at the World's.

DAVENPORT, ALMA *(b. 1947) U.S. Ice Dance medalist with Roger Berry (b. 1946).*

In a year of transition in U.S. Ice Dancing, 1967, as Lorna Dyer and John Carrell finally took the Gold, Alma Davenport and Roger Berry gained the Silver Medal and relative newcomers Judy Schwomeyer and James Sladky in 3rd place. All three couples went to the World Championships, where Dyer and Carrell took the Silver, while Davenport and Berry placed 9th. One place ahead of them, in a preview of things to come, were Schwomeyer and Sladky, who would dominate American Ice Dancing for the next five years. Alma Davenport and Roger Berry, happy with their Silver Medal and good timing, retired from amateur skating.

DAVIES, ANNE *(b. 1931) U.S. medalist in both Ice Dance and Pairs with* CARLETON HOFFNER *(1931).*

With partner Carleton Hoffner, Anne Davies was a double-threat skater in both Ice Dancing and Pairs from 1945 to 1950. The couple first gained a Bronze Medal in Ice Dancing in 1945 and became U.S. Champions the following year. In 1947 and 1948 they were 2nd to Lois Waring and Walter Bainbridge. At the same time, they were skating as a Pair and in 1949 concentrated on that effort, successfully gaining the Bronze Medal both at the U.S. Championships and at the World Competition in Paris. They capped their amateur career in 1950 with a U.S. Bronze in both Ice Dance and Pairs, a rare feat of strength and control.

DAVIS, SCOTT *(b. 1972) U.S. Champion.* A native of Montana who skates out of the Broadmoor Skating Club in Colorado Springs, Scott Davis participated in his first national competition at the age of 14 in 1986, coming in 2nd in the Novice division. By 1990, he was U.S. Junior Champion and became Senior Champion for the first time in 1993, winning over the more experienced Mark Mitchell. Davis finished 6th at the 1993 World Championships and seemed poised to make his move to the medal platform in 1994. That became even more likely when he retained his U.S. title in 1994 over Brian Boitano, who had been reinstated as an amateur.

At the 1994 Olympics, Davis got off to a fine start, coming in 4th in the technical short program. Two of the skaters ahead of him were regarded as inconsistent free-skating competitors, given to flubs; instead it was Davis who suffered the attack of nerves, missing important jumps and ending up in 7th place. At the World Championships he encountered the same problems and finished 8th.

Davis was unable to retain his U.S. title in 1995, as a newly confident Todd Eldredge continued his comeback to win the Gold Medal for the first time since 1991. As Silver Medalist, Davis once again went to the World Championships and initially seemed in good shape, coming in 3rd in the short program behind Eldredge and defending World Champion Elvis Stojko of Canada. But Davis once again fell apart in the long program and ended up in 7th place as Stojko repeated as World Champion, Eldredge took the Silver and France's Phillipe Candeloro collected another Bronze.

The 1996 U.S. Championships proved a great disappointment for Davis. He did not skate dreadfully, but he was not in top form either and ended up in 4th place. Rudy Galindo won the Gold Medal, Eldredge took the Silver and young Dan Hollander (who had been 7th the previous year) snatched the Bronze. The skating world began to wonder if Davis was finished in performance, although he could still dazzle in practice sessions and was generally regarded as the best spinner the sport had since Ronnie Robertson in the 1950s. Anyone inclined to dismiss his future chances needed to be reminded of the story of Paul Wylie. Wylie, who had suffered from a similar problem with competition nerves, became Olympic Silver Medalist in 1992 after many had given up on him.

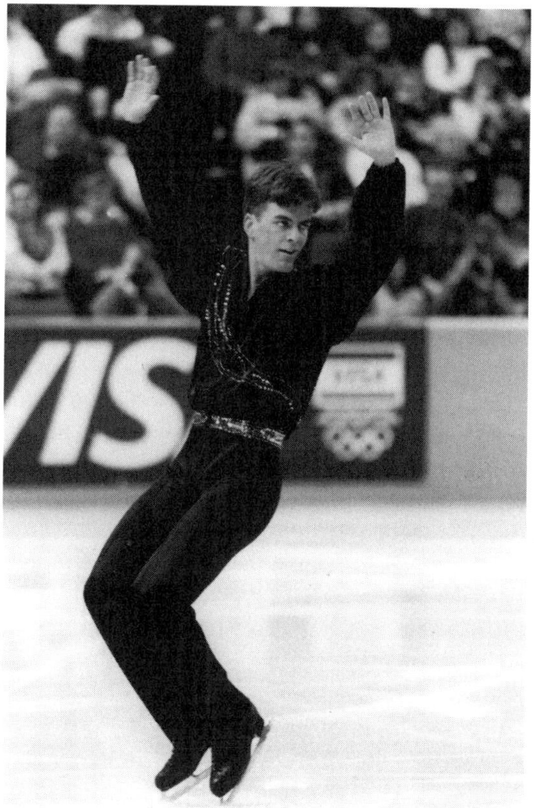

Scott Davis won his second U.S. Championship in 1994.
(Courtesy Michelle Harvath)

DEAN, CHRISTOPHER *See* TORVILL, JAYNE.

DEATH SPIRAL

This classic element of the Pairs skating repertoire was invented by Charlotte, the German show skater and movie actress who began her career before the First World War. The man positions himself at a central point, like the upright on a protractor, and draws the woman in a circle around him. She is balanced on one skate and bent far over backward so that her head nearly touches the ice. The woman's outstretched arm is supported at the wrist by the man as she also clasps his wrist. The woman may travel on either edge of either skate blade, usually in a backward direction but occasionally forward. The man bends at the knees as he supports the woman, while her free leg can be held in a number of positions that add elements of individual style.

The two couples usually regarded as the greatest practitioners of the death spiral were rivals for the World and Olympic Championships in 1964, West Germany's Marika Kilius and Hans Jurgen Baumler and the Soviet Union's Ludmila and Oleg Protopopov. The Soviets won the Olympic Gold, and the Germans captured the World title that year. The Germans performed the death spiral with exciting speed and the Soviets with exaggerated balletic slowness.

DE LEEUW, DIANE *(b. 1953) Dutch World Champion and Olympic Silver Medalist.*

In 1974, sturdy Dutch skater Diane De Leeuw took the World Bronze Medal at Munich, West Germany. The Gold Medalist was East Germany's Christine Errath, Bronze Medalist the previous year; the U.S.'s Dorothy Hamill won the Silver Medal, moving up from a 4th place finish in 1973. It was widely believed that with another year's seasoning, Hamill could beat Errath, but instead 1975 brought an upset: Diane De Leeuw won the Gold Medal, Hamill again found herself in 2nd and Errath fell to 3rd.

De Leeuw was excellent at school figures, but her free-skating, while athletic, was not particularly artistic. At the 1975 World Championships, however, she proved once again an old rule of competition: consistency counts for a great deal. Many times skaters who were inherently less talented than their nearest competitors won because they did not make any mistakes; that was certainly true in 1975. A year later at the Olympics and again at the World Championships, Dorothy Hamill skated with consistency equal to her talent and won the Gold Medal at both competitions. Diane De Leeuw retired that year with the Olympic Silver Medal and the World Bronze Medal.

DEMMY, LAWRENCE *See* WESTWOOD, JEAN.

DENNY, DOREEN *See* JONES, COURTNEY.

DE VRIES, VIKKI *(b. 1962) U.S. medalist.*

Vikki de Vries skated at a time when the depth of talent among U.S. women figure skaters was the greatest it had ever been. Rosalyn Sumners, Elaine Zayak and Tiffany Chin would all win World medals, but all three of these women were also inconsistent. In 1982, de Vries skated cleanly at the U.S. Championships to garner the Silver Medal behind Rosalynn Sumners and ahead of Elaine Zayak, who had been the previous year's champion and who would win the World Gold Medal that year. De Vries was 7th at the World Championships. With a U.S. Silver to her credit, she turned professional.

DEWHURST, JOAN *(b. 1930) British Ice Dancer with John Slater (b. 1931).*

When Ice Dancing was first included in the World Championships in 1952, the British were the discipline's dominant force; in fact, British Ice Dancers won 12 out of the 15 Ice Dance World medals in the first five years—the other three were taken by U.S. couples: Carol Peters and Daniel Ryan won two Bronze Medals and Carmel and Edward Bodel one. Joan Dewhurst and John Slater placed 2nd among British dancers in 1952 behind Jean Westwood and Lawrence Demmy. They were also 2nd at World's, taking the Silver Medal in both 1952 and 1953.

DIDOMENICO, MARIA *See* WATSON, JILL.

DIESTELMEYER, WALLACE *See* MORROW, SUZANNE.

DIJKSTRA, SJOUKJE *(b. 1941) Dutch World and Olympic Champion.*

Sjoukje Dijkstra was larger-boned and heavier than most women figure skaters usually are, but she was also a great athlete with a remarkable musical sense. She took her first World medal in 1959, a Bronze, and came back the next year to win not only the World Silver (behind Carol Heiss) but also the Silver at the 1960 Olympics at Squaw Valley, California. Her first World Championship was delayed by the cancellation of the 1961 competition because of the deaths of the American team in a plane crash at Brussels, but she won the title with authority in 1962 and retained it through the rest of her amateur career.

Excellent at school figures, Sjoukje Dijkstra (pronounced Skookie Dikestra) also performed jumps more powerfully than usual for woman skaters until Debi Thomas more than 30 years later. In 1964, two-time World Champion Dijkstra went to the Olympics at Innsbruck, Austria with a chance to repeat the parlay accomplished by two previous Olympic Gold Medalists, Tenley Albright and Carol Heiss of the United States: to win the Silver Medal at one Olympics and the Gold at the next. In addition to the pressure of Olympic competition, Queen Juliana of the Netherlands traveled to Austria to watch Dijkstra compete. Unruffled as always, Sjoukje skated the finest free program of her career to win the Gold Medal, the first won by the Netherlands since 1948 when Fanny Blankers-Koen took four Gold Medals in women's track. Dijkstra then went on to take the World Gold for the third time. She left amateur skating as a national heroine and turned professional to skate with Holiday on Ice.

DINEEN, PATRICIA AND ROBERT *(b. 1940, d. 1961; b. 1935, d. 1961) Sister-and-brother U.S. Ice Dance medalists.*

Patricia and Robert Dineen were the Bronze Medalists in Ice Dance at the U.S. Figure Skating Championships in 1961 behind Diane Sherbloom and Larry Pierce, and Dona Lee Carrier and Roger Campbell. All three couples were killed with the rest of the American team in a plane crash at Brussels on the way to the World Championships.

DIVIN, KAROL *(b. 1941) Czech Champion, World and Olympic medalist.*

Karol Divin, though a fine skater both in school figures and in free-skating—when he was "on," was inconsistent in both of these disciplines at a time when there were a half-dozen men capable of winning World or Olympic medals. His first international medal came with one of his very best showings, at the 1960 Olympics at Squaw Valley, California. Four-time U.S. and World Champion David Jenkins took the Gold Medal, as expected, but Tim Brown of the United States, who had been 3rd at the World's the year before and 2nd for two years before that, faltered and fell to 5th; the two "Alains" of France—Giletti and Calmat—also did not skate their best. Therefore, Karol Divin took the Silver and Canada's Donald Jackson won the Bronze. A few weeks later at the World's—which both David Jenkins and Tim Brown skipped—Divin faltered and Giletti, Jackson and Calmat took the medals in that order.

The 1961 World's were canceled because of the deaths of the entire American team in a plane crash at Brussels, but 1962 was a battle royal between Divin and Jackson for the Gold. Divin had finished his free-skating before Jackson took the ice, and it was clear that it would take a spectacular performance for Jackson to overtake him. Jackson responded by landing the first triple lutz ever performed in competition and in general skated one of the most legendary free programs in figure-skating history to snatch the Gold from Divin. Alain Calmat took the Bronze.

DMITRIEV, ARTUR *(b. 1968) Olympic and World Pairs Champion with Natalia Mishkutenok (b. 1971) and Olympic Pairs Champion with Oksana Kazakova (b. 1975)*

Artur Dmitriev earned a unique place in skating history at the 1998 Winter Olympics in Nagano, Japan: He became the first man to win Olympic Gold Medals in pairs skating with two different partners. During a highly successful career with his first partner, Natalia Mishkutenok, the pair won World Bronze in 1990, the World Championships in 1991 and 1992, and took Olympic Gold in 1992. After a brief stint on the professional circuit, Dmitriev and Mishkutenok had themselves reinstated as amateurs for the 1994 Olympics, at which they placed 2nd. Mishkutenok then retired and, after a year's hiatus, Dmitriev found a new partner, Oksana Kazakova.

By 1997 Kazakova and Dmitriev had become World Bronze Medalists. After only three brief years of partnership, Dmitriev entered his third Olympic contest and Kazakova her first, and together the two made Pairs skating history.

DOAN, PAULETTE *(b. 1943) Canadian Ice Dancer with Kenneth Ormsby (b. 1942).*

Paulette Doan and Kenneth Ormsby won the Canadian Bronze in 1962, then succeeded Virginia Thompson and William McLachlan as Canadian Champions in 1963. Immediately laying claim to the previous champions' world ranking as well, they took the Bronze Medal at the 1963 World Championships in Cortina, Italy. The following year, they were again the Canadian Champions and gained the Silver Medal at Dortmund, East Germany, behind the Czechoslovakians Eva Romanova and Pavel Roman, who won their third successive Gold Medal.

DORAN, DANIEL *(b. 1966) U.S. medalist.*

A fine free-skater with dash and musicality, Daniel Doran was nevertheless hampered throughout his amateur career by nerves and injuries that cost him several trips to the medal platform. In 1986 he took the U.S. Bronze Medal and was widely expected to go on to a splendid amateur career. He was 8th at that year's World Championships, one place higher than U.S. Silver Medalist Scott Williams. But the following year, Christopher Bowman vaulted into 2nd place at the Nationals behind Brian Boitano, and the Bronze went to Scott Williams. Most disappointingly, Doran did not qualify for the 1988 Olympics; the three team places were filled by Boitano, Paul Wylie and Bowman. Doran made one final attempt to win the U.S. Championship in 1989 after Boitano turned professional, but his best competitive performance earned Doran the Silver behind Bowman. He did not skate up to his potential at the World's, placing only 7th in a competition that saw Bowman win the Silver Medal.

DU BIEF, JACQUELINE *(b. 1930) French World Champion.*

French Champion Jacqueline du Bief took the European title in 1951 and the Silver Medal at the World Championships that year behind Great Britain's Jeanette Altwegg. In 1952 she repeated as European Champion, but she fell back a place at the Olympic Games; Jeannette Altwegg took the Gold Medal and the U.S.'s Tenley Albright surprised the skating world by taking the Silver. At that year's World's, however, du Bief had three things in her favor: Altwegg, having both a World and an Olympic Gold Medal to her credit, skipped the World Championships to turn professional, and Albright was unable to compete because of an injury; in addition, the competition was held in du Bief's home city, Paris.

Jacqueline du Bief wore a then-daring costume for the 1952 Olympics.
(Courtesy World Figure Skating Museum)

Du Bief was a very musical skater, and without doubt she had the sexiest aura projected by a woman skater up to that time, one that she heightened with revealing costumes. Always an audience favorite, Paris accorded her a tumultuous reception and, skating her very best, she easily won the Gold Medal over Sonya Klopfer and Virginia Baxter, both of the United States. She immediately turned professional, wowing Ice Capades audiences in extremely low-cut costumes bedecked with jewels and feathers. Few woman skaters have ever played up innate sensuality on ice to the extent that Jacqueline du Bief did.

DUCHESNAY, ISABELLE AND PAUL

(b. 1964, 1962) Canadian-born World Ice Dance Champions who skated for France.

The French Canadian brother-and-sister Ice Dance team of Isabelle and Paul Duchesnay caused controversy by deciding to skate for France: They felt that Canada did not provide sufficient encouragement and backing. Gaining their first World Medal, the Bronze, in 1989 behind two Soviet couples, Marina Klimova/Sergei Ponomarenko and Maria Usova/Alexander Zhulin, they moved past Usova and Zhulin in 1990 to take the Silver Medal.

A daring and original Ice Dance team, the Duchesnays attracted former Olympic Gold Medalist Christopher Dean's attention; he heightened their special talents to help them gain the World Championship in 1991, overcoming both Klimova/Ponomarenko and Usova/Zhulin. The 1992 Olympics were held in Albertville, France and their adopted country fully expected them to win a Gold Medal for France. But judges that year proved more conservative—or their dancing was *too* daring this time—and the Gold Medal was awarded to Klimova and Ponomarenko as the largely French audience howled in protest. The Duchesnays got the Silver, and the Bronze went to Usova and Zhulin. Feeling cheated, the Duchesnays skipped the World Championships and turned professional.

DUISCH, LARRY

(b. 1947) U.S. Pairs skater with Page Paulsen (b. 1946) and Sheri Trapp (b. 1951).

Larry Duisch simply enjoyed competing for the fun of it, whether he won a medal or not. He was good enough, however, to twice take a U.S. Bronze Medal in Pairs, first in 1966 with Page Paulsen and again in 1970 with Sheri Trapp. Only two U.S. Pairs teams were eligible for World competition in those years, but to have captured two U.S. Bronze Medals five years apart was an unusual accomplishment in itself.

DUNGJEN, JASON *See* INA, KYOKO.

DUNN, JACK *(b. 1917) British Champion and ice-show star.*

Jack Dunn was only the third British male to take a solo World medal, preceded by Edgar Syers (the Bronze in 1899) and John Page (the Bronze in 1926). Dunn went them one better to take the World Silver Medal in 1935 behind Austria's Karl Schafer. Dunn then made way for Britain's Graham Sharp, who would take three World Silvers and then the Gold in 1939. Dunn, tall and handsome, went on to a successful career as the male lead in a number of British-stage skating spectaculars based on famous fairy tales, playing the dashing prince to a number of leading ladies, including British World Champion Cecilia Colledge.

DUNN, ROSALIE *(b. 1904) U.S. Ice Dance medalist.*

Before 1936 when Ice Dancing was reorganized into the modern competitive format, Rosalie Dunn won a number of medals with several different partners in the old two-dance competition in which separate medals were given for each dance. She accumulated two Bronze and five Gold Medals from 1923 to 1928, usually in the waltz.

DURBROW, KATHERINE *(b. 1917) U.S. medalist.*

In 1937, Katherine Durbrow was the U.S. Bronze Medalist behind Maribel Vinson (who took the Gold for the 9th time) and Silver Medalist Polly Blodgett. The following year, she became the 7th of eight partners with Joseph Savage to win a medal in Ice Dancing in the course of 11 years. Durbrow and Savage won the Silver Medal.

DWYER, RICHARD *(b. 1931) U.S. Medalist and show performer.*

Richard Dwyer took the U.S. Bronze medal in 1950. But with World Champion Dick Button committed to skating for two more years and future World medalists James Grogan and Hayes Alan Jenkins to compete against as well, Dwyer opted to turn professional, joining the Ice Capades as a feature soloist. Dwyer, a spectacular jumper, had an exceptionally elegant and fluid style that served him well in the Ice Capades for a quarter-century.

DYER, LORNA *(b. 1943) U.S. Ice Dancer with King Cole (b. 1942) and John Carrell (b. 1944).*

Lorna Dyer took her first U.S. Bronze Medal in 1962 with King Cole (his real name). The following year, she changed partners, joining forces with John Carrell; during the next several years this team made a steady climb both in United States and international Ice Dancing, skating with greater security, finesse and style with each passing year.

They first scored a U.S. Bronze Medal in 1963 and placed 8th that year at the World Championships. The following year, they placed 3rd in the United States, but a 5th-place finish at the World's (three places better than U.S. Champions Sally Schantz and Stanley Urban) was a clearer indication of their progress. In both 1965 and 1966 they were both U.S. Silver and World Bronze medalists. In 1967, they became U.S. Champions and World Silver Medalists. Having gained the national title and recognizing that it was unlikely they could surpass the British team of Diane Towler and Bernard Ford internationally, they retired at the height of their form and turned professional for a short period to recoup the costs of their amateur career.

E

EDGES

What makes figure skating unique is that the blade on each skate has two edges, with a hollow in between them. The entire blade is only one-eighth inch thick, and the width of the edges is measured in centimeters, but because each edge is very sharp, it can grip the ice securely when the body is properly aligned. When school figures are being traced, only one edge of each blade should ever touch the ice at one time. If both blades are on the ice, the resulting "flat" will bring heavy point deductions. In free-skating, there are times when the blade is flat against the ice, with both edges gripping the surface—when performing spins, for example, or in preparation for the stuntlike back flip. But footwork, spirals and jumps all call for use of single edges. A skater who can lean at a steep angle during a spiral is saluted for having very deep edges, which adds to the excitement of the move because it looks as though the skater is on the verge of falling over.

The skate edge on the outer side is called an outside edge; the edge between the feet is an inside edge. A "back outside edge" means that the skater is moving backward on an outer edge.

EIGEL, HANNA *(b. 1938) Austrian World medalist.*

Although the figure-skating world focused on the intense competition between Americans Tenley Albright and Carole Heiss in the mid-1950s, a similar situation existed in Austria, where Hanna Eigel and Ingrid Wendl contended for both national and international supremacy. In 1955, Hanna Eigel won the World Bronze behind Albright and Heiss, but in 1956 Ingrid Wendl took both the Olympic and World Bronze, as Albright and Heiss split the Olympic and World Championships between them. With Albright's retirement, Eigel took the 1957 World Silver Medal behind Heiss but ahead of 3rd-place Wendl. Eigel also married that year; as Hanna Walter, she took the Bronze in 1958, Wendl the Silver and Heiss the Gold. Walter closed out her career with a final Silver at World's in 1959, with Heiss again winnng the Gold and the Netherlands' Sjoukje Dijkstra taking the Bronze.

EIGHTS *See* SCHOOL FIGURES.

EISLER, LLOYD *See* BRASSEUR, ISABELLE.

EKSTROM, KAJ AF *See* HERRIKSON, ELNA.

ELDREDGE, TODD *(b. 1971) U.S. Champion.*

At the 1990 U.S. Championships, Todd Eldredge was the surprise Men's Gold Medalist over Paul Wylie and Mark Mitchell; reigning champion Christopher Bowman did not compete because of an injury, but the victory was still a major accomplishment for 18-year-old Eldredge. At the World's, where a recovered Bowman took the Bronze, Eldredge finished a very respectable 5th. The next year, Eldredge, the son of a commercial fisherman in Chatham, Massachusetts, repeated as national champion with Bowman taking the Silver; the two skaters switched positions at the World's, Eldredge taking the 1991 World Bronze and Bowman dropping to 5th.

Eldredge seemed on target for an Olympic medal in 1992, but he developed a lower-back problem that prevented him from competing at the Nationals. Bowman took his second U.S. Gold Medal; Paul Wylie garnered Silver and Mark Mitchell Bronze. U.S. skating officials named Eldredge to the Olympic and World team instead of Mitchell anyway because he was a World medal holder. This caused some bad feeling in U.S. skating circles, especially when it proved that Eldredge's back was not fully healed and he placed 10th. At the World's, he climbed only to 7th.

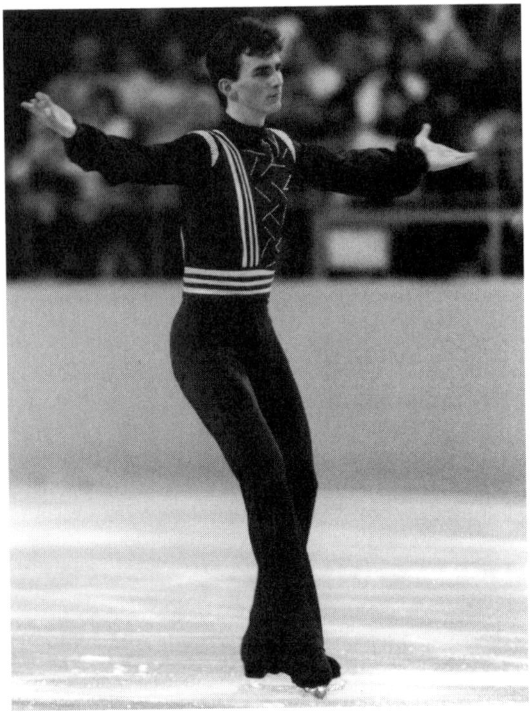

Todd Eldredge won his first U.S. Championship in 1990.
(Courtesy Paul Harvath)

He then suffered a crisis of confidence and skated so badly at the 1993 Nationals that he only came in 6th, nearly persuading Eldredge to give up skating. Regaining enthusiasm he believed he could win one of the two 1994 Olympic-team spots despite the return to amateur competition of Brian Boitano. An attack of the flu just before the U.S. Championships and a 104-degree temperature left Eldredge so weak that he finished 4th.

In various competitions preceding the 1995 U.S. Championships, he beat former Olympic Gold Medalists Viktor Petrenko and Alexei Urmanov, Olympic and World Bronze Medalist Philippe Candeloro and reigning U.S. Champion Scott Davis; at the U.S. Championships, he beat Davis to become the U.S. Men's Champion for the third time. Brimming with confidence, he won the short program in the World Championships and, despite some problems with the long program, took the overall lead. But reigning World Champion Elvis Stojko of Canada, who was skating with a leg injury, against doctors' advice, skated brilliantly and took the Gold again, leaving Eldredge with the Silver Medal.

In 1996, Eldredge toured in shows extensively, ending shortly before the National Championships. Although the U.S. Figure Skating Association gave permission to the top U.S. amateurs to make these lucrative tours, some officials were concerned that such commercial ventures were taking precedence over U.S. Championships training. They were proven correct: Nicole Bobek, for example, withdrew in midcompetition because of an ankle injury that had not received proper rest. Eldredge himself was clearly not in peak form because of limited time to work on his new competitive routines. Eldredge might have won anyway because his chief rival, former U.S. Champion Scott Davis, who had also been on tour, continued to suffer from nerves. However, the almost-forgotten Rudy Galindo, Kristi Yamaguchi's former partner in winning the 1989 and 1990 U.S. Pairs Championships, gave electrifying performances in both the short and long programs before a hometown San Jose, California crowd. Galindo, who had never finished better than 5th in the Men's competition, suddenly found his form at the age of 26 to become the oldest U.S. Men's Champion in 70 years. Eldredge again took the Silver Medal position and Dan Hollander the Bronze; Scott Davis was off the podium entirely for the first time since his 1993 win.

It was generally assumed that World Champion Elvis Stojko would flourish before a home-country audience at the 1996 World Championships in Edmonton, Alberta, Canada, but he appeared to put too much pressure on himself and badly botched the short program, putting him in 7th place and almost out of medal contention. The other main threats were the Ukraine's Viacheslav Zagorodniuk, who had just won the European Championships; Russia's young jumping phenomenon, Ilya Kulik, who had been the European Champion in 1995 but slipped back to 3rd place in 1996; and Russia's Alexei Urmanov and France's Philippe Candeloro, both 1994 Olympic Gold and Bronze Medalists who had been erratic recently. Of course there was Rudy Galindo, out to prove that his U.S. victory was not a fluke.

Eldredge worked extremely hard after the U.S. Championships and skated superbly in both the World's short and long programs, jumping with dynamism and security and making his strongest artistic showing ever. His long-delayed ascendancy to the crown of World Champion was a clear-cut one. Kulik took the Silver with a bravura display, and Galindo's Bronze demonstrated that he was a genuine force; Stojko was 4th and Urmanov 5th. It was clear that the Men's division would be the most difficult through the 1998 Olympics, but by finally winning a World Championship, Todd Eldredge was as well placed as any of this elite group of male skaters. But the intensity of male competition was again emphasized in 1997, when Stojko took the World title, with Eldredge a close second.

ELTSOVA, MARINA *(b. 1973)*

Russian Pairs World Medalist with Andrei Bushkov (b. 1971).

Marina Eltsova and Andrei Bushkov were deprived of a chance to skate in the 1994 Olympics when the Russian teams who had won the last two Olympics, Ekaterina Gordeeva/Sergei Grinkov and Natalia Mishkutenok/Artur Dmitriev were both reinstated as amateurs. Neither of these 1994 Gold and Silver Medal Olympic winners skated at the 1994 World Championships, however, and Eltsova and Bushkov took the Bronze behind a third Russian couple, Evgenia Shishkova and Vadim Naumov, and Canada's Isabelle Brasseur and Lloyd Eisler.

Eltsova and Buskov did not win a medal at either the European or World Championships in 1995 but came back strong to win the World Championship in 1996. In 2nd place behind 1995 European Champions Mandy Woetzel and Ingo Steuer of Germany, after the short program, they gave a sterling long-program performance to take the 1996 Gold Medal with Woetzel and Steuer pushed back to the Silver and America's Jenni Meno and Todd Sand repeating as Bronze Medalists.

ENGELMANN, HELENE *(b. 1897)*

Austrian World Pairs Champion with both Karl Mejstrik (b. 1895) and Alfred Berger (b. 1902).

One of the longest top-flight amateur careers in figure-skating history belonged to Helene Engelmann. She and her partner, Karl Mejstrik, made their first World medal a Gold, winning the 1913 championship over Finland's Ludowicka and Walter Jakobsson, who already had two World Silvers and a Gold Medal. In 1914, however, the two pairs ended up in reversed position. No World Championships were held for the next seven years due to World War I, but the Jakobssons were on hand for the 1922 renewal of the World Championships in Davos, Switzerland and so was Helene Engelmann and a new partner, Alfred Berger. Engelmann and Berger prevailed, with the Finnish husband-and-wife team taking the Silver Medal.

Engelmann and Berger did not attend the World competition in 1923, which was won by the Jakobssons, but in the Olympic year of 1924, the two couples who had alternated championships a full decade earlier had a final showdown. Engelmann and Berger came out on top at both the Olympics in Chamonix, France and the World's at Manchester, England. The difficult and dangerous lifts that are the hallmark of Pairs skating today were not performed when Helene Engelmann and the Jakobssons pursued their great rivalry—their programs were closer to ice dancing in many respects, although separate jumps and spins were performed. Nevertheless, their ability to remain at the top of their sport for more than a dozen years was remarkable.

ERRATH, CHRISTINE *(b. 1954) East German World Champion.*

The first woman skater of prominence to emerge from the communist East German sports machine, Christine Errath took four World medals in successive years from 1973 to 1976: In 1973 she took the World Bronze, as did her compatriot Jan Hoffmann in the Men's division; both skaters then took the World Gold Medal in their divisions in 1974. But Errath's rise was concurrent with that of the U.S.'s Dorothy Hamill, who took the Silver Medal that year, and the Netherlands' 1974 Bronze Medalist Diane de Leeuw. In 1975 de Leeuw took the Gold with Hamill repeating as Silver Medalist and Errath falling back to the Bronze. It would prove to be Hamill's year in 1976 as she became both Olympic and World Champion while Erath and de Leeuw traded places on the medal platform—Errath took the Silver at the World's after de Leeuw bested her at the Olympics. Seldom have the three top women skaters been so evenly matched, but Hamill gained a small but decisive edge when it counted most—in the Olympic year.

EXHIBITION PROGRAMS

Even before there were formal figure-skating competitions, skaters put on exhibitions. The American dancer who became the father of modern figure skating, Jackson Haines, went to Europe in 1864 to perform skating exhibitions for paying audiences in several countries. Settling in Vienna, he popularized this new sport and taught many skaters who later organized skating clubs. Norwegian speed skater Axel Paulsen—also an extraordinary stunt skater who jumped over barrels and the like—toured Europe first in the late 1870s, inventing what was to become the classic figure-skating jump, the axel, along the way. As skating grew in popularity, early skating clubs in Europe put on exhibitions of Ice Dancing and solo performances that eventually coalesced in the 1880s in the form of actual competitions.

The beginning of competitions also brought new rules, and while at first these differed from country to country, they were codified prior to the 1896 birth of the World Championships. In the 20th century the rules have become increasingly specific, evolving in part to maintain a clear distinction between amateur competition and professional performance skating. To this day, many rules—restrictions some would say—apply to amateur skating but do not apply to exhibition performances, whether amateur or professional.

Amateur rules affecting what moves can be used in a program, what kind of music is permitted and even what kinds of costumes may be worn are not applicable to exhibition performances. For example, the backward sommersault that is performed by many men and a few women in exhibition is absolutely forbidden in amateur skating because it is considered both a danger and a distraction to other skaters.

Ice dancers are not permitted to raise their partners in a true lift in competition. The woman can be raised off the ice, but her waist must not be higher than her partner's shoulder. Ice dancers constantly push the parameters of this rule even in competition, but they are not bound by it in exhibition programs and often use moves that are more common to Pairs skating. No throw lifts or jumps are used in Ice Dancing by common agreement; Such moves would undermine the distinction between Ice Dancing and Pairs Skating too deeply.

One most obvious distinction between competition and exhibition performances lies in the realm of music. In amateur competition, no vocals can be used on the performance tape; a medley of Beatles songs or a Whitney Houston hit must be an orchestrated version without vocals. Vocals are commonly used in exhibition performances by amateurs, however, ranging in form from Bette Midler singing "You Are the Wind Beneath my Wings" through Carl Orff's choral composition, *Carmina Burana.* This gives skaters much more freedom in setting a mood or delineating character in exhibition programs, and they often take advantage of it. Professional competitions also allow the use of vocal music, but among amateur judges and officials the bias against it remains strong.

The line between costuming for amateur competition and that for exhibitions or professional shows has been growing less distinct for the past decade (see COSTUMING for further discussion), but even here there are some dividing lines. For example, the World and Olympic Bronze Medalist from France, Philippe Candeloro, has an exhibition program in which he appears on the ice in a huge American flag scarf that he removes to skate the rest of his number naked to the waist. This would not be permitted in competition nor would a bare midriff for a woman, although the gauzy costumes that are sometimes worn in competition seem to verge on flouting this rule.

There is currently a movement to allow skaters to move back and forth between professional careers and amateur competition at will. While this kind of situation already exists in such Olympic sports as basketball, there are powerful voices opposing such a change in figure skating. Should it occur, it seems likely that the forces trying to retain the integrity of figure skating as an amateur sport will simply make the short program's technical content so difficult that any skater who has been a professional for very long would have an extremely difficult time making the grade. Exhibition programs are rarely as difficult as those required in competition.

F

Alexandr Fadeev of the Soviet Union became World Champion in 1985.

(Courtesy Michael Rosenberg)

FADEEV, ALEXANDR *(b. 1964) Soviet World Champion.*

One of the steadiest of Soviet male skaters during the past 25 years, Alexandr Fadeev had the misfortune to see his accomplishments eclipsed by the headline-grabbing "battle" between Canada's Brian Orser and the United States' Brian Boitano. In 1984, Fadeev took the World Bronze behind Scott Hamilton and Brian Orser, who had also finished in the same position at the Olympics in which Fadeev had been edged for the Bronze by Czechoslovakia's Josef Sabovcik.

In 1985, following Hamilton's departure for a professional career, Brian Orser was widely expected to succeed to the World title, but Orser was struck by a case of nerves that would so often hamper him, and Fadeev skated cleanly, if less spectacularly, to take the World Gold. Orser took 2nd, and new U.S. Champion Boitano held 3rd. In 1986, the order of finish was Boitano, Orser and Fadeev; in 1987, Orser, Boitano and Fadeev.

Fadeev won the Soviet Championship again in 1988, but perhaps disheartened by what seemed an inevitable 3rd place behind Boitano and Orser, he faltered at the Olympics, with his expected Bronze going instead to teammate Viktor Petrenko. The unforgiving Soviet sports authorities immediately decreed that to be the end of Fadeev's career, but in fact, he had held his own remarkably well in the most competitive World events since the extraordinary level set in the mid-1950s by Americans Hayes Allen Jenkins, Ronnie Roberston and David Jenkins.

FALK, PAUL *See* BARAN, RIA.

FASSI, CARLO *(b. 1930) Italian World medalist, and important coach in the United States.*

Between 1950 and 1960, American men so dominated figure skating that only six non-Americans won World medals of the 30 that were awarded in the Men's division. One who managed to challenge the U.S. bandwagon was Italy's Carlo Fassi, who took the World Bronze Medal in 1953 behind the U.S.'s Hayes Alan Jenkins and James Grogan.

Fassi then emigrated to the United States and settled in Denver, Colorado, where he molded many champions, including Peggy Fleming and Dorothy Hamill. Fassi worked in conjunction with his wife, Christa, who teaches younger skaters. Fassi did not take on pupils until they had a degree of excellence that marked them as potential champions. His regimen was tough, but in addition to hard technical training, he was expert at putting a high-gloss finish on skaters that gave them the showmanship and artistic maturity necessary to winning international medals. Also widely admired for his ability to encourage off-the-ice friendships between his students who were in direct competition with one another on the ice, Fassi was a molder of character, not just of technique; Most major coaches insist that character is as much a part of the ability to win championships as talent is.

Carlo Fassi died suddenly during the 1997 World Championships, his loss mourned by skaters, fellow coaches and judges. The judges were acutely aware that figure skating had lost someone profoundly dedicated to upholding the highest standards of the sport.

FAUVER, WILLIAM *(b. 1956) U.S. Pairs medalist with Alice Cook (b. 1957).*

In the crowded field behind U.S. Champions Tai Babilonia and Randy Gardner, William Fauver joined with Alice Cook in 1976 to take the U.S. Silver Medal in Pairs Skating. The achievement ensured a trip to the World Championships and the Olympics at Innsbruck, Austria, where the couple placed 9th and 12th, respectively.

In an unusual show of skating fervor, William Fauver came back five years later with another partner, Lea Ann Miller, to win U.S. Pairs Medals in 1981. Silver Medalists in 1981, 1983 and 1984 —with a Bronze in 1982—the couple had placings of 19th, 8th, 7th and 10th at the World Championships during those years and were 10th at the 1984 Olympics in Sarajevo, Yugoslavia.

FENTON, GERALDINE *(b. 1935) Canadian Ice Dancing Champion with William McLachlan (b. 1938).*

From the first World Championship, in 1952, to include Ice Dancing, through 1960, four British couples won the Gold Medal. Four U.S. couples also won medals, but the most consistent medalists, behind the Britons, were the Canadian Champions Geraldine Fenton and William McLachlan, who were on the medal podium from 1957 to 1961. Polished and technically expert, they lacked only the innovative qualities of the successive British couples, which was hardly surprising because the British were chiefly responsible for the development of the discipline. Fenton and McLachlan won the World Silver Medal in 1957, 1958, and 1960, taking the Bronze in 1959 and 1962.

FINNEGAN, LYNN *(b. 1939) U.S. medalist.*

An exciting free-skater, Lynn Finnegan was always held back by her problems with school figures. She would often beat several young women in free-skating; yet when the scores were totaled, her lower marks in school figures would give the medals to those she had outshone in free-skating. In 1958, however, she skated the figures well enough to gain

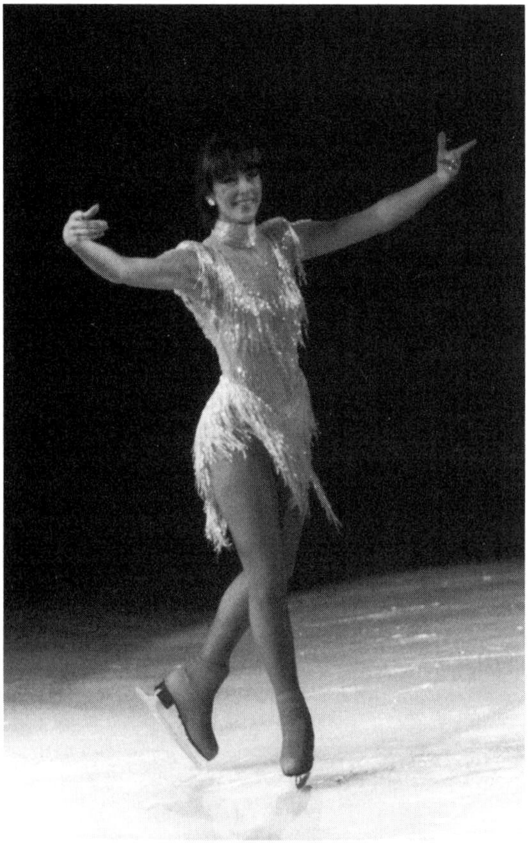

Peggy Fleming, 1968 Olympic Champion, was still performing in 1991.
(Courtesy Paul Harvath)

the U.S. Bronze Medal behind Carol Heiss and Carol Wanek. That put her on the World team for 1959, and she finished 6th overall in that competition. She subsequently skated professionally for a short period.

FISHER, VICTORIA *(b. 1944) U.S. medalist.*

In the year following the 1961 plane crash that wiped out the American figure-skating team at Brussels, Victoria Fisher gained the U.S. Bronze Medal. At the World Championships that year, she finished 16th.

FLEMING, PEGGY *(b. 1948) U.S., World and Olympic Champion.*

When all the top U.S. skaters were killed at Brussels in a plane crash in 1961, the gloomy prediction was that it would be a decade before the United States produced another World Champion. But Peggy Fleming was just 12 at the time and winner of the Pacific Coast Juvenile Championship, her first skating medal. She developed with extraordinary speed, becoming U.S. Champion just three years later in 1964 and placing 6th at that year's Olympic Games and 7th at the World Championships. In 1965 she won her second U.S. title and became the World Bronze Medalist at the age of 15.

Part of her success lay in the fact that she was one of the masters of the school figures in skating history, invariably mentioned in the same breath with the exemplary British compulsories exponent from the 1930s, Cecilia Colledge. Often described as fragile in appearance, Fleming was deceptively strong and became an extraordinary free-skater as well. The word *grace* is inextricably linked with her name, and to this day people will talk of an artistically inclined young skater as "being in the Peggy Fleming mold." She could also do any jump more athletic skaters could, often with greater technical assurance if not quite the height of a skater like East Germany's Gaby Seifert. Fleming's spins, particularly her supremely expressive lay-back spin, were held up as models of perfection.

Peggy Fleming was never seriously challenged during her five-year reign as U.S. Champion, from 1964 to 1968. She held the World title from 1966 to 1968 with Gaby Seifert finishing 2nd each time. The East German could give Fleming a close contest in free-skating, but by then Fleming was always so far ahead in points from her school-figures performance that there was no chance of catching her. Coached by the great Carlo Fassi at the Broadmoor Skating Club in Colorado Springs, she was always completely ready for competition and so deeply focused that she was never afflicted with the nerves that have derailed so many other skaters in international events.

At the 1968 Olympics in Grenoble, France Fleming amassed an insurmountable lead of 77.2 points in the school figures and then went out and skated a difficult free program with the intensity of someone in 2nd place, turning in her finest performance ever before a worldwide television audience. Her program included a spread-eagle takeoff into a double axel with another spread-eagle finish that no one else had mastered, even among the men.

A household name at 20, Fleming handled the transition to professional skating with aplomb. She toured with the Ice Follies, starred in several television specials and continued to skate in exhibitions into the mid-1990s. She also became a television commentator at U.S., World and Olympic competitions; tentative at first, she took this assignment with great seriousness, working with a vocal coach to deepen her light voice and develop an incisive style laced with dry humor that perfectly meshed with that of Dick Button, with whom she often worked. Button himself had a telling comment to make about her skating: "With some skaters there is a lot of fuss and feathers, but nothing is happening. With Peggy, there's no fuss and feathers—and a great deal is happening."

The Associated Press Female Athlete of the Year in 1968, Fleming has since been elected to the Ice Skating Hall of Fame (which includes speed skaters and hockey players), the World Figure Skating Hall of Fame, the United States Figure Skating Hall of Fame and the U.S. Olympic Hall of Fame.

FLIP JUMP

The flip is a variation on the loop jump, but instead of taking off from the back outer edge of the right foot, the toe pick of the skate is used to propel the skater into the air. This adds to the upward thrust, giving the jump greater height than a regular loop. The right leg is extended to the rear, the toe pick is dug into the ice and a full revolution is made in the air before landing on a back outside edge of the right foot as in the loop. The leg must be straight as the toe pick comes into contact with the ice, which puts a lot of pressure on the knee because the leg is being used almost like the pole in a pole vault. Skaters nursing a knee injury avoid the jump for obvious reasons.

The flip is often called a toe loop because of the use of the pick. See also LOOP JUMP.

FLORA, BETH AND KEN *(b. 1963, 1962) U.S. Pairs medalists.*

The Floras skated when U.S. Pairs skating was at its peak—just as the U.S. Championship was handed on from Tai Babilonia and Randy Gardner to Kitty and Peter Carruthers. The younger sister-and-brother team of Beth and Ken Flora still managed to gain a U.S. Bronze in 1981 as the Carrutherses took their first national title and Lea Ann Miller and William Fauver took the Silver.

FLYING CAMEL *See* CAMEL SPIN.

FLYING SIT SPIN *See* SIT SPIN.

FORD, BERNARD *See* TOWLER, DIANE.

FORD, MICHELLE *(b. 1955) U.S. Ice Dancer with Glenn Patterson (b. 1953).*

Michelle Ford and Glenn Patterson won the U.S. Bronze Medal in Ice Dancing in 1974, 1975 and 1977. They did not go to the World Championships because, after a decade in which U.S. Ice Dancers placed well enough at the World's to guarantee three openings on the World Team, there were now only two slots available. This was not altogether due to a diminishment in the quality of U.S. Ice Dancing but also the result of increasing international interest in the discipline. The competition was simply tougher, especially from Soviet-bloc countries.

FORNEY, MARTIN AND PHYLLIS

(b. 1933, 1934) Brother-and-sister U.S. Ice Dance team.

Winners of the U.S. Silver Medal in Ice Dancing in 1954, and of the Bronze in 1955, the Forneys also did well in the World competition, placing 6th both years.

FORTUNE, KRISTIN *(b. 1943)*

Champion U.S. Ice Dancer.

In 1965 and 1966 Kristin Fortune and partner Dennis Sveum were the first repeat winners of the U.S. Ice Dancing Gold Medal since 1958–59. An unusual off-performance at the World's in 1965 brought them only 5th place, while American Silver Medalists Lorna Dyer and John Carrell took the Bronze Medal, but they came back in 1966 to capture the World Silver, with their teammates again taking the Bronze.

FOTHERINGILL, JERRY AND JUDI-ANNE *(b. 1944, 1945) Brother-and-sister U.S. Pairs Champions.*

Coming into the limelight after the deaths of the U.S. World Team members in a plane crash at Brussels in 1961, this vivacious brother-and-sister team were so full of fun that they did a great deal to lift the gloom that pervaded U.S. skating. They took the U.S. Silver Medal in 1962 and won the U.S. Championships in 1963 and 1964. They placed 10th, 8th and 7th at the World Championships during those years and finished 7th at the 1964 Olympics.

FOURS

This skating form involves teams of two Pairs couples competing against other teams of four. Fours has never been officially recognized by the International Skating Union, but Fours events have been held intermittently at the national championships in a number of countries. There have been a dozen such events at the U.S. Championships in 1924, 1925, 1934, 1935, 1939, 1940, 1945, 1946, 1947, 1948, 1950 and, after a hiatus of 40 years, in 1991. The event has usually been requested by a group of skaters, and although such competitions are largely a matter of having some fun, medals are awarded. The teams have often included a mix of older and younger skaters. For example, the winning team in 1934 included Theresa Weld Blanchard, a six-time Ladies' Champion in the 1920s as well as Pairs Champion with Nathaniel Niles from 1924 through 1927; Suzanne Davis, who won the Ladies' title in 1934; Frederick Goodridge, who had been the Men's Silver Medalist in 1927–28 and an Ice Dance Bronze Medalist in 1932; and Richard Hapgood.

FOX, BERNARD *(b. 1919) U.S. Pairs Champion.*

With his partner Joan Tozzer (b. 1921) (who was simultaneously U.S. Ladies' Champion), Bernard Fox was U.S. Pairs Champion from 1938 to 1940 after taking the Bronze in 1937. Their skating was more decorous and far less athletic than we are now used to in Pairs skating. The great advances in this discipline pioneered a decade earlier by Pierre Brunet and Andrée Joly were only beginning to take hold in the United States. No U.S. pairs or Men's division skaters attended either the 1937 or 1938 World Championships in Europe as Hitler's ambitions became clear, so Fox and Tozzer's international potential was never tested.

FOX, CAROL *(b. 1959) U.S. Ice Dancing medalist with Richard Dalley (b. 1959).*

The sparkling partnership of Carol Fox and Richard Dalley brought them great popularity and seven successive Ice Dancing medals from 1978 to 1984. While the couple did not have the finesse or technical assurance of Judy Blumberg and Michael Seibert, U.S. Champions from 1981 to 1985, their contrasting style, zippy and fun loving, found many admirers and gained them Silver Medals in

1978, 1979, 1981 and 1984 and Bronze Medals in 1980 and 1983. They made five trips to the World Championships, with their best placement a 5th in 1982. They also took 5th place at the 1984 Olympics in Sarajevo, Yugoslavia.

FRANKS, SHERYL *(b. 1959) U.S. Pairs Medalist with Michael Botticelli (b. 1958).*

While Tai Babilonia and Randy Gardner reigned as U.S. Champions, the steady team of Sheryl Franks and Michael Botticelli won the Bronze Medal for four successive years, 1977–80. They were consistently 9th in the World, except for 1980 when they placed 10th. But 1980 also brought their best performance on the international stage when they placed 7th at the Winter Olympics in Lake Placid, New York. Initially stunned by the withdrawal of Babilonia and Gardner due to Randy's groin injury, they found something extra in themselves and skated the finest long program of their career.

FRATIANNE, LINDA *(b. 1959) U.S. and World Champion.*

In 1976, Linda Fratianne was the U.S. Silver Medalist behind Dorothy Hamill, topping a number of older skaters, including Bronze Medalist Wendy Burge. She was also 5th at the World Championships, an impressive achievement for a skater previously unknown to most international judges. The next year, she not only succeeded Hamill as U.S. Champion but also as World Champion, besting East Germany's Anett Poetzsch and West Germany's Dagmar Lurz. For the next three years, Fratianne would retain her U.S. title, with Lisa Marie Allen taking the Silver each time, but she was to have tougher competition at the World's. Anett Poetzsch turned the tables at the 1978 World's to win the Gold with Fratianne taking the Silver; in 1979, however, she was back on top over Poetzsch.

The U.S. and East German women were very different skaters, Fratianne holding the artistic edge and the athletic Poetzsch the slightly stronger jumper. Their meetings were exciting duels down to the last decimal point, with the outcome often in doubt until the judges' decision was announced. But it was Poetzsch who took the big prize, the 1980 Olympic Gold Medal, as Fratianne took the Silver over Dagmar Lurz. At that year's World's, Fratianne faltered and took only the Bronze behind Poetzsch and Lurz. She then went on to a splendid professional career. Fratianne was always quite frank with the press: During the 1994 Harding/Kerrigan imbroglio, for example, she told a television reporter that there had been a cutthroat aspect to figure skating for a long time, that even 20 years earlier some skaters and their coaches had been full of dirty tricks to unnerve and even "accidentally" injure their competitors during practice and precompetition warm-ups. She said this without any bitterness, simply stating a matter of fact.

Linda Fratianne succeeded Dorothy Hamill as the queen of American figure skating.
(Courtesy Michael Rosenberg)

FREE LEG

The free leg is whichever one is not in contact with the ice while skating. The control and positioning of the free leg is something that judges pay extremely close attention to, and the skater using the free leg correctly will almost always get the higher score. What's more, the use of the free leg can affect both technical and artistic scores.

In school figures, involving the laying down and retracing of intricate variations on the figure eight and skated with only one foot on the ice at a time, the positioning of the free leg should conform to complex rules of style. But the line between style and technique is blurred here, for the incorrect positioning of the free leg will not only look awkward but will affect the skater's balance and thus cause a sloppy tracing on the ice. Nevertheless, among the very finest exponents of school figures, when two top skaters lay down equally well-formed circles on the ice and retrace them with equal fidelity, one skater will likely be closer to "textbook" form in the positioning of the free leg. In such cases the skater with the better style will gain a tenth of a point here and there, which can be crucial when the scores are totaled and may well make the difference between a Gold and a Silver medal.

In free-skating, it is easier for an audience without special expertise to see how well a skater is using the free leg. For instance, in a camel spin where one leg is extended to the rear at a right angle to the leg on which the skater is spinning, is the skater's leg absolutely straight and held directly parallel to the ice, or does it wobble during the spin or droop a little below the horizontal position? Wobbling or drooping, if they are pronounced, may result in a small deduction in the technical score or influence a small difference in the artistic scores between two skaters.

The steadiness of the free leg is also important when spirals are being performed. Here the judges' eyes will look for matters of line. The skater whose entire body—from the steady angle at which the free leg is held aloft to the stretch of the back and the configuration of the arms in front—creates a particularly graceful line will gain points. An audience can *see* such grace even if the fine points are not fully appreciated.

The correct use of the free leg is particularly crucial in the performance of jumps. When a skater falls while doing a jump, television commentators will often point out during a replay of the jump that the skater's free leg is not properly positioned while the skater is rotating in the air, noting that this failure makes a fall almost inevitable. The problem may be hard to spot for the audience at the skating arena, but slow-motion replay will make it obvious. The arena audience can easily spot a landing that has gone astray, even when the skater does not actually fall. For example, a skater may slightly "two-foot" a landing, bringing the free leg down and touching the ice with that skate to retain balance at the same moment that the landing leg hits the ice. This is always cause for a point deduction.

Without a touch-down of the free leg, there may also be another problem: If the free leg is not fully extended behind the skater following the landing, creating a graceful line from the hand extended in front to the tip of the free leg skate, the jump has not been given an exemplary finish. There are exceptions to this extension of the leg, however: In a combination jump, the final extension of the leg is omitted; instead, the skater must use the free leg to launch immediately into the second jump in the combination. Another exception occurs when a skater shifts immediately into a spread eagle following the landing of a jump. This difficult maneuver, a highlight of Peggy Fleming's 1968 Olympic Gold Medal performance, is a situation in which the spread eagle is a more difficult substitution for the extension of the free leg to the rear.

Skaters who do not extend the free leg gracefully or for a sufficient length of time after completing a jump usually lose artistic rather than technical points. Correct use of the free leg, creating a graceful flow that holds a program together, has been one of the hallmarks of great skaters from the beginning. It is not an issue that judges want to compromise on, although there have been occasions in the past when skaters who did not use the free leg especially well have won because of jumping success that in a given competition simply has not been matched by anyone else.

FROTHINGHAM, CLARA *(b. 1902)*

U.S. Ice Dancer.

Clara Frothingham was the kind of amateur skater who competed for the fun of it on and off over the years when she didn't have other matters, like having children, to distract here. She was an ice dancer in the period after the First World War when that event was more informal than the other disciplines. There were usually two dances chosen for competition at the Nationals, with medals being awarded for each dance. For many years the competitive dances were the waltz and the fourteen step, although the latter was replaced by an original dance beginning in 1930.

Clara Frothingham took her first medal in 1921, winning the Silver in the waltz with Sherwin Badger. For many years she did not compete; when she did, she skated with several different partners: She took two Bronze Medals in the fourteen step in the early 1920s and then won the Gold Medal in the original dance in 1930 and 1932, both times with George Hill; she won a Silver and a Bronze in the waltz in 1931 and 1932, partnered first by Harold Hartshorne and then Frederick Goodridge. She did not compete for the next three years, returning in 1936, the first year in which the modern Ice Dancing competitive format was used in the United States. In her hometown of Boston, Massachusetts, partnered by Ashton Parmenter, she came away with the U.S. Bronze Medal, 15 years after winning her first medal in the waltz.

FUCHS, GILBERT *(b. 1875)* *German who was first World Champion.*

Gilbert Fuchs was the first figure-skating World Champion: He traveled to St. Petersburg, Russia from his hometown of Munich, Germany in 1896 and defeated Austria's Gustav Hugel (who would go on to win three World Championships) and Russia's Georg Sanders. Fuchs, who entered medical school at the time of his victory, did not defend his title the following year; Hugel won. He competed again in 1898 in Stockholm, Sweden and then skipped two years before returning to take the Silver Medal behind Sweden's Ulrich Salchow in 1901. By then a practicing physician, he did not compete from 1903 to 1905 but did in 1906, 10 years after Fuchs' first Gold Medal. He spent the year before the Munich competition, practicing assiduously, and again he became World Champion, ahead of Germany's much younger Heinrich Berger and Sweden's Bror Meyer.

Fuchs' achievement in winning World Championships 10 years apart without even competing in seven of the intervening years has never been equaled in the sport. Ulrich Salchow, Sonja Henie and Irina Rodnina (with two different partners) were World Champions 10 times, but they competed every year, except for one-year absences by Rodnina and Salchow—the latter's absence happening to coincide with Fuchs' second Gold Medal. After his second Gold, Fuchs did compete twice more, taking the Bronze in 1907 and the Silver in 1908. Salchow was the winner both times.

FUHRMAN, GALE AND JOEL

(b. 1955, b. 1953) U.S. Pairs team.

Sister-and-brother Gale and Joel Fuhrman took the U.S. Silver Medal in Pairs during the transition year of 1973, the first competition following the retirement from amateur skating of three-time U.S. Champions JoJo Starbuck and Ken Shelley, and the year before Tai Babilonia and Randy Gardner took their first Silver Medals. The winners in 1973 were another sister-brother team, Melissa and Mark Militano. The Militanos finished 8th at World's, the Fuhrmans 13th.

G

GALINDO, RUDY *(b. 1969) U.S. Pairs Champion and Men's Champion.*

Starting out as a singles skater, Rudy Galindo took the Bronze Medal in the National Junior Championship in both 1985 and 1986 and won the Gold Medal at the World Junior Championships in 1986, topping his 2nd-place finish of the previous year. Moving to the senior level of competition, he was well back in the ranks, but he had begun to skate Pairs with Kristi Yamaguchi and in 1989 and 1990 concentrated on that collaboration to splendid results: The couple took the U.S. Gold both years. Although only 5'6", Galindo was very strong from weightlifting and had no difficulty in executing spectacular lifts with the petite Yamaguchi.

The couple took 5th place at the World Championships in both 1989 and 1990, but by the latter year, Yamaguchi, who had continued with her solo skating as well, moved up to 4th place in the World's and had been national title runner-up to Jill Trenary for two years. Yamaguchi decided to concentrate on her solo skating, which paid off with two World Championships and an Olympic Gold. Galindo resisted the temptation to continue with a new partner in Pairs and also concentrated on solo skating.

But Galindo's career as a solo skater met with seemingly endless frustration. His record at Nationals speaks for itself: 1991, 11th place; 1992, 8th; 1993, 5th; 1994, 7th; 1995, 8th. In other competitions, flashes of his true ability showed: 2nd at both the 1992 Prague Skate and the 1993 U.S. Olympic Festival and winning an international competition in Vienna in 1994. But most of the top competitors did not take part in these events, and he seemed to be making no progress at the U.S. Nationals.

In addition, his personal life was shadowed by tragedy: In 1992, his older brother, George, developed full-blown AIDS and moved back to the San Jose, California trailer where Rudy lived with his father; it was Rudy who chiefly cared for him. Their father, who was a diabetic, suddenly died of a heart attack in 1993, and then George died in the fall of 1994. That December, Rudy's coach Rick Inglesi also died of AIDS.

His older sister Laura had been a competitive skater, too, and was a coach at the San Jose rink. Rudy started to work for her in 1995 and saved enough money to put together music and costumes. He couldn't afford repairs on his car and rode his bicycle to the rink and to the gym where he worked out, averaging 14 miles a day on his bike. His sister coached him without a fee. He wouldn't have been able to enter the 1996 Nationals at all for lack of funds if the competition hadn't been scheduled for his hometown of San Jose.

He was placed 3rd by the judges in the short program behind Todd Eldredge and Scott Davis.

The crowd booed this result and many skating reporters thought he should have been ranked at least 2nd. But after so many years of lackluster performance, the judges needed further convincing. There was also the fact that Rudy was openly gay, and there was little doubt that that fact made some in the skating establishment nervous. In the long program, skated to Tchaikovsky's *Swan Lake*, Galindo performed eight triple jumps, including two triple-triple combinations, carried out in a deeply artistic style recently out of fashion with male skaters. Hardened reporters for national magazines and major newspapers wrote afterward about the "hairs standing up" at the backs of their necks and of the tears streaming down the cheeks of other skaters as they watched. There was pandemonium in the arena as the audience gave him a screaming standing ovation. Seven of the nine judges placed him 1st with Eldredge 2nd and young Dan Hollander 3rd. Twice before Rudy Galindo had been National Pairs Champion, but this title was his alone, and it had come after six years of heartbreak. Only four other men in the history of U.S. figure skating had been both Pairs and Men's Champions; most recently, in 1972, Ken Shelley held both titles simultaneously.

Within days, Galindo had a $500,000 skating contract, a regular training stipend from the U.S. Figure Skating Association and a new role as a national figure in the gay rights movement. This was heady stuff, and it brought many new pressures, but at 26, Galindo, the second-oldest man ever to become National Champion in the sport, also had the maturity to carry the load. He went to the World Championships, where judges who hadn't laid eyes on him in years awarded him the Bronze Medal behind Todd Eldredge and Russia's Ilya Kulik. As several reporters noted, he had disproved F. Scott Fitzgerald's famous dictum that there are no second acts in American life.

GANSON, DEBBIE *See* HISLOP, BRAD.

GARDNER, RANDY *See* BABILONIA, TAI.

GAUTSCHI, GEORG *(b. 1904) Swiss Olympic medalist.*

At the first official Winter Olympics at Chamonix, France in 1924, Switzerland's Georg Gautschi won the Bronze Medal behind two famous male skaters, Sweden's Gillis Grafstrom and Austria's Willy Boeckl. In subsequent years Gautschi was often just behind the leaders, but he did not take another medal until 1930, when he won the World Bronze behind Austria's Karl Schafer and the U.S.'s Roger Turner.

GEEKIE, HELEN *(b. ?) U.S. medalist.*

With the retirement of Sonya Klopfer and Virginia Baxter, Helen Geekie was able to fulfill her dream of winning a U.S. medal, taking the Bronze in 1952, the first year of Tenley Albright's five-year reign as national champion. Carol Heiss, just 12, was junior Champion and would move up to take the Silver Medal behind Albright the next year.

GENOVESI, JUDY *(b. 1956) U.S. Ice Dance Champion.*

Partnered by Kent Weigel, Judy Genovesi won a U.S. Silver Medal in Ice Dancing behind Colleen O'Conner and Jim Millns in both 1975 and 1976. After taking both the World and Olympic Bronze in 1976, O'Conner and Millns turned professional, clearing the way for Genovesi and Weigel to gain the U.S. Gold in 1977. That year Genovesi and Weigel had their best showing at the World's, finishing 9th, and retired from amateur skating.

GERHAUSEN, JANET *(b. 1932) U.S. Pairs medalist.*

Skating with John Nightingale, Janet Gerhausen was the U.S. Silver Medalist in Pairs in both 1951 and 1952 behind Karol and Peter Kennedy, who were also World Silver Medalists. While not in the same extraordinary class as the Kennedys, Gerhausen and Nightingale finished a respectable 8th at the 1951 World's, 5th in 1952 and 6th in the 1952 Olympics.

GERKEN, DEBBIE *(b. 1948) U.S. Ice Dancer with Raymond Tiedmann (b. 1947).*

This Ice Dance team took the U.S. Bronze Medal in 1968 and 1969, the first two years of the five-year reign of Judy Schwomeyer and James Sladky as national champions. When the latter couple placed 4th at the 1968 World's and U.S. Silver Medalists Vicki Camper and Eugene Heffron came in 7th, they opened the way for the eligibility of a third U.S. couple the following year. By repeating as Bronze Medalists, Gerken and Tiedmann earned a trip to the 1969 World Championships in Colorado Springs, where they finished 9th, one placement better than U.S. Silver Medalists Joan Bitterman and Brad Hislop, while Schwomeyer and Sladky became World Bronze Medalists.

GILBERT, RICHARD *See* LEWIS, BETTY.

GILETTI, ALAIN *(b. 1938) French World Champion.*

Few skaters can equal the doggedness of Alain Giletti. He was among the top half-dozen male skaters in the world for a decade. He had more disappointments than great successes, yet he kept at it year after year until he finally achieved his dream and became World Champion. He was good at school figures but not as good as Hayes Alan Jenkins, against whom he competed again and again. He was a solid free-skater with a smooth artistic style, but although he couldn't equal the jumps of such rivals as Ronnie Robertson and David Jenkins of the United States or Canada's Donald Jackson, he was always a threat and he never gave up.

Giletti's first World Medal came in 1954, when he took the Bronze behind Hayes Alan Jenkins and James Grogan of the United States. He had won the European Championship that year and would do so for the next six years, but it was not until 1958 that he was able to take a second World Bronze, this time behind the younger Jenkins brother, David, and his teammate Tim Brown. The next year Giletti was out in the cold again, as Jenkins took the Gold, Canada's Donald Jackson the Silver and Tim Brown the Bronze. He was unable to break through at the 1960 Olympics either, won by Jenkins with Czechoslovakia's Karol Divin taking the Silver and Jackson the Bronze. But when David Jenkins turned professional and skipped the World Championships that year, Giletti had his chance; all he had to do was beat Jackson and Divin. With the finest and final performance of his amateur career, he became World Champion with Jackson 2nd and fellow Frenchman Alain Calmat 3rd. Perseverance had finally paid off.

GLOCKSHUBER, MARGOT *(b. 1949) West German Pairs Skater with Wolfgang Danne (b. 1941).*

Successors to Marika Kilius and Hans Baumler as West German Pairs Champions, Margot Glockshuber and Wolfgang Danne were not in quite the same class, but they did manage to become runners-up to the Protopopovs at the World's in 1967, edging out the Americans Cynthia and Ronald Kauffman. At the 1968 Olympics, the Protopopovs and another Soviet couple, Tatiana Zhuk and Alexandr Gorelik, were 1st and 2nd, but Glockshuber and Danne took the Bronze when the Kauffmans had an unexpectedly bad outing. At that year's World's, however, the Kauffmans prevailed to take the Bronze behind the two Russian couples. Still, the Olympic Bronze gave Glockshuber and Danne the credentials to pursue a brief professional career.

GOBL, MARGARET *See* NINGEL, FRANZ.

GOODRIDGE, FREDERICK *(b. 1909) U.S. Medalist.*

U.S. Silver Medalist behind Roger Turner in both 1928 and 1929, in New Haven and New York, Goodridge did not make the expensive journey overseas to the World Competitions in Berlin and London those two years, nor did he attend the 1928 Olympics in St. Moritz, Switzerland. The 1928 World's were in fact the first ever attended by U.S. male skaters, and the best Roger Turner could do was 5th, although he would subsequently win two World Silvers.

GOOS, DOROTHY *(b. 1924) U.S. medalist.*

In 1943, Dorothy Goos won two medals at the U.S. Championships, taking the Silver Medal in the Ladies' Competition behind Gretchen Merrill and also garnered a Bronze in Pairs with partner Edward Lemaire (b. 1923). In 1944, Goos was again the Silver Medalist behind Gretchen Merrill.

GORDAN, MARTIN *(b. 1883) German World medalist.*

Martin Gordan won the Bronze Medal at the 1902 World Championships in England. Because Ulrich Salchow was the Gold winner, this might have seemed quite satisfactory, but the Silver Medalist was a woman, Britain's Madge Syers; she was given permission to enter because there was no competition for women. Gordan's dismay was tempered by the fact that Salchow gave Madge Seyers his own Gold Medal in tribute. Gordan again took the Bronze in 1904, this time beaten by Salchow and countryman Heinrich Burger.

GORDEEVA, EKATERINA *(b. 1972) Soviet/Russian two-time Olympic Gold Medalist with partner Sergei Grinkov (1967–95).*

Ekaterina Gordeeva was only 14 and Sergei Grinkov 19 when they won their first World medal, taking the Gold at the 1986 World Championships over their Soviet teammates, 1985 winners Elena Valova and Oleg Vasiliev. There was such disparity in the height of the two winning partners that some commentators thought they looked a bit odd at times, but the height and weight difference also allowed Grinkov to toss Gordeeva around in the air above his head in spectacular fashion. They won again over Valova and Vasiliev at both the 1987 World Championships and the 1988 Olympics, but a slight backlash set in at the 1988 World's, and the Gold there went to Valova and Vasiliev by a narrow margin.

Gordeeva and Grinkov won two more World Championships over Canadian couples Cindy Landry and Lyndon Johnson in 1989 and Isabelle Brasseur and Lloyd Eisler in 1990. By this time, Gordeeva was a young woman, the height discrepancy had narrowed considerably and the pair had developed a fluid elegance that distinguished them clearly from any other couple in the world. They then married and turned professional.

Another Soviet couple with a polar opposite acrobatic style, Natalia Mishkutenok and Artur Dimitriev, won the 1991 and 1992 World Gold as well as the 1992 Olympics and also turned professional. Then both couples applied for reinstatement of their amateur status to compete in the 1994 Olympics, to the irritation of Brasseur and Eisler, who had become World Champions in 1992 and expected to cap their career with Olympic Gold. Despite two bobbles on jumps by Grinkov in the long program, the classical purity of his and Gordeeva's performance won the day, with a disgruntled Mishkutenok and Dimitriev, the audience favorites, 2nd and a furious Brasseur and Eisler 3rd. Then the two Russian couples returned to their professional careers, and the Canadians also entered the professional ranks.

In the fall of 1995, the figure skating world was deeply shocked by the death of Sergei Grinkov, who collapsed of a heart attack while practicing. After a period of mourning, Ekaterina Gordeeva turned to solo skating with remarkable success, her solid jumps and great artistry making possible an entirely new career in figure skating.

GORELIK, ALEKSANDR *See* ZHUK, TATIANA.

GORSHKOV, ALEKSANDR *See* PAKHOMOVA, LUDMILA.

GRAFSTROM, GILLIS *(1893–1938)*
Swedish three-time Olympic Gold Medalist.

Despite competing in only three World Championships, all of which he won, Gillis Grafstrom proved himself the dominant male figure skater of the 1920s by taking three Olympic Gold Medals and by adding significantly to the repertoire of figure-skating elements. Because the World Championships were not held from 1915 to 1921 because of World War I, Grafstrom was already 26

The Swedish master Gillis Grafstrom, three-time Olympic Champion in the 1920s.
(Courtesy World Figure Skating Museum)

years old when he took his first international title at the Summer Olympic Games of 1920 in Antwerp, Belgium. There, the existence of an indoor rink allowed figure skating to be contested, as had also been the case in London in 1908. Grafstrom's first Olympic Gold Medal was won over Norway's Andreas Krogh and Martin Stixrud, neither of whom competed again.

Grafstrom, however, was just beginning. He won the World title at the resumption of that competition in Stockholm, Sweden in 1922 over Austria's Fritz Kachler and Willy Boeckl, who would take the Gold and Silver the following year at the World's in Vienna. Grafstrom skipped the 1923 competition but returned to capture both the Olympic and World titles again in 1924, with Boeckl placing 2nd both times. He did not compete at the World's in 1925–27; Boeckl won all three Gold Medals. But Grafstrom was again at the Olympics in 1928 to seek a third Gold Medal and successfully held off another strong challenge by Boeckl. He skipped the 1928 World's because of an injury; Boeckl took his fourth title and retired. At the age of 35, Grafstrom came back to take a final World Gold in 1929 over the rising Austrian star Karl Schafer, only 19, who would go on to win the next seven World Championships. That was not, however, Grafstrom's last competition: He showed up at the 1932 Olympics in Lake Placid, New York to defend his Olympic title for the third time. Hampered by a leg injury and his 38 years, he had to settle for the Silver, as Schafer took the first of two Olympic Golds.

One reason that Grafstrom was able to win titles after not competing for several years throughout his amateur career was that he was one of the sport's great innovators: Like Dick Button 25 years later, Grafstrom always had something new to unveil to the skating world when he competed—he invented the spiral, which was quickly taken up by women skaters, and both the change sit spin (during which the skater changes legs in the middle of the spin) and the more spectacular flying sit spin (which involves jumping into the spin). All three of these elements became essential free-skating moves. It was Grafstrom whom Dick Button had in mind—and whom he himself had emulated—when he first issued his standard by which to judge skating greatness: leaving the sport different and better than the skater had found it at the beginning.

GRAFSTROM SPIN

A spin that retains the name of its inventor, Gillis Grafstrom (see above). It is a camel spin in which the raised free leg is bent upward at the knee instead of extended in a straight line behind the skater.

GRAHAM, HUGH AND MARGARET ANNE

(b. 1933, 1934) U.S. Pairs medalists; Hugh also men's medalist.

The brother-and-sister team of Hugh and Margaret Anne Graham took the U.S. Silver Medal in Pairs in both 1953 and 1954 behind Carole Ormaca and Robin Greiner. In those years, World team members were selected on the basis of their placement in the previous year's National Championships; the Grahams thus competed in 1954 in Oslo, Norway where they finished 5th, one place behind Ormaca and Greiner.

Margaret Anne then quit skating to marry, but Hugh continued to skate the next year in the men's division. He was competing in the strongest men's division in U.S. skating history, including Hayes Jenkins, David Jenkins and Ronnie Robertson. Robertson was unable to perform at the U.S. Championships because of an injury, and Hugh took the U.S. Bronze Medal for 1955. All four skaters were allowed to compete at the World's because the United States had taken the Gold and Silver Medals as well as 4th and 5th place at the 1954 World Championships. In 1955, Hayes Jenkins won the World Gold, Ronnie Robertson the Silver and David Jenkins the Bronze; Hugh Graham was 10th.

GREEN, HILARY *(b. 1952) British Ice Dancer with Glyn Watts (b. 1949).*

In 1973, it had been three years since a British Ice Dancing couple had won a World Medal—a failure that had occurred only once in the previous 17 years. But Hilary Green and Glyn Watts again put the British on the Ice Dancing medal platform by taking the World Bronze that year behind the Soviet Union's four-time Gold Medalists Ludmila Pakhomova and Aleksandr Gorshkov and West Germany's Angelika and Erich Buck. The following year they gained the Silver behind Pakhomova and Gorshkov, but in 1975 fell back to 3rd again as another Soviet couple, Irina Moiseeva and Andrei Minekov, became World Champions. The U.S.'s Colleen O'Connor and Jim Millns, who had been only 7th the previous year, showed enormous improvement and seized the Silver. With Pakhomova and Gorshkov back in competition in 1976, Green and Watts were pushed back to 4th at the Olympics and the World's, with the Silver going to Moiseeva and Minekov and the Bronze to O'Connor and Millns at both competitions.

GREENOUGH-SMITH, DOROTHY *(b. 1878) British Olympic medalist.*

At the first Olympic figure-skating events ever in London in 1908, Dorothy Greenough-Smith took the Bronze Medal behind her pioneering compatriot Madge Syers and Silver Medalist Elsa Rendschmidt of Germany. When she competed again at the World Championships in 1912, she not only earned the Silver Medal but also became the first woman to perform an axel in competition, for its time a daring assault on the rules of femininity that stifled the Ladies' Division until the 1920s. Her jump may even have cost her the Gold Medal which went to Hungary's Opika von Horvath, but it earned her an honored place in figure-skating history.

GREGORY, SCOTT *(b. 1960) U.S. Ice Dance Champion.*

With two different partners, Scott Gregory was U.S. Ice Dancing Medalist from 1982 to 1988. His first partner was Elisa Spitz (b. 1964). The couple took the Bronze Medal in 1982 and 1984 but edged Carol Fox and Richard Dalley for the Silver in 1983. Fox and Dalley beat them the other two years, with Judy Blumberg and Michael Seibert winning the Gold each year. Gregory and Spitz were 8th, 7th and 11th at the World's during these years. When Elsa Spitz retired from amateur skating, Gregory teamed with Suzanne Semanick. They took the Bronze in 1985 and the Silver in 1986 and were U.S. Champions in 1987 and 1988. They were 5th at the World's in 1986 and 1987 and placed 6th at the 1988 Olympics.

GREINER, ROBIN *(b. 1933) U.S. Pairs Champion.*

Without winning a previous medal, Robin Greiner and partner Carole Ormaca became U.S Pairs Champions in 1953 and retained the title through 1956. They maintained a steady 4th place at the World's in 1953–1956 and finished 5th at the 1956 Olympics. Carole Ormaca then retired, but Greiner came back to win the U.S. Silver Medal in 1958 with Sheila Wells.

GRINER, WENDY *(b. 1951) Canadian World medalist.*

No Canadian woman had won a World medal of any kind since Barbara Ann Scott in 1948 until Wendy Griner captured the World Silver in 1962, behind Sjoukje Dijkstra. She then retired from competition, leaving the field to her strong Canadian challenger, Petra Burke, who would become World Champion three years later.

GRINKOV, SERGEI *See* GORDEEVA, EKATERINA.

GRIP

This term is used in reference to various kinds of handholds used by Pairs skaters in performing lifts, throw jumps and death spirals, as well as to the clasps specific to particular Ice Dance forms such as the waltz or the tango. In Pairs skating, the grip is a matter of practicality, with the grip determined by the tensile requirements of a given maneuver. Thus the grip may take the form of a simple hand clasp, the fingers may be intertwined for added strength or the hands may be placed over one another's wrists, as in performing a death spiral. There are practical considerations in Ice Dancing, too, but here the grip also becomes an element of style and extends to the ways in which the partners' arms are placed around one another, with certain placements required for the idiomatic expression of specific dance forms.

GRISCHUK, OKSANA (PASHA)

(b. 1971) Russian Olympic and World Ice Dance Champion with Evgeny Platov (b. 1969).

Oksana Grischuk and Evgeny Platov came to the fore in 1992 when they won the World Bronze behind two other couples from the former Soviet Union, Marina Klimova/Sergei Ponomarenko and Maria Usova/Alexander Zhulin. In 1993, they moved up to the Silver behind Usova and Zhulin. With the return of Great Britain's Jayne Torvill and Christopher Dean, the 1984 World and Olympic Champions and the continued presence of Usova and Zhulin, the 1994 Olympics promised to be an extraordinary competition. In fact, it proved to be the most controversial Ice Dance competition in years, with the judges being second-guessed at every turn.

Torvill and Dean narrowly edged Grischuk and Platov for the European title. At the Olympics, the start of the Free Dance found the Britons and Usova and Zhulin tied for the lead, with Grischuk and Platov very close behind. The Gold Medal would be won by the couple that prevailed in the free dance. The judges chose Grischuk and Platov, but many spectators and experts thought the winners should have been Usova and Zhulin, the Silver Medalists, and an even larger group of dissenters were convinced that Torvill and Dean had been the clear winners. At the World Championships, Usova and Zhulin and Torvill and Dean were absent, allowing Grischuk and Platov to easily win the Gold Medal over France's Sophie Moniotte and Pascal Lavanchy, with Finland's Susanna Rahkamo and Petri Kokko taking the Bronze.

In 1995, Evgeni Platov was hampered by a serious cartilage problem that kept the couple out of the European Championships, which were won by the Finns, narrowly beating Moniotte and Lavanchy. But Grischuk and Platov returned for the World Championships and despite being slightly less precise than usual because of Platov's injury, won their second World Championship over the Finnish and French couples. Grischuk and Platov went on to win World Gold in 1996 and 1997, ahead of Krylova and Ovsiannikov and Shae-Lynn Bourne and Victor Kraatz both years. At the 1998 Olympics in Nagano, Japan they became the first ice dancers to repeat as Gold Medalists since the sport was inaugurated as part of the Winter Games in 1976, prevailing over Anjelika Krylova and Oleg Ovsiannikov, also of Russia, and Marina Anissina and Gwendel Peizerat of France.

GROGAN, JAMES

(b. 1923) Superb U.S. and World medalist.

For several years, James Grogan was the second-best male skater in the world. Unfortunately for him, he competed against U.S. skaters Dick Button and Hayes Alan Jenkins year after year. Grogan won his first U.S. medal, a Bronze, the second year of Button's long tenure as U.S. Champion. After that, except for 1950, when he was injured, he was 2nd to Button four times in the U.S. competition and twice at the World's, in 1951 and 1952.

In 1949, 1951 and 1952, Hayes Alan Jenkins was right behind Grogan as U.S. Bronze Medalist, and in 1952, it was Button, Grogan and Jenkins, in that order, at the World's. At the 1952 Olympics, Button took his second Gold Medal, while Austrian Helmut Seibt took the Silver; Grogan was the Bronze Medalist and Hayes Alan Jenkins was 4th. In 1953, and again in 1954, Jenkins was both U.S. and World Champion, with Grogan the World Silver Medalist. He missed the 1953 U.S. competition because of injury and retired after his Silver Medal performance at the World's in 1954. (At that time, national titles were decided after the World competition rather than before, as is the case now).

In the course of his amateur career, James Grogan amassed a total of 10 U.S., World and Olympic medals. He, Button and Jenkins were all friends as well as rivals. In 1952, when they were 1st, 2nd and 3rd in the world, Button, Grogan and Jenkins ushered in a period of U.S. dominance of male skating that would persist until 1958, with U.S. skaters always first and second in the world (as well as possessors of all three medals in 1955 and 1956). James Grogan was never the U.S. or World Champion, but he was a standout American male figure skater.

GROSS, MANUELA *(b. 1957) Major East German Pair skater first with Uwe Kagelmann (b. 1952) and then with Uwe Bewersdorf (b. 1957).*

Manuela Gross and Uwe Kagelmann were surprise winners of the Olympic Bronze Medal in 1972 and then took the World Bronze in 1973. The couple was then somewhat eclipsed by another East German Pair, Romy Kermer and Rolf Osterreich, who became East German Champions and took the World Bronze in 1974. The next year, Kermer and Osterreich were the World Silver Medalists behind the Soviet Union's Irina Rodnina and Alexandr Zaitsev, with Gross and Kagelmann taking the World Bronze for a second time.

Gross and Kagelmann earned a second Olympic Bronze in 1976 behind Rodnina and Zaitsev and Kermer and Osterreich, but they did not make the medal platform at the World's. With two Olympic and two World Bronzes, Uwe Kagelmann then retired; Manuela Gross married, but she was shortly back in competition, skating under her married name of Manuela Mager and with a new partner, Uwe Bewersdorf. They took the World Silver behind Irina Rodnina and Alexandr Zaitsev in 1978, were out of the running in 1979 and then took the Olympic Bronze and another World Silver in 1980. Manuela Gross Mager thus became the only Pairs skater ever to win three Olympic medals aside from Irina Rodnina and Andrée and Pierre Brunet.

GUHEL, CHRISTINE AND JEAN-PAUL *(b. ?, ?) French Ice Dance team.*

In 1960, the French sister-and-brother Ice Dance team of Christine and Jean-Paul Guhel became the first couple from anywhere but Great Britain, Canada or the United States to win a medal in the World Ice Dancing competition since its inauguration in 1952. Their Bronze Medal that year came at the expense of Margie Ackles and Charles Phillips of the United States, who found themselves in 4th place for the second year in a row. The Gold Medal that year went for the second time to Doreen Denny and Courtney Jones of Great Britain (British couples had taken every Gold Medal since the start of World competition), and the Silver was taken by Virginia Thompson and William McLachlan of Canada.

In 1961 competition was canceled because of the deaths of the American team in a plane crash at Brussels, and when competition resumed in 1962, the Guhels were expected to fight it out for the Gold chiefly with the Canadians because Denny and Jones had retired. But instead the victors were Eva Romanova and Pavel Roman of Czechoslovakia, who would win three more times, although the Guhels were able to beat the Canadians for the Silver. The Guhels then retired, and it would be 28 years before another French team took an Ice Dancing medal.

GUSTAFSON, PATTI *See* KOLLEN, PIETER.

H

HADLEY, ILLA RAY AND RAY JR.

(1942–61 [twins]) U.S. Pair medalists.

The Hadley twins were the 1960 U.S. Bronze Medalists in Pairs behind Nancy and Ron Ludington and Maribel Owen and Dudley Richards but gaining them a berth on the Olympic team; they finished 11th. In 1961 they moved up a notch, taking the U.S. Silver behind Owen and Richards. They were then killed in the plane crash at Brussels on the way to the World Championships.

HAGAN, BARRY

See KROHN, KIM.

HAIGLER, CHRISTINE

(b. 1948) U.S. medalist.

Young Christine Haigler became the U.S. Silver Medalist in 1963 behind Lorraine Hanlon, one of several skaters who moved into the gaps left by the deaths of the American World Team at Brussels in 1961. She finished 19th at the World Championships that year, but she proved the next year that she was a skater of international quality. Although she was only 3rd at the U.S. Championships behind Peggy Fleming and Albertina Noyes, she took 7th place at the 1964 Olympics and 5th at the World Championships, one place behind Fleming at the Olympics and two ahead of her at the World's. In 1965, she won the U.S. Silver Medal behind Fleming, and placed 4th at the World's, as Fleming took the Bronze Medal. She then retired from skating.

HAINES, JACKSON

(b. 1835) Pioneering U.S. dancer and figure skater.

The second U.S. figure-skating club was formed in New York City in 1860, following the lead of Philadelphia. One of its members was Jackson Haines, who had been trained in the ballet. He had a host of ideas about developing figure skating beyond the sedate and rigid exercises that were then in fashion. But his ideas were not well received in the United States (the last important Western country to hold national championships in the sport, at the late date of 1914). He left for Europe in 1864 and performed on skates to music in numerous countries. Like the United States, England was initially resistant to his ideas, but he met with enthusiastic receptions on the Continent.

He met with particular success in Vienna; the Austrians were enchanted by his performances to Strauss waltzes. A skating club was formed in 1867 in Vienna, where he taught for several years. His popularity was such that he performed on a small artificial rink in Giacomo Meyerbeer's opera *Le Prophète*, and his picture adorned a score of the composer's ballet *Les Patineurs*. Haines was the first skater known to use blades that were screwed to the sole of the boot; this afforded the kind of stability necessary to perform his inventive new move, the sit spin, a basic element in the figure skating repertoire to this day. He died at the age of 39 on a trip to Finland. He was buried in 1875 at Gamla-Kareby, Finland, his tomb inscribed with the words "The American Skating King."

The "Viennese School" of figure skating that Jackson Haines created had taken hold across Europe and finally in England by the 1890s, and its triumph opened the way to the establishment of the World Championships in 1896.

The "father of modern figure skating," American Jackson Haines, circa 1870.
(Courtesy World Figure Skating Museum)

HAMILL, DOROTHY *(b. 1956) U.S., World and Olympic Champion.*

Dorothy Hamill, the youngest of three children of Carol and Chalmers Hamill, grew up in Riverside, Connecticut but first skated on a pond behind her maternal grandparent's home in Wellesley, Massachusetts when she was eight years old. She immediately asked to take lessons, starting with a local teacher and then with former Czech champion Otto Gold, spending summer 1966 under his tutelage at Lake Placid, New York. Her rapid development then brought her to Swiss coach Gustav Lussi, again at Lake Placid, in 1967. That fall she began a daily commute from Riverside to New York City to study with former U.S. Champion Sonya Klopfer Dunfield. The reward for her intense training was National Novice Championship in 1969.

Hamill lived with friends in New York and was privately tutored in her schoolwork to spend as much time as possible practicing. When she became Eastern Junior Ladies' Champion and National Junior Silver Medalist in 1970, Coach Carlo Fassi invited her to the Broadmoor Skating Club in Colorado Springs. She spent most of the next several years there and earned her high school diploma at Colorado Academy. Under Fassi's strict guidance, she moved up steadily in the National Senior Ladies' ranks, taking 5th in 1971, 4th in 1972 and 2nd in 1973 to five-time Champion Janet Lynn, who turned professional later that year.

At her first World Championship in 1972, Hamill finished 7th but moved up to 4th the following year; in 1974 she took her first U.S. Championship as well as the World Silver Medal. At home in the United States, Hamill was not strongly challenged, but major international competition came from East Germany's Christine Errath and the Netherlands' Dianne de Leeuw. The three young women were quite different as skating personalities but so closely matched in talent that they held the three top World positions from 1974 to 1976, each of them taking the World title once:

Errath was champion in 1974 and de Leeuw in 1975 with Dorothy in 2nd place both times. The suspense of the 1976 Olympic year was who would take the Olympic Gold.

When a U.S. skater has a real chance of taking the Olympic Gold Medal, the press pays attention. This was particularly true in 1976 because Dorothy Hamill was the only U.S. skater who had a legitimate possibility of triumphing—the U.S. Ice Dance Champions Colleen O'Connor and Jim Millns were contenders for the Bronze, possibly the Silver, but they were up against two former Soviet World Champion teams, and in Men's and Pairs' competition no American had finished above 5th at the World's in several years. Hamill's hairstyle even received attention: a long-standing problem with her very fine hair was finally solved by having it cut short in a style that would soon sweep the world.

Hamill was an athletic skater in the Carol Heiss mold, but in the past two years she had developed artistically to give her style a more fluid, feminine line. The combination of strength and grace always appeals to judges, but with those strong adversaries, she would have to skate nearly flawlessly throughout the competition. Hamill did just that in the school figures and short program, bringing herself into the free-skating final with a small edge: it was now her championship to win or lose. Jumping superbly and flashing her well-known smile, she merited the Gold Medal. Both Silver Medalist de Leeuw and Bronze Medalist Errath also skated very well.

Dorothy Hamill, still smiling a decade after her 1976 Olympic victory.
(Courtesy Paul Harvath)

With the Gold Medal in her pocket, the question was whether to skate at the World Championships: A loss could cut into her obvious commercial potential as a professional. Like Britain's Gold Medalist John Curry, Hamill had "never won [the World Championship] and I thought things would be incomplete without it," she said. Both she and Curry took their World titles in splendid style; Errath and de Leeuw still challenged her, but their Olympic order of finish was reversed, Errath taking the Silver this time.

Having a face that television cameras love, Dorothy Hamill's championship season gave her a vast new public following. Her cheerful, steady presence on camera made her the most sought-after figure skater for commercial endorsements in the sport's history. Her professional skating career, which she began with a million-dollar Ice Capades contract, has been particularly long-lived and has embraced several television specials, professional competitions, a creative period with John Curry and his Ice Dancing company and innumerable special appearances in fund-raising exhibitions for amateur skaters.

After her first marriage to Dean Martin Jr. ended in divorce, she married Dr. Kenneth Forsythe, a sports-medicine specialist and former Canadian Olympic skier; their daughter, Alexandra, was born

Olympic Gold Medalist Scott Hamilton, always the picture of glee on ice.
(Courtesy Paul Harvath)

a year later. In 1993, together with her husband and businessman Ben C. Tinsdale, she bought the financially troubled Ice Capades, in which she had skated on and off for eight years. Revamping the company, she opened with a full-evening story-on-ice called *Cinderella. . . Frozen in Time,* featuring herself as Cinderella and former British Pairs Champion Andrew Naylor as Prince Charming. The company was acquired by a media conglomerate in 1994.

Dorothy Hamill still wears her hair in the fashion that attracted so much attention at the 1976 Olympics. "I'm kind of stuck with it," she told a reporter, laughing, in 1994.

HAMILTON, SCOTT *(b. 1958) U.S. World and Olympic Champion.*

The extraordinary background of Scott Hamilton was first revealed to the U.S. public during the 1980 Winter Olympic Games' opening ceremonies at Lake Placid, New York. The bearer of the U.S. flag during the parade of nations was customarily chosen by a vote of the entire U.S. Olympic contingent. In 1980 this singular honor was bestowed on 21-year-old Bronze Medalist in men's figure skating Scott Hamilton because of the great odds he had overcome to reach that point: He had already accomplished what for many years of his life had seemed impossible—he had become an athlete.

Scott was adopted six weeks after birth by Ernie and Dorothy Hamilton of Bowling Green, Ohio where his father was an associate professor of biology at Bowling Green University. Everything had seemed fine until, at the age of two, Scott stopped growing. It took years to discover the problem: a rare medical condition called Schwachman's syndrome caused an improper absorption of nutrients due to a paralysis of the intestine.

He was nine when his older sister, Susan, took him to a rink and he first put on ice skates. At that point he was still wearing a permanent feeding tube, but he enjoyed skating, and it obviously agreed with him. His doctors are not sure why, but the combination of exercise and the lower temperatures of the rink atmosphere somehow restored his health. He began to grow at a more normal rate, although he would never be taller than 5'3". That was big enough: Hamilton developed a wiry physique that was packed with power. Nevertheless, his rise through the amateur ranks was slower than he would have liked—especially because his mother, who had done so much for him when he was ill as a child, died of cancer in 1978 before he had won a senior medal. In 1979 he had expected to be able to take his first U.S.

Senior medal and win one of three places in the men's division of the World team, but he came in 4th and missed out.

At that point he switched coaches, putting himself in the hands of Don Law of Philadelphia, who put him through the most rigorous year of training he had ever experienced. That brought Hamilton the 1980 U.S. Bronze and a trip to the Olympics, where he came in 5th. U.S. Champion Charlie Tickner was 3rd, and U.S. Silver Medalist David Santee was 4th. All three took the same places at the World's.

In 1981, a newly confident Hamilton vaulted over Santee to become U.S. Champion for the first time. Even more impressively, he took the first of four successive World Gold Medals. There was no stopping him now. He became so dominant that he was expected to win the Olympic Gold Medal in 1984 with ease. Being the prohibitive favorite is daunting enough at the Olympics, but things were made much more difficult when Hamilton developed an ear infection that affected his balance. It didn't bother him during the school figures, and he piled up points to take first place. But in the short program Brian Orser of Canada beat him. Orser had been a distant 7th after the figures but now moved into 5th place. Then in the free-skating, Orser gave a dazzling performance skating just before Hamilton. Feeling wobbly from the ear infection, Scott turned a planned triple jump into a double and did not have his customary verve throughout his program. Once again, Orser was 1st and he was 2nd. But the combined scores still put Hamilton in 1st place. Olympic Gold Medal in hand and his illness behind him, he won his fourth World title handily.

Scott Hamilton's outgoing personality and imaginative ideas about choreography made him a natural as a professional skater. He was also able to make fuller use of his acrobatic skating skills. Famous for his high-flying Russian split jump, he could make more use of it than in a competitive program, and he wowed audiences with his terrific back flip, which wasn't allowed in competitive skating at all. Equally adept at serious and comic routines, he won numerous professional competitions and remains one of the biggest draws in professional skating a decade later. He also made himself a respected name as a skating commentator for CBS, covering many competitions, including the 1992 and 1994 Olympics. The little boy who stopped growing had become one of the most popular male figure skaters of all time.

In 1997, Hamilton was diagnosed with testicular cancer and withdrew from performing to undergo treatment. In keeping with his history of overcoming medical problems and always looking on the bright side, he returned to the professional circuit in September of 1997.

HAMULA, GAIL *(b. 1956) U.S. Pairs medalist with Frank Sweiding (b. 1954).*

Gail Hamula and Frank Sweiding were the Silver Medalists at the U.S. Championships in both 1977 and 1978, behind Tai Babilonia and Randy Gardner. Babilonia and Gardner were the World Bronze Medalists both years, while Hamula and Sweiding were 7th in 1977 and then slipped to 10th in 1978.

HAND-TO-HAND LOOP LIFT

A basic Pairs lift that calls for both partners to skate backward with their hands interlocked on either side. As the woman skates on a back outside edge, she is lifted into a loop jump position, her legs stretched apart. Her partner turns with her as a full loop revolution is made and then lowers her once again to a back outside edge. Advanced Pairs skaters use double and triple revolution versions of this lift.

HANLON, LORRAINE *(b. 1946) U.S. Champion.*

Junior Ladies' Champion in 1961, the year the American team was killed in the plane crash at Brussels, Lorraine Hanlon became U.S. Silver Medalist in 1962 and U.S. Champion at the age of 17 in 1963. She was 10th at the World Championships both years.

HARDING, TONYA *(b. 1970) U.S. Champion whose career ended in scandal.*

A skater with the talent to become a World Champion, Tonya Harding's career was marked by serious ups and downs and ended in a blaze of tabloid headlines. She was 5th in her first two National Seniors competitions in 1987 and 1988 and then gained the U.S. Bronze in 1989. Although she did not go to the World's because only two Americans were eligible that year, Harding won two sidebar competitions, Skate America and the Nations Cup. In 1990, however, she plummeted to 7th place at the U.S. Championships, falling all over the ice. Yet, the following year she became national champion over Kristi Yamaguchi and Nancy Kerrigan and was part of a surprise sweep of the World Championships, as Yamaguchi took the Gold Medal, Harding the Silver and Kerrigan the Bronze.

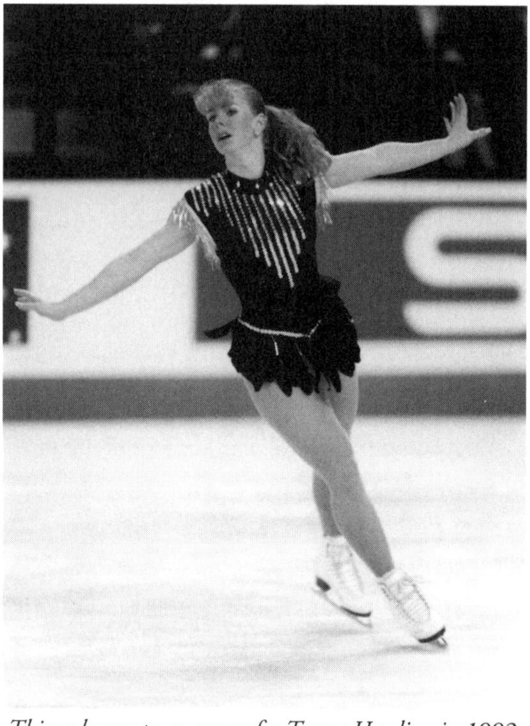

Things began to go wrong for Tonya Harding in 1992.
(Courtesy Paul Harvath)

She was not at her best in 1992, taking the U.S. Bronze behind Yamaguchi and Kerrigan, placing a disappointing 4th in the Olympics at which Yamaguchi and Kerrigan were the Gold and Bronze Medalists and collapsing to 6th place at the World's, where Yamaguchi and Kerrigan were 1st and 2nd. Things did not improve in 1993. Kerrigan became U.S. Champion and two skaters who had not previously won U.S. medals, Lisa Ervin and Tonia Kwiatkowski, took the Silver and Bronze, with Harding finishing 4th and losing out on a chance to compete at the World's. Although Kerrigan fell apart at the World Championships under the pressure of being the favorite, it later became clear that Harding had developed an intense resentment of Kerrigan's overall success.

As the U.S. Championships were getting under way at Detroit, Michigan in 1994, Nancy Kerrigan had just come off the ice after a practice session when a man appeared out of nowhere and whacked her across her left knee with a hard instrument. The resulting injury made it impossible for her to defend her U.S. title and at first seemed likely to keep her out of the Olympics as well. Harding somewhat coolly expressed her sympathy and went on to skate her best in three years, winning the national championship for a second time with young Michelle Kwan and Nicole Bobek taking the Silver and Bronze Medals. The U.S. Figure Skating Association named Kerrigan as the second member of the Olympic Ladies' team, along with Harding, pending Nancy's recovery.

There had been veiled speculation that Harding might have been involved in the attack on Kerrigan, and shortly after the Nationals a confession by Harding's bodyguard made it clear that in fact the attack had been masterminded by Harding's ex-husband, Jeff Gilooley, with whom she was again living. Harding denied any advance knowledge of or participation in the plot, but the story became the subject of intense television and tabloid speculation; even serious newspapers gave it major play. Was Harding really not involved? Would she be allowed to skate at the Olympics?

How would Kerrigan and other U.S. team members deal with the situation?

The Olympic skating events took place amid a media frenzy. Kerrigan, fully recovered, gave the best performances of her life in both the short and the long program and lost the Gold Medal to Ukraine's Oksana Baiul by one-tenth of a point in a very controversial decision. Harding skated badly in the short program, held up the proceedings during the long program with a tearful display of a broken shoelace to the judges and finished 8th overall. "I'm really glad Nancy skated great," she said. "I hope she did it not only for herself but for her country and our team."

Less than three weeks later, Tonya Harding pleaded guilty to a charge of hindering the prosecution in the attack on Nancy Kerrigan. She was given probation but slapped with fines that amounted to $160,000. Finally the young woman who had wanted so much to be a World Champion was stripped of her 1994 U.S. title, taken off the World team and banned from all officially sanctioned competitions and exhibitions for life.

Much had been made in the press of Tonya Harding's broken home, her estrangement from her mother, her troubled marriage and her money problems. There was much talk in the skating world about her extremely uneven competition record and about her tendency to have equipment failures during competition—the broken lace at the Olympics was only the last of several such incidents. Editorial writers talked about a breakdown of character. There were suggestions that skating had become too cutthroat a sport because of all the money that had become available to champions. But on this last subject, former U.S. and World Champion Linda Fratianne said that some competitors had been out to sabotage other skaters by any means short of hiring hitmen when she was competing 20 years earlier. Even before that, Dorothy Hamill noted in her autobiography that an unnamed European competitor and her coach had driven a car straight at her and her coach as they were walking along a road on the eve of a World Championship, causing them to dive into a ditch. The Tonya Harding story had just gone further in exposing the dark side that exists in any highly competitive endeavor.

What seemed saddest to many in the skating world was that Tonya Harding had been on the edge of greatness as a skater. She was one of only two women, along with Midori Ito of Japan, who could perform a triple axel. At her best, as in 1991, she had been 2nd in the world and had always had the potential to be number one. But something had gone terribly wrong.

HARTSHORNE, HAROLD *(1918–61)*

Major U.S. Ice Dancer in early years of sport.

Prior to 1936, the U.S. Ice Dancing competition involved separate competitions for two dances, with medal winners for each category. From 1936, when the competition was first reorganized along modern lines, through 1944, Harold Hartshorne was a medalist every year—but with three different partners: First, he and partner Nettie Prantel were Silver Medalists in 1936 and national champions the two following years; then they split up with some acrimony. Second, in 1939 Hartshorne and Sandy MacDonald took the Gold Medal; Nettie Prantel was runner-up, partnered by Joseph Savage. The results were the same in 1940: Hartshorne and MacDonald were again champions in 1941 but fell to second in 1942. In 1943 he rejoined forces with Nettie Prantel, who had not competed for two years, and they won the Bronze. But this reunion lasted only a year. Third, Hartshorne and third partner, Kathe Mehl, won the Silver Medal to finish his career in 1944. He was one of the most important figures during the first decade of modern Ice Dance competition in the United States and was elected to the U.S. Figure Skating Hall of Fame in 1981.

HAUPT, OLLIE JR. *(b. 1920)* *U.S. medalist.*

At the age of 18, Ollie Haupt Jr. won the U.S. Bronze Medal in 1938. In 1939 and 1940 he was the Silver Medalist, first behind Robin Lee and then Eugene Turner. The United States did not send a team to the World Championships from 1937 to 1939 and no event was held from 1940 to 1946, so Haupt was unable to test himself against international competition.

HEAD-BANGER

This move in Pairs skating invariably causes audiences to gasp. The woman is raised above the head of the male partner as they skate in tandem and then dropped precipitously to one side, headfirst, so that her head almost brushes the ice. The momentum carries her through an arc that brings her upright again and she lands beside the man on her outer skate. It is a dangerous move that requires absolute trust on the part of the woman skater that her partner will judge the height of the drop precisely.

Quite aside from the danger involved, the move works well only when the height differential between the partners is within certain parameters. If the man is a lot taller than the woman, the effect is lessened. If the woman is too tall, the element of danger becomes prohibitive. Thus the head-banger is not too often used in the Pairs repertoire. The chief exponents of it in recent years have been the United States Champions Todd Sand and Jenni Meno, who performed the move to great effect at the 1994 Olympics and World Championships.

HEASLEY, VICKI

See WAGGENHOFFER, ROBERT.

HECKERT, JOANNE *(b. 1946) U.S. Pairs medalist with Gary Clark (b. 1945).*

Joanne Heckert and Gary Clark took the U.S. Bronze Medal in Pairs in 1965 behind the two sister-and-brother teams of Vivian and Ronald Joseph and Cynthia and Ronald Kauffman. At the World Championships, Heckert and Clark placed 9th as the Josephs won the Silver Medal.

HEFFRON, EUGENE

See CAMPER, VICKI.

HEISS, CAROL *(b. 1940) U.S., World and Olympic Champion.*

A native of Ozone Park in New York City, Carol Heiss began to skate at a very early age and showed immediate promise. She was taken on as a pupil by Andrée Joly Brunet, who then passed Heiss on to her husband, Pierre Brunet. Even then, when Carol was seven, her coach was convinced that she had the talent to reach the top of the skating world within 10 years.

National Novice Ladies' Champion at 11, Heiss took the Junior title the next year. Moving up to the Senior level in 1953, she came in 2nd to Tenley Albright, as she would many times over the next few years. At her first World Championships that year, she came in 4th. In 1954, Heiss missed the World Championships because of a serious cut below her calf that resulted from a collision with her younger sister, Nancy, during a practice session. By the time Nationals were held, however, she had healed well enough to take the Silver Medal again behind Tenley Albright.

The press began to make a good deal of a "rivalry" between the two U.S. skaters, but it appeared to exist mostly on the side of Heiss, who at five years younger than Albright had developed very quickly as a skater. In 1955, Albright was 1st at both the World's and Nationals with Heiss a close 2nd. The following year, 1956, the Olympics were skated first, the World's second and the Nationals third. This time Albright was injured just a few days before the start of the Olympics. But she prevailed in Cortina, Italy even so, becoming the first American woman to win an Olympic Gold Medal in skating. She had beaten Heiss by only 1.5 points.

At the World Championships, Heiss finally triumphed, winning the Gold, while Albright, whose injury was still bothering her, came in 2nd. The results were again reversed, however, at the U.S. Championships. Albright retired with five successive U.S. Championships.

It was now Carol Heiss' turn to dominate, and despite the death of her mother in October 1956, Carol went on to four successive national titles, five World titles and the Olympic Gold medal in 1960. A mature young woman now, skating with both athleticism and feminine charm, she brushed aside her competition as no woman had done since Sonja Henie. Like Henie, she answered the call of Hollywood, but the result, an unfortunate vehicle called *Snow White and the Three Stooges*, was not a box-office success.

Married to former Olympic Champion Hayes Alan Jenkins, Heiss settled down to raise a family and coach her sport. As a coach or judge, she is often seen at competitions, still flashing the bright smile she wore so many times as an undisputed queen of her sport.

HEISS, NANCY *(b. 1942) U.S. medalist.*

Nancy Heiss did not have the natural talent for figure skating that her older sister Carol so abundantly possessed, but she stuck to it even in the shadow of her sister's fame. She usually finished 4th at the U.S. Championships but also made three trips to the World Championships in 1957–59, finishing 8th, 6th and 8th. In 1959 she also had her best competition ever and placed 2nd to her sister at the U.S. Championships. That fulfilled her goals and she retired from skating.

HEITZER, REGINE *(b. 1945) Austrian World medalist.*

An extremely reliable skater good at both school figures and free-skating, Regine Heitzer was a competitor who might well have become World Champion at another time but had to compete against Sjoukje Dijkstra of the Netherlands year after year. Heitzer first appeared on the World medal platform in 1962 to accept the Bronze as Dijkstra gained her first World Championship. During the next three years and at the 1964 Olympics, Heitzer was runner-up to Dijkstra until the Dutch champion retired after her Olympic and World victories in

1960 World and Olympic Champion Carol Heiss.
(Courtesy World Figure Skating Museum)

1964; then Heitzer decided to compete one more year with the expectation of finally becoming World Champion. She was, however, thwarted by Canada's Petra Burke, 1964's World and Olympic Bronze Medalist. The 3rd-place medalist in 1965 was a 16-year-old American named Peggy Fleming, who gave Regine Heitzer a sufficient enough challenge for the Silver to persuade the Austrian to retire while she was at least the number-two skater in the world.

HENIE, SONJA *(1912–69)*

Legendary Norwegian skater and movie star.

Born in Oslo (then Kristiana), Norway, Sonja Henie learned to ski practically as soon as she could walk, as is the case with most Norwegians. But she was also interested in ballet and began to take lessons at five from Love Krohn, teacher of the great Russian ballerina Anna Pavlova. It was Pavlova rather than a skater whom Henie claimed as her greatest influence. She began to skate at the age of six and became the figure skating champion of Norway at 10, a title she would continue to hold through 1936, 14 years later.

In 1924, as a still tiny 12-year-old, Sonja Henie competed in her first of four Olympics. She finished 5th of 7 skaters at this first official Winter Olympics in Chamonix, France and attracted much attention. Her next international appearance was at the 1926 World Championships at Stockholm, Sweden, where she came in 2nd to five-time World Champion Herma Jaross-Szabo, a great woman skater in the sport's history. A year later, Henie dethroned Jaross-Szabo and became Gold Medalist in every subsequent competition she entered. No one beat her during the next decade, although some argue that U.S.'s Maribel Vinson should have won in 1928 but that the entirely European contingent of judges simply would not let a non-European win the Gold.

Henie took the lead in changing the nature of her sport: she introduced dance routines into free-skating at the 1928 Olympics in St. Moritz, Switzerland, was the first woman to wear truly short skirts, well above the knee, and had remarkable spinning abilities—19 different spins in her repertoire that she could keep going almost indefinitely, achieving up to 80 revolutions.

By the time she retired at 24 years old from competition after the 1936 season, Sonja Henie had won 14 national championships, 8 European Championships (a competition inaugurated in 1929), 10 World Championships and 3 Olympic Gold Medals, a record equaled only by 1970s Russian Pairs skater Irina Rodnina.

Henie then started to tour with her own skating show, but she wanted something bigger. In 1927 she had made a Norwegian movie called *Seven Days for Elizabeth* and soon headed for Hollywood, rented a rink and managed to attract an audience filled with Hollywood stars. Twentieth Century-Fox signed her to a contract immediately and by the winter of 1936 her first Hollywood musical, *One in a Million*, was in theaters. An immediate hit at the box office, Henie ranked 3rd behind Shirley Temple and Clark Gable as a box-office draw in 1938. Teamed with such upcoming male stars as Tyrone Power, Don Ameche and John Payne, she made a series of successful films, including *Thin Ice* (1937), *Happy Landings* (1938) and *Sun Valley Serenade* (1942).

With these movies, Henie became the first figure skater to reach a mass-market audience and to make large amounts of money. As her Hollywood career began to decline in the mid-1940s, she produced a touring ice show, in which she also appeared. By the mid-1950s, she had retired from performing, but her business deals, especially in real estate, proved to be extremely successful; at her death in 1969 her total fortune was estimated at $47 million.

Before her death, Henie and third husband Nils Onstad made a gift to Norway of a museum that celebrated her career and was dedicated to the arts. The Norwegian government was less than thrilled about this museum, which opened in Oslo in 1968. For one thing, it is considered bad form in Norway for even the most famous athletes to flaunt their individual achievements. Beyond that, the country's interest in winter sports is primarily focused on skiing and speed skating. Ironically, the country that produced the first figure skater to become an international celebrity has only a passing interest in figure skating. Since Sonja Henie

Sonja Henie captured her first World Championship at 14, in 1927.
(Courtesy World Figure Skating Museum)

retired from competition in 1936, no Norwegian has won a World or Olympic medal in the sport.

HERBER, MAXIE *See* BAIER, ERNST.

HERRIKSON, ELNA *(b. 1904) Swedish Pairs skater with Kaj af Ekstrom (b. 1902).*

In the years 1923–24 there were so many highly accomplished Pairs that six different couples took medals at the two World Championships and one Olympics contests. Sweden's Elna Herrikson and Kaj af Ekstrom were one of three couples who won two medals. Finnish husband-and-wife Pair Ludowika and Walter Jakobsson won the 1923 World Gold and the 1924 Olympic Silver, and previous World Champions Helene Engelmann and Alfred Berger of Austria won both the Olympic and World Gold in 1924. Herrikson and Ekstrom took the World Bronze in both 1923 and 1924, but they missed out on an Olympic medal, with the Bronze going to France's Andrée Joly and Pierre Brunet, at the beginning of a career that during the next eight years would revolutionize Pairs skating with spectacular new lifts.

HERZ, JENNY *(b. 1886) Austrian World medalist.*

Jenny Herz took the first two World Silver Medals behind the pioneering Great Britain's Madge Syers in 1906 and 1907. At the 1906 competition Herz became the first woman to perform the sit spin invented by U.S. skating visionary Jackson Haines, who had spent many years living in Herz's home city of Vienna, laying the foundations of modern figure skating.

HICKINBOTTOM, DAVID *See* SAWBRIDGE, JANET.

HICKOX, LAURIE AND WILLIAM *(b. 1944, 1943, d. 1961) U.S. Pair.*

Laurie and William Hickox won the U.S. Pairs Bronze Medal in 1961 and were one of three sister-and-brother skating teams killed in an airplane crash at Brussels on the way to the World Championships that year.

HILL, GEORGE *(b. 1907) U.S. medalist.*

One of the stalwarts of 1930s U.S. figure skating, George Hill won the U.S. Bronze Medal four times, in 1930, 1931, 1934 and 1936. He competed internationally only twice, at the 1931 World's, where he placed 11th, and at the 1936 Olympics, where an uncharacteristically disastrous performance put him in 22nd place.

Hill's real strength was as a Pairs skater, however. Teaming with nine-time U.S. Ladies' Champion Maribel Vinson, he won the U.S. Silver Pairs Medal in 1930–33 and the Gold Medal in 1933 and 1935–37. The couple did not compete in 1934: Maribel took the year off from skating before returning to reclaim her two U.S. Championships three more times. Hill and Vinson competed at only two World Championships, in 1931 and 1936, as well as the 1936 Olympics, finishing 5th each time.

In addition, Hill won several U.S. Ice Dancing medals, including the original dance competition with Clara Frothingham twice, in 1930 and 1932, and the Bronze in 1931.

HILL, PRISCILLA *(b. 1960) U.S. medalist.*

Priscilla Hill won the U.S. Bronze Medal in 1977, as Linda Fratianne took the first of her four U.S. titles. Lisa-Marie Allen was the Silver Medalist that year and for the next two, but then Hill once again gained the medal stand in 1981 behind the young Elaine Zayak. This time she edged Lisa-Marie Allen to win the Silver Medal. In 1978, Hill was 9th in the world; in 1981 she moved up to 7th.

HISLOP, BRAD *(b. 1950) U.S. Pairs skater.*

Partnering Joan Bitterman (b. 1949), Brad Hislop was the U.S. Silver Medalist in Ice Dancing in 1969, as Judy Schwomeyer and James Sladky took their second U.S. Championship. Switching partners, he teamed with Debbie Ganson (b. 1951) the following year, but they fell back to 3rd behind Schwomeyer and Sladky and Anne and Harvey (Skip) Miller. Hislop was 10th in the world with Bitterman in 1969 and 9th with Ganson in 1970.

HOFFMANN, JAN *(b. 1954) East German major competitor 1973–1980.*

Finely disciplined in school figures with a smooth if unspectacular free-skating style, all-round skater Jan Hoffmann was in the international medal hunt for seven successive years. Consistency was his great strength—if other leading skaters faltered, he was almost always in a position to claim a medal on points. In 1973, he took the Bronze at the World's, and the following year became World Champion over the Soviet Union's Sergei Volkov—another skater of similar style—and Canada's unique Toller Cranston. Injury kept Hoffmann out of the 1975 competition; a year later he was still not back to his best, failing to gain a medal at the 1976 Olympics and then taking the Bronze at the World Championships as John Curry skated into legend.

Hoffmann kept at it, however, and was World Silver Medalist in both 1977 and 1978 behind Soviet Union's Vladimir Kovalev the first year and the U.S.'s Charlie Tickner the second. In 1979, it was Kovalev again in 1st, the surging Robin Cousins in 2nd and Hoffmann taking his third World Bronze. The suspense in 1980 as to whether the steady Hoffmann or the free-skating whiz Robin Cousins would prevail was almost as great as for the Brian Boitano/Brian Orser confrontation eight years later.

At the 1980 Olympics, Cousins was 4th in school figures but moved up to 2nd behind Hoffmann after the short program. Hoffmann gave the best free-skating performance of his life and the Gold Medal seemed to be his, but skating 13th, Robin Cousins' display of free-skating dazzled to push him out front; Hoffmann was awarded the Silver. At the World Championships, Hoffmann, prevailed, becoming World Champion for the second time in his career.

Much has been made of Hoffmann's scoring as a judge at the 1994 Olympics, in which he placed Oksana Baiul above Nancy Kerrigan in the free-skating artistic score to give Baiul the Gold Medal. It was little noted that Jan Hoffmann himself had lost the Gold Medal to Robin Cousins in 1980 by the same one-tenth of a point.

HOFFNER, CARLETON *(b. 1932) U.S. medalist in both Ice Dance and Pairs.*

With partner Anne Davies, Carleton Hoffner was an important skater in two disciplines from 1945 to 1950. The couple gained a Bronze Medal in Ice Dancing in 1945 and became U.S. Champions the following year. In 1947 and 1948 they were 2nd to Lois Waring and Walter Bainbridge; at the same time, they were skating as a Pair, and in 1949, that effort produced excellent results—the Bronze Medal both at the U.S. Championships and at the World competition in Paris. They capped their amateur career in 1950 with a U.S. Bronze in both Ice Dance and Pairs, a rare feat.

HOLLANDER, DAN *(b. 1972) U.S. medalist.*

After medaling in the U.S. Junior Men's Competition in 1994, Dan Hollander was 7th at the 1995 U.S. Championships. In 1996, he took the U.S. Bronze Medal behind Rudy Galindo and Todd Eldredge, edged out former U.S. Champion Scott Davis for the 3rd position and gained his first trip to the World Championships. There, his inexperience at the top level showed, and he came in 10th. Still a developing skater, Hollander had moved up quickly and showed great future potential.

HOLMES, JULIE LYNN *(b. 1950)*
U.S. Ladies' medalist.

A steady skater, proficient at figures and with a smooth free-skating style, Julie Holmes was runner-up to Janet Lynn at the U.S. Championships for four successive years, 1969–72. Her consistency stood her in good stead at World competitions, where she finished ahead of Janet Lynn on every occasion when they both competed. In 1969, Holmes was 4th, while Lynn was 5th; in 1970, Holmes took the Bronze Medal and Lynn, having a bad year, fell to 6th place; in 1971, Holmes won the Silver Medal behind Austria's Beatrix Schuba and Lynn was 4th. Julie Holmes lacked Janet Lynn's extraordinary charisma, and at her best Lynn could also outskate her, but in terms of consistency under pressure, Holmes demonstrated sterling competitive qualities year in and year out. It was only at the 1972 Olympics that Lynn did better on the world stage, taking the Bronze Medal; steady as ever, Holmes was 4th.

HOLT, ANNE AND AUSTIN *(b. 1932)*
Twin U.S. medalists.

Anne and Austin Holt gained the U.S. Bronze Medal in Pairs in 1952 behind Karol and Peter Kennedy, who won their fifth Gold Medal, and Janet Gerhausen and John Nightingale.

HORNE, RICHARD *See* PANKEY, JANE.

HORWITZ, LEO *See* SZABO, CHRISTA VON.

HUBLER, ANNA *(b. 1887) Early Pairs Champion with Heinrich Burger (b. 1881) from Germany.*

The first World Pairs Championship was held in St. Petersburg, Russia in 1908. Anna Hubler and Heinrich Berger won the Gold Medal over Great Britain's Phyllis and James Johnson. The same result prevailed at the first Olympic figure-skating competition in London, England that year. Hubler and Berger did not defend their World title in 1909 but regained it in 1910 in their home city of Berlin, winning over Finland's Ludowicka Eilers and Walter Jakobsson, who would continue to compete well into the 1920s.

HUFF, THOMAS *See* SUSMAN, ERICA.

HUGEL, GUSTAV *(b. 1876) Austrian skating pioneer.*

Influenced by the U.S. figure-skating innovator Jackson Haines, who spent much time in Vienna from the mid-1870s, Gustav Hugel was one of the leading pioneers of figure skating as a European sport. He won the first World Silver Medal in 1896 at St. Petersburg behind Germany's Gilbert Fuchs, and took the Gold Medal in Stockholm, Sweden the following year. In 1898, the Gold Medal went to Sweden's Henning Grenander, with Hugel taking the Silver. Hugel captured the Gold again in 1899 and 1900, both times edging Sweden's Ulrich Salchow, and then retired from competition.

HULTEN, VIVI-ANNE *(b. 1914)*
Swedish World medalist.

Vivi-Anne Hulten was one of those who gave Sonja Henie a serious challenge during Henie's long reign at the top of women's figure skating; Hulten took the Silver Medal in 1933. In subsequent years, she would take the World Bronze three times, in 1935, 1936 and 1937, as well as the Olympic Bronze in 1936.

II

ICE DANCING

Ice Dancing occupies a curious place in figure-skating history: the precursor of all figure skating, it was the last of the four disciplines to be included in World and Olympic competition. Before figure skating became an organized sport, and before the development of school figures, it was a social sport in which top-hatted men and ladies in long, full dresses paraded around the ice. These skaters found a place for elements of ballroom dancing, but soon the most talented couples expanded on a casual kind of skating to give birth to what came to be called Pairs skating. But because early Pairs skating from the late 1880s to the First World War was essentially what we now know as Ice Dancing, there was no reason to have special competition for those who persisted in practicing ballroom turns on ice.

But the old traditions were kept alive, especially in Great Britain and the United States. Both countries did have Ice Dance competitions at their national championships. In the United States, these competitions involved two separate dances, usually the waltz and the fourteen step. Medals were given to the top three couples for each dance. Thus in 1921, Theresa Weld Blanchard and Nathaniel Niles won Gold Medals for both the waltz and the fourteen step. (They were also Pairs Champions that year, and Blanchard was Ladies' Champion while Niles was Men's Silver Medalist—a very good year for them.) In 1929, the idea of an original dance was introduced, much like the set pattern performed between the compulsories and the free dance in today's competitions. In the modern format of a three-part competition as established in 1936 in the United States, technical compulsories take place first, followed by a set pattern and a concluding free dance.

In the meantime, Pairs skating had moved further and further away from Ice Dancing in format, with spectacular lifts, side-by-side jumps and spins and other developments that turned it into an entirely new kind of skating. Those who loved Ice Dancing began to agitate for their form of figure skating to be included in the World Championships; that finally happened in 1952. From 1952 to 1960, every World medalist was British, American or Canadian, with the British taking every Gold Medal and 15 out of a possible 24 medals. The United States was second with six medals and the Canadians had three. This was only to be expected because these three countries, and especially Great Britain, had done the most to not only keep Ice Dancing alive but to develop it into a distinctive figure-skating discipline.

In 1960, a French couple finally took a Bronze Medal, and the following year, Czechoslovakia's Eva Romanova and Pavel Roman won the Gold Medal. By 1970, Soviet skaters were starting to win, and the West Germans were also making a strong showing. Ice Dancing had become truly international and was rewarded by being included in the

Olympics starting in 1976. Although there have been many great Ice Dancing couples during the past 40-odd years, Jayne Torvill and Christopher Dean of Great Britain are given the greatest credit for popularizing the sport with the public.

INA, KYOKO *(b. 1972) U.S. Pairs skater with Jason Dungjen (b. 1967).*

This Pair began to skate together in 1991. Born in Japan, Ina had won that country's Ladies' Junior title in 1987, and Dungjen had competed in the Senior Men's division in the United States. He had previous experience as a Pair, having won the U.S. Junior Pairs title with his sister Susan in 1983. Ina and Dungjen became U.S. Silver Medalists in 1994, then took Silver again in the 1995 and 1996 Nationals. They also gained a very respectable 8th place at the 1995 World Championships. In 1996 they moved up to 6th place at the World's and went on to become U.S. Champions in 1997.

INA BAUER

Named for an Austrian champion of the 1970s who never quite managed to win a World medal but who was an innovative free-skater, the move Ina Bauer originated is a variation on the spread eagle. Instead of placing the outward-turned feet parallel to one another so that the skater travels in a semicircle, the leading foot is placed farther forward than the other, causing the skater to move across the ice in a straight line. It is usually used at the beginning or end of a step sequence, adding a punctuation mark to the footwork.

INNER EDGE *See* EDGES.

INTERNATIONAL SKATING UNION

The ISU, as it is usually called, was founded at a meeting in Holland in 1892, which was attended by representatives from Austria, Germany, Sweden, Great Britain, the Netherlands and Hungary. This group has expanded to include more than 30 nations around the world. The new organization sponsored the first World Championships, held in St. Petersburg, Russia in 1896 and oversees the event to this day. It has specific committees to deal with each of four major disciplines: Men's, Ladies', Pairs and Ice Dancing. These committees decide the elements that should be included in the short program for soloists and Pairs and the dances that will be required in the technical compulsories for the Ice Dance competition. Skaters work throughout the year to perfect these various required elements, which are automatically adopted for national competitions as well.

The ISU also has the responsibility for selecting the international panels of judges for the World Championships and the referees who are in charge of the panels during competition. It has the authority to punish judges deemed to have issued marks erratically or prejudicially. A judge can be banned from the panels for a set term of years or banished perpetually. The ISU has even banned all judges from a given country—the Soviet Union—for conspiring to rig the outcomes of competition by orchestrating their marks.

The ISU can also make rules concerning music, costuming and particular elements of the skating repertoire. For example, it ruled in 1982 that women could not perform more than five triple jumps in a free-skating program, called the "Zayak rule" by outside commentators because it was so obviously aimed at Elaine Zayak of the United States, who performed seven triples in winning the 1982 World Championships. The rule was later rescinded. The ISU has also banned the performance of the back flip in competition.

Finally, the ISU is the ultimate arbiter of changes in the sport that range from the elimination of school figures in competition after 1988 to the question of how much and what kinds of income a skater can have and still retain amateur status.

ITO, MIDORI *(b. 1968) Japanese World Champion.*

Midori Ito was the first Japanese skater to make a mark in international competition and that country's first World Champion in the sport. Although the Japanese were sufficiently enthusiastic about figure skating for the World Championships slated for Tokyo in 1977 and 1985 (the 1972 Winter Olympics in Sapporo had given figure skating a big boost), the paucity of experienced teachers and coaches slowed the development of Japanese skaters. But in the late 1980s, Midori Ito quickly made a great impression on the figure-skating world with her extraordinary jumping ability. Short in stature, she was nevertheless extremely strong and was able to jump higher than many women much taller than she. In addition, she had great technical ability and was the first woman to perform the triple axel.

Although she was considered a possible World Champion as early as 1987, Ito had two problems: One was a weakness in school figures, the other a style that strongly emphasized athleticism over artistry, always a drawback in the eyes of international judges. These problems kept her off the medal podium until 1989, when school figures were finally completely excised from World competition, with the short program now counting for one-third of the total and the long program, also known as the free-skate, accounting for the other two-thirds.

In 1989, Ito was also helped by the retirement from amateur competition of Katarina Witt, Elizabeth Manley and Debi Thomas, but she skated so powerfully that she might have even beaten that trio, easily winning the World Gold Medal over West Germany's Claudia Leistner and the U.S.'s Jill Trenary. But at the following year's World's, Trenary bested her, and Ito fell back to 2nd place.

Ito's 1991 World's performance was marked by a disaster: She skated too far into the corner to perform her required combination jump and actually skated off the ice, crashing into a television camera behind a makeshift barrier. She was not hurt, but the penalty for not completing the combination set her too far back to overcome the deficit in the long program. In 1992 Ito took the Silver Medal at the Olympics in Albertville, France, beaten by the technique and artistry of America's Kristi Yamaguchi. She then turned professional and was a Japanese television commentator at the 1994 World Championships in Chiba, Japan. Here, she was able to exult in the victory of the second Japanese World Champion, Yuka Sato.

Midori Ito dropped to second at the 1990 World Championships.

(Courtesy Paul Harvath)

J

JACKSON, DONALD *(b. 1939)*

Canadian World Champion.

Emerging into the international skating spotlight at the end of the 12-year period dominated by the U.S.'s Dick Button, Hayes Alan Jenkins and David Jenkins, Donald Jackson was destined to make his own great contribution to figure skating. The first World Medal for the Canadian Champion came in 1959 when he took the Silver Medal at Colorado Springs behind David Jenkins, with the U.S.'s Tim Brown in 3rd place. At the 1960 Olympics, Jackson won the Bronze Medal with David Jenkins winning the Gold and Czechoslovakia's Karol Divin edging him for the Silver. Turning professional immediately, Jenkins skipped the World Championships, which were won by France's Alain Giletti with Jackson taking the Silver.

The 1961 World Championships were cancelled because of the deaths of the U.S. team in a plane crash at Brussels. In summer 1961, Jackson began to work on a triple-lutz jump. The last step forward in jumping had been taken by Dick Button a decade earlier when he mastered the first triple jump, the loop; because of the more difficult takeoff involved, the triple lutz had eluded skaters in the intervening years. Jackson conquered it and landed it successfully five times before the Canadian Championships, but at that competition he two-footed the landing. Should he attempt it at the World Championships?

As it happened, Karol Divin skated before Jackson at the 1962 World's at Prague, Czechoslovakia in the final free-skating portion of the competition. Divin received extremely high marks. It looked as

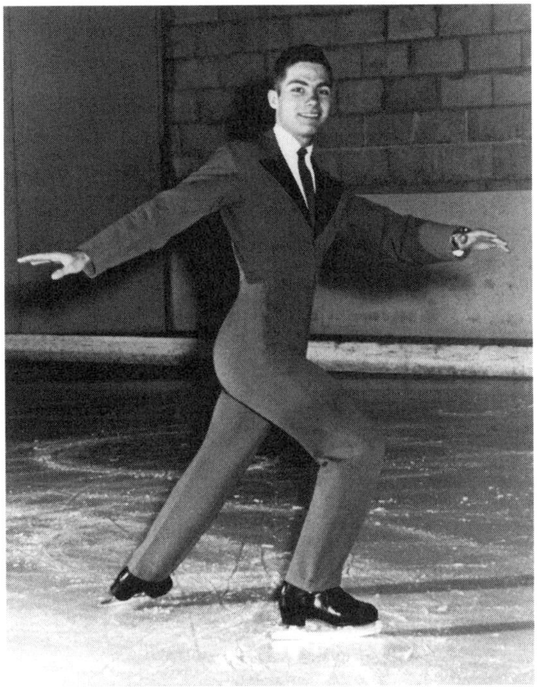

Canada's World Champion Donald Jackson, a legendary jumper.

(Courtesy World Figure Skating Museum)

though he would win the Gold Medal on his home ice unless Jackson gave the performance of his life. Jackson not only successfully landed the triple lutz for a *Guinness Book of Records* first but also skated with an overall excitement that brought him seven scores of perfect 6.0 from the judges—a record that has never been equaled by a solo skater. Jackson then turned professional, continuing to thrill international audiences through the 1960s.

JACKSON, JOE JR. *(b. 1923)*

Professional skating clown.

Probably the best-known skating clown aside from "Mr. Frick," Joe Jackson Jr. was an Ice Capades fixture in the 1940s and the 1950s. With the persona of an endlessly persevering tramp, he made two generations of children (and their parents) roar with laughter at his attempts to master such obstacles as riding a bicycle on ice.

JACOBY, DONALD *(b. 1930) Major U.S. Ice Dancer with Virginia Hoyns (b. 1932) and Andrée Anderson (b. 1938).*

Donald Jacoby won his first U.S. Ice Dance medal, taking the Silver with partner Virginia Hoyns in 1951. They took another Silver Medal in 1953 and were 5th at the World's both that year and the next. Virginia Hoyns then retired, but with new partner Andrée Anderson, Jacoby came back to win the Silver Medal again in 1957.

Jacoby and Anderson became U.S. Champions in 1958 and took the World Bronze Medal as well behind repeat champions June Markham and Courtney Jones of Great Britain and the Canadian team of Geraldine Fenton and William McLachlan. Retaining their U.S. title in 1959, Jacoby and Anderson moved up to take the Silver Medal at the World's, behind Courtney Jones and his new partner Doreen Denny but beating the Canadians this time around. Jacoby and Anderson then turned professional.

JAKOBSSON, LUDOWIKA AND WALTER *(b. 1884, 1882) Finnish World Pairs Champions before and after World War I.*

In 1910, Walter Jakobsson and Ludowika Eilers (they married two years later) competed against the two couples who had won the first and second World Championships in Pairs, 1908 winners Anna Hubler and Heinrich Burger of Germany, and 1909 winners Phyllis and James Johnson of Great Britain. Jakobsson and Eilers came away with a Silver Medal, with the Germans in 1st place and the British husband-and-wife team in 3rd. The following year, they won the Gold, but because of the small number of competitors no other Pairs medals were awarded. In 1912 and 1913, the newly married Jakobssons were Silver Medalists, the Gold going to the Johnsons in 1912 and to Austria's Helene Engelmann and Kurt Mejstrik in 1913. With World War I looming, the Jakobssons took the Gold Medal in 1914 over the Austrians; Christa von Szabo and Leo Horwitz, also of Austria, were the Bronze Medalists in both 1913 and 1914.

World figure-skating competition did not resume until 1922 in Davos, Switzerland. The Jakobssons, now in their 30s, were back, but so was Helene Engelmann with a new, younger partner, Alfred Berger; that couple edged the Finns for the Gold. In 1923, the Jakobssons competed in the World Championships for the last time, again winning the Gold Medal over Norway's Alexia and Yngvar Byrn and Sweden's Elna Henrikson and Kaj af Ekstrom; both couples were nearly two decades younger than the Jakobssons.

The Jakobssons also won the 1920 Olympics at Antwerp, Belgium, beating the Byrns and Phyllis Johnson and her new partner Basil Williams. They competed again in 1924 at Chamonix, France, the first true Winter Olympics site, but could only manage the Silver, beaten again by Engelmann and Berger. The Bronze Medalists were the young Andrée and Pierre Brunet, who would revolutionize Pairs skating during the remainder of the decade.

It should be noted that the rivalries with Helene Engelmann and Phyllis Johnson and their two partners were extremely friendly. The kind of intense personal and national competition that marks figure skating to this day did not really begin to take hold until the mid-1920s.

JARMON, JOHN *See* WATSON, MARY J.

JELINEK, MARIA AND OTTO *(b. 1938, 1937) Czech-born Canadian Pair World Champions.*

In 1955, Maria and Otto Jelinek, together with their parents, fled communist Czechoslovakia and settled in Canada. In 1957, the sister-and-brother team were Canadian Silver Medalists behind Barbara Wagner and Robert Paul, and at that year's World Championships, Wagner and Paul became Gold Medalists for the first of four successive times, while the Jelineks took the World Bronze. The two Canadian couples finished with the same placements again in 1958. In 1959, Marika Kilius and her new partner Hans Jurgen Baumler took the Silver for West Germany behind Wagner and Paul, and the U.S. Champions, Nancy and Ronald Ludington, were the Bronze Medalists, with the Jelineks finishing 4th. The same order of finish occurred at the 1960 Olympics, but at that year's World competition, the West Germans and the U.S. pair faltered. Wagner and Paul took their fourth Gold Medal and the Jelineks won the Silver, with the West Germans earning the Bronze.

Wagner and Paul, as well as the Ludingtons, then turned professional. In 1961, the World Championships were scheduled to be held in Prague, Czechoslovakia. The communist government made noises about refusing to allow the former Czech citizens entry or possibly even arresting the Jelineks if they entered the country. The matter was still unsettled when the entire U.S. World team was killed in a plane crash at Brussels, Belgium on the way to Prague, leading to the cancellation of the World Championships for that year.

The International Figure Skating Union decided to hold the 1962 World Championships in Prague. The matter of allowing the Jelineks to skate unimpeded was strongly pressed by the governments of Canada, the United States and Great Britain. They issued stern diplomatic warnings concerning the Jelineks, who were now Canadian citizens. The Czech government finally guaranteed safe passage, and the Jelineks gave the performance of their lives before an ecstatic audience of their former countrymen. The defectors became Champions of the World in the country they had fled and then returned to their adoptive home as Canadian national heroes.

Iron Curtain refugees, Maria and Otto Jelinek won World Gold for Canada.

(Courtesy World Figure Skating Museum)

JENKINS, DAVID *(b. 1936) U.S., World and Olympic Champion.*

David Jenkins won his first senior medal at the U.S. Championships in 1954, taking the Silver Medal behind his older brother Hayes, who garnered his second U.S. Men's title. He then went on to place 4th at the World's as Hayes took his second World title. In 1955, David was again the U.S. Silver Medalist but moved up to take the World Bronze in a U.S. sweep that had Hayes 1st and Ronnie Robertson 2nd. In the Olympic year of 1956, David was third in the United States behind Hayes and Ronnie Robertson, with the same order of finish prevailing at both the Olympics and the World Championships, the only complete sweep during an Olympic year ever achieved by U.S. skaters.

Like his older brother, David started off with some weakness in school figures that he eventually overcame. Shorter and more compact, David was a more athletic skater than his brother; Hayes was one of the most elegant male skaters of all time. After Hayes Alan Jenkins and Ronnie Robertson turned professional following the 1960 competitive season, David Jenkins dominated male skating as thoroughly as his brother had. He won the U.S. and World Championships four years straight, 1957–60, plus the 1960 Olympic Gold Medal, and had triple and double jumps "of a standard which no European could match," as British skating writer Howard Bass put it. Jenkins was not quite as seriously challenged by perennial U.S. Silver Medalist Tim Brown as his brother Hayes had been by Ronnie Robertson. Often, the margin of victory for Hayes had been his school figures, with Robertson, a superb jumper and great spinner, surpassing him in free-skating. David Jenkins could not be topped as a free-skater during his championship reign.

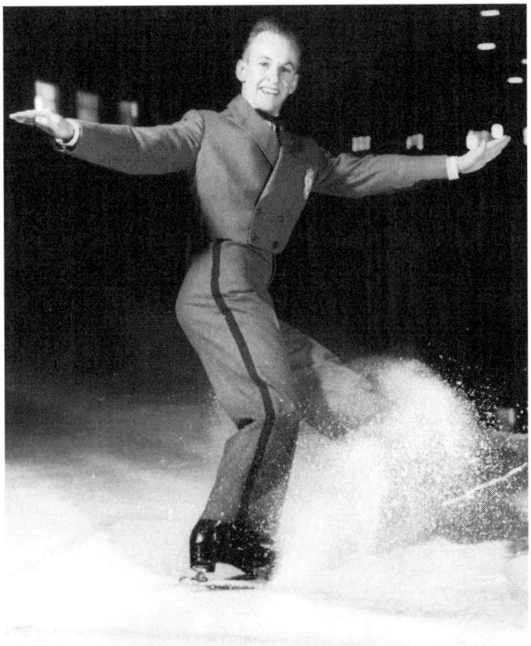

Younger Jenkins brother, David, was 1960 Olympic Champion.
(Courtesy World Figure Skating Museum)

JENKINS, HAYES ALAN *(b. 1933) U.S., World and Olympic Champion.*

Hayes Alan Jenkins won the Bronze Medal at the U.S. Championships in 1949, as Dick Button took the fourth of his seven Gold Medals and James Grogan took his second Silver. Hayes was 6th that year at his first World Championship. The next year Grogan was out with an injury and Hayes was the U.S. Silver Medalist as well as the World Bronze winner behind Button and Hungary's Ede Kiraly. With Grogan's return in 1951, Hayes was pushed back to the U.S. Bronze and 4th place at the World's, with Grogan the Silver Medalist behind Button at both events. Hayes was again 3rd in the United States in 1952, and finished 4th at the Olympics (Austria's Helmut Seibt took the Olympic Silver behind Button and ahead of Grogan), but the World Championships was the first U.S. sweep ever in Men's Competition, with Button, Grogan and Jenkins finishing one, two, three.

Hayes was somewhat weak in school figures in his career's early years, but he worked at them with great dedication until they eventually became his greatest strength. As a free-skater, he developed an enormous style and was also a fine jumper; he also possessed what teammates described as an amazingly good flying sit spin, but it was his extremely proficient school figures that gave him the winning edge. He won the U.S. Championship, also taking the World title, four years in succession, from 1953 to 1956, capping his career with the Olympic Gold Medal in 1956.

His greatest challenges came not from European skaters but from his teammates James Grogan and Ronnie Robertson. Grogan was the Silver Medalist at the World Championships in both 1953 and 1954; yet it was Robertson who gave Jenkins the greatest challenge. Despite a weakness in school figures, Robertson, a great free-skater, was capable of performing acrobatic jumps and spinning so fast that he almost seemed to disappear. He often had the highest marks for free-skating, with Hayes Alan Jenkins 2nd, but in those days, with school figures counting 60 percent of the total, Jenkins was always able to hang on. In 1955 and 1956, Hayes Jenkins, Robertson, and Hayes' younger brother David made up an invincible trio in international competition, with Hayes taking the Gold, Robertson the Silver and David the Bronze at the 1955 and 1956 World Championships and the 1956 Olympics.

Although Robertson was the more spectacular free-skater, Hayes Jenkins probably had a greater influence, his smoothness and elegance being sometimes compared to that of Fred Astaire.

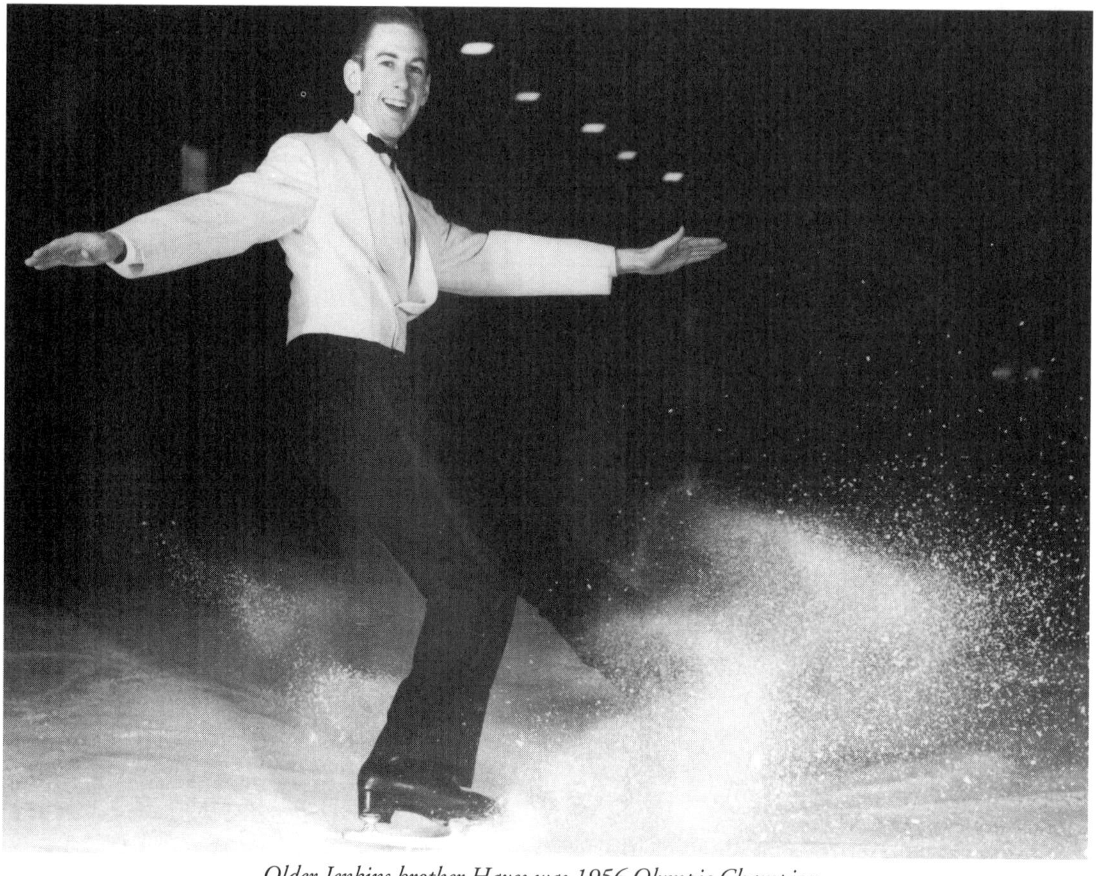

Older Jenkins brother Hayes was 1956 Olympic Champion.
(Courtesy World Figure Skating Museum)

While Robertson's success depended upon unique athletic ability, Hayes Jenkins set a standard for a kind of manly grace that has since been emulated by many U.S. and European champions. Jenkins and Robertson both joined the Ice Capades after the 1960 season. Although Robertson continued that career for many years, during the two seasons they performed together, Jenkins got top billing. He was after all the Gold Medalist.

JOHANSSON, RICHARD *(b. 1882) Swedish medalist.*

At the beginning of the period dominated by his countryman Ulrich Salchow, Johansson was part of a Swedish sweep of the medals at the first Olympic figure-skating competition in London in 1908. Salchow won the Gold Medal, Johansson the Silver, and Per Thoren the Bronze.

JOHNS, JOHNNY *(b. 1952) Versatile U.S. medalist.*

Johnny Johns first attracted national attention as an Ice Dancer, winning the Bronze Medal with partner Mary Campbell in 1971 and 1972 and then becoming national champion and ranking 6th at the World Championships in 1973. Even as Johns took the Gold Medal in U.S. Ice Dancing, he was also competing in the Pairs competition and became one of the few skaters to win medals in two disciplines simultaneously by taking the 1973 U.S. Bronze in Pairs with Emily Benenson.

The U.S. Pairs Champions in 1973 were Mark and Melissa Militano, who had placed 2nd the three previous years. With a Gold Medal in hand, Mark retired, and Johnny Johns took his place as Melissa's partner. The new team was equally successful, becoming national champions in 1974 and 1975. In 2nd place both years was the new young team of Tai Babilonia and Randy Gardner. Johns and Militano also competed respectably at the World Championships, finishing 8th in 1974 and 6th in 1975. They then left the field open to Babilonia and Gardner.

Before retiring, Johns and Militano firmly imprinted their names on Pairs-skating history by performing the first successful throw triple loop in Pairs competition, adding a new measure of difficulty and excitement to their discipline.

JOHNSON, JAMES AND PHYLLIS

(b. 1874, 1886) British husband-and-wife World Pairs Champions.

At the first Olympics to feature figure skating—the London Games in 1908—Phyllis and James Johnson won the Silver Medal in Pairs behind Germany's Anna Hubler and Heinrich Burger, edging another British husband-and-wife team, Madge and Edgar Syers. (Madge Syers won the Ladies' Gold Medal as well as the Pairs Bronze.) That year marked the first Pairs competition at the World Championships, in St. Petersburg, Russia and the Johnsons were again Silver Medalists behind the Austrians. The following year, the Johnsons became World Champions at Stockholm, Sweden, beating two Swedish couples, Valborg Lindahl/Nils Rosenius and Gertrud Strom/Richard Johanson. In 1910 at Berlin, the Johnsons were Bronze Medalists, as Anna Hubler and Heinrich Burger took another Gold, and Ludowika Eilers and Walter Jakobsson won the Silver. The Johnsons gained a second World Championship in 1912 (they did not compete in 1911) over the now-married Ludowicka and Walter Jakobsson. That was their last competition together, but Phyllis returned to Pairs competition at the 1920 Olympics with her husband's blessing and a new partner, Basil Williams, to take the Olympic Bronze.

Phyllis Johnson also had an important solo skating career prior to her marriage, as Phyllis Squire; she won the 1904 British Championship over the male defending titlist H. M. Morris, to whom she had been runner-up the year before. Subsequently, she won three World Ladies' medals, the Bronze in 1912 and 1914 and the Silver in 1913; all three competitions were won by Hungary's Opika von Horvath.

JOLY, ANDRÉE *See* BRUNET, PIERRE.

JONES, COURTNEY *(b. 1936) Major British Ice Dancer with June Markham (b. 1937) and Doreen Denny (b. 1940).*

The first decade of World Ice Dance competition was largely dominated by British skaters, who had championed the discipline for years before it was accepted on the same level as the Men's, Ladies' and Pairs divisions. With June Markham, Courtney Jones took his first World medal in 1956 in a sweep headed by Gold Medalists Pamela Weight and Paul Thomas and rounded out by the Bronze Medalists Barbara Thompson and Gerard Rigby. That Silver Medal was followed by the Gold in 1957 over Canada's Geraldine Fenton and William McLachlan and the U.S.'s Sharon McKenzie and Bert Wright. Jones and Markham successfully defended their title in 1958 against the Canadians, with another U.S. couple, Andrée Anderson and Donald Jacoby taking the Bronze.

June Markham retired after that victory and Jones took a new partner, Doreen Denny. It usually takes even the best ice dancers a year or two to become a completely meshed team at the start of a new partnership, but Jones and Denny were an exception, winning the World Gold Medal in 1959 as though they had been together for years, while the U.S.'s Anderson and Jacoby this time edged the Canadians for the Silver. In 1960, Jones and Denny repeated as World Champions a final time, with William McLachlan taking the Silver with his own new partner Virginia Thompson.

Courtney Jones' retirement from competition after the 1960 victory hardly ended his contribution to Ice Dancing, however. At the Queen's Ice Club in London, Jones worked together with Peri Horne to a new set dance pattern called the Starlight Waltz. There were already two standard waltz patterns, the Viennese Waltz and the Westminister Waltz, introduced in 1934 and 1938 respectively; the Starlight Waltz joined them as a required Ice Dance pattern to be used in competition, with the choice among them made by the International Skating Union each year, months in advance of the World Championships. A fourth waltz, the Ravensburg, was added in 1973. Jones and Horne's Starlight Waltz is regarded as the easiest of the four, but that only means that it is judged with particular severity.

For his contributions to Ice Dancing, Courtney Jones was inducted into the World Figure Skating Hall of Fame in 1986.

JOSEPH, RONALD AND VIVIAN *(b. 1944, 1948) U.S. Pairs Champions.*

Brother and sister Ronald and Vivian Joseph were already poised to challenge older skaters when the U.S. team was killed in a plane crash at Brussels on the way to the 1961 World Championships. The following year, the Josephs won the U.S. Bronze Medal in Pairs, in 1963 they moved up to the Silver behind Judianne and Jerry Fotheringill and finished right behind them at the World's, taking 8th place. In 1964, the Fotheringills were again U.S. Champions with the Josephs in 2nd place, but later that year, the Fotheringills placed 8th in the Olympic Competition, while the Josephs surged ahead to 4th place, and were then moved up to 3rd after the Silver Medalist Pair team of Marika Kilius and Hans Baumler was disqualified. At the 1964 World's, the Josephs also placed 4th ahead of the 8th-placed Fotheringills. In 1965, the Josephs became U.S. Champions and then skated brilliantly to take the World Silver Medal behind the Protopopovs, who had won the Olympic Gold the previous year. The Josephs realized they could not do better than that against the already nearly legendary Soviet Pair and so turned professional.

JUDGE SELECTION

It must first be understood that skating judges are essentially critics, and like many critics in the arts, often they cannot do what they are criticizing. Judges are not usually former champions, partially because many of those become teachers and coaches, like Carol Heiss and John Nicks, or have gone into broadcasting, like Dick Button and Peggy

Fleming. By and large, judges are also-rans, with a keen interest in the sport and the free time to become involved in the administrative side of skating. Some of these individuals are superb judges who work very hard at keeping up with new moves and probing the fine points of skating excellence. There are also judging "schools," usually held in the summer months, at which judges can hone their expertise, generally in the hope of becoming a judge at the higher levels of the sport. But a persistent problem is that judges are often middle-aged or older and have never performed some of the newer, more difficult moves that are constantly being developed. When Dick Button decided that he would attempt the first triple jump at the 1952 Olympics, he and his coach spread the word in advance to reporters to make sure that the judges would see it and recognize it for what it was. That kind of precompetition advertising of a new move still takes place.

Judges tend to develop an expertise in one of the four disciplines to the exclusion of the others. Ice Dance judges in particular are likely to be specialists. That has always been true of school figure judges as well. The pool of judges from which to select at the top level of the sport is not large, but it is large enough to make it possible to ban a judge who too obviously exhibits national prejudice or who, more rarely, seems not to be of sufficient competence.

Judges at the national level are chosen by the skating associations of each country. At the World Championships and the Olympics, judges are selected by the International Skating Union, which has unquestioned power to discipline errant judges. It must be understood that what is looked for in a good judge is consistency, not necessarily conformity with other judges. Audiences at competitions will boo when they think the judges' scores are too low, and they may develop an animosity toward a given judge whose marks seem particularly low. But if a judge marks all skaters somewhat lower than the majority, that does not mean that individual is a bad judge. It may in fact be an indication that he or she is a particularly good judge with exacting standards. If a judge gives lower marks to all skaters, there is still a consistent standard at work, but when a judge gives suspiciously high marks to one skater and suspiciously low ones to another, questions of bias are raised.

Judging is not as good as it ought to be—almost everyone in the skating world agrees on that, even many judges. But it is far more honest than it was in the 1920s and 1930s, when there were many scandals involving prearranged collusion. Judges are human, like the skaters they mark. There are mistakes all around.

JULIN-MAUROY, MAGDA *(b. 1894)*

Swedish Olympic Champion.

When figure skating was included in the Olympic Games for the second time at Antwerp, Belgium in 1920, there had been no World Championship competition since 1914; two years before the World's resumed. At these 1920 Games, Magda Julin-Mauroy made her only appearance at an international competition and skated away with the Gold Medal, beating her countrywoman Svea Noren, who had won the World Bronze in 1913.

JUNIOR CHAMPIONSHIPS

Junior Championships are the last step before joining the Senior ranks and competing for national championships. They are held on a regional basis each year around the country, for example, New England's Junior Championship, the Mid-Atlantic Junior Championship. The medalists at each regional competition then compete for the National Junior titles, at the same time and in the same arena where the Senior Championships are held. World Junior Championships are held each year separate from the regular World Championships.

Surprisingly few skaters go from being Novice Champion to Junior Champion to Senior Champion in the space of a few years. A sudden spurt of growth can temporarily derail a young skater on the way up, and some skaters develop more slowly but end at a higher peak. Becoming U.S. Junior Champion in any division of the sport means that a skater has real talent, but this accomplishment is no guarantee of going all the way to the top.

K

KADAVY, CARYN *(b. 1966) 1980s U.S. and World medalist.*

Caryn Kadavy's story is that of a hard-luck skater but with a happy ending. Her flowing, feminine style brought her four U.S. medals in successive years, the Bronze in 1985, 1987 and 1988 and a Silver in 1986, years of great strength among U.S. women, with Tiffany Chin, Debi Thomas (twice) and Jill Trenary winning the U.S. Championships. Kadavy held her own in this elite company: Without quite the jumping ability of Thomas or Trenary nor the delicacy of Chin, she nevertheless had great charm on the ice and was more musically attuned than any of them. She proved how good she could be at the memorable World Championships of 1987 where Debi Thomas and Katarina Witt dueled for the second consecutive year for the Gold; Witt reclaimed the top spot she had relinquished to Thomas the previous year. Amid the hubbub of this rivalry, Kadavy skated to a richly deserved Bronze Medal, putting herself in good position to win an Olympic medal the following year.

But at the Olympics, she came down with a flu that left her with a high fever and so weak that she had to withdraw from the competition. She had not fully regained her form by the time the World's came around and so finished 7th. It was a sad conclusion to a fine amateur career, but Kadavy was still offered a good professional contract on the basis

Caryn Kadavy had her greatest successes as a professional.
(Courtesy Michael Rosenberg)

of her demonstrable audience appeal and free-skating abilities.

The transition to professional skating did not prove easy, however. A vastly more rough-and-tumble world than Kadavy was used to, she felt uncomfortable in it. For a time, by her own admission, her skating was simply wan, but she kept at it, skating with several different touring groups; gradually, she adjusted. In 1993 and again in 1994, Kadavy won the Hershey Kisses Pro-Ams (Professionals vs. Amateurs). She went on to become the 1996 Canadian Professional Champion, and in 1997 won the Ladies Professional Championship.

KAGELMANN, UWE *See* GROSS, MANUELA.

KAISER, OTTO *See* SCHOLZ, LILLY.

KARPONOSOV, GENNADI *See* LINICHUK, NATALIA.

KASPAR, FELIX *(b. 1905) Austrian World Champion.*

As Austria's Felix Kaspar set off for the Olympic Games in Garmisch, Germany in 1936, he was very much in the shadow of his compatriot Karl Schafer, who had been the World Champion for the past five years, but he was to make a mark for himself that year. Shafer won the Gold Medal, as expected, with Ernst Baier taking the Silver (as well as the Pairs Gold with Maxie Herber), but Kaspar garnered the Bronze. Showing it was no fluke, he then took the Bronze at the World Championships in Paris, where Schafer won the Gold for a sixth time, followed by Great Britain's Graham Sharp.

With the retirement of Schafer, Kaspar succeeded to not only the Austrian title but also the World Championship in 1937, with Sharp 2nd. Kaspar beat back Sharp again in 1938 for a second Gold Medal and then retired as Austria was annexed by Hitler's Germany.

KAUFFMAN, CYNTHIA AND RONALD *(b. 1947, 1945) American Pairs Champions.*

Sister and brother Cynthia and Ronald Kauffman won their first U.S. medal in Pairs in 1964, taking the Bronze behind two other teams of siblings, Judianne and Jerry Fotheringill and Vivian and Ronald Joseph. Three American couples were eligible for the Olympics and World Championships that year; the Kauffmans demonstrated their promise by placing 8th at the Olympics and 7th at the World's, where they finished one place ahead of the Fotheringills. The following year they were 2nd to the Josephs at the Nationals and moved up to 6th at the World's.

Becoming U.S. Champions in 1966, for the first of four successive times, they also took the first of three consecutive World Bronze Medals. Unfortunately, they had a bad outing at the 1968 Winter Olympics and placed a disappointing 6th, although they successfully defended their World Bronze that year. At the 1969 U.S. Championships, they retained their title against a strong challenge by the up-and-coming JoJo Starbuck and Ken Shelley and placed 4th at the World Championships in their final competition before turning professional.

The Kauffmans were one of the first major Pair combinations who had a marked height differential between them, with Ronald nearly a foot taller than his sister. Instead of letting this height difference hold them back, they developed a style that took advantage of it. One of their innovations was the Kauffman spin: Ronald performed a camel spin, passing his free leg completely over Cynthia as she performed her own spin. This move has become a standard for Pairs skaters with a similar height differential.

KAUFFMAN SPIN *See immediately above.*

KEELEY, KATY *(b. 1968) U.S. Pairs skater with Joseph Mero (b. 1967).*

Katy Keeley and Joseph Mero took the U.S. Bronze Medal in Pairs twice, in 1987 as Jill Watson and Peter Oppegard wrested the national title from Gillian Wachsman and Todd Waggoner, and again in 1989 when Kristi Yamaguchi and Rudy Galindo took the first of their two titles. Keeley and Mero did not compete in the World Championships because only two U.S. couples were eligible during their U.S. medal years, 1987 and 1989.

KAZAKOVA, OKSANA *See* DMITRIEV, ARTUR

KEKESY, ANDREA *See* KIRALY, EDE.

KELLEY, GREGORY *(b. 1943, d. 1961) U.S. medalist killed at Brussels.*

Gregory Kelley didn't look like a figure skater: He had the compact, muscular body of a college wrestler, but when he put on a pair of skates he zipped around the rink with the explosiveness of a cannon ball. Few male skaters have ever had such speed or jumped with such dynamism.

U.S. Junior Champion at 16, Kelley joined the senior ranks in 1960 and got to go to the World Championships in Vancouver, Canada because the three top U.S. men retired after the Olympics (David Jenkins, who had won the Gold Medal and Tim Brown and Robert Brewer, who had placed 5th and 7th). Showing his stuff, Greg Kelley placed 9th. At the 1961 Nationals, Kelley won the U.S. Silver Medal right behind Bradley Lord, a skater in the elegant tradition of Hayes Alan Jenkins. Both were killed in a plane crash at Brussels on their way to the World Championships.

KELLEY, SUSAN *(b. 1957) U.S. Ice Dancer.*

In their first year as U.S. Ice Dancing medalists (they took the Bronze at the U.S. Championships in Colorado Springs), Susan Kelley and partner Andrew Stroukoff became a part of the 1976 U.S. team at the first Winter Olympics to include Ice Dancing as an official medal sport. Young and somewhat inexperienced, they took 17th place, but just being part of this very special occasion for ice dancers was in itself a reward. In 1977 they were U.S. Silver Medalists and moved up to 12th place in the World's. In 1978 they were again U.S. Bronze Medalists.

KENNEDY, KAROL AND PETER *(b. 1928, 1929) Major American Pair in post–World War II years.*

The sister-and-brother team Karol and Peter Kennedy were Massachusetts natives. Dashing, athletic and possessed of a very American sense of fun, they exemplified the fresh new wave in U.S. skating that made such an impact in the post-World War II years. The hallmark of the Kennedys' skating was speed, a quality now often seen in Pairs skaters, but then a revelation on the international skating scene.

They first came to major attention in 1946 when they won the U.S. Silver Medal. In 1947 they repeated that placement and also won the Silver Medal as the World Championships resumed in Stockholm, Sweden. For the next five years, 1948–52, the Kennedys were the unbeatable U.S. Champions. Internationally, they had a difficult year in 1948, with an Olympics 6th place and a World Championships 4th place, but from then on they were always on the medal podium at international competitions.

The Kennedys were the World Silver Medalists three more times, in 1949, 1951 and 1952, and in 1950 became the first U.S. Pair to become World Champions, a triumph achieved only once in the years since, when Tai Babilonia and Randy Gardner took the World Gold in 1979. In 1952 they capped their career with an Olympic Silver Medal, barely edged by their chief rivals, another sister-and-brother team, West Germany's Ria and Paul Falk.

Karol and Peter Kennedy, America's most successful Pairs team.
(Courtesy World Figure Skating Museum)

The Kennedys had a considerable influence on Pairs skating in Europe as well as in the United States and Canada. Speed, daring and pizzazz marked most of the top Pairs for a decade, until the Protopopovs brought a return to classicism in the 1960s.

KERNER, ROMY *(b. 1954) East German Pairs Champion and World medalist with Rolf Osterreich (b. 1953).*

In 1974, Romy Kerner and Rolf Osterreich succeeded Manuela Gross and Uwe Kagelmann as East German Champions and, like their predecessors the previous year, took the World Bronze Medal at Munich, West Germany. The next two years, they were World Silver Medalists behind the Soviet Union's Irina Rodnina and Alexandr Zaitsev and took the Olympic Silver as well in 1976. They were extremely proficient technically but did not break any new ground as skaters.

KERRIGAN, NANCY *(b. 1969) U.S. Champion and Olympic and World Silver Medalist.*

Nancy Kerrigan's first senior U.S. medal came in 1991 when she took the Ladies' Bronze at the U.S.

Two-time Olympic Silver Medalist Nancy Kerrigan shows off her elegant line in 1993.
(Courtesy Michelle Harvath)

Championships behind Tonya Harding and Kristi Yamaguchi. She made an immediate impression on international judges, also winning the World Bronze that year in a U.S. sweep that saw Yamaguchi win the Gold and Tonya Harding the Silver. The following year she advanced to the U.S. Silver as Yamaguchi became U.S. Champion, with Harding slipping to 3rd place. At the 1992 Olympics, won by Yamaguchi, Japan's Midori Ito ranked 2nd, and Kerrigan won the Bronze Medal. Kerrigan was also 2nd to Yamaguchi at the World Championships, with China's Lu Chen taking the Bronze.

With Yamaguchi turning professional, Kerrigan became the favorite to win the World Championship in 1993. She won the U.S. title with confidence over Lisa Ervin and Tonia Kwaitkowski, but the World Championships proved a disaster. Though she skated a clean short program that put her in lst place, an attack of nerves interfered with her long program and she ended in 5th place. She prepared for the 1994 Olympic competition as the Winter and Summer Games were realigned to fall two years apart instead of occurring simultaneously.

Despite the interruptions of filming commercials that had come her way after her 1992 successes, Kerrigan kept to a grueling practice schedule and was reported to be skating her best ever. Then, as the U.S. Championships got under way in Detroit, Michigan in January 1994, she was struck heavily across her left knee by an unknown assailant after a practice session. Television pictures of her clutching her knee and crying, "Why? Why?" shocked the nation. The resulting injury prevented her from competing at the Nationals, where Tonya Harding took the Ladies' Gold Medal, but the U.S. Figure Skating Association named Kerrigan to the Olympic and World Team pending a full recovery.

The hunt for her assailant, aided by the confession of Tonya Harding's bodyguard, pointed to a plot to injure Kerrigan that was hatched by Harding's former husband, Jeff Gilooley, with whom Harding was again living. A firestorm of media attention erupted, the main question being whether Harding herself was a party to the plot. While Harding was hounded by the media, press focus on Kerrigan was also intense. Shielded by her close and loving family, she was able to concentrate on recovering and returning to top skating form;

she gave only a few, carefully controlled press conferences.

Nevertheless, intense pressures were exacerbated by the open question of Harding's degree of involvement; with Harding's denial that she had known anything about the attack in advance, and with only circumstantial evidence and media speculation against her, the U.S. Figure Skating Association avoided the issue of whether to remove Harding from the Olympic team. That only fueled the media frenzy as the inevitable meetings between the two U.S. skaters at the Olympics, on and off the ice, became the focus of endless television, tabloid and newspaper stories. Olympic officials refused to alter training schedules, and although Kerrigan and Harding had to practice at the same time, there were no incidents of any kind. Kerrigan's practice went very well, while Harding had difficulty with her jumps.

On February 23, in Hamar, Norway the Ladies' competition began with the short program. Harding's chances for a medal evaporated early with a dismal performance that eventually put her in 10th place. Nancy Kerrigan was flawless, and the judges put her in 1st place, followed by reigning World Champion Oksana Baiul of Ukraine and European Champion Surya Bonaly of France. The *New York Times* sports columnist George Vecsey summed up the general reaction when he wrote: "Whether or not she wins the Gold Medal tomorrow night, Nancy Kerrigan will never have a greater night. This was the night she showed great courage. This was the night Nancy Kerrigan came back. This was not the night Nancy Kerrigan beat Tonya Harding. This was the night Nancy Kerrigan beat every beautiful and talented skater in the world."

But even with Tonya Harding out of the running for a medal, the anticipation of the final long program competition was intense. Could Kerrigan withstand the pressure of being in 1st place? Would she fall apart, the way she had at the World Championships the previous year?

The worries proved unfounded: Kerrigan's long program was nearly flawless, she doubled one triple jump in her long program, but otherwise performed all her planned triple jumps. It looked as though the Gold Medal was hers. Oksana Baiul had not yet skated, but she had been slightly off form at the European Championships, coming in second to Bonaly, and she had been injured in an accident during practice the previous day. With an injection of pain killers, however, she skated with all her usual artistic flair, although there were a couple of technical bobbles. The judges were split down the middle, and the difference was finally one-tenth of a point in the artistic scores—the former East German World Champion Jan Hoffmann gave that point to Baiul. Ironically, Hoffmann had lost the Olympic Gold Medal to Great Britain's Robin Cousins in exactly the same way in 1980 by one-tenth of a point.

The judges' decision to give Baiul the Gold and Kerrigan the Silver was the most controversial in many years. There were partisans on both sides of the debate, and seemingly objective commentators were equally split. But Kerrigan was able to turn professional with as much acclaim as though she had won the Gold. Her televised skating spectaculars drew huge audiences, and her performances on lengthy tours and in professional competitions were extremely well received. It was noted, too, that she and Oksana Baiul toured together and seemed to have formed a genuine friendship.

Kerrigan herself summed up her approach to the rigors of touring this way: "It's not about being famous. I come from a working family. We do our jobs."

KILIUS, MARIKA *(b. 1943) Major West German Pairs skater; World Champion with Hans Jurgen Baumler (b. 1940).*

Vivacious, pretty and a fearless athlete, Marika Kilius amassed six World and two Olympic medals from 1956 to 1964 with two different partners. This West German dynamo won her first World medal, a Bronze, in 1956, partnered by Franz Ningel. The next year, the couple improved to take the Silver. But this was not a happy personal relationship, and Kilius took a new partner, Hans Jurgen Baumler, with whom she would eventually reach new heights.

Kilius and Baumler were famous for their dramatic death spiral. Marika had blond hair, which she wore piled on top of her head in a way that was not only becoming but also allowed the couple to pull off a wonderfully theatrical trick. As Kilius leaned far backward over the ice during the spiral, the exquisite timing and control between the two partners made it possible for her to sweep the ice with her hair so that when she was brought erect again there were always ice crystals glistening like some diadem on top of her head.

The couple took the Silver Medal at the 1959 World's, as well as the Silver at the 1960 Olympics, although they fell back to the Bronze at that year's World Championships. The World's were canceled in 1961 because of the deaths of the U.S. team in a plane crash at Brussels, and Kilius and Baumler did not compete in 1962. Then in 1963, they reappeared to become World Champions. The following year brought a fierce battle between the couple and Soviet Pair Oleg Protopopov and Ludmila Belousova. The Soviets prevailed at the Olympics with a legendary Gold Medal performance, but Kilius and Baumler showed how good they really were by winning the World Championship once again; the Soviets took 2nd place this time.

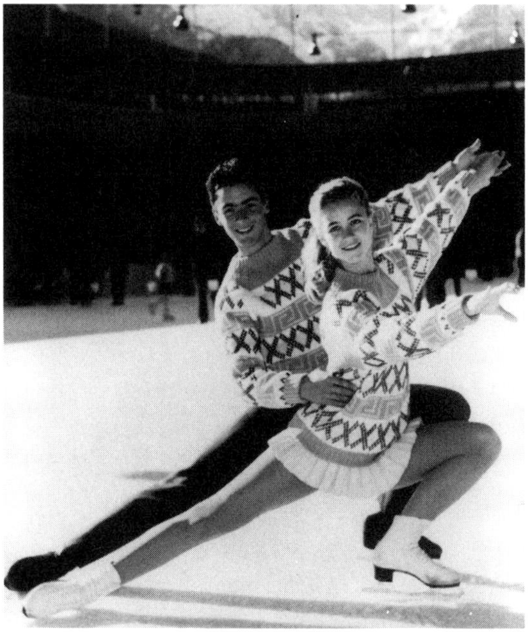

Marika Kilius and Hans Baumler, West Germany's World Champion Pairs Team.
(Courtesy World Figure Skating Museum)

Kilius and Baumler then turned professional, joining the Ice Capades, in which they were an enormous hit. But they had made an unfortunate mistake: It was proven after the Olympic Games that they had signed their Ice Capades contract just before the games began. Amid much controversy, they were stripped of their Olympic Silver, which went to 3rd-place finishers Debbi Wilkes and Guy Revell of Canada, and the Bronze was awarded to the U.S.'s Vivian and Ronald Joseph. Kilius and Baumler said that they had thought that because they were not actually going to perform professionally until after the Olympics, there was no problem about signing the contract beforehand. Public opinion was on their side of this issue, and they are usually listed as the Silver Medalists in reference books.

KIRALY, EDE *(b. 1930) Hungarian solo World medalist; World Pairs Champion with Andrea Kekesy (b. 1929).*

Ede Kiraly was the last individual to win World medals in two skating divisions simultaneously. This was an uncommon feat in the first 40 years of the century, but a half-dozen skaters were able to accomplish it. Since Ede Kiraly managed it in 1948 and 1949, it has never recurred, although a few people have tried.

In 1948, Kiraly won the World Bronze Medal as a solo skater, while also taking the World Silver in Pairs with his partner Andrea Kekesy. The difficulty of this double success was pointed up by the fact that while in that year's Olympics at St. Moritz, Switzerland, Kiraly and Kekesy also took the Silver Medal, Kiraly was unable to reach the medal stand in the Men's individual competition. In 1949, he and Kekesy became World Pairs Champions. He also won the Men's Silver behind

Dick Button and ahead of Austria's Edi Rada, who had beaten him for the Bronze at the Olympics the year before. Andrea Kekesy then retired, but Kiraly took one more shot at the Men's World title in 1950, only to be bested again by Dick Button.

KLIMOVA, MARINA *(b. 1967) Soviet World Champion Ice Dancer with Sergei Ponomarenko (b. 1961).*

After gaining a Bronze Medal at the 1984 Olympics, Marina Klimova and Sergei Ponomarenko took the World Silver Medal from 1985 through 1988 behind Soviet Champions Natalia Bestemianova and Andrei Bukin. The audience sometimes clearly preferred their verve to the flowing classicism of Bestemianova and Bukin, but so far as the judges were concerned, the latter represented perfection of its kind. The two couples were also the Gold and Silver Medalists at the 1988 Olympics, with Canada's Tracy Wilson and Robert McCall the Bronze Medalists as they had been at the previous three World Championships.

With the retirement of Bestemianova and Bukin, Klimova and Ponomarenko came into their own, but they were not as dominant as their predecessors. They captured the World Championship in 1989 and 1990, winning over the new Soviet team of Maia Usova and Alexander Zhulin, and the French brother-and-sister team of Isabelle and Paul Duchesnay in 1990; the latter two couples reversed position for the Silver and Bronze in 1990. The Duchesnays were actually Canadian born but skated for France because of what they felt to be early slights by the Canadian skating establishment. In 1991, they snatched the Gold Medal away in Munich, Germany with Klimova and Ponomarenko taking the Silver, and Usova and Zhulin the Bronze. The Duchesnays had Christopher Dean as their choreographer, and his imaginative work suited their daring style beautifully. But in 1992, they became a little too daring for the judges, who gave the Olympic Gold Medal to Klimova and Ponomarenko before an enraged audience in Albertville, France. The Duchesnays were so disgusted with what they saw as a sudden turn to conservatism by the judges that they withdrew from the World Championships. Klimova and Ponomarenko closed out their amateur career with a third Gold Medal.

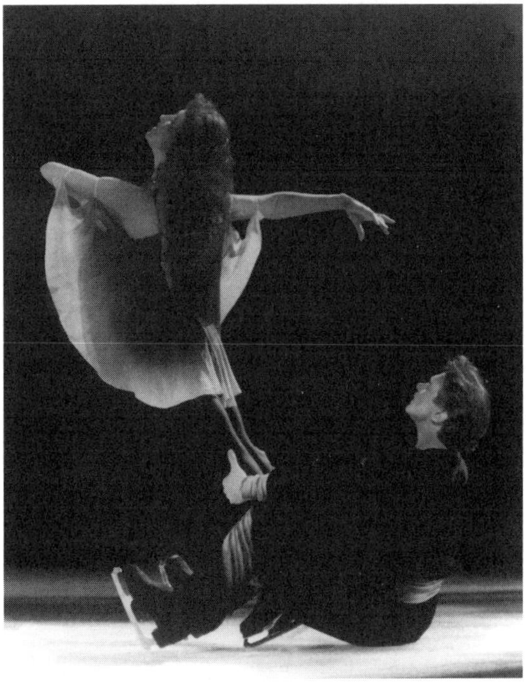

Marina Klimova and Sergei Ponomarenko won World Silver or Gold eight times.

(Courtesy Michael Rosenberg)

KLOPFER, SONYA *(b. 1934) U.S. Champion.*

Described by Dick Button as "the most dynamic free-skater of her day," Sonya Klopfer was nevertheless competing at a time—the late 1940s and early 1950s—when there was great depth among U.S. women skaters, including Yvonne C. Sherman, Virginia Baxter and the young Tenley Albright. In 1950, Klopfer was unable to overcome the school-figures lead built up by Sherman and had to settle for the U.S. Silver Medal. At the World Championships that year she was 5th as Sherman garnered the Bronze Medal. In 1951, with Sherman's retirement, Klopfer became U.S. Champion and took the World Bronze Medal. She withdrew from the national competition in 1952, which was won by Tenley Albright, but Klopfer did skate at both the Olympics and the World Championships. She was only 4th at the Olympics as Albright took the Silver Medal, but at World's, which Albright missed because of an injury, Klopfer won the Silver Medal behind France's Jacqueline du Bief, while teammate Virginia Baxter took the Bronze Medal.

It was clear that Albright combined both Sherman's strength in school figures and Klopfer's own gift for free-skating. Klopfer thus took advantage of an offer to star in a grand British-stage ice show and turned professional. The show, called *Cinderella on Ice*, was a great hit, and Klopfer continued to headline similar productions in England for the next several years.

KNAPP, ROSALIE *(b. 1905) U.S. medalist.*

Rosalie Knapp was the U.S. Silver Medalist in 1924 behind Theresa Weld Blanchard, taking her sixth title. There was no Bronze Medalist that year because of a small pool of competitors. The following year, Knapp was pushed back to Bronze as Beatrix Loughran won the first of three consecutive national championships, with Blanchard 2nd.

KNIGHT, DONALD *(b. 1945) Canadian Champion.*

The third Donald in a row, after Jackson and McPherson, to reign as Canadian Champion, Donald Knight also captured the World Bronze in 1965. No other Canadian Men's Champion took a World Medal until Toller Cranston's Bronze in 1974.

KOCH, INGE *(b. 1919) German Pairs skater with Gunther Noach (b. 1918).*

Inge Koch and Gunther Noach were a world-class Pair who were always in the shadow of their older compatriots, the great Maxi Herber and Ernst Baier. But they did win two World Bronze Medals on the eve of World War II, in 1938 and 1939, as Herber and Baier gained their third and fourth World titles.

KOKHO, PETRI *See* RAKHAMO, SUSANNA.

KOLLEN, PIETER *(b. 1941) U.S. Ice Dance and Pairs medalist, with Dorothyann Nelson (b. 1942); Pairs medalist with Patti Gustafson (b. 1943).*

In the downcast circumstances of the U.S. Championships in 1962 following the deaths of the U.S. World team the year before, Pieter Kollen and Dorothyann Nelson shone in two different disciplines, winning the Gold Medal in Pairs Skating and taking the Silver in Ice Dancing. They also helped buoy the depleted U.S. team at the World Championships, finishing 8th in Pairs and 7th in Ice Dancing. Dorothyann Nelson then retired, but Pieter Kollen competed again in 1963 in Pairs with a new partner, Patti Gustafson. They took the Bronze Medal at the U.S. Championships and were 9th at the World's.

KOTHMAN, SULLY *(b. 1933) U.S. Pairs medalist with Kay Servatius (b. 1931) and Lucille Ash (b. 1934).*

Sully Kothman won the U.S. Bronze first with Kay Servatius in 1953 behind new Pairs Champions Carole Ormaca and Robin Greiner and the sister-brother team of Margaret and Hugh Graham. Kay Servatius then retired from skating, and Sully formed a new partnership with Lucille Ash, which resulted in another Bronze Medal in 1954. In 1955 and 1956, Kothman and Ash were runners-up to Ormaca and Greiner. They acquitted themselves confidently in international competition, finishing

8th in 1955 and 6th in 1956 at the World's, and placing 7th at the 1956 Olympics.

KOVALEV, VLADIMIR *(b. 1954)*

Soviet World Champion.

The most successful Soviet male skater of his time, Vladimir Kovalev was also prone to sudden collapses in competition that gave the Soviet sports authorities fits. In 1972, Kovalev took his first medal at the World Championships, capturing the Bronze, while Soviet Champion Sergei Chetverukhin garnered the Silver and Czechoslovakia's Ondrej Nepela took his second of three consecutive Gold Medals. It was not until 1975 that Kovalev took another World Medal, this time the Silver behind compatriot Sergei Volkov and the following year placed 2nd to John Curry at both the Olympics and World's.

Becoming World Champion in 1977, Kovalev went to pieces the following year and was shut out by the U.S.'s Charlie Tickner, East Germany's Jan Hoffmann and Great Britain's Robin Cousins, in that order, as Soviet officials screamed at him in public. Kovalev came back to win his second World Championship the next year, and the Soviets made no secret of the fact that they expected him to become the Soviet Union's first Olympic Gold Medalist in the men's division in 1980. The pressure obviously got to him: He did much less well than usual in school figures and fell all over the ice during the short program. Team officials packed him unceremoniously back to Moscow without even allowing him participate in the long program. They would not let him attend the World Championships either. Kovalev never appeared in another competition.

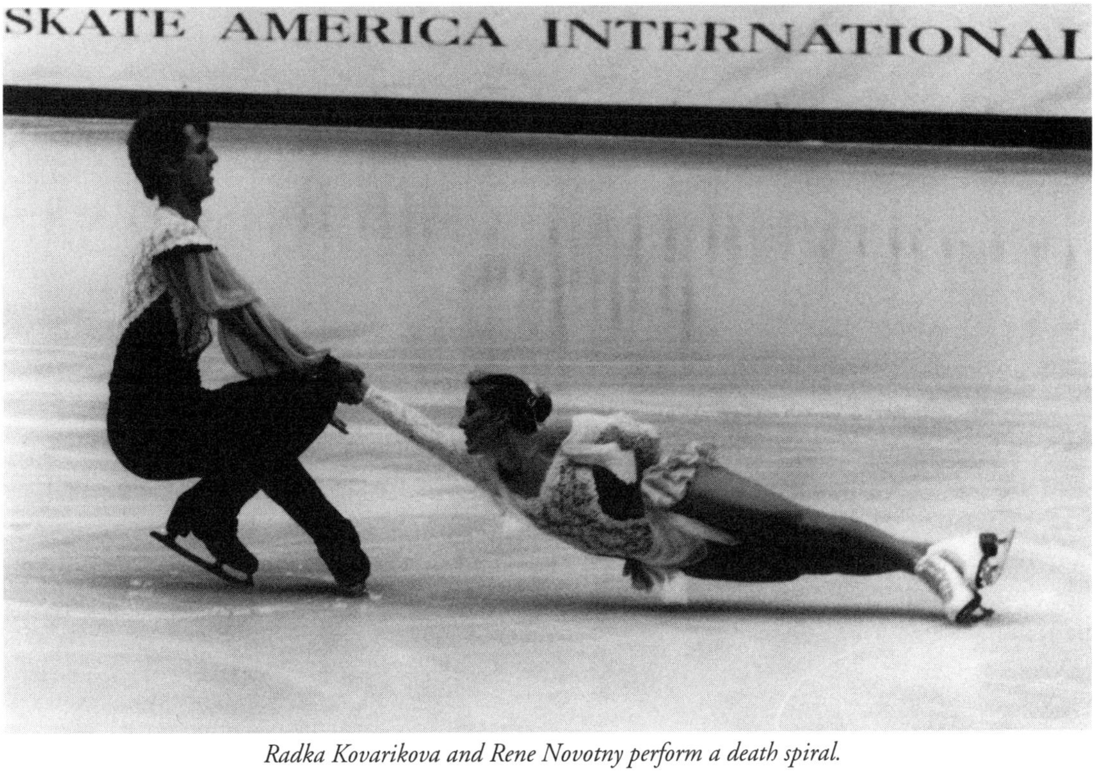

Radka Kovarikova and Rene Novotny perform a death spiral.
(Courtesy Michael Rosenberg)

KOVARIKOVA, RADKA *(b. 1975) Czech Republic World Pairs Champion with Rene Novotny (b. 1963).*

When Radka Kovarikova was only 17, she and her partner, Rene Novotny, then 29, took their first World Medal in Pairs, the Silver at Oakland, California behind Natalia Mishkutenok and Artur Dmitriev of Russia. Both pairs skated that year under the banner of the amalgamated countries that had just been liberated from the Soviet Union. In 1993, Kovarikova and Novotny failed to gain a medal, as was also the case at the 1994 Olympics, where the return to amateur skating of the 1988 and 1992 Olympic winners, Ekaterina Gordeeva and Sergei Grinkov and Mishkutenok and Dmitriev, both of Russia, pushed the newer skaters back into the pack. But in 1995 at Birmingham, England, Kovarikova and Novotny finally managed to break through to the Gold Medal, topping Shiskova and Naumov and the U.S.'s Jenni Meno and Todd Sand. The couple then turned professional.

KRAATZ, VICTOR *See* BOURNE, SHAE-LYNN.

KRAVETTE, RON *See* SEMANICK, SUZANNE.

KROGH, ANDREAS *(b. 1898) Norwegian medalist.*

Because there were no World Championships held from 1915 through 1921, Norwegian Champion Andreas Krogh had only one chance to shine in the international arena—the 1920 Olympics in Antwerp, Belgium, where the existence of an artificial rink made possible the inclusion of skating among the normal track-and-field competitions. He took the Silver Medal behind Swedish skater Gillis Grafstrom. Krogh's compatriot, Martin Stixrud, took the Bronze. These were the only two medals ever won by male Norwegian skaters in the Olympics.

KROHN, KIM *(b. 1961) U.S. Ice Dancer.*

During a very strong period for U.S. ice dancers, topped by partners Judy Blumberg/Michael Seibert and Carol Fox/Richard Dalley, Kim Krohn and her partner Barry Hagan managed to take the Bronze Medal in 1981, but they were then supplanted by Scott Gregory and Elisa Spitz in 1982.

KRONBERGER, LILLY *(b. 1890, d. 1967) Hungarian World Champion.*

One of the most colorful figures of early figure skating, Lilly Kronberger was World Champion from 1908 to 1911. From a wealthy aristocratic Hungarian family, she spared no expense on costumes, dazzling European figure-skating circles with her lavish outfits. But she was also a splendid skater and did much to further the use of music as an accompaniment to the free program. Tired of dealing with indifferent and underrehearsed musicians provided at competitions, she astonished and captivated Vienna at her 1911 swan song by bringing her own brass band with her from Hungary—and graciously had the band play for her fellow Hungarian and Silver Medalist, Opika von Horvath, as well. From then on, the host cities saw to it that musicians put in sufficient rehearsal time with the competing skaters.

KRYLOVA, ANGELIKA *(b. 1973) Russian Ice Dancing Champion and Olympic medalist with Oleg Ovsiannikov (b. 1970)*

Known for their expressive style, Ice Dance team Angelika Krylova and Oleg Ovsiannikov had each skated at the world level before partnering in 1995 to place 5th at the World's. From there they soared ever higher, taking World Silver in 1996 and again in 1997, also the year they became Russian National Champions. Continuing their success in 1998, they were again Russian Champions, and Silvered at the Olympics in Nagano, Japan.

KUBICKA, TERRY *(b. 1955) U.S. Champion.*

An exuberant free-skater, Terry Kubicka was U.S. Silver Medalist in 1974 and 1975 and became U.S. Champion in 1976. Like most U.S. men's competitors of the time, Kubicka was not at his best in school figures. Although that did not prevent him from shining among U.S. skaters who shared their weakness, it held him back in World and Olympic competition, which was dominated by such school-figure perfectionists as John Curry and Jan Hoffmann. At the World's, Kubicka was 12th, 7th and 6th in 1974–76 and took 7th place at the Olympics. He made a considerable impact in 1976, however, with a free-skating routine to music from Andrew Lloyd Webber's *Jesus Christ Superstar.* It was one of those special matches between skater and music that brought roars of approval from the audience. At the 1976 World's, he became the first skater to perform a backflip (backward somersault) in competition, but it was thereafter banned as being too dangerous.

KUCHIKI, NATASHA *(b. 1976) U.S. Pairs Champion with* TODD SAND *(b. 1963).*

Natasha Kuchiki and Todd Sand were U.S. Silver Medalists in Pairs in 1990, and, in 1991 they became U.S. Champions and World Bronze Medalists behind Russia's Natalia Mishkutenok and Artur Dmitriev and Canada's Isabelle Brasseur and Lloyd Eisler. But in 1992 they slipped to 3rd in the United States, 6th at the Olympics and 8th at the World's. Todd Sand then split with Kuchiki to became partners with Jenni Meno.

KULIK, ILYA *(b. 1977) Russian World and Olympic medalist.*

Ilya Kulik became the World Men's Junior Champion at the age of 16 in 1994 and moved into the senior ranks with resounding success by winning the 1995 European Championship over more-experienced skaters, including his own countryman and 1994 Olympic Gold Medalist Alexei Urmanov. At the 1995 World Championships, however, he missed the required combination jump in the short program, which put him out of medal contention. At the 1996 European Championships, he was 3rd behind the Ukraine's Viacheslav Zagorodniuk and another young Russian, Igor Paskevitch, but at the 1996 World Championships he excelled: In the short program, skating to the theme from the U.S. movie, *The Addams Family,* he combined speed, presence and huge jumps to top the U.S.'s Todd Eldredge and Urmanov. In the long program he was ranked 2nd behind Eldredge and ended up with the Silver Medal; the U.S.'s Eldredge and Rudy Galindo won the Gold and the Bronze, while Urmanov faded to 5th and Canada's defending World Champion Elvis Stojko was unable to move higher than 4th after a disastrous short program. By taking 2nd place in such company, the young Kulik made it clear that he would be a major threat to the established order. The next year, although he dropped to 5th place at the World's, he became the Russian National Champion. In 1998 he further fulfilled the promise of his talent and took the Gold at the Olympics in Nagano, Japan, ahead of Canada's Elvis Stokjo and Philippe Candeloro of France.

KWAN, MICHELLE *(b. 1980) U.S. medalist.*

Tiny Michelle Kwan was thrust into the spotlight at age 13 in 1994 when she was named as a backup to the U.S. Olympic and World team because of the uncertain availability of both Tonya Harding and Nancy Kerrigan in the aftermath of the physical attack on Kerrigan just before the 1994 U.S. Championships. A fast-rising skater from Los Angeles, Kwan placed 6th at her first National Senior Championship in 1993 and took 1st place at that year's U.S. Olympic Festival (where younger skaters get a chance to win their first major title).

At the 1994 U.S. Championships, with Kerrigan out because of her injury, Kwan was runner-up to Harding. With questions abounding about Harding's involvement in the Kerrigan attack and Kerrigan herself a physical question mark for a while,

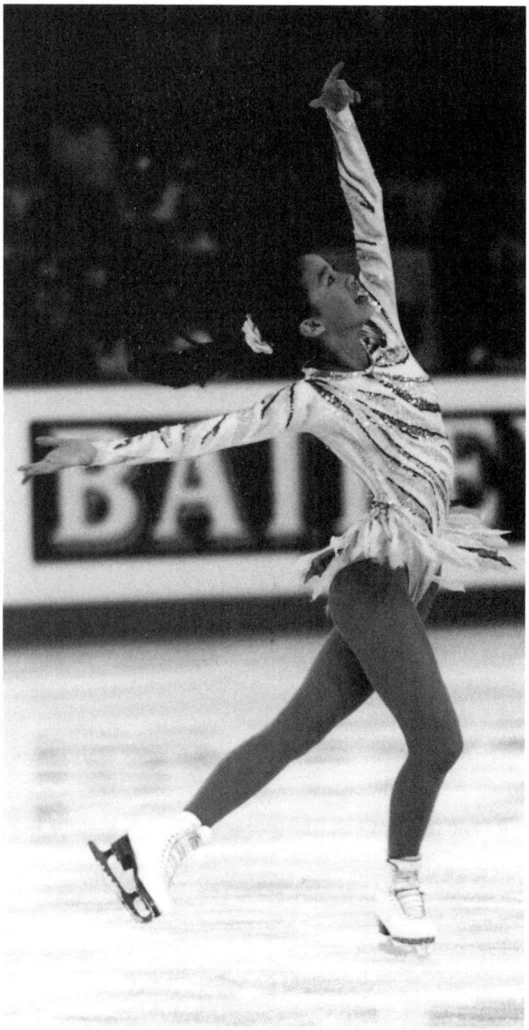

Michelle Kwan on the verge of stardom in 1995.
(Courtesy Michelle Harvath)

Kwan was sent to Europe to continue training before the Olympics in case she was needed as a last-minute replacement. That proved unnecessary, but Nancy Kerrigan then passed on going to the World Championships and Tonya Harding's plea bargain in the Kerrigan attack case removed her from the team at the last minute.

Kwan did the job required of her as a substitute at the 1994 World's, taking 8th place, with a top ten finish necessary to ensure the presence of two women representing the United States at the 1995 World's.

Kwan, even though only 14, was favored to gain the national title on her own in 1995. But 17-year-old Nicole Bobek, the previous year's Bronze Medalist, who had a reputation for not skating up to par, pulled herself together under her eighth coach, Richard Callaghan, and won the U.S. Gold with a technically polished program that complemented her widely recognized artistic ability. As the Silver Medalist, Kwan did, however, attend the World Championships. Bobbles in her short program appeared to have knocked her out of medal contention. She was the last to skate in the final group during the long program competition, and by that time, the medal order seemed to be set, with China's Lu Chen taking the Gold, Nicole Bobek the Silver and France's Surya Bonaly the Bronze. But Kwan skated a clean, strong program that brought her the 3rd highest scores, and the standing suddenly changed. Bobek had been 1st in the short program, but now Kwan had edged her in the long, and as a result the computer showed Lu Chen still with the Gold but Bonaly taking the Silver and Bobek the Bronze. Michelle Kwan had not yet won a World medal, but she had set her U.S. rival and the World judges on notice that she would be a force to be reckoned with for years to come.

Indeed, Kwan's ascendancy came sooner than expected. Unlike many other skaters, she turned down a chance to tour during the period leading to the 1996 National Championships. Her coach persuaded her parents that even at 15, Michelle needed a more adult image to be taken with absolute seriousness by the judges, so for the first time she used adult makeup, a sexier costume, and took the somewhat daring step of skating to Richard Strauss' music for the biblical temptress Salome. There were those in the skating world who wondered if this was a little too adult, but Kwan skated the program with a new maturity and great technical assurance. With Nicole Bobek's withdrawal because of an ankle injury, Kwan won with ease, becoming the youngest U.S. Ladies' Champion in 32 years. Tara Lipinski, who was a Silver Medalist at the Junior Ladies' Championship the previous year, was 2nd at the age of 13, and 26-year-old Tonia Kwiatkowski was 3rd. Because Bobek and Kwan had both finished in the top five at the World Championships the previous year, all three U.S. medalists were allowed to compete at the 1996 Championships in Edmonton, Canada.

At Edmonton, Kwan, China's Lu Chen (the defending World Champion), and Russia's Irina Slutskaya (who had just dethroned France's Surya Bonaly as European Champion) were so closely bunched after the short program that it was possible for any one of them to win the title; everything would depend on the long program. Slutskaya, who had performed the most difficult jump in the short program, a triple lutz-double loop combination, was not quite as secure in the long program, so the choice for the Gold Medal was between Kwan and Lu Chen. Both skated beautifully and each received two perfect 6.0s for artistry, but the remaining artistic marks were divided in Kwan's favor—seven 5.9s to Chen's four 5.8s. Kwan thus became third-youngest World Champion ever, after Sonja Henie (who won her first title at 14) and Oksana Baiul (who was also 15 but a few months younger than Kwan when she won in 1993).

In 1997, Kwan was beset by the problems that often affect very young World Champions. She herself said that she had lost the sense of fun she had always taken into competition. She was badly affected by nerves at the U.S. Championships and lost her title to the even younger Tara Lipinski. At the World's, Kwan had a bobble in the short program but won the long program. Lipinski, with a flawless short program and second place in the long program, took the World title also, setting up a major confrontation for the 1998 Olympics with Kwan, although China's Lu Chen, Russia's Irina Slutskaya and even America's Nicole Bobek were also serious contenders.

Kwan arrived at the 1998 Winter Games in Nagano having recently recovered from an injury to her foot. She skated well, though conservatively, and was in 1st place after the short program, with Lipinski taking 2nd. Kwan entered the long program with a perceived advantage over Lipinski, in that artistic marks, Kwan's strength, serve as a tie-breaker. However, Lipinski's long program was more technically challenging than Kwan's; the younger skater performed perfectly and showed an unexpected artistry. Though Kwan's long program was also perfect and skated with her usual elegance, it was not as difficult as Lipinski's, and Kwan had to settle for the Silver ahead of China's Chen Lu.

KWIATKOWSKI, TONIA *(b. 1971)*

U.S. medalist.

Coached by former Olympic Champion Carol Heiss Jenkins since she was nine years old, Tonia Kwiatkowski's performances in practice have long promised a major success that has never quite materialized. Trying to carry a double major in college and a full skating schedule seemed to take a toll. In 1993, she did become the U.S. Bronze Medalist behind Nancy Kerrigan and Lisa Ervin but then slipped to 5th in 1994. In 1995, Kwiatkowski was in 1st place after the short program but ran into problems in the long program and ended up with another Bronze behind Nicole Bobek and Michelle Kwan.

In 1996, Kwiatkowski was Silver Medalist behind Michelle Kwan and ahead of 13-year-old Tara Lipinski and then made her first trip to the World Championships. There she did well, ending up in 8th place as Kwan became World Champion and Lipinski finished 15th.

L

LADIES' COMPETITION *See* WOMEN'S COMPETITION.

LAMAR, JUDY ANNE *(b. 1940) U.S. Ice Dance medalist.*

A fine skater, Judy Lamar had great difficulty finding Ice Dance partners because of her six-foot height. In 1959, Ron Ludington, the two-time U.S. Pairs Champion (with his wife, Nancy), agreed to take on the added responsibility of partnering Judy Lamar in Ice Dancing. A natural skater who went on to become a major coach, Ludington partnered Lamar to the U.S. Bronze in Ice Dancing as well as a 9th place finish at the World's. At the same time, he and his wife retained the U.S. Pairs title and became the first U.S. Pair in seven years to take a World medal, winning the Bronze.

LANCON, BURT *See* WATSON, JILL.

LANE, JON *See* SAWBRIDGE, JANET.

LANNOY, MICHELINE *(b. 1925) Belgian World Champion Pairs Skater with Pierre Baugniet (b. 1925).*

As the World Championships resumed following World War II at Stockholm, Sweden in 1947, Micheline Lannoy and Pierre Baugniet became the first (and only) skaters from Belgium ever to win a World Championship, beating U.S. sister-and-brother team Karol and Peter Kennedy, who would become World Champions themselves in 1950. At the 1948 Olympics and World Championships, Lannoy and Baugniet again triumphed, beating Hungary's Andrea Kekesy and Ede Kiraly in both competitions.

LASSO LIFT

As both Pairs partners skate forward, with the woman in front of the man, the man lifts the woman and twirls her over his head in a wide lassolike circle and deposits her again on the ice, now skating backward.

LAVANCHY, PASCAL *See* MONIOTTE, SOPHIE.

LAY-BACK SPIN

The classic woman's spin calls for the skater to spin on one foot while the free leg is bent at the knee and extended behind her, with the arms raised in a ballet arabesque over the head. The back should be deeply arched, with the shoulders and head thrown backward. This spin is a benchmark criteria in scoring artistic impression. There have been numerous World and Olympic Champions whose lay-back spin has been merely well done, but when a skater excels at it, you are likely to be watching a skater whose artistic marks are her margin of victory.

A great lay-back spin has about it a grace and loveliness that can give spectators goose bumps. Among post-World War II skaters who have been noted for their lay-back spins are such World Champions as Canada's Barbara Ann Scott and the U.S.'s Tenley Albright, Peggy Fleming, Linda Fratianne, and Rosalyn Sumners, as have Switzerland's Denise Biellmann and the Ukraine's Oksana Baiul. In 1961, on the final page of the *Life* magazine issue that reported on the plane crash that killed the entire U.S. figure-skating World team, there was a photograph of the new 16-year-old U.S. Ladies' Champion, Laurence Owen, who was killed in that Brussels crash, performing a breathtaking lay-back spin at the National Championships. Even at 16 she was already famous for it.

LEE, ROBIN *(1919–97) U.S. Champion.*

Following Roger Turner's seven-year run as U.S. Men's Champion, Robin Lee won the Gold Medal five successive times beginning in 1935. He had previously won the Bronze Medal in 1933 and the Silver in 1934. Lee competed in the World Championships only twice, placing 9th in 1933 and 8th in 1936, and was 12th at the 1936 Olympics.

LEMAIRE, EDWARD *See* GOOS, DOROTHY.

LENZ, SANDY *(b. 1961) U.S. medalist.*

Skating during a period in which there was a large number of world-class U.S. women skaters, Sandy Lenz took the U.S. Bronze in 1980 and placed 9th at that year's Olympics.

ETTENGARVER, JOHN *(b. 1928) U.S. medalist.*

In 1947, John Lettengarver placed 2nd to Dick Button at the U.S. Championships; James Grogan took the Bronze. The following year, Grogan moved past Lettengarver at the U.S. Championships to take the Silver, but Lettengarver shone at both the Olympics and the World Championships, taking 4th in both contests.

LEWIS, BETT *(b. 1947) U.S. Pairs skater with Richard Gilbert (b. 1946).*

Betty Lewis and Richard Gilbert won the U.S. Bronze Medal in Pairs in 1967 behind repeat medalists Cynthia and Ronald Kauffman (Gold) and Susan Berens and Roy Wagelein (Silver). Lewis and Gilbert were 13th at that year's World's and were beaten out for the U.S. Bronze the following year by the up-and-coming JoJo Starbuck and Kenneth Shelley.

LEWIS, CLARALYNN *(b. 1938) U.S. medalist.*

Claralynn Lewis was the Bronze Medalist at the U.S. Championships in 1957 as Carol Heiss won the first of four Gold medals. At the World's that year, Lewis was 5th. In 1958 she did not win a U.S. medal, but she gained a berth on the World team and placed 10th.

LIBERMAN, JOEL *See* MUNSTOCK, GRACE.

LINICHUK, NATALIA *(b. 1956) Soviet Ice Dancer with Gennadi Karponosov (b. 1950).*

Throughout their amateur careers, Natalia Linichuk and Gennadi Karponosov strongly rivaled their fellow Soviet Ice Dancers Irina Moiseeva and Andrei Minekov, known in the skating world as Min and Mo. Linichuk and Karponosov took the World Bronze Medal in 1974 but didn't win a World medal again for two years. Instead, Moiseeva and Minekov became World Champions in 1975 and took the Silver in 1976 and the Silver at the 1976 Olympics. The Gold Medal at both the World Championships and Olympics in 1976 was taken by the third great Soviet team of that period, Ludmila Pakhomova and Alexandr Gorshkov, who had been World Champions in 1970–1974 but did not compete in 1975. The latter couple then retired, but the rivalry between the two other Soviet couples continued for several more years. In 1977, Min and Mo were World Champions, with Linichuk and Karponosov taking the Bronze. In 1978, the latter team won the Gold with Moiseeva and Minekov right behind them for the Silver. They took the Gold again in 1979; Moiseeva and Minekov earned the Bronze this time and the Hungarian team of Krisztina Regoeczy and Andras Sallay seized the Silver Medal. At the 1980 Olympics, Linichuk and Karponosov won the Gold, just beating the Hungarians, while Moiseeva and Minekov took the Bronze. At the World's, the Hungarians prevailed to become World Champions, with Linichuk and Karponosov 2nd and Moiseeva and Minekov 3rd. The level of Ice Dancing competition in 1980 is regarded as the most extraordinary in figure-skating history, with 4th place at the World's and 5th at the Olympics going to a British couple named Torvill and Dean; they succeeded to the World Championship the following year, after the retirement of both the Hungarians and Linichuk and Karponosov.

LIPINSKI, TARA *(b. 1983) U.S. medalist.*

After placing second in the National Junior Ladies' Championship in 1995, Tara Lipinski moved into senior competition to capture the Bronze Medal in San Jose in 1996, behind Michelle Kwan and Tonia Kwiatkowski, who was twice her age. Extremely poised both on and off the ice, Tara was widely heralded as a future Olympic Champion. She received a setback at the 1996 World Championships, however, finishing 15th as Kwan became World Champion and Kwiatkowski placed 8th.

In 1997, Lipinski moved to the forefront, however. Michelle Kwan succumbed to the pressures of being World Champion and made mistakes in both her short and long programs at the U.S. Championships, opening the way for Lipinski to take the Gold Medal. At the World Championships, Kwan had a mistake in the short program, and although she won the long program, Lipinski was ahead in points after a flawless short program, becoming the youngest World Champion since Sonja Henie. These developments set up a major showdown for the 1998 Olympics.

In an event that captured the public's imagination and served as the centerpiece of the 1998 Winter Games, the contest between Lipinski and Kwan at Nagano was closely fought: Lipinski's technical precision and daring opposed Kwan's more mature skating style and natural artisty—no one could predict the outcome, and the suspense captivated audiences around the world. Though Lipinski's program lacked the sophistication of Kwan's —Lipinski skated to the theme from the Disney movie *Anastasia,* while Kwan chose a piano concerto by Rachmaninoff—in the end, through a combination of perfect technical execution, an unexpected burst of grace and a challenging series of jumps, Lipinski's performance edged out the beautiful but slightly cautious skating of Kwan, and Lipinski took the Gold, breaking Sonja Henie's record as the youngest Olympic Gold Medalist in the sport's history.

Though the world looked forward to continued competition between the two great American skaters, Lipinski declined to compete at the 1998 World's, and shortly afterward announced plans to join the professional skating circuit.

LITTLEFIELD, YVONNE *(b. 1944)*

U.S. Ice Dancer with Roger Campbell (b. 1940) and Peter Betts (b. 1935).

With Roger Campbell, Yvonne Littlefield won the U.S. Bronze in Ice Dancing in 1960 and placed 8th at the World's. But the couple did not get along and split up. In a twist of fate, this was to prove fortunate for Yvonne Littlefield, who was unable to win a U.S. medal in 1961 with her new partner, Peter Betts; Roger Campbell, however, won the Silver with his new partner, Dona Lee Carrier. Because they had not won a medal, Littlefield and Betts did not make the U.S. team that was killed in the plane crash at Brussels on its way to the 1961 World Championship. Carter and Campbell died in that crash.

Littlefield and Betts subsequently won the U.S. Gold in 1962 and placed 8th at the World's. In 1963, they had to settle for the Silver behind Sally Schrantz and Stanley Urban. After placing a disastrous 17th at the World Championships, they retired from amateur skating.

LITZ, THOMAS *(b. 1941) U.S. Champion.*

Tommy Litz's first U.S. senior medal found him in the top spot as 1963's national champion. Scott Allen, the more experienced Silver Medalist, came back to beat him in 1964, however. Litz placed a respectable 6th at both the Olympics and the World Championships and then turned professional for a short period.

LOCHEAD, JAMES *(b. 1924) Versatile U.S. medalist.*

With Marcella May (b. 1923), James Lochead was the U.S. Ice Dance Champion in both 1943 and 1944; in 1945, the couple took the Silver. At the same time, Lochead and May pulled off the feat of winning the U.S. Pairs Bronze in 1944–45. To top off his very versatile career as a figure skater, Lochead took the U.S. Silver Medal in the Men's competition in 1946.

LOOP JUMP

The first full-revolution jump taught to beginning skaters, the loop in itself is quite straightforward. It is very often combined with other jumps to make up the combination jumps that are a required technical element of the short program in competition. Single loop jumps were being performed as early as the 1880s, although it is not known who originated the maneuver.

The skater enters a loop jump while moving backward on the right foot, holding the ice with the outer edge of the blade. The upper body is turned so that the right shoulder is to the rear and the left to the front, with both arms extended just below shoulder level parallel to the line that the jump will take. That line is held steady until the skater actually leaves the ice, at which time the body is rotated in the air for one revolution before landing on the same leg and the same back outer edge. As the skater lands, the free leg should be quite close to the landing leg, but at the moment of landing, the free leg is extended backward in a straight line but arched slightly to give a nice line. If the free leg is loose and flailing when the skater lands or too great an arc is covered by the free leg away from the body, a deduction is likely to be made by the judges even if the skater doesn't fall—which can easily happen because the flailing leg is a sign that the jump is not fully under control.

At the moment of landing, the left arm should be held forward and the right arm back in order to "check" or control the rotation of the body. Once the back edge is secure, the arms can be extended to either side to give a visual finish to the idea of flight. Very experienced skaters may spread the arms without using the checking motion, but while this can be very graceful, it also means that the body will continue to turn on the ice in a circle, which causes a loss of speed. That may be no problem, depending upon what the next element of the choreography is.

The two-revolution double loop has the same takeoff and landing as a single loop except that the skater must complete two full revolutions in the air. This jump had become a standard jump for the top male competitors during the 1930s; the women champions were expected to do it by the late 1940s. It was the U.S.'s Dick Button who began to up the ante in terms of loops: In 1949, he performed the first double loop-double loop combination in competition, that is, two double loops in succession without any additional preparation in between, with the landing of one double leading directly into the takeoff for the second. He carried that move a step further in 1950 by performing a triple double loop, three separate jumps in quick succession.

Button, who had also performed the first double axel, requiring two-and-one-half revolutions, was determined to attempt the triple loop at the 1952 Olympics. He had learned to increase the speed of his rotation in double loops by crossing his feet at the ankles while in midair, just as one would cross one's feet doing a spin on the ice. Clearly that would also be essential to mastering a triple loop.

Even so, Button encountered a major problem: the more he practiced a triple loop without actually getting it, the more the effort derailed his entire repertoire of jumps. He decided to give up. But in December 1951 on a spur-of-the-moment attempt, he accomplished it. Although the landing was two-footed, he now had the feel of it. Although he sometimes missed it even in practice, he decided to include it at the Olympics, where he did it perfectly, making skating history and assuring his second Olympic Gold Medal.

To date, the quadruple loop has not been successfully landed in competition, although there are several men who have tried and landed it in practice. Among the women, French Champion and two-time World Silver Medalist Surya Bonaly has also landed it in practice, but she has not tried it in competition. Nevertheless that breakthrough now seems inevitable.

LOOPS *See* SCHOOL FIGURES.

LORD, BRADLEY *(b. 1940, d. 1961)*

U.S. Champion.

Bradley Lord placed 4th at the U.S. Championships in both 1959 and 1960. Because recent U.S. placements at the World Championships had been very strong (at least two U.S. men had been medalists for a decade), four places were available on the U.S. World team. Lord came in 8th in 1959 and 6th in 1960; in 1961 he succeeded David Jenkins as U.S. Champion. An elegant skater in the mold of David Jenkins' older brother, Hayes Alan Jenkins, Lord was widely considered a potential World Champion, but he was killed on the way to the 1961 World Championships in a plane crash at Brussels.

LOUGHRAN, BEATRIX *(1900–75)*

U.S. Ladies' and Pairs Champion.

Along with Theresa Weld Blanchard and Maribel Vinson, Beatrix Loughran was a versatile skater who had a major impact on U.S. figure skating in the 1920s and 1930s. The height of her solo-skater success brought her three national Ladies' titles between the reigns of the older Blanchard and the younger Vinson. She won her first U.S. Senior medal in 1922, placing 2nd to Blanchard, an order of finish repeated the following year. In 1924 she was unable to compete in the U.S. Championships because of an injury but did take the Silver Medal at that year's Olympics and won the Bronze at the World's. (Blanchard, who had repeated as U.S. Champion was 4th at the Olympics and did not compete at the World's.)

In 1925, Loughran beat Blanchard to take her first U.S. Gold Medal. The same result occurred in 1926, with the fast-rising Vinson taking the Bronze. In 1927, Loughran won again, with Vinson 2nd and Blanchard slipping to 3rd. That was the last U.S.

Ladies' competition Loughran entered, although she did compete in the 1928 Olympics, taking the Bronze Medal behind Norway's Sonja Henie and Austria's Fritzi Burger.

Beatrix Loughran had also begun to skate in Pairs and took the U.S. Silver Medal in 1927 with Raymond Harvey. She then changed partners and renewed her efforts, winning the U.S. Gold in 1930 with Sherwin Badger, who had been the U.S. Men's Champion from 1920 to 1924. Drawing on their solo-skater strengths, the couple also won the World Bronze in 1930. They repeated as U.S. Champions in 1931 and 1932, topping Vinson and George Hill both times. Loughran and Badger did not compete in the World's in 1931 but in 1932 again took the Bronze Medal and captured the

Versatile Beatrix Loughran, a U.S. Champion in both the Ladies' and Pairs divisions.
(Courtesy World Figure Skating Museum)

Olympic Silver behind the great French Pair Andrée and Pierre Brunet. Loughran then retired having amassed a total of nine U.S., three World and two Olympic medals.

LU CHEN *(b. 1972) Chinese World Champion. (Note: Although her name is listed as Lu Chen in Western records, the skater prefers the traditional Chinese name order, in which the last name appears first: thus Chen Lu).*

Chen Lu was regularly among the top half-dozen women skaters in the world from the start of the 1990s. She took her first World medal in 1992, winning the Bronze behind the U.S.'s Kristi Yamaguchi and Nancy Kerrigan. In 1993, she was again the Bronze Medalist, this time topped by the Ukraine's Oksana Baiul and France's Surya Bonaly. At the 1994 Olympics, she repeated her win of the Bronze, this time behind Baiul and Kerrigan. Injured shortly afterward, Chen Lu was unable to compete at the 1994 World Championships.

The 1995 World's found Chen Lu in 3rd place after the short program, with the U.S.'s Nicole Bobek in 1st place and Russia's Olga Markova in 2nd; Surya Bonaly placed 4th after a nervous performance. In the long program, skater after skater had problems, but Chen Lu not only displayed her usual artistic grace and astonishing footwork, she also nailed her jumps. This mature and lovely performance brought her the Gold Medal; Bonaly moved up to 2nd and Nicole Bobek earned the Bronze Medal. In 1994, Chen Lu became the first Chinese to win an Olympic medal in figure skating; in 1995 she became the first to be crowned World Champion.

Defending her World title at Edmonton, Canada in 1996, Chen Lu found that her chief competitors were the new U.S. Champion Michelle Kwan and the new European Champion Irina Slutskaya of Russia. All three were sufficiently solid in the short program that the final outcome depended entirely on the long program. Chen Lu skated with her customary grace and technical assurance and received two perfect 6.0s for artistry, as well as four 5.8s. That put her in 1st place, with Slutskaya in 2nd, but with Kwan still to skate. The judges had left a little room for Kwan to receive higher marks, but to gain them the 15-year-old would have to skate better than she ever had before. She did just that, scoring two perfect 6.0s, but also seven 5.9s for artistry and gaining the World title over Chen Lu and Slutskaya. This was not, however, a matter of Chen Lu skating badly but rather of Kwan surpassing herself. At the time it was clear that any of the three medalists had the potential to win the World's in 1997 and the Olympics in 1998. However, in 1997 Chen Lu was seriously injured; she returned to competition before she was fully recovered and did not do well at the World's.

Known for her exquisite arm placement, Chen Lu became World Champion in 1995.
(Courtesy Paul Harvath)

In 1998, Olympic audiences had the pleasure of seeing her skate slowly but exquisitely at the Nagano contest, where she took the Bronze, behind Gold Medalist Tara Lipinski and Silver Medalist Michelle Kwan.

LUDINGTON, RONALD AND NANCY ROUILLARD *(b. 1934, 1938)*

U.S. Pairs Champions.

Ron Ludington and Nancy Rouillard were roller-skating competitors as a team before taking up figure skating. Although it is highly unusual for people who come late to figure skating to rise to championship level, Ron and Nancy were extraordinary athletes who applied themselves to their new sport under the tutelage of Maribel Vinson Owen, nine-time U.S. champion and four-time U.S. Pairs Champion. Once they had acclimated themselves, they moved straight to the top, taking their first medal in 1957 by capturing the U.S. Championship. That year they were 4th at their first World Championships.

They were also married that year and went on to win the U.S. Gold thrice more successively. At the 1958 World's, the Ludingtons were 5th but captured the Bronze Medal in 1959 behind three-time World Champions Barbara Wagner and Robert Paul of Canada and Marika Kilius and her second partner, Hans Jurgen Baumler. At the 1960 Olympics, they won the Bronze Medal behind these same two couples. The Ludingtons had a disastrous World Championships that year, finishing only 6th, but they then went on to skate professionally together. Subsequently divorced, they were inducted into the U.S Figure Skating Hall of Fame together in 1993 as Nancy Luddington Graham and Ronald Ludington.

Ron Ludington also won a U.S Bronze in Ice Dancing in 1959 with Judy Lamar; the couple finished 9th at the World Championships even as

Nancy and Rod Ludington were four-time U.S. Pairs Champions.
(Courtesy World Figure Skating Museum)

Ron and Nancy were taking the World Bronze in Pairs. He became a major coach, most notably for Kitty and Peter Carruthers.

LURZ, DAGMAR *(b. 1959) West German World and Olympic medalist.*

Dagmar Lurz, a top women's figure skater during the late 1970s, often found herself just behind the medal leaders, for example as Bronze Medalist at the 1977 World Championships behind the U.S.'s Linda Fratianne and East Germany's Anett Poetzsch. While those two women exchanged places as Gold and Silver Medalists during the next two years, Lurz was unable to repeat as a medalist. She hit her top form at exactly the right time, however, taking the Olympic Bronze in 1980 behind Poetzsch and Fratianne, and the World Silver behind Poetzsch but ahead of Fratianne.

LUSSI, GUSTAV *(b. 1905) Major Swiss-born American coach.*

Immigrating to the United States before World War II, Swiss-born Lussi was known as a great taskmaster among skating coaches. Few skaters were willing to submit to the rigorous training Lussi conducted at Lake Placid, New York in summer and Philadelphia in winter.

Dick Button, one of his pupils, later wrote, "He did everything with great fervor—running a lumber camp, hunting moose, building a Swiss chalet in the mountains near Lake Placid, or collecting objets d'art in Europe." Lussi was adamant that Button perfect school figures; as the years passed, he also encouraged Button to experiment with the jumps and spins Button would become the first skater ever to master—the double axel, the triple loop and the flying camel. Although Lussi worked with other champion skaters, it was through Button he helped to revolutionize figure skating in the post–World War II years.

LUTZ JUMP

Invented in the 1930s by an otherwise obscure Italian skater named Tomas Lutz, this jump is one of only two (the other being the walley) that employs a clockwise rotation in the air. It requires a speedy, curving approach on the back outside edge of one skate, usually the right. You can spot a lutz coming because the skater's head is turned, looking over the opposite shoulder from the skating foot for a long-held moment. The takeoff is aided by a quick tap of the toe-pick of the free-leg skate. Following the clockwise rotation, in which the legs are held particularly close together in the air, the skater lands on the back outside edge of the opposite foot from that used for takeoff.

The double lutz began to be performed commonly by men in the mid-1930s. The first triple lutz

Effervescent Janet Lynn, five-time U.S. Ladies' Champion.
(Courtesy World Figure Skating Museum)

in competition was unveiled under dramatic circumstances in Prague at the 1962 World Championships. Canadian Donald Jackson was involved in a very tight contest for the Gold Medal with hometown favorite Karol Divin, who had already skated his free program and achieved very high marks. There had been some question as to whether Jackson should risk the jump, which he had only recently mastered, but with the closeness of the scores, it was essential to winning. He landed it cleanly, skated the rest of his program brilliantly, and took the Gold Medal.

The triple lutz is often a "money" jump for women because almost none of them can perform the triple axel, now crucial to male skaters. It was Nancy Kerrigan's big jump in competition, and one she performed with particular flair. When she missed it at the 1993 World Championships, where she was the favorite, she ended up in 5th place, but she nailed it at the 1994 Olympics.

Brian Boitano developed a spectacular variation on the lutz, which he began to perform in 1988, his Olympic Gold Medal year. During his triple lutz, while in rotation, he raises one arm high above his head in a move that in ballet is called an *arabesque en l'air*. It gives great elegance to the jump and is also exceedingly difficult because the raising of the arm can easily disrupt the rotational balance. He is the only person as of 1996 to have performed this variation, and in his honor it is known as the tano lutz, using the final syllables of his name.

LYNN, JANET *(b. 1953) Charismatic, extremely popular U.S. Champion.*

Born Janet Nowicki in Chicago, the future champion began to skate almost as soon as she could walk and took part in her first exhibition performance at the age of four in a group number at Chicago Stadium. By age seven, she was living away from home part of the year, staying with the slightly older skater Jada Steinke to be close to her coach Slavka Kohout, who worked out of Rockton, Illinois, but her close-knit family was never far away. She used her mother's maiden name Lynn instead of Nowicki, which was constantly being misspelled and mispronounced. Janet was always forthright about the name change; in her own mind her name was still Nowicki.

In 1964, at 11, she became the youngest girl to pass the rigorous eighth and final test administered by the USFSA, and two years later she was National Junior Ladies' Champion at Berkeley, California. The only skater to perform a triple salchow, which at the time had been mastered only by the world's top skaters, Lynn gave early evidence of a jumping ability that was to thrill audiences and impress judges for years to come.

Moving up to senior level, Lynn gained 3rd place in 1968 and vaulted into 1st place in 1969, bypassing her competition. That year she beat Canada's Karen Magnussen for the North American title but had disappointing results in the World Championships. Despite the absence of both Magnussen and Czechoslovakia's Hana Maskova due to injuries, Lynn was unable to do better than 5th place, falling behind Julie Holmes, in 4th, whom she had beaten for the national title. Gaby Seyfert of France took the Gold Medal.

The World Championships were to remain a problem for her. Although she continued to reign as U.S. Champion, something always seemed to go wrong at the World's. In 1970, Seyfert and Austria's Beatrix Schuba were again in 1st and 2nd place, while Holmes moved up to 3rd and Lynn dropped back to 6th. Part of the problem was an inconsistency in school figures, which meant that she always had to make up ground in the free-skating. Lynn made an effort to remedy this weakness by working with the great New York-based coach Pierre Brunet, who had previously had World Champions Carol Heiss and Donald Jackson under his tutelage. But in 1971 her free-skating went awry under the pressure and she rose only to 4th place, while Schuba took the Gold, Holmes the Silver and Magnussen the Bronze.

The year 1972 brought both World and Olympic challenges. Lynn beat Holmes for the national title for the fourth year in a row, and there were widespread predictions that she would finally take not only World but Olympic Gold, especially because of Schuba's weakness in free-skating. Schuba's lackluster performance at Lyon, France the previous year had even drawn boos, but she won the Gold anyway on her enormous lead in the figures.

The Olympics at Grenoble, France preceded the World's. Lynn did well in school figures placing 3rd, but once again Schuba's technical mastery in this discipline was very strong; with some improvement evident in her free-skating, she took the Gold Medal. Magnussen won the Silver and Lynn was left with the Bronze, an order of finish repeated at the World's in Calgary, Canada.

By this time, international-level disappointments had taken their toll, and Lynn nearly quit skating. But she had always had a very strong religious faith, and after considerable soul-searching, she continued, taking her fifth National title. With Schuba's retirement, only Magnussen seemed to stand in her way. In 1973, Lynn skated her best figures ever, taking 2nd in that discipline, but in the short program of required jumps and spins, which she should have aced, two falls landed her in 12th position. She came out on top in free-skating, but the terrible short program kept her from the Gold. A Silver Medal would mark the end of Lynn's amateur career.

Lynn's international-level travails had not dimmed her country's affection for her, however; her popularity was such that the Ice Follies offered her a three-year contract for an unheard of $1.5 million. She proved to be the kind of draw she was expected to be, putting the Ice Follies on a much firmer basis in its rivalry with the Ice Capades. In 1974, Janet Lynn finally took the top spot in a World competition, becoming the World Professional Champion.

LYONS, SHELBY *(b. 1981) U.S. Pairs medalist with Brian Wells (b. 1970).*

In 1994, Brian Wells, who had never won a U.S. medal, needed a new partner if he was to continue in Pairs skating. He traveled a total of 9,000 miles to skating rinks across the United States and found what he was looking for in 12-year-old Shelby Lyons. He persuaded her family to move from Oswego, New York to Colorado Springs, and the couple set about putting together an effective partnership, while Shelby continued with training as a solo skater as well.

These efforts paid off in 1996, when Lyons and Wells captured the U.S. Bronze Medal in Pairs, with a long program that contained the first side-by-side triple loops ever performed in competition by a U.S. pair. To cap their success, Shelby also became the Junior Ladies' Champion.

M

MCCALL, ROBERT *See* WILSON, TRACY.

MACDONALD, SANDY *(b. 1920) U.S. Ice Dance Champion.*

When 1938 U.S. Ice Dance Champions Harold Hartshorne and Nettie Prantel split up, Hartshorne immediately found a new partner in Sandy MacDonald. MacDonald proved an excellent match for the experienced Hartshorne, and the couple won the U.S. Gold in 1939, beating Prantel and her new partner Joseph Savage. In 1940, MacDonald and Hartshorne turned back another challenge by Prantel, now skating with George Boltres. MacDonald and Hartshorne won their third title in 1941, but in 1942 were beaten by Edith Whetstone and Alfred Richards, who had been the Bronze Medalists the previous year. With three Gold Medals and a Silver, Sandy MacDonald then retired from competition.

MACHADO, CATHERINE *(b. 1937) U.S. medalist and show skater.*

Cathy Machado had the unenviable task of competing against two of the U.S.'s most accomplished women skaters, Tenley Albright and Carol Heiss. In 1955 and 1956, when Albright and Heiss were the U.S. Gold and Silver Medalists as well as the two top Ladies' competitors in the world, Machado had to be content with winning two U.S. Bronze Medals. She was 10th in 1955 and 6th in 1956 in the World's and 8th at the 1956 Olympics. Although she was somewhat weak in school figures, Machado had her own style in free-skating and a charisma to go with it. It was clear that Heiss was going to continue as an amateur through the next Olympics; Albright, however, agreed to a limited schedule of appearances with the Ice Capades as a professional while she attended Harvard Medical School. That left an opening for a free-skater of audience appeal in the professional ranks, so Cathy Machado signed an Ice Capades contract that brought her fine success over a number of years.

MCKELLEN, GORDON *(b. 1953) U.S. Champion.*

An engaging, ever-smiling competitor, Gordie McKellen became the U.S. Bronze Medalist at the age of 18 in 1971. He repeated in that position the following year and then leapt to the Gold Medal in 1973, remaining U.S. Champion through 1975. It was a very strong period in international men's skating: Czechoslovakia's Ondrej Nepela, East Germany's Jan Hoffmann, Soviets Chetverukin, Kovalev and Volkov, and Canada's Toller Cranston were among the world's top skaters. McKellen never did win a World or Olympic medal, but he improved one place in the standings each year at the World Championships, from 9th in 1971 to 5th in

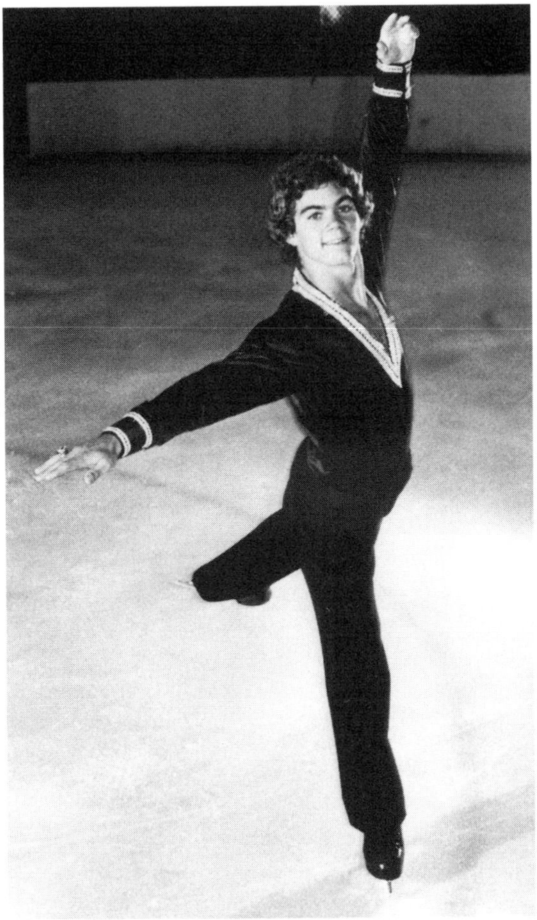

Popular three-time U.S. Champion Gordon McKellen. (Courtesy World Figure Skating Museum)

1975. Although not among the world's great skaters, McKellen was an extremely well-liked young man, as popular among skaters as he was with audiences.

MCKENZIE, SHARON *(b. 1937) U.S. Ice Dance Champion.*

With her partner Bert Wright, Sharon McKenzie skated to the U.S. Gold in Ice Dancing in 1957 without having won any previous medals. At World's, the couple took the Bronze Medal. Two other U.S. couples, Joan Zamboni/Roland Junso and Carmel Bodel/Edward Bodel, were 4th and 6th. That year's Silver Medalists, who would become U.S. Champions the following year, Andrée Anderson and Donald Jacoby did not compete at the 1957 World Championships, because the roster was based on the previous year's standings. In this highly competitive field, Sharon McKenzie and Edward Bodel opted to turn professional immediately, appearing with the Ice Capades for several years.

MCKINSTRY, JULI *(b. 1953) U.S. medalist.*

In 1973, Janet Lynn became U.S. Champion for the fifth time and then retired. In 2nd place was Dorothy Hamill, winning her first U.S. Ladies' medal and on the verge of becoming three-time national champion. Juli McKinstry took the Bronze Medal in 1973 and the next year would be 2nd to Hamill. At the World's, McKinstry was 9th in 1973 and 8th in 1974.

MCLACHLAN, WILLLIAM *See* FENTON, GERALDINE.

MCPHERSON, DONALD *(b. 1940) Canadian World Champion.*

Donald McPherson had been in the shadow of his compatriot Donald Jackson for a number of years before he leapt to the top in 1963. Jackson had been World Silver Medalist in 1959 and 1960, won the Olympic Bronze in 1960 and had become World Champion in 1962; McPherson had always been the runner-up in Canada and just behind the leaders at World competition. In 1963, he succeeded the now-professional Jackson by topping France's Alain Calmat, winner of two World Bronze Medals, and West Germany's upcoming Manfred Schnelldorfer for the World Gold. McPherson turned professional himself immediately afterward.

MADDEN, GRACE AND J. LESTER

(b. 1911, 1909) Sister-and-brother U.S. Pairs Champions.

Grace and J. Lester Madden were among the mainstays of U.S. figure skating during the 1930s. As a Pair, they won the U.S. Bronze Medal in 1931 and the Silver in 1933, were U.S. Champions in 1934 and won the Silver Medal three more times, in 1935, 1937 and 1938. They competed internationally only in 1936, having a bad outing that brought them 11th place at the 1936 Olympics, but they garnered a very respectable 6th at that year's World Championships. As a couple, the Maddens were Bronze Medalists in the original dance in 1933 and Silver Medalists in the same event in 1934 when separate medals were still awarded in two different dance events.

J. Lester Madden also competed in the Men's division, taking the Bronze in 1929 and four successive Silver Medals, behind champion Roger Turner in 1930–33; he concluded with a final Bronze Medal in 1935. Madden competed at the World Championships only twice, achieving 7th place in 1930 and 6th in 1932; he was 7th at the 1932 Olympics.

MAGER, MANUELA

See GROSS, MANUELA.

MAGNUSSEN, KAREN

(b. 1951) Canadian World Champion.

An athletic skater with big jumps but also a solid performer in school figures, Karen Magnussen was something of a nemisis for the U.S.'s Janet Lynn: Every time they met in competition, Lynn was the favorite, but in World and Olympic contests, Magnussen always came out ahead. She was as cool and collected as Lynn was nervous, and that quality paid off for her again and again.

In 1971, Magnussen took the World Bronze behind Austria's Beatrix Schuba and the U.S.'s Julie Holmes, while three-time U.S. Champion Lynn finished 4th. In 1972 the order of finish at both the Olympics and the World Championships was Schuba 1st, Magnussen 2nd and Lynn 3rd. In 1973, Lynn finally came up with a performance at the World Championships that was almost worthy of her talent, but Magnussen had never been better and became World Champion; Lynn took the Silver.

MAGUIRE, IRENE

(b. 1929) Versatile U.S. medalist.

With Frank Davenport, Irene Maguire took her first U.S. medal in 1948, a Bronze in Ice Dancing. She then changed partners, joining forces with Walter Muelhbronner to achieve a remarkable double accomplishment: the Silver Medal in both Ice Dancing and Pairs, in 1949 and 1950 behind the already established U.S. Champions Lois Waring and Walter Bainbridge in Ice Dancing and Karol and Peter Kennedy in Pairs. Although other U.S. skaters had competed in both disciplines before and others would in the future, few were as solid as Maguire and Muelhbronner in the two different forms.

MALMBERG, KATH

(b. 1956) U.S. medalist.

U.S. Bronze Medalist in both 1974 and 1975, Kath Malmberg also did well at the World Championships, taking 7th in 1974 and 5th in 1975. But with Wendy Burge besting her for the Silver in 1975 and Linda Fratianne showing enormous promise, Malmberg retired from skating in 1976 to concentrate on college.

MANDATORY DEDUCTIONS

In the short program for Men, Ladies and Pairs, every skater must perform certain jumps, spins and other moves that have been set in advance. If a skater fails to do any of these moves or does them badly (a two-footed landing, for example), the judges must make a deduction. Thus, if a combination jump is missed, 0.8 is automatically deducted, while a fault in its performance results in a deduction of 0.4–0.7 points. For a missed solo jump or a combination spin, the mandatory deduction is 0.6, with a fault being penalized 0.3–0.5.

MANLEY, ELIZABETH *(b. 1966)*
Canadian Olympic Silver Medalist.

A troubled career, plagued by physical and emotional problems, came to a glorious moment of fulfillment for Elizabeth Manley at the 1988 Olympic Games at Calgary. All the attention was on the duel for the Gold Medal between East Germany's Katarina Witt and Debi Thomas of the United States. Thomas had taken the 1986 World Gold, with Witt second, and then their places had been reversed in 1987. But at the 1988 Olympics in her home country, Elizabeth Manley gave the performance of her life in the long program, after placing third in the short program. Manley, who had been training eight hours a day the entire year leading up to the Olympics, was cheered throughout the long program by wildly enthusiastic Canadians in the audience. She ended up placing first in the long program, with Witt second and Thomas third, giving Manley the Silver Medal.

Elizabeth Manley went on to a long and successful professional career.

MASKOVA, HANNA *(b. 1946)*
Czechoslovakian World medalist.

Hanna Maskova was a steady all-round skater who had the misfortune to skate in the shadow of the great Peggy Fleming and East Germany's flashy Gabriele Seyfert. She did win World Bronze Medals in 1967 and 1968 as well as the Olympic Bronze in 1968. All three times the order of finish was Fleming, Seyfert and Maskova. Challenged by future World Champion Beatrix Schuba of Austria in 1968, she retired from competition.

MAY, MARCELLA *See* LOCHEAD, JAMES.

MAYER, RACHEL *(b. 1973) U.S. Ice Dance medalist with Peter Breen (b. 1969).*

Rachel Mayer and Peter Breen, Junior Champions in 1989, were the 1992 U.S. Silver Medalists in Ice Dancing behind April Sargent and Russ Witherby. In a period during which Ice Dancing was totally dominated by Soviet/Russian and European couples, they were able to finish only 15th at the 1992 World Championships and Olympics.

MEEKER, MARILYN *See* PIERCE, LARRY.

MEHL, KATHE *(b. 1924) U.S. Ice Dance medalist.*

In 1943, Kathe Mehl was taken as a new partner by Harold Hartshorne, who had won five U.S. Ice Dancing Championships with other partners. Mehl and Hartshorne took the Silver Medal in 1943. Mehl then changed partners and won the U.S. Gold Medal in 1945 with Robert Swenning, under her new married name of Kathe Williams.

MENO, JENNI *See* SAND, TODD.

MEN'S COMPETITIONS

At its beginning in the 1880s, as with so many other sports, figure skating featured a competition for men only, in a number of European countries, usually overseen by clubs that had originally been formed to sponsor and regulate speed-skating contests. Such basic elements as the figure-eight variations known as the bracket and the counter had first been laid down by H.E. Vandervell in England in 1880–81, and skaters were already experimenting with simple jumps and spins.

It may be difficult for young people to understand why the variations on the figure eight, known as the school figures, counted for 60 percent of the score at figure-skating competitions until the 1970s. The fact is that school figures had been fully laid out by the beginning of the 20th century, while the triple jumps that are now central to competition did not begin to be mastered until the middle of the century (Dick Button performing the first triple, a loop jump, at the 1952 Olympics) with the triple axel coming into play as late as 1976. Moreover, school figures were basic to learning the control of the two edges of the hollowed-out figure-skate blade and remain so to this day.

In 1892, the International Skating Union was formed to create universal rules for both speed and figure skating, with each discipline governed by separate committees. It was under the sponsorship of the ISU that the first World Championships for figure skating were held in 1896 in St. Petersburg, Russia, an event won by Germany's Gilbert Fuchs. Constrained by his medical practice, Fuchs entered the competition only three more times, winning a Bronze Medal in 1898, a Silver in 1901 and, most remarkably, a second Gold Medal in 1908.

That figure skating had become a truly international sport in Europe was demonstrated by the fact that during the first decade of competition, the events were held in Russia, Sweden, England and Switzerland. Competition sites branched out to Germany, Czechoslovakia, Austria and Finland before the First World War. The nationalities of medalists during the World Championships' first decade included competitors from Germany, Sweden, Russia, Norway, Austria and Great Britain. The British medalist was a woman, Madge Syers, who—to everyone's shock except her own—won the Silver Medal in 1902, an event that led to the creation of a Ladies' competition in 1906.

The two dominant skaters in the Men's competition prior to the beginning of the First World War were, aside from Fuchs, Austria's Gustav Hugel, who won three Gold Medals, Sweden's Ulrich Salchow, who won ten, and Austria's Fritz Kachler, who took two Golds and a Silver just before the war. Kachler won another Gold in 1923, but the three dominant skaters between the wars were Sweden's Gilles Grafstrom, who won each time he entered, in 1922, 1924 and 1929; Austria's Willy Boeckl, winner of four successive Gold Medals from 1925 to 1928; and his countryman Karl Schafer, winner of seven consecutive Golds from 1930 to 1936. Still another Austrian, Felix Kaspar, won in 1937 and 1938, and Great Britain's Graham Sharp took the final Gold before World War II, in 1939.

Figure skating became popular in the United States later than in Europe, with the first national championships for Men, Ladies and Pairs held in 1914. No American man competed in the World Championships until 1928, when Roger Turner finished 5th. Turner won the Silver Medal in 1930 and 1931. After World War II, a new generation of young U.S. skaters took charge of the World Championships with a vengeance, starting with Dick Button's five-year reign from 1948 to 1952 (he had been the Silver Medalist behind Switzerland's Hans Gerschwiler in 1947), followed by Hayes Alan Jenkins, winner of four successive World Championships, and his younger brother David, who won the next three. All three of these men also won the Olympic Gold Medal, Button doing it twice. Even more remarkable, U.S. male skaters swept the medal roster in 1952, 1955 and 1956 at the World Championships as well as at the 1956 Olympics. From 1947 to 1959, they collected 26 of a possible 42 World and Olympic Medals.

After that extraordinary period, no one country dominated the Men's division in the World Championships in the same way, although the only man to win four consecutive World Championships was the U.S.'s Scott Hamilton (Canada's Kurt Browning won four, but they were not consecutive). The bravura jumps and innovative style that U.S. male skaters introduced following World War II are now the standard everywhere. Over the past quarter century, there have been so many accomplished male skaters that their number inevitably includes many who won only one or two Gold Medals, including Jan Hoffmann of East Germany, Vladimir Kovalev of the Soviet Union, and Brian Orser of Canada. Indeed, the level of competition has been so high that the two most influential male skaters, Great Britain's John Curry and the U.S.'s Brian Boitano, despite winning the Olympic Gold Medal, took only one

World Gold in Curry's case and two in Boitano's. A third major figure, Britain's Robin Cousins, never won a World Championship, although he did win the Olympic Gold.

MEREDITH, GERTRUDE *See* SAVAGE, JOSEPH.

MERO, JOSEPH *See* KEELEY, KATY.

MERRILL, GRETCHEN *(b. 1925)*

Dominant U.S. Champion.

Gretchen Merrill, a protégée and pupil of nine-time U.S. Champion Maribel Vinson, took her first U.S. Ladies' medal in 1941, winning the Silver behind Jane Vaughn. The following year brought the same result, but Merrill ascended to the national title in 1943 and went on to win it five more times in succession. There were of course no World Championships during the war years, but when they resumed in 1947, Merrill made a great impression in Europe. She was at the time on the Best Dressed List of American Sportswomen, and her glamour garnered much attention in the European press. She was already a little past her peak as a skater, however, and Canada's Barbara Ann Scott took the World Gold Medal, with Great Britain's Daphne Walker in 2nd place, Merrill having to content herself with the Bronze. In 1948, although she retained her U.S. title, she was only 8th at the Olympics and did not compete in the World Championships.

Yvonne Sherman, who was runner-up to Merrill in the 1948 U.S. Championships, did better than Merrill at the Olympics, taking 6th and repeating that position at the World Championships. It was clear that Sherman was very likely to beat Merrill for the U.S. title the following year, but Merrill did not take the easy way out and retire as reigning champion. A true sportswoman, she admitted to the press that she was likely to be beaten but said that that was the way it should be—the upcoming champion should have the opportunity to win her crown in competition and not have it pass to her by default. Indeed, in 1949, Yvonne Sherman beat Gretchen Merrill for the U.S. Gold Medal, and Merrill then retired with a grace not often seen in any sport.

MEYER, BROR *(b. 1886) Legendary Swedish-born teacher and coach.*

Bror Meyer won only one World medal—the Bronze in 1906—but in his own way was as influential as Swedish innovator Ulrich Salchow, who won every World Championship but one (in which he did not compete) from 1901 to 1911. Meyer's influence was felt as teacher and coach at St. Moritz, Switzerland and Manchester, England prior to World War I, in Canada and the United States during the war years and then back in Europe for the next 30-odd years.

Only a few great skaters have been good teachers—Great Britain's Cecilia Colledge (who taught in America) and nine-time U.S. Champion Maribel Vinson were the most notable. The finest teachers are usually second-, even third-rank skaters during their amateur careers, but they have the patience to train others step by step and the gift of inspiring students to reach heights they themselves could not have achieved.

Meyer was such a man. He possessed the added ability to encourage the development of new kinds of jumps, spins and footwork. His work in North America during the First World War, together with that of Irving Brokaw, is credited with the U.S. talent that exploded during the 1920s and led to the United States becoming the world's foremost figure-skating power.

MICHELSON, RHODA L. *(b. 1942, d. 1961) U.S. medalist.*

When Barbara Roles, U.S. Silver Medalist the previous year, was unable to compete in 1961, Rhoda Michelson was able to win the U.S. Bronze Medal. But what initially seemed like good fortune for

Michelson turned out to have a tragic ending: She was killed in a plane crash at Brussels along with the rest of the U.S. World team.

MILEY, JEANNE *(b. 1971) U.S. Ice Dance medalist with Michael Verlich (b. 1970).*

U.S. Ice Dancing has been the weakest area of figure skating during the 1990s, with no team establishing a clear dominance or managing to create a strong presence in World competition since 1990. Jeanne Miley and Michael Verlich were among several couples to show promise, winning the U.S. Bronze in 1991, but they proved unable to develop further.

MILITANO, MARK AND MELISSA *(b. 1949, 1951) U.S. Pair Champions.*

The brother-and-sister Pair team of Mark and Melissa Militano gained national notice by taking the U.S. Bronze Medal in 1969, the final year of Cynthia and Ronald Kauffman's four-year reign as national champions. The Silver Medalists were JoJo Starbuck and Ken Shelley, who would take over as national champions beginning in 1970. For each of the next three years, Starbuck and Shelley took the top spot, while the Militanos were 2nd. With Starbuck and Shelley turning professional after 1972, the Militanos became national champions in 1973. Gold Medal in hand, Mark retired, but Melissa would go on to further triumphs.

She formed a new team with Johnny Johns, 1993 U.S. Ice Dancing Champion with Mary Campbell as well as Pairs Bronze Medalist with Emily Benenson. The new team of Militano and Johns were Pairs Champions in 1974 and repeated in 1975. In 2nd place both years were Tai Babilonia and Randy Gardner. Militano and Johns did respectably at the World's, taking 8th and then 6th (she and her brother had been 8th, 8th, 6th, 9th and 8th).

They retired after the 1975 competitions but not before firmly imprinting their names on Pairs-skating history by performing the first successful throw triple loop in Pairs competition, which added a new measure of difficulty and excitement to their discipline.

MILLER, ANNE AND HARVEY ("SKIP") *(b. 1951, 1950) Sister-and-brother U.S. Ice Dance medalists.*

Anne and Skip Miller won the U.S. Silver Medal in Ice Dancing five successive times, from 1970 to 1974. The first three years, they were beaten by Judy Schwomeyer and James Sladky, who went on to take World Silver or Bronze Medals each of those years, while the Millers placed 10th, 9th and 7th at the World's. In 1973, following the retirement from competition of Schwomeyer and Sladky, Mary Campbell and Johnny Johns, who had taken the U.S. Bronze the previous two years, vaulted over the Millers to take the Gold. Campbell and Johns took 7th at the World's, while the Millers fell back to 10th. They took their final U.S. Silver in 1975 and were 13th at the World's as the new U.S. Champions, Colleen O'Connor and Jim Millns, placed 7th.

Anne and Skip Miller were a lively dance team who were always popular with audiences, but their pop-oriented style was not as much admired by judges, particularly in international competition.

MILLER, LEA ANN *See* FAUVER, WILLIAM.

MILLNS, JIM *See* O'CONNOR, COLLEEN.

MINENKOV, ANDREI *See* MOISEEVA, IRINA.

MIRROR JUMPS

This term is used to describe any jump performed separately by the members of a Pair when the jump is done in opposite directions, with one skater rotating in the air to the left and the other to the right. This requires that each skater take off from a different foot. Mirror jumps are much less often seen than shadow jumps, in which the partners rotate in the same direction. When mirror jumps are performed, the skaters land at a considerably greater distance from one another, which requires the use of speed and additional linking choreography to bring them back together.

MISHKUTENOK, NATALIA *(b. 1971)*

World and Olympic Pairs Champion with ARTUR DMITRIEV*(b. 1968), from the Soviet Union.*

Natalia Mishkutenok and Artur Dmitriev were the World Bronze Medalists in Pairs in 1990 behind fellow Soviets Ekaterina Gordeeva and Sergei Grinkov, and Canada's Isabelle Brasseur and Lloyd Eisler. Gordeeva and Grinkov turned professional in 1991, and Mishkutenok and Dmitriev took their place as World Champions, beating Brasseur and Eisler and the U.S.'s Todd Sand and his first partner, Natasha Kuchiki. They repeated as World Champions in 1992 over Czechoslovakia's Radka Kovarikova and Rene Novotny and Brasseur and Eisler. They also became Olympic Champions in 1992 over their fellow Russian skaters Elena Bechke and Denis Petrov and over Brasseur and Eisler.

Mishkutenok and Dmitriev then skated as professionals but turned around and had themselves reinstated as amateurs for the 1994 Olympics. Gordeeva and Grinkov had done the same, and the two Russian couples finished 1st and 2nd, with Gordeeva and Grinkov taking the Gold. Mishkutenok and Dmitriev actually skated a technically more difficult long program, but the judges preferred the classicism of Gordeeva and Grinkov over the jazzier performance of Mishkutenok and Dmitriev. Brasseur and Eisler were the Olympic Bronze Medalists. Mishkutenok then retired and, in 1995, Dmitriev took a new partner, Oksana Kazakova.

MITCHELL, JOAN *See* SPECHT, BOBBY.

MITCHELL, MARK *(b. 1968) U.S. medalist.*

A native of Connecticut, Mark Mitchell began to skate at the age of six and became National Junior Champion in 1986. A dogged skater who kept at the sport despite several injuries over the years he won the U.S. Bronze Medal in 1990 and 1992 and the Silver Medal behind Scott Davis is 1993. He did not attend the 1992 Olympics because a place on the Olympic team was reserved for Todd Eldredge, who had been U.S. Champion the two previous years but was still recovering from an injury at

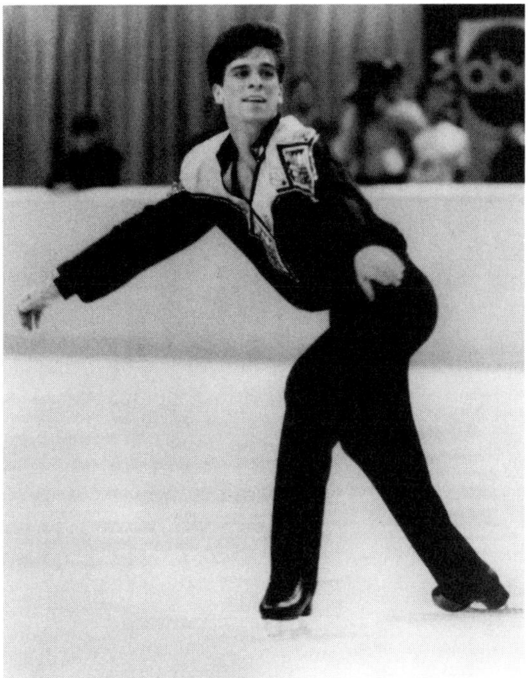

Mark Mitchell won several U.S. medals in the early 1990s.

(Courtesy Michael Rosenberg)

championships time. The 1992 U.S. Champion, Christopher Bowman, and Silver Medalist Paul Wylie made up the rest of the Olympic team, with Wylie capturing the Olympic Silver. Wylie had said he would not attend the World Championships to make room for Mitchell on the team; Mark placed 5th at that competition, moving up to 4th in 1993. In 1994, Mitchell was 4th in the United States behind Scott Davis, the reinstated Brian Boitano and Aren Nielsen.

MOHAWK

A mohawk is an abrupt change of direction on a single skate from, say, a right forward inside edge to a back outside edge. It does not have the half-circle approach and conclusion that distinguish a three-turn but is done in a straight line, with the hips and arms being used to propel the quick turn from forward to backward skating, or vice versa. It is used while performing footwork and sometimes as a lead into a jump.

MOISEEVA, IRINA *(b. 1955) Soviet World Champion Ice Dancer with Andrei Minenkov (b. 1955).*

When five-time World Champion ice dancers Ludmila Pakhomova and Aleksandr Gorskov took a year off from competition in 1975, the great depth of Soviet Ice Dancing was demonstrated as the previous year's 3rd-place Soviet national competitors claimed the World Championship for themselves: Irina Moiseeva and Andrei Minenkov were a livelier and less classically oriented team, but they had the usual degree of Soviet technical prowess.

Pakhomova and Gorskov returned for the 1976 Olympic year, pushing Moiseeva and Minenkov back into 2nd place in both contests (with the U.S.'s Colleen O'Connor and Jim Millns in 3rd at both competitions). Pakhomova and Gorskov then retired, and Moiseeva and Minenkov once again seized the World crown. To everyone's surprise, they did so performing their final free dance to a medley from *West Side Story*, the first time Soviet skaters had ever used American music. But it seemed perfectly appropriate that they should break the mold because the couple were the most open and friendly Soviet skaters anyone could remember, to the degree that they were affectionately called Min and Mo by Western European and North American skaters.

Ice Dancing reached an apex during the coming years, and Moiseeva and Minenkov found themselves winning the Silver in 1978 and 1981 and the Bronze in 1979, 1980 and 1982. The World Champions during those years were still another Soviet couple, Natalia Linichuk and Gennadi Karponosov (1978–79), the Hungarians Krisztina Regoeczy and Andras Sallay (1980) and Great Britain's Jayne Torvill and Christopher Dean (1981–82). But Moiseeva and Minenkov were always in the medal hunt. No Soviet skaters were as well liked until Viktor Petrenko came on the scene in late 1980s.

MONIOTTE, SOPHIE *(b. 1971) French Ice Dance World Medalist with Pascal Lavanchy (b. 1970).*

For years, Sophie Moniotte and Pascal Lavanchy skated in the shadow of Isabelle and Paul Duchesnay, the daring Canadian ice dancers who, with dual citizenship, chose to compete under the flag of France. Nevertheless, Maniotte and Lavanchy's elegance on the ice often had them in the top five couples at World and Olympic competition. They were devoted to one another as partners; Lavanchy did not seek a new partner even when Maniotte was unable to skate for more than a year because of a major leg injury and it was questionable whether she would ever compete again. Their dedication to one another and the sport was finally rewarded in 1995 when they won the World Bronze Medal behind Russia's Oksana Grischuk and Evgeny Platov and Finland's equally persevering Susanna Rahkamo and Petri Kokko.

MOORE, TOM *(b. 1938) U.S. medalist.*

Tom Moore won the U.S. Bronze Medal in both 1957 and 1958. David Jenkins was the Gold Medalist and Tim Brown the Silver in both of those years, and they also went on to place 1st and 2nd at the World's. Tom Moore was 5th at the 1957 World's, but plagued by a nagging leg injury, he placed 12th in 1958 and retired after that competition.

MORGENSTERN, SONYA *(b. 1951) East German.*

Although the East German skater never won a medal in World competition because she was weak in school figures, Sonya Morgenstern was a fine free-skater and holds the honor of being the first woman to complete a triple jump in competition. At the 1972 World Championships in Long Beach, California she entered the history books with her successful attempt at a triple salchow, which has become the most important jump in the repertoire of world-class women skaters.

MORROW, SUZANNE *(b. 1926) Canadian World and Olympic Pairs medalist with Wallace Diestelmeyer (b. 1925).*

In 1948, the second postwar World Championships and the first Olympics since 1936 took place at Davos, Switzerland. The Pairs competition that year was particularly intense (the U.S.'s Dick Button and Canada's Barbara Ann Scott clearly dominated the Men's and Ladies' divisions). Canadian Champions Suzanne Morrow and Wally Diestelmeyer were the Bronze Medalists at both competitions; they were beaten for the Silver both times by Andrea Kekesy and Ede Kiraly of Hungary. Both couples were noted for their tremendous speed, but the judges gave the Gold Medals to Belgium's Micheline Lannoy and Pierre Baugniet.

MUCKELT, ETHEL *(b. 1903) British Olympic medalist.*

At the first official Winter Olympic Games in Chamonix, France in 1924, British Champion Ethel Muckelt took the Bronze Medal behind Austrian skater Herma Plank-Szabo and the U.S.'s Beatrix Loughran. Also among the seven women competing was a tiny 12-year-old from Norway, Sonja Henie, who would place 5th but would go on to win the next three Olympics.

MUEHLBRONNER, WALTER *See* MAGUIRE, IRENE.

MUNSTOCK, GRACE *(b. 1905) U.S. Pairs medalist with Joel Liberman (b. 1904).*

During the nine-year reign of Theresa Blanchard and Nathaniel Niles as U.S. Pairs Champions, which began in 1918, Grace Munstock and Joel Liberman gave them a serious challenge in 1924, taking the Silver Medal. They then won the Bronze Medal in 1925 and 1926.

MURRAY, SUNA *(b. 1955) U.S. medalist.*

Suna Murray took the U.S. Bronze Medal behind Janet Lynn and Julie Holmes in both 1971 and 1972. She was 10th at the World's in 1971 and 12th at the 1972 Olympics. Her best international success occurred at the 1972 World's when she moved up to 8th place.

MUSIC

Music has been an integral part of free-skating since the U.S. "father" of modern figure skating, Jackson Haines, wowed the citizens of Vienna, Austria by skating to Strauss waltzes in 1866. In the early years of the World Championships, the city where the competition was held assembled a band or small orchestra to play the music chosen by the competitors, who would bring sheet music with them. Without much time for rehearsal, the results were often ragged, and the tempos might not be what the skater wanted. In 1911, reigning World Champion Lily Kronberger of Hungary, whose parents were wealthy landowners, astonished the skating community by bringing her own brass band with her to Vienna from Hungary.

Recorded music was always used after World War I, which greatly increased the variety of usable compositions. There are some limitations embedded in the rules, however. Vocal music cannot be used in amateur competition, although skaters often choose it for their exhibition programs. A number of restrictions apply to ice dancers: In the compulsory dances that form the competition's first part, all Ice Dance couples perform their technical displays to the same music, chosen by the International Skating Union's Ice Dance committee. The set pattern must be performed to a particular kind of music—a waltz one year, a rhumba the next—but the skaters may select any composition that adheres to the chosen musical form.

Considerable freedom exists for the free dance, although the rules state that the choice must be a composition that could be performed off the ice on a dance floor. This can cause problems. Although Great Britain's Jayne Torvill and Christopher Dean were able to get away with their daring choice of Ravel's rhythmically insistent *Bolero* at their triumphant 1984 Olympic performance, some judges marked down the U.S.'s Judy Blumberg and Michael Seibert, costing them the Bronze Medal at the same competition, for skating to Rimsky-Korsakov's *Schéhérezade,* even though both couple's choices had been officially approved.

Even in solo skating, where the latitude is much broader, a skater's choice of music can help or hinder the chance of attaining high artistic marks. Music appreciation is subjective: If a judge dislikes a particular piece or kind of music, he or she is likely to give slightly lower marks, even though such personal prejudice should not be allowed to affect the scores. Beyond that, it is a matter of how well a skater uses the music that has been chosen: Does the music suit the skater's style? Does it offer sufficiently varied tempos to show off the skater's mastery of both athletic and lyrical elements? Does the skater make the most of the possibilities inherent in the piece of music, using choreography that expresses it fully?

Although there have been champion skaters in the past who have had "tin ears" and done surprisingly little with the musical aspects of figure skating, it has become increasingly imperative that skaters be musically inclined. Because the tie-breaking score is the artistic rather than the technical one, the more musical skater has a built-in advantage. It is the difference—only one-tenth of a point in each case—that gave the Olympic Gold Medal to Robin Cousins over Jan Hoffmann in 1980 and Oksana Baiul over Nancy Kerrigan in 1994. It's not that Hoffmann and Kerrigan lacked musicality, but rather that Cousins and Baiul have exceptional ability when it comes to interpreting a musical score.

The ability to draw the most out of a musical score has both subtle and dramatic elements. A slight turn of the head or wrist at the right moment, when put together with many other similar subtleties, can collectively impart a sense of grace and rhythm that is almost subliminal and yet clearly "felt" by both judges and spectators. At the other end of the spectrum, to be able to land a triple axel at the precise moment that the cymbals crash on the soundtrack gives a sense of excitement that is immediately palpable to anyone watching.

Some musical scores are chosen again and again by skaters because they simply work extremely well and are beloved by audiences. Various selections from Bizet's opera *Carmen* are commonly used by both women and men, the women choosing the Habanera and men the Toreador march. Medleys of songs by pop music stars—without the vocals for amateur competition—are often chosen, with the Beatles, Neil Diamond and Stevie Wonder among the favorites.

Broadway music and the movie scores are heard at every competition. In the former category, the specially arranged score from *Mack and Mabel* provided Torvill and Dean with one of their greatest triumphs, while France's Philippe Candeloro had a great success with the score from *The Godfather*, using it for both his short and long program in 1994 and acting it to the hilt.

Some skaters try to use music native to the country where the competition is taking place in order to enhance audience response, for example, a Russian Pair skating to Leonard Bernstein's *West Side Story* in the United States, or an American woman using Offenbach's *Gaîté Parisienne* in France. But finally, it's not the music itself but what the skater does with it that counts.

N

NAGY, LAZLO AND MARIANNE

(b. 1927, 1929) Hungarian brother-and-sister World and Olympic Pairs medalists.

The first half of the 1950s was an exciting period in Pairs skating with so many top teams that no one couple managed to dominate for more than a year or two at a time. Among the stellar teams of the period were three brother-and-sister teams: the Kennedys of the United States, the Falks of East Germany and the Nicks of Great Britain, all of whom won World Championships, along with Canada's Frances Dafoe and Norris Bowden and Austria's Elizabeth Schwartz and Kurt Oppelt, all winning between 1950 and 1956. After this, Canada's Barbara and Robert Paul Wagner reigned for four straight years.

A fourth brother-and-sister team, Hungary's Lazlo and Marianne Nagy, never quite challenged for the top spot, but they were often on the medal podium. They took World Bronze Medals in 1950, 1953 and 1955 and accomplished the considerable feat in this very competitive period of also taking the Olympic Bronze Medal in both 1952 and 1956.

NAUMOV, VADIM

See SHISHKOVA, EVGENIA.

NELSON, DOROTHYANN

See KOLLEN, PIETER.

NELSON, FRANKLIN

See ARNOLD, SIDNEY.

NELSON, JULIUS

(b. 1904) U.S. medalist.

Julius Nelson was the U.S. Bronze Medalist in 1923, behind four-time winner Sherwin Badger and Chris Christensen, who would become champion in 1926.

NEPELA, ONDREJ

(1951–89) Czech World and Olympic Champion.

There was a large contingent of exceptionally young skaters, especially on the U.S. team, at the 1964 Olympics in Innsbruck, Austria. Because of the deaths of the U.S. medalists three years before, there were five U.S. skaters who had not yet turned 16, including Peggy Fleming and Scotty Allen, who won the Bronze Medal while still two days shy of his 15th birthday. But the youngest skater of all was not an American but a 13-year-old Czechoslovakian, Ondrej Nepela, his country's Silver Medalist behind Karol Divin.

Small and slender, Nepela finished a distant 15th, but he would be back for two more Olympics in the years to come. In 1968, he moved up to 5th place, and the following year, at 18, he became the World Silver Medalist at Colorado Springs, behind Tim Wood of the United States. In 1970, he was again 2nd to Wood at Ljubljana, Yugoslavia and in 1971 became the first man from Czechoslovakia to become Champion of the World. In 1972 he was both World and Olympic Gold Medalist and again took the World title in 1973.

Nepela was a whiz at school figures, which always gave him an initial advantage, but despite his slim frame, he was surprisingly strong and was noted for the height he achieved in his jumps. Also one of the least nervous skaters of his time, he wasn't nervous at his first Olympics at the age of 13, and he remained coolly collected when he won it all eight years later.

NICKS, JENNIFER AND JOHN

(b. 1932, 1930) British sister-and-brother World Pairs Champions.

In the 1950 World Pairs Championships, all three medalists were sister-and-brother teams. The Gold Medalists were the U.S.'s Karol and Peter Kennedy, Great Britain's Jennifer and John Nicks were the Silver Medalists and the Bronze went to the Hungarians Marianne and Lazlo Nagy. In 1951, both the Kennedys and the Nicks were pushed back a place as the German team of Ria and Paul Falk rocketed to the top, another sister/brother sweep. These standings were repeated in 1952, but the Nicks faltered slightly at that year's Olympics, and the Nagys won the Bronze there.

With both the Falks and the Kennedys turning professional, the Nicks continued to compete for an additional year, which paid off as they became World Champions over Canada's Francis Dafoe and Norris Bowden with the Nagys again Bronze Medalists. The Nicks thus became the first Britons to hold the World title in Pairs since Phyllis and James Johnson in 1912. There have been no British World Pairs medalists since the Nicks.

John Nicks, however, has had a continuing influence on Pairs skating: He immigrated to the United States and became a highly acclaimed coach in the Los Angeles area. As they took the Gold Medal in 1979, his pupils Tai Babilonia and Randy Gardner became the first from the United States since the Kennedys to win the World Championships. John Nicks also coached 1994–95 U.S. Champions and 1995 World Bronze Medalists Todd Sand and Jenni Menno.

NIELSEN, AREN *(b. 1968) U.S. medalist.*

A native of Kansas City, Missouri, Aren Nielsen was runner-up for the National Junior title in 1988 and then moved to the senior level, where he remained until he attained 4th place in 1993. The slight 5'4" skater always had fine artistic marks, but competition nerves often undid him, causing falls on crucial jumps and bringing down his technical scores. In 1994 he was the U.S. Bronze Medalist behind Scott Davis and Brian Boitano. Only two places were open on the Olympic team, but Boitano did not compete at the World Championships; Nielson competed in his stead, placing 13th.

NIGHTINGALE, JOHN *See* JANET GERHAUSEN.

NILES, NATHANIEL *(b. 1886) U.S. Men's and Pairs Champion.*

Along with his Pairs partner Theresa Weld Blanchard, Nathaniel Niles was a preeminent figure in the first two decades of U.S. competitive skating. At the first U.S. Championships in 1914, Bronze Medalist Niles was also the Silver Medalist with the then Theresa Weld in Pairs; at the second competition in 1918, he was U.S. Champion in both Men's and Pairs. Niles won the Men's Gold Medal twice more, in 1925 and 1927, and was Silver Medalist behind Sherwin Badger in 1920–23 and again in 1924 was runner-up to Chris Christensen in 1926.

At the same time, he and Theresa Weld Blanchard (she married in 1921) were the U.S. Pairs Champions without a break from 1919 through 1927 and Silver Medalists behind Maribel Vinson and Thornton Coolidge in 1928 and 1929.

Niles competed internationally only a few times, as was generally the case with U.S. skaters before the late 1920s. He was 6th in the Men's competition at the 1920 Olympics and again in 1924; competing for fun in 1928, he was 15th. In Pairs, Niles and Blanchard were 4th in 1920, 5th in 1924 and 9th in 1928. At the World's, he competed only once in the Men's division, finishing 10th in 1928, but he and Blanchard were 7th in Pairs in 1928, 6th in 1930 and 8th in 1932.

In addition, he and Blanchard competed often in the old format two-dance competitions, starting in 1914 when they won the Gold Medal in the waltz competition. Over the years they won five more Ice Dance Gold Medals, five Silvers and two Bronzes; the last was won in 1932, 18 years after their first Gold.

Nathaniel Niles became a competition judge as well as the long-term president of the U.S. Figure Skating Association. He was elected to the U.S. Figure Skating Hall of Fame in 1978.

NINGEL, FRANZ *(b. 1936) West German World Pairs medalist.*

As the first partner of Marika Kilius, Franz Ningel became the World and Olympic Bronze Medalist in 1956. The following year the couple won the World Silver behind new champions, Barbara Wagner and Robert Paul of Canada. Ningel then retired, while Marika took Hans Jurgen Baumler as a new partner. Ningel returned briefly to competition, however, winning the World Bronze with Margaret Gobl in 1962.

NOACH, GUNTHER *See* KOCH, INGE.

NOFFKE, WALTER *See* SCHUBACH, DORIS.

NOREN, SVEA *(b. 1895) Swedish World medalist.*

Svea Noren won the World Bronze Medal in 1913 behind Hungary's Opika von Horvath and Great Britain's Phyllis Johnson. Her next medal came in 1920, when figure skating was once again included in the Summer Olympics. Here Noren won the Silver Medal behind her teammate Magda Julin-Mauroy, just edging the U.S.'s Theresa Weld. When the World Championships resumed for the first time since 1914 at Stockholm in 1922, the home-country skater was the Silver Medalist behind Austria's Herma Plank-Szabo. In 1923, Noren took a final medal, the Bronze behind Plank-Szabo and another Austrian, Gisela Reichmann.

NOVICE CHAMPIONSHIPS

The second level of competition for young skaters, Novice Championships are held regionally around the United States (as is also the case in other countries). The regional Gold and Silver Medalists compete for the National Novice titles in their respective divisions. National Novice Gold Medalists move up to the Junior Championships, provided they have passed the series of tests that are required for entry into Juniors. Even those who do not win medals at the Novice level may eventually move up after passing the Junior tests. But there is a good deal of attrition at the Novice level, as young skaters realize that they do not have the talent necessary to success.

O

O'CONNOR, COLLEEN *(b. 1953)*

U.S. Ice Dance Champion with Jim Millns (b. 1949).

The first U.S. Ice Dancing medal won by Colleen O'Connor and Jim Millns was the Gold in 1974. In 4th place the previous year, they leaped over Silver Medalists Anne and Skip Miller, who again finished 2nd. At the World's, they placed a respectable 7th; they might well have gained a higher standing, but international Ice Dancing judges are notorious for being less than generous with couples they are seeing for the first time.

Repeating as U.S. Champions in 1975, O'Connor and Millns showed their true quality in capturing the World Silver Medal behind the Soviet Union's Irina Moiseeva and Andrei Minenkov. Both couples benefited by the absence that year of five-time World Champions Ludmila Pakhomova and Aleksandr Gorskov. When this premier Soviet couple returned in 1976 for the first Olympics at which Ice Dancing was officially contested, they pushed the other Soviet couple and the U.S. couple back one place to Silver and Bronze, a ranking that also held true at the World Championships. But even Bronze Medals were a signal accomplishment in this rarefied company, and O'Connor and Millns then turned professional with a sense of great achievement.

Colleen O'Connor and Jim Millns, America's only Olympic Ice Dance medalists.
(Courtesy World Figure Skating Museum)

OLD SMOOTHIES *Mature Ice Dance team of Irma Thomas and Orrin Markhus, whose ages were never revealed; starred in Ice Capades.*

For 20 years from the mid-1940s into the 1960s, Irma Thomas and Orrin Markhus were hugely popular stalwarts of the Ice Capades. Known as the Old Smoothies, they always skated a stellar solo number and participated in the central story ice ballet that was mounted each year, playing roles such as the parents of Prince Charming in Cinderella.

Their solo act was fundamentally the same each year, although the music and costumes changed. Portly, bald-headed Orrin Markhus, in an elegant tailcoat, glided around the ice primarily to waltz music with the slender Irma Thomas, whose evening dresses revealed only her skates. They performed no special tricks but, followed by a spotlight, they gave a sense of consummate grace and ease. The high point of their act, which always brought huge, affectionate applause, occurred when Irma raised the handkerchief that was always present in her right hand and gently mopped Orrin's glistening brow. The Old Smoothies were a shining example of how much can be achieved with a very simple performance done with an absolute mastery of style.

OLSON, MADELON *(b. 1926) U.S. medalist.*

Madelon Olson won the U.S. Ladies' Bronze Medal in 1945 and 1946 behind Gretchen Merrill and Yvonne C. Sherman both times. Due to the suspension of the World Championships during World War II, she did not get a chance to test her talent in the international arena.

OLYMPIC COMPETITION *See* WINTER OLYMPICS.

O'NEILL, CLAIRE *(b. 1938) U.S. Ice Dance medalist with John Bejshak (b. 1937).*

Claire O'Neill and John Bejshak won the U.S. Silver Medal in Ice Dancing in 1958 as Andrée Anderson and Donald Jacoby took the first of two national titles. They were 8th at the World Championships that year, where Anderson and Jacoby took the Bronze Medal.

OPPEGARD, PETER *See* WATSON, JILL.

OPPELT, KURT *See* SCHWARTZ, ELIZABETH.

ORGANISTA, OLGA *(b. 1909) Hungarian World Pairs medalist with Sandor Szalay (b. 1908).*

Olga Organista and Sandor Szalay took the World Bronze Medal while they were Hungarian Champions in 1929 behind Lilly Scholz/Otto Kaiser and Melitta Brunner/Ludwig Wrede, the two Austrian teams. In 1931, they were the Silver Medalists behind Emilie Rotter and Laszlo Szollas, who had also displaced them as Hungarian Champions.

ORMACA, CAROLE *(b. 1936) U.S. Pairs Champion with Robin Greiner (b. 1932).*

Without winning a previous medal, Carole Ormaca and Robin Greiner became U.S. Pairs Champions in 1953; they retained the title through 1956. Ormaca and Greiner maintained a steady 4th place at the World Championships from 1953 to 1956 and were 5th at the 1956 Olympics. They were extremely reliable skaters, lacking only that extra dash of brilliance that wins World medals.

ORMSBY, KENNETH *See* DOAN, PAULETTE.

ORSER, BRIAN *(b. 1961) Canadian World Champion.*

Brian Orser was Canadian Men's Champion for nine successive years from 1980 to 1988, a reign unequaled by any male skater in any other country in figure-skating history. From 1983 through 1988, he was always on the medal platform at the World Championships, as he was at the 1984 and 1988 Olympics. But this extraordinary amateur career was also marked by great frustration: Again and again Orser found himself just short of a Gold Medal in international competition.

He won his first World medal in 1983, taking the Bronze at Helsinki, Finland behind the U.S.'s Scott Hamilton and East Germany's Norbert Schramm. A brilliant jumper whose free-skating was always marked by tremendous energy, Orser was always a favorite with audiences: No male skater ever equaled his ability to make eye contact with the spectators despite the speed with which he skated, and there are many competitions at which his rapport with the audience had him a clear favorite among the attending fans.

Orser's weakness was school figures, which still counted 30 percent throughout his amateur career; they often held him back. This was particularly true at the 1984 Olympics when, in the figures, he did even less well than usual, coming in 7th, a grave disadvantage. His chief competition was three-time World Champion Scott Hamilton, but Hamilton was suffering from an ear infection that affected his balance and hampered his free-skating. First after the school figures, Hamilton was second to Orser, who won the short program, which counted 20 percent. Orser's free-skating program was brilliant; Hamilton's was less than his best. Once again it was Orser 1st and Hamilton 2nd, but because of Orser's weak score in school figures, Hamilton still won the Olympic Gold and then, recovered from his ear infection, went on to win the World Championship for a fourth time.

The following year the Soviet Union's Alexandr Fadeev, another expert in school figures, was World Champion with Orser second and U.S. Champion Brian Boitano third. In 1986, Boitano became World Champion with Orser taking the Silver medal and Fadeev the Bronze. Now 25, Orser finally gained the World Championship in 1987, moving past a technically expert but bland Boitano. The stage was set for the 1988 Olympics and what the press quickly dubbed "The Battle of the Brians."

The contest between the two Brians made for good copy, but it was in no way a grudge match: Orser and Boitano had known one another since the 1978 World Junior Championships and had become good friends. They had many common interests aside from skating, which they never talked about in terms of their own training or programs. Orser made it clear that he badly wanted to win: Not only did he already have an Olympic Silver Medal from 1984, but the 1988 games were being held in his own country, at Calgary. He was the best hope for a Canadian Gold Medal, and he wanted it to cap his long career. Boitano, on the other hand, insisted that his own interest was simply in skating his very best. He felt that figure-skating judging always had a subjective element to it. Provided he did his best, he maintained, who got the Gold Medal was in the hands of fate.

Working harder than he ever had before to prepare himself for the Olympics, Orser had consulted a sports psychologist for two years and made even greater use of him now. Aside from his school-figures weakness, he had been adversely affected by nerves in the past, flubbing jumps that he had done countless times without fault in practice. He was determined that this time he would not beat himself.

The school figures went as expected: the Soviet Union's Fadeev was in first place; Boitano, helped by a superlative third figure, was in second; and Orser was happy to be in third. At the U.S. Championships, Boitano's imaginative short program had been a stunning success, but at the Olympics he skated it more cautiously, and Orser came in first with a bravura display of technical authority. Everything would be decided by the free-skating.

Of the six final skaters, Boitano drew the first slot, exactly what he had hoped for: He could skate for himself without knowing what Orser accom-

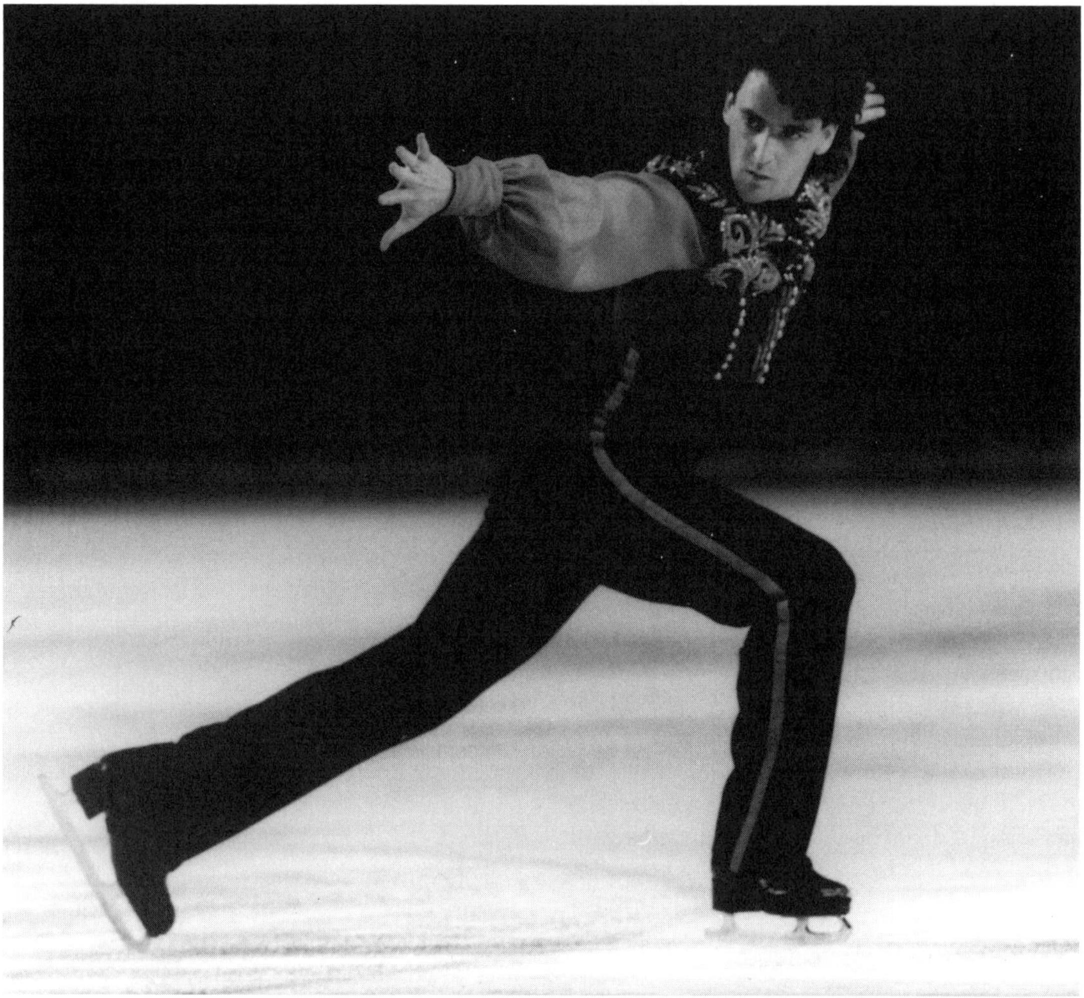

1987 World Champion Brian Orser competing professionally in 1990.
(Courtesy Paul Harvath)

plished. For the past year, Boitano had worked with the Canadian choreographer and former Canadian Ice Dance Champion Sandra Bezic to inject more emotion and greater projection into his free-skating. The result was the finest program he had ever skated, technically flawless and theatrically potent. Television viewers were treated to an expression of utter joy as he completed his program. He had indeed done the best of which he was capable.

Two slots later was Orser's turn. Skating to "The Bolt" by Russian composer Shostakovich, Orser started off brilliantly, with tremendous energy and breathtaking jumps. Then little more then halfway through, he landed with a slight bobble after a triple flip. It was barely noticeable, but in such a tight competition, television commentator Dick Button immediately noted that it could cost him dearly. At the end of the program he substituted a double axel for a triple. Ordinarily that would not have cost him anything, but in this case it accentuated a sense that he was tiring.

In the end, five judges put Boitano 1st, and four voted for Orser. The Gold went to Boitano, and Orser had a second Olympic Silver medal. The order of finish would be the same at the World Championships in Budapest. During a long amateur career, Orser amassed nine Canadian Championships, a World Bronze Medal, four World Silver Medals, two Olympic Silvers and a single World Gold Medal. It was one of the most impressive accomplishments in the history of men's skating, but it was not all that Orser had believed himself capable of.

Brian Orser went on to a fine professional career that still continues, wowing audiences with his jumps and sparkling personality, but here too he has been overshadowed by Boitano, who continued to develop artistically in ways that Orser did not attempt.

OSTERREICH, ROLF *See* KERNER, ROMY.

OUTSIDE EDGE *See* EDGES.

OVERHEAD LIFT

There are many Pairs lifts in which the woman moves through the air higher than her partner's head, but some of these are performed with the woman to one side of the man, as in the cartwheel lift, or where the woman revolves in the air without support, as in the triple twist lift—the woman rotates horizontally three times before being caught by her partner. In a true overhead lift, however, the woman is supported directly above the man's head.

The first overhead lift was invented by German solo and Pairs skater Ernst Baier, who was Pairs Champion of the World with Maxi Herber from 1936 to 1939. Here, the woman is supported above the man by a hand placed in her armpit as he rotates on the ice. These days, the overhead lift most commonly seen in competition is the one-hand overhead lift, where the man supports the woman with one hand placed in her pelvic region. The man's arm is fully extended upward, and he rotates on the ice throughout the lift.

OVSIANNIKOV, OLEG *See* KRYLOVA, ANJELIKA.

OWEN, LAURENCE *(b. 1945, d. 1961)*

U.S. Champion.

The younger daughter of the nine-time U.S. Ladies' Champion Maribel Vinson Owen, Laurence Owen began to skate as soon as she could walk. Coached by her mother, who had taken Tenley Albright to her World and Olympic titles, she was U.S. Junior

Maribel Y. Owen, Maribel Vinson Owen and Laurence Owen, a family of champions.
(Courtesy World Figure Skating Museum)

Ladies' Champion at 13 and took the Bronze Medal as a Senior competitor in 1960 at 15. She was 6th at that year's Olympics, won by Carol Heiss, and 9th at the World Championships, where her trick knee gave her problems. She was already regarded as a very likely future World and Olympic Champion, with her very solid school figures and a free-skating style that combined feminty with athleticism in a highly charismatic way.

In 1961 Owen was the youngest woman to become the Ladies' U.S. Champion since her mother; she was 16, her mother had been 15. But she, her mother, and older sister Maribel Jr. were killed along with all the other members of the U.S. World Figure Skating Team at the Brussels, Belgium airport, where they were to change planes to continue on to Prague, Czechoslovakia. The issue of *Life* magazine that covered the crash had on its final page a photograph of Laurence performing her trademark lay-back spin at the National Championships.

OWEN, MARIBEL VINSON *(b. 1913, d. 1961) U.S. Champion won more medals than any other U.S. skater in history.*

Born the year before the first U.S. Figure Skating Championships were held, Maribel Vinson became the Ladies' Champion of the United States just 15 years later. That was 1928, and she won the championship year after year for a total of nine times without ever being beaten. In 1934, she did not compete, interrupting her string of victories, which made it possible for her friend Suzanne Davis, Silver Medalist behind her twice, to win a Gold Medal.

Owen also competed in five World Championships and two Olympic Games. This was the period of Sonja Henie's domination of women's figure skating, but many skating experts of the period, not just Americans, felt that Owen should have won at least three of the competitions in which the Norwegian triumphed. In those days there were often no U.S. judges on the World and Olympic panels; even when there were, they had little effect. This problem did not just affect Owen: No American ever won a World or Olympic Gold Medal until after World War II, when the criteria for selecting judges were changed.

Even so, Maribel Vinson managed to win a few medals. She was runner-up to Sonja Henie at the 1928 World Championships and took the Bronze in 1930 and an Olympic Bronze in 1932. She was also 4th in 1931 and 1932 and 5th in 1934 at the World's and placed 4th at the 1928 Olympics.

But this indefatigable champion was not content with merely winning solo championships; she also competed in Pairs, first with Thornton Coolidge and then with George Hill. With Coolidge, she was U.S. Pairs Champion in 1928 and 1929; with Hill, she won the U.S. Silver in 1930–32, the Gold in 1933 and, after her absence in 1934, came back to win the national title three more times, 1935–37, after which she finally retired from competition. With Hill, she competed twice at the World's, coming in 5th both times, in 1931 and 1936; they were also 5th at the Olympics.

For the fun of it, she also occasionally competed in the U.S. Dance event and won a Silver Medal in the fourteen step in 1929 and a Bronze in the waltz and original dance combined in 1930, both with J. Lester Madden. This diversity of experience gave her the groundings to become one of the best American figure-skating teachers in subsequent years.

After retiring from amateur competition, she married former Canadian Champion Guy Owen; they skated professionally as a Pair for a brief period, and then she turned her attention to teaching. She had been a member of the Skating Club of Boston since childhood, but the club did not allow members to teach, a rule that so annoyed her that she built her coaching career at other public rinks in Massachusetts. Her venues for teaching eventually included the public Boston rink that formed the Commonwealth Skating Club; Worchester in midwestern Massachusetts; Lynn, southeast of Boston; and for a time once-a-week evening sessions at the new outdoor rink built in

1952 at Phillips Academy, Andover. Owen also taught skating at Harvard College, where skating was offered as an official athletic-requirement option in keeping with the success of Harvard's own Olympic Champion Dick Button, who had been given a varsity letter in figure skating to honor his achievements.

Maribel Vinson Owen's greatest triumph as a coach was with Tenley Albright. Although also a Boston Skating Club member, Albright was taught by Owen from the start, rather than by former British World Champion Cecilia Colledge, the club's senior skating instructor. Owen once said, "The tough part was getting her to smile while she skated." The coach was famous for exhorting her pupils at the top of her lungs from the sidelines, and she got Albright to smile; she also guided her to five U.S. titles, two World Gold and two Silver Medals, and an Olympic Silver and Gold Medal.

Another great success came with Ron and Nancy Ludington, former roller skaters who took to the ice very late. Owen coached them to four U.S. Pairs titles and World and Olympic Bronze Medals. At the same time she coached her elder daughter, also called Maribel, and Dudley Richards in Pairs. During the last three years that the Luddingtons were U.S. Champions, Maribel Jr. and Dudley Richards won the U.S. Bronze Medal twice and the Silver in 1960. They then succeeded the Ludingtons as U.S. Pairs Champions in 1961.

Her younger daughter Laurence (see above) developed under her mother's tutelage into a figure skater of rare ability to become U.S. Champion in 1961. In addition to schooling champions, Owen also wrote sports coverage of major skating events for the *Boston Globe* and the *New York Times* and published a classic instructional book on the sport. She was the sole support of her family for many years; she had divorced Guy Owen, who died of a heart attack a year later.

When the plane carrying the U.S. World figure skating team crashed at Brussels, Belgium on the way to the World Championships in 1961, a generation of figure skaters was lost, as well as several other coaches. But the loss of the entire Owen skating family hit particularly hard—there had never been another like them. The only way members of the surviving skating community could begin to console themselves was to note that at least Maribel had seen both her daughters win the national titles that she herself had held so many times.

OWEN, MARIBEL Y. *(1941–61) U.S. Pairs Champion.*

The press referred to Maribel Vinson Owen's elder daughter as Maribel Jr.; her friends called her Little Maribel, although she was several inches taller than her mother. She hated school figures, so her mother guided her into Pairs. She won her first U.S. medal in 1956, taking the Bronze with partner Charles Foster (b. 1938) when only 15. But Owen was still growing, and a change of partners proved necessary. Dudley Richards, a former Men's Bronze Medalist and already in his 20s, proved to be the perfect answer. The team were U.S. Bronze Medalists in 1958 and 1959, Silver Medalists in 1960, and attained the national title in 1961. At the World's, they were 6th in 1959 but fell to 10th with a difficult outing in 1960, when they were also 10th at the Olympics. The problems had been solved by the next year when they became national champions. They were also engaged to be married at the time of their death in the Brussels, Belgium plane crash.

P

PAIRS COMPETITION

Pairs skating was inaugurated as a World Championship event in 1908, only two years after the first Ladies' competition and a dozen years after Men's competition began in St. Petersburg, Russia in 1896, but what was then called Pairs bore little resemblance to the sport as it is now practiced. Pairs partners skated almost entirely in tandem, their bodies close together, arms intertwined in various ballroom-dance holds. They were quite formally attired, with both men and women wearing hats, often top hats for the men, although those gave way to more casual styles. The women, of course, wore voluminous long skirts.

In the years before and just after the First World War, two introduced elements involved separate skating: The partners would perform the same moves, usually some kind of spiral, modest spin or rudimentary jump, like the half-turn waltz jump, at opposite ends of the rink; such moves had to be chosen according to the abilities of the least ac- complished of the two skaters. Given the narrow range of elements performed, it was in no way necessary for the two skaters to have achieved any kind of real expertise as solo skaters, although it was not uncommon for at least one of the partners to have won solo World medals. Great Britain's Phyllis Johnson, for instance, who was twice World Pairs Champion with her brother James, in 1909 and 1912, won a Ladies' World Bronze in 1912 and a Silver in 1913; Austria's Heinrich Burger, World Pairs Champion with Anna Hubler in 1908 and 1910, won the World Men's Silver Medal in 1904 and 1906 and the Bronze in 1908. But there was often a very considerable disparity between the overall skating talent of Pairs partners.

A more complex and daring form of Pairs skating was initially performed by younger skaters at the 1922 and 1923 World Championships, but the Gold Medalists at both competitions were holdovers from the ranks of prewar medalists, with Austria's Helene Engelmann winning in 1922 with Alfred Berger, just as she had with her previous partner, Karl Mejstrik in 1913, and Finland's Ludowicka and Walter Jakobsson taking the title in 1923, as they had in 1914.

The true birth of modern Pairs skating came at the 1924 Olympics. The top two winners were still the old-guard skaters Engelmann and Berger and the Jakobssons, but the Bronze Medal went to the young French couple Pierre Brunet and Andrée Joly, who soon married. The performance they gave at the Olympics introduced daring new lifts and separate jumps; they dazzled many and outraged some judges, which is why they were only the Bronze medalists. They would go on to win the Olympic Gold Medal in both 1928 and 1932.

The Brunets consolidated a number of trends in creating a new form of Pairs skating. At the previous year's World Championships, Britain's

T.D. Richardson and his wife had performed what they called shadow skating, in which they skated separately most of the time, one partner creating a shadow of the other's moves. But the Brunets were far more technically assured; they created a number of lifts that had never been seen before. Their new approach to Pairs skating was also espoused over the next few years by two Austrian couples. The more accomplished was Herma Jaross-Szabo and Ludwig Wrede, who in fact beat the Brunets for the World Gold in 1925 and took another Gold Medal in 1927, when the Brunets did not compete. Jaross-Szabo, one of the greatest women skaters of all time, was five times Ladies' Champion of the World in the 1920s in addition to her efforts in Pairs.

The second Austrian couple, Lilly Scholz and Otto Kaiser, was second only to the Brunets in the daring nature of their lifts. They were third at the 1925 World's behind Jaross-Szabo/Wrede and the Brunets, second behind the latter couple during the Brunets' 1927 absence and second to the Brunets at both the Olympics and World's in 1928. They won the World Gold in 1929, another year when the Brunets did not skate because of Andrée's second pregnancy.

By the 1928 Olympics, all the major Pairs skaters were in the Brunet mold, although none could beat the French couple, either then, in 1932 nor at the two additional World Championships the Brunets entered, in 1930 and 1932. In the years since 1928, many new and more spectacular lifts have been added to the Pairs repertoire, as well as the difficult throw jumps, while the side-by-side jumps have progressed from singles to triples. The major differences within Pairs skating in the past several decades, however, have been in matters of style. The athletic North American style, which developed in both the United States and Canada and became the hallmark of such European World Champions as Marika Kilius and Hans Jurgen Baumler of West Germany, has produced many World and Olympic Gold medalists.

In 1962, an alternative style was introduced by the Soviet Union's Ludmila and Oleg Protopopov. Soviet skaters had never previously won a World medal in Pairs, but the Protopopovs' balletic and hauntingly lovely approach brought them the World Silver in 1962 behind Otto and Maria Jelinek (the Canadians who had fled communist Czechoslovakia) and the Silver again in 1963 behind Kilius and Baumler. The latter couple and the Protopopovs squared off in 1964 in two of the most exhilarating Pairs competitions of all time, according to many who were there, with the Soviet couple taking the Olympic Gold and the West Germans the World Gold. The Protopopovs went on to take the next four World Championships and a second Olympic Gold and to perform professionally for another two decades.

The Protopopovs were succeeded as Soviet, World and Olympic Champions by Irina Rodnina and her two partners, Alexei Ulanov and and Alexandr Zaitsev; with both of them during a 10-year period, Rodnina pursued the athletic North American style. Other Soviet couples retained more of the Protopopov balletic approach but were not as successful. In recent years, Russia's Ekaterina Gordeeva and Sergei Grinkov, winners of the Olympic Gold Medal in both 1988 and 1994, have moved toward a fusion of the two styles, using daring lifts but emphasizing a classical line. This is also the approach, unusual in North American skaters, of 1995 U.S. Champions and World Bronze Medalists Jenni Meno and Todd Sand. International judges currently seem to favor this fusion, but the history of Pairs skating suggests that further changes will inevitably occur.

PAKHOMOVA, LUDMILA *(1947–86)*

Soviet Ice Dance World and Olympic Champion with Aleksandr Gorskov (b. 1950).

The first Soviet couple to become Ice Dance World Champions, Ludmila Pakhomova and Aleksandr Gorskov not only dominated their sport for years but also extended its technical and artistic vocabulary, introducing "a more classical, smoother performance heavily influenced by Russian Ballet," in the words of British skating reporter Howard Bass.

They won their first World medal in 1959, taking the Silver behind the last of the British tradionalists, Diane Towler and Bernard Ford, who won their fourth straight World Championship before retiring.

In 1970, Pakhomova and Gorskov won their first World Championship at Ljubljana, Yugoslavia, beating the U.S.'s Judy Schwomeyer and James Sladky and East German sister-and-brother team Angelika and Erich Buck. The Soviet couple won again four consecutive times (1971–74) and then took the year off in 1975, only to return as magisterial as ever in 1976 to win the first Olympic Gold Medal awarded in Ice Dancing and take back their World Championships from fellow Soviets Irina Moiseeva and Andrei Minenkov.

Blending Russian ballet style with the ballroom tradition of England and America, they established a style that is prevalent among Russian ice dancers to this day. They also created, together with their coach Elena Tschaikowskaja, a new basic dance called the Tango romantica, introduced in 1974 and soon included among the list of compulsory ice dances. Accentuating one of their own great strengths, the Tango romantica requires the use of especially deep edges.

PANKEY, JANE *(b. 1953) U.S. Ice Dance medalist with Richard Horne (b. 1952).*

In 1973, the year following the retirement of five-time U.S. Ice Dance Champions Judy Schwomeyer and James Sladky, Jane Pankey and Richard Horne took the U.S. Bronze Medal. Right behind them were Colleen O'Connor and Jim Millns, who would become U.S. Champions the following year, as well as several other challengers. This would prove to be Pankey and Horne's only medal.

PAPEZ, IDI *(b. 1914) Austrian Pairs Champion and World medalist with Karl Zwach (b. 1913).*

Succeeding Melitta Brunner and Ludwig Wrede as Austrian Pairs Champions in 1931, Idi Papez and Karl Zwach gained the World Bronze Medal that year. The 1932 Olympic year brought the return to competition of Andrée and Pierre Brunet of France and Beatrix Loughran and Sherwin Badger of the United States, who had been the Gold and Bronze Medalists in 1930 and who recaptured those honors in 1932. These couples were also Gold and Silver Medalists at the Olympics; Hungary's Emilie Rotter and Lazlo Szollas won the Bronze at the Olympics and the Silver at the World's. The team of Papez and Zwach were shut out in both events.

Only the Hungarians continued competing in 1933, taking the World Gold Medal as they also had in 1931, but this time Papez and Zwach were able to move up to the Silver Medal. After they repeated as Silver Medalists in 1934 behind the Hungarians, they retired. Ilse and Erich Pausin took their place as Austrian Champions and as World Silver Medalists.

PARKER, MARJORIE *See* SAVAGE, JOSEPH.

PARMETER, ASHTON *See* FROTHINGHAM, CLARA.

PATTERSON, GLENN *See* FORD, MICHELLE.

PAUL, ROBERT *See* WAGNER, BARBARA.

PAULSEN, PAGE *See* DUISCH, LARRY.

PAUSIN, ERICH AND ILSE *(b. 1917, 1916) Major Austrian Pairs Champions and World medalists.*

Brother-and-sister Erich and Ilse Pausin succeeded Idi Papez and Karl Zwach as Austrian Pairs Champions in 1935, and went on to claim their fellow Austrians' place as World Silver Medalists that year at Budapest, Hungary where the hometown team of Emilie Rotter and Lazlo Szollas took the Gold. At the Olympics the following year in Garmisch, Germany, the Pausins took the Silver, while the Hungarians fell to 3rd place, but the new German sensations Maxi Herber and Ernst Baier took the Gold Medal, with the judges giving them seven 1st-place votes to the Pausins two. The Pausins would finish 2nd to the German couple three more times, in 1937–39. The Pausins always gave the Germans a strong challenge, but the latter always proved too strong technically; Herber and Baier built on the more athletic style that was introduced by the French Pair the Brunets and was sustained by the deep experience of Ernst Baier—he had also won two World Bronze, two World Silver and an Olympic Silver Medal in the Men's division between 1931 and 1936.

PAWLIK, EVA *(b. 1927) Austrian World and Olympic Silver Medalist.*

Although the World Championships had resumed in 1947, the shape of figure skating to come could be seen more clearly in the 1948 Olympic year. Canada's Barbara Ann Scott, who had become World Champion the previous year, was the expected winner of the Olympic Gold Medal and repeat World Champion. Austria's Eva Pawlik gave her a good challenge in both competitions, however. It might seem surprising that Pawlik then retired, two Silver Medals in hand, but she was probably wise to do so: Among the women competing that year were three who would become World Champions during the next four years—Alena Vrzanova of Czechoslovakia, Jeannette Altwegg of Great Britain and Jacqueline du Bief of France—as well as the U.S.'s Yvonne Sherman, who would win a Silver and a Bronze. Pawlik was a worthy Silver Medalist, but she had been trained according to an older tradition. The future of women's skating was all around her as she garnered her two Silver Medals.

PEIZERAT, GWENDEL *See* ANISSINA, MARINA.

PEPPE, AUDREY *(b. 1918) U.S. medalist.*

Audrey Peppe won the U.S. Bronze Medal in 1936 and placed 12th at that year's Olympics and 13th at World's. Although she did not win a U.S. Medal in 1937, she was the sole U.S. representative at the World's, placing 12th. In 1938 and 1939, she won the U.S. Silver Medal behind Joan Tozzer, but neither of them competed at the World Championships, as World War II loomed in Europe.

PERA, PATRICK *(b. 1950) French World and Olympic medalist.*

At the age of 18, France's Patrick Pera made a dazzling debut as an international medalist, taking the Bronze at both the Olympics and the World Championships. He seemed destined to one day claim a World title, like countrymen Alain Giletti and Alain Calmat, who won the Gold Medal in 1960 and 1964. But Pera was not quite able to equal their success: He was again Bronze Medalist in 1969 but missed the medal stand in 1970; in 1971, he gave a strong challenge to Czechoslovakia's Ondrej Nepala but ended up with the Silver. After taking another Olympic Bronze in 1972 behind Nepela and the Soviet Union's Sergei Chetverukhin, whom he had beaten for the World Silver the previous year, Pera retired from competition.

PETERS, CAROL ANN *(b. 1932) U.S. Ice Dancing Champion with Daniel Ryan (b. 1930).*

Carol Ann Peters and Daniel Ryan won the U.S. Bronze Medal in Ice Dancing in 1951, improved to the Silver Medal in 1952 and became U.S. Champions in 1953. At the first World Championships to include Ice Dancing in 1952, they took the Bronze behind British couples Jean Westwood/ Lawrence Demmy and Joan Dewhurst/John Slater.

The same order of finish prevailed in 1953, after which Peters and Ryan turned professional for a short period. Their World Bronze medals were no small accomplishment because the British were, at that time, the acknowledged leaders in that aspect of the sport—the World Champion couple would be British for the rest of the decade.

PETKEVICH, JOHN MISHA

(b. 1949) U.S. Champion.

Always called Misha, Petkevich was a daring free-skater who usually had audiences rooting for him. He took the U.S. Bronze in 1968, the Silver behind Tim Wood in 1969 and 1970, won the U.S. Championship in 1971 over Kenneth Shelley and then was pushed back to the Silver again by Shelley in 1972. Like Dick Button two decades earlier and Paul Wylie 20 years later, Petkevich was a full-time student at Harvard during most of his amateur career. He often won the highest scores in free-skating but was held back by weaker school figures; in international competitions he was regularly afflicted by nerves. He was 6th at the 1968 Olympics, 5th at the 1969–71 World Championships, 5th at the 1972 Olympics and just missed capping his career with a World Bronze in 1972 when he was edged by the Soviet Union's Vladimir Kovalev.

Following his retirement from amateur competition in 1972, Petkevich was for several years a television commentator at national and international competitions.

PETRENKO, VIKTOR

(b. 1969) World and Olympic Champion from Ukraine.

Viktor Petrenko succeeded Alexandr Fadeev as Champion of the Soviet Union in 1988 and immediately made a mark on men's skating by winning the Olympic and World Bronze as the U.S.'s Brian Boitano and Canada's Brian Orser took Gold and Silver at both championships. Petrenko did not win a World medal in 1989 but took the World Silver the next two years behind Canada's Kurt Browning, fending off challenges from two U.S. Bronze Medalists, Christopher Bowman in 1990 and Todd Eldredge in 1991.

Petrenko had always been remarkably independent, insisting upon remaining in his home city of Odessa. This fact, he would later say, helped him in 1992 following the collapse of the Soviet Union, as he skated under two different umbrella groups of former Soviet countries: One was formed for the Olympics and the other for the World Championships, although Petrenko wished that he could have been skating under the flag of his native Ukraine.

Kurt Browning was the favorite for the 1992 Olympics, but he was incapacitated for a time by an injury that prevented him from defending his Canadian title. He claimed to have recovered sufficiently by the time of the Olympics, but it was clear that he had not. He was out of the medal hunt after a botched performance in the short program. That made Petrenko, who won the short, the new favorite, followed by Petr Barna. A surprising 3rd after the short program was the U.S.'s Paul Wylie, who had a long history of falling apart at World Championships. Wylie's long program was good this time out, while Petrenko seemed to tire (he had always had some problems with stamina in the long program). Many observers thought Wylie had won, but the judges gave Petrenko the Gold, Wylie and Silver and Czechoslovakia's Petr Barna the Bronze.

At the World Championships, Petrenko skated better than he ever had in a long program and took the Gold with no doubters to object. Wylie was not there, having previously promised to skate only in the Olympics, giving his place on the World Team to the U.S. Bronze Medalist Mark Mitchell, who finished 5th. The Silver went to a healthier Kurt Browning and the Bronze to his young Canadian rival Elvis Stojko.

Petrenko went on to the expected success as a professional. He had always been interested in American music and dance styles and put that to good use in jazzy show numbers. He also had a great following among young women, which continued even after he married his coach's eldest daughter in 1992. One of skating's true gentlemen, Petrenko was noted for his assistance to other skaters: He came to the rescue of the young Ukrainian orphan, Oksana Baiul, persuading his coach to take Oksana into her home and providing financial assistance. She became World and Olympic Champion in 1994.

Like Brian Boitano, Katarina Witt and several other top skaters, Petrenko applied for reinstatement as an amateur for the 1994 Olympics. Like Boitano, he had an uncharacteristically bad outing in the short program, placing 9th, but his long program pulled him up to 4th overall. He then returned to touring as a professional, remaining a major draw among the galaxy of top stars with whom he appeared.

PHILLIPS, CHARLES

See ACKLES, MARGIE.

PIERCE, LARRY

(1937–61) U.S. Ice Dance Silver Medalist with Marilyn Meeker (b. 1941), and Gold Medalist with Diane Sherbloom (b. 1943, d. 1961).

Larry Pierce won the U.S. Silver Medal in Ice Dancing in 1960 partnering Marilyn Meeker; the couple were 5th at that year's World Championships. Pierce then changed partners, and with Diane Sherbloom developed enough to become U.S. Champion in 1961. The couple seemed to have a chance for a Bronze Medal at the World Championships that year, but they were killed with the rest of the U.S. World team en route to Prague in a plane crash at Brussels.

PLANK-SZABO (later JAROSS-SZABO), HERMA

(b. 1902) Austrian World and Olympic Champion.

When the World Championships resumed following World War I, at Stockholm, Sweden in 1922, Herma Plank-Szabo was the Ladies' Gold Medalist, a title she would successfully defend four times. The Austrian school of figure skating was at the time the most modern and sophisticated in existence, and Herma Plank-Szabo defeated one challenger after another—Svea Noren of Sweden, her fellow Austrian Gisela Reichmann, Ellen Brockhofft of Germany twice and finally 13-year-old Sonja Henie of Norway in 1926. But Henie, with her imaginative spins and great appeal, finally turned the tables in 1927, pushing the now married Jaross-Szabo back into second place. By then, however, Jaross-Szabo had a 1924 Olympic Gold Medal to go with her five World Golds.

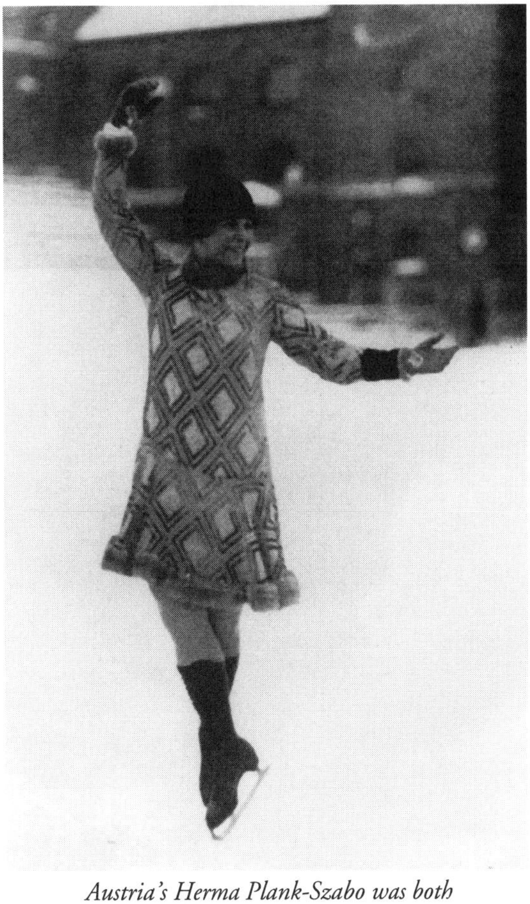

Austria's Herma Plank-Szabo was both World Ladies' and Pairs Champion in 1925.
(Courtesy World Figure Skating Museum)

She had also accomplished something no other skater ever has: In 1925, she not only was Ladies' Champion of the World but also Pairs Champion with Ludwig Wrede. In 1926, the couple won the World Bronze in Pairs and repeated as World Champions in 1927 even as Herma was losing her Ladies' title to Henie. While a few other skaters, both women and men, have held national titles in both Singles and Pairs simultaneously, Jaross-Szabo is the only person to pull off this unusual feat at the World Championship or Olympic level.

PLATOV, EVGENY *See* GRISCHUK,OKSANA.

POETZSCH, ANETT *(b. 1959) East German World and Olympic Champion.*

Anett Poetzsch of East Germany and Linda Fratianne both reached their full flowering as skaters in 1977 and would remain in a great struggle for primacy through 1980. Both were skating prodigies, demonstrating unusual ability when remarkably young; Anett performed her first triple salchow in competition when she was only 13. At the 1977 World Championships, the two young women arrived as freshly crowned national champions, Linda Fratianne succeeding Dorothy Hamill, Anett Poetzsch succeeding Christine Errath. Errath and Hamill had each defeated the other in World Championships, and so it was to be for Fratianne and Poetzsch.

Fratianne won the first round, taking the 1977 World Gold while Poetzsch won the Silver; in 1978, their positions were reversed. In 1979, Fratianne again prevailed, but in 1980, Poetzsch dominated, winning both the Olympic and World Gold Medals, with Fratianne taking the Olympic Silver and the World Bronze. The two skaters were very evenly matched in all ways, but Anett Poetzsch was the more daring free-skater. One move that always drew gasps from the audience was a spread eagle in a layback position, her upper body horizontal to the ice.

After Anett Poetzsch retired from amateur competition in 1980, she married the brother of her successor as East German and, eventually, World and Olympic Champion, Katarina Witt.

POSPISIL, DONNA J. *See* BRUNET, JEAN-PIERRE.

PRANTELL, NETTIE *(b. 1917) Major U.S. Ice Dance Champion.*

Nettie Prantell first won an Ice Dance medal in 1930 when she took the U.S. Bronze in the waltz with partner Roy Hunt (b. 1916). At this time there were two separate dance competitions, one for the waltz and the other for original dance, with medals awarded in each category. The couple were Silver Medalists in the waltz in 1932, and took the Gold Medal in 1934 and 1935. In 1936 a new Ice Dance competition along the lines still used today was inaugurated, and Prantell was the Silver Medalist with a new partner, Harold Hartshorne (see separate entry); they won the Gold in 1937 and again in 1938. Hartshorne and Prantell then split, and he won the next two competitions with Sandy MacDonald, while Prantell took the Silver in 1938 and 1939 with Joseph Savage (see separate entry), and then another Silver with George Boltres (b. 1919) in 1940.

PREISSECKER, OTTO *(b. 1907) Austrian World medalist.*

In the period from the resumption of the World Championships in 1922 through 1929, medals in the Men's division were won by eight different Austrians, with at least two medals going to Austrians every single year. The dominant Austrian skater was Willy Boeckl with a Bronze, two Silvers and four Golds; Otto Preissecker, however, took three medals—a Bronze in 1925 and the Silver behind Boeckl in 1926 and 1927, the latter year being one of two in which Austrian men swept the awards; future World Champion Karl Schafer took the Bronze that year. Preissecker's position during this period was like that of the U.S.'s James Grogan after

World War II: Grogan could never beat Dick Button for the U.S. Championship, just as Preissecker could never beat Boeckl for the Austrian title; yet both men were the second best in the world.

PROTOPOPOV, LUDMILA AND OLEG *(b. 1935, 1932) Soviet European World and Olympic Pairs Champions.*

Oleg Protopopov did not begin to skate until he was 15, a very late age for a future champion. He had survived the Nazi siege of Leningrad (St. Petersburg) which lasted from September 8, 1941, to January 27, 1944, and resulted in the death of at least a million citizens.

Once he began to skate, Protopopov developed very quickly, but his training was interrupted when he served in the Russian navy. He was allowed to perform with a Leningrad partner in the Soviet Championships in 1953. A 3rd-place finish brought a dispensation from the navy that made it possible for him to continue his figure-skating training in Moscow.

Protopopov met Ludmila Belousova in Moscow in 1954 at the rink where they both trained. Then 19, she too had begun to skate late, at the age of 16. They decided to skate together, but no coach was interested in them because of their age. At first they had to go it alone, often skating outdoors under freezing winter conditions, but they were so well matched as a Pair that they overcame their late start. Married in 1957—although she continued to use her maiden name in competition—they competed at the European and World Championships for the first time in 1958, placing 10th at the European's and 13th at World's. By the 1960 Winter Olympics they had moved up to 9th.

By 1962, they had advanced to a new level, placing second to West German stars Marika Kilius and Hans Jurgen Baumler at both the European and World Championships. They retained that position for the next two years and then captured the Gold Medal at the 1964 Winter Olympics, beating the West Germans for the first time. Kilius and Baumler once again took top place at the 1964 World's but then turned professional. The Protopopovs were already in their late 20s, but they would go on to dominate Pairs skating for the next four years, becoming recurrent Soviet, European and World Champions and taking another Gold Medal at the 1968 Olympics.

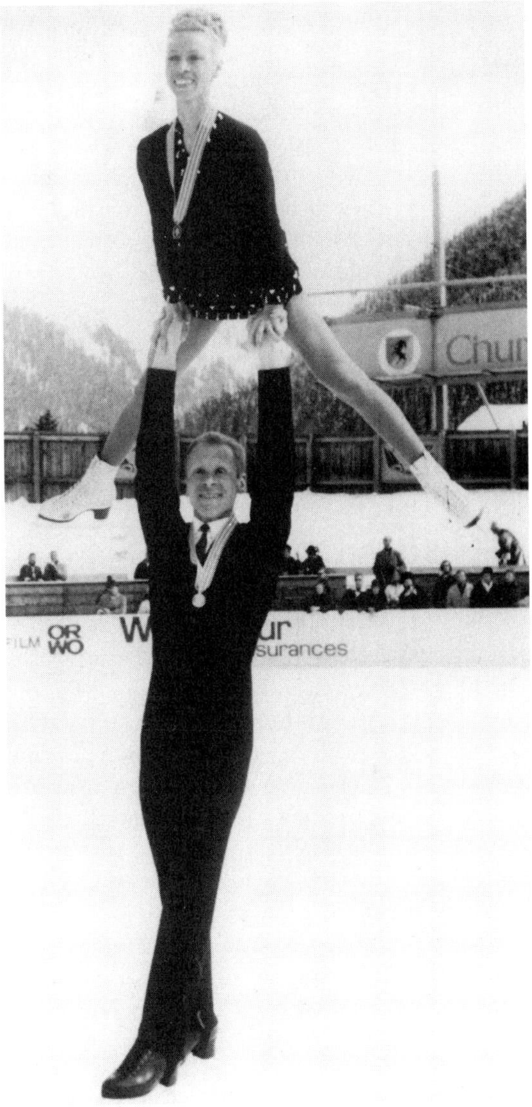

The legendary Protopopovs demonstrate an overhead lift.

(Courtesy World Figure Skating Museum)

One word that is always used in describing the skating of the Protopopovs is *elegance.* Although they had had no ballet training and continued to be self-taught, working without a coach throughout their long career, they succeeded as no skaters had before in transferring the feel of ballet movement to the ice. One aspect of achieving that elegance was the extraordinary slowness with which they could carry out difficult maneuvers so that they almost seemed to be moving in slow-motion at times. But that almost languid, floating quality was based on two very highly developed athletic qualities. The first was Oleg's very great strength. Tall and slender, he never gave any appearance of effort, but the tensile strength of his back, arms and shoulders was remarkable. In addition, both skaters had phenomenal control of their skating edges; Ludmila, in particular, was noted for the very steep angles at which she could skate while maintaining perfect balance.

The chief rivals of the Protopopovs in the earlier part of their career were the West German World Champions, Marika Kilius and Hans Jurgen Baumler, who were famous for their death spiral. The Protopopovs managed to make even more of this classic move, adding a greater degree of balletic grace to it and inventing a new variation: Ludmila used the inside foot instead of the outside, where once again Oleg's great strength and her very deep edges made a gravity-defying move possible.

The Protopopovs carried balletic Pairs skating as far as it could go. Because no one could equal them in terms of grace and slowness of execution, their competitors, particularly Irina Rodnina, who with her first partner, Alexsei Ulanov, supplanted the Protopopovs as Soviet, European and World Champions in 1969, emphasized speed. Rodnina's 10-year reign at the top of Pairs skating changed the esthetics of Pairs skating toward quickness to such a degree that the balletic qualities of the Protopopovs would likely seem out of place today. Yet no one who has watched the sport continuously during the past 40 years would put the Protopopovs anywhere but at the top of the discipline; they achieved something that was sublime —and legendary.

When the Protopopovs won their second Olympic Gold in 1968, Oleg was 36 and Ludmila 33. No one else has ever won an Olympic skating medal at such a relatively advanced aged, and the difficulty of doing so was emphasized by the experiences of Brian Boitano, Katarina Witt and Torvill and Dean at the 1994 Olympics. As Rodnina and Ulanov came into their ascendency the following year, the Soviet sports czars began to pressure the Protopopovs to stop competing and become coaches. They turned professional instead, skating with a Leningrad show troupe starting in 1973. On a tour abroad in 1979, they defected in Switzerland and were given political asylum. Now 47 and 44 years old, they skated with the Ice Capades for three years and proved an enormous box-office draw. With various other troupes they continued performing for at least part of the year, winning many professional medals along the way, and did not stop performing until Oleg was 59 years old, in 1992. To the very end, they could reduce an audience to an awed hush.

PRUESCH, ARTHUR *(b. 1920) U.S. medalist.*

Arthur Preusch was the U.S. Silver Medalist behind Arthur Vaughn, Jr. in 1943. No Men's competition was held for the next two years because of World War II, but Preusch combined with Janette Ahrens in 1944 to gain a Silver Medal in the Pairs competition.

PUNSALAN, ELIZABETH *See* SWALLOW, JEROD.

R

RADA, EDI *(b. 1926) Austrian World and Olympic medalist.*

In 1948, as Dick Button won the U.S., European, World and Olympic Men's Figure Skating crowns, Austria's Edi Rada was the Bronze Medalist at the European Championships and the Olympics; the previous year's World Champion, Switzerland's Hans Gerschwiler took 2nd place. Rada was also in 3rd place going into the free-skating at the World Championships, but a skate blade loosened during his performance and he had to withdraw; Ede Kiraly of Hungary took the Bronze instead. A daring but sometimes wild free-skater, Rada then finished 3rd at the 1949 World Championships, with Dick Button and Kiraly winning Gold and Silver. Rada then retired from amateur skating.

RAHKAMO, SUSANNA *(b. 1966) Finnish Ice Dancer with Petri Kokko (b. 1967).*

Like Norway, Finland is so obsessed with skiing and speed skating that there have been few important figure skaters from the country, but Susanna Rahkamo and Petri Kokko have recently been major exceptions to that rule. At their first appearance in an international competition, they finished in last place at the European Championships in 1986. In the intervening years, however, they have gradually perfected their skills and have risen slowly but steadily through the ranks of ice dancers. Along the way, they developed an individualistic style, lively and amusing, that endeared them to audiences, if not always to the judges. In 1994, they finally reached the top rank of ice dancers, taking 4th place at the Olympics in Lillehammer, Norway and the Bronze Medal at the World Championships in Chiba, Japan. In doing so, they sparked a new interest in figure skating in Finland; it didn't hurt that Rahkamo's father was mayor of the capital city of Helsinki.

In 1995, Rahkamo and Kokko won the Gold Medal at the European Championships, although they were aided by the absence of Olympic Champions Oksana Grischuk and Evgeny Platov of Russia, because of his nagging knee injury. The Russians returned to the ice for the World Championships, but Rahkamo and Kokko, skating to the Beatles' score for *A Hard Day's Night*, challenged them strongly enough to become the clear audience favorites. In the end, however, the Russians took the Gold and the Finns the Silver. According to NBC television commentator Sandra Bezic, herself a former Canadian Ice Dance Champion, the difference was in the greater difficulty of the Russian program, although she saluted the charm of the Finns, whose popularity she thought stemmed in part from the fact that their performances almost seemed to be "sending up the stuffy world of Ice Dancing."

REFEREE

At competitions a referee oversees each panel of judges. The referee is appointed by the national or international governing body under whose auspices the competition is being held. At U.S. competitions he or she is chosen by the U.S. Figure Skating Association; the International Skating Union makes the appointment at the World Championships and Olympics. The referee is always someone who has had wide experience as a judge but in this position does not take part in the marking of competitors. This does not mean that the referee doesn't make a judgment about the competitors, however; it is part of his or her job to take note of the marks that are issued by the judges and in essence to judge them. If one or more judges appears to be giving marks that unduly reflect national prejudice, the referee has the power to recommend to the governing body that the judge(s) be questioned about the marks given, beginning a process that can lead to the suspension of the judge, or even all judges from the country, for a period of time.

In addition, the referee deals directly with the competitors if problems arise, such as music that cuts off in the middle of a performance or a skate blade that comes loose. In a famous instance of the former problem, the music that the Soviet Olympic Pairs Champion Irina Rodnina and her partner Alexandr Zaitsev were skating to during their long program at the 1973 World Championships went dead two-thirds of the way through their performance. They kept skating, and the referee was subsequently criticized for not stopping them, but according to the rules, Rodnina and Zaitsev themselves should have requested that they be allowed to start again from the point where the music stopped once the technical malfunction was fixed.

If a problem occurs early in a program, the referee may even allow the skater to start over. This was the case at the 1994 Olympics when Tonya Harding stopped early in her long program and showed the judges the problem she was having with her skate lace. There were those who felt Harding should simply have been disqualified because she had a history of disruptive equipment problems and because, except in very unusual circumstances, a skater is held responsible for keeping his or her skates or costumes in perfect order.

The referee is also responsible for taking charge if an injury should occur on the ice and to make every effort to prevent such an injury by making sure that the ice has been thoroughly cleared of all flowers or other tributes that have been thrown at the previous skater—a practice that many officials believe should be banned outright, although it would be hard to control without even greater disruption as culprits were removed from their seats. As it stands, the referee has the power to delay the competition until he or she feels confident that it is safe to proceed.

REGOECZY, KRISZTINA *(b. 1959)*

Hungarian Ice Dancer teamed with Andras Sallay (b. 1958).

Ice Dance team Krisztina Regoeczy and Andras Sallay showed a theatrical flair that often made them audience favorites. In 1978 they gained the World Bronze Medal in a strong field, surpassed only by two Soviet couples, Natalia Linichuk and Gennadi Karponosov, who had taken the Bronze the previous year, and defending World Champions Irina Moiseeva and Andrei Minenkov, who had to be satisfied with the Silver. The following year, in one of the tightest overall competitions of the period, Linichuk and Karponosov repeated as World Champions, while Regoeczy and Sallay took the Silver, pushing the other Soviet couple back to the Bronze.

The 1980 Olympics brought a repeat of the previous year's World Championship order of finish, but at the 1980 World's, the Hungarians finally won out over both Soviet couples, becoming the first non-Soviet World Ice Dance Champions in a decade. The Hungarians then retired, to be replaced as World Champions the next year by their good friends Jayne Torvill and Christopher Dean of Great Britain, with whom they had shared training under coach Betty Callaway for the past two years.

REITER, ERIC *(b. ?) U.S. medalist.*

Eric Reiter became U.S. Silver Medalist in 1936 behind repeat Gold Medalist Robin Lee. In 13th place at the 1936 Olympics and 11th at the World Championships, he won the U.S. Silver two more times, in 1937 and 1938, but no U.S. men competed in the World's after 1936 until the championships resumed after World War II.

RENDSCHMIDT, ELSA *(b. 1886) German Olympic and World medalist.*

At the first Olympic Games to include figure skating, in London in 1908, Elsa Rendschmidt won the Silver Medal behind Great Britain's Madge Syers. At that year's third World Championship, which included women's competition and was held in Troppau, Czechoslovakia, Syers did not defend her title, and Rendschmidt again finished 2nd, this time to Hungary's Lilly Kronberger. Rendschmidt did not compete in 1909 but was once more runner-up to Kronberger at Berlin in 1910.

REVELL, GUY *See* WILKES, DEBBI.

REYNOLDS, R. TODD *See* COURTLAND, KAREN.

RICHARDS, DUDLEY *(1934–61) U.S. Men's medalist and Pairs Champion.*

Dudley Richards was one of the rare skaters who competed in two World Championships even before winning a U.S. medal. Because the United States had had three of the top five placements at the 1950 World Championships, with Dick Button the Gold Medalist and Hayes Jenkins the Bronze Medalist, four U.S. men were eligible in 1951. Dudley Richards, who was 4th at the U.S. Championships, proved he belonged at the World's by placing 5th. He did the same the following year, but he did not go to the Olympics because only three spots were open. In 1953, he won the U.S. Bronze Medal behind Hayes Jenkins and Ronnie Robertson and placed 6th at the World's.

After a period of not competing, he returned to win a U.S. Bronze Medal in 1958 as the new Pairs partner of Maribel Owen. They were Bronze Medalists again in 1959 and were 6th at that year's World Championships. In 1960, Owen and Richards moved up to the U.S. Silver Medal behind four-time Champions Ron and Nancy Ludington. Both couples were coached by Owen's mother, Maribel Vinson Owen, who had been U.S. Pairs Champion three times and Ladies' Champion a still-unmatched nine times. Dudley and his partner placed 10th at both the Olympics and the World Championships in 1960. Then with the retirement of the Ludingtons, Owen and Dudley became U.S. Pairs Champions in 1961. Engaged to be married, they were killed along with the rest of the U.S. World team in a plane crash at Brussels.

RICHARDSON, T.D. *(b. 1900) British skating expert and author.*

A proponent of what he called shadow skating, which involved a man and woman performing the same jumps, spins and other elements in tandem but without touching, T.D. Richardson played a significant role in the development of modern Pairs skating. He and his wife Mildred were members of the British team at the first official Winter Olympics in 1924 as Pairs skaters. As judge and skating official for several decades, he was deeply knowledgable (and opinionated) about the sport and wrote a half-dozen books on figure skating.

RITTBERGER, WERNER *(b. 1891)*

German World medalist.

Coming to the fore just after the retirement from competition of his notable German predecessors Gilbert Fuchs and Heinrich Burger, Werner Rittberger was second to Ulrich Salchow, as the Swede won his 9th and 10th World titles in 1910 and 1911 and then took another Silver Medal in 1912 behind the new champion, Austria's Fritz Kachler.

ROBERTSON, RONALD *(b. 1933)*

U.S., World and Olympic medalist and Ice Capades star.

Universally regarded as one of the greatest spinners who ever skated, Ronnie Robertson had his first taste of glory at the 1953 U.S. Championships, taking the Silver Medal as Hayes Alan Jenkins won the Gold Medal for the first of four successive times. Robertson was relatively weak in school figures, which then counted for 50 percent of the judges' total marks. Although he improved his school figures, he was never able to beat Hayes Jenkins, who after a slow start, mastered those figure eights completely. Jenkins was also a superb free-skater with a distinctive style, but Robertson beat him in the free-skating portion of the program several times.

A jumper with the snap of a circus acrobat, Robertson's ace-in-the-hole was his spinning. He could revolve so fast that he almost seemed to disappear at times, moving at a greater speed than the eye could quite take in. He electrified audiences and even made judges shake their heads in near disbelief. But in the 1950s even more than now, judges preferred the "complete" skater, which Hayes Jenkins was, and he always managed to edge out Robertson, even if only by the slimmest of margins.

After taking his first U.S. Silver, Robertson placed 4th at the 1954 World Championships. The following year he was the U.S. Bronze Medalist as Hayes Jenkins and his younger brother David finished 1st and 2nd. That year, Robertson was 5th at the World Championships, due to lapses in his figures. In 1955, he was kept out of the U.S. Championships with an injury but was named to the World team anyway and won the Silver Medal, as Hayes Jenkins took his third World Championship. David Jenkins won the World Bronze to complete a U.S. sweep.

In 1956, Hayes Jenkins won the U.S., Olympic and World Gold, Robertson the Silver in all three competitions and David Jenkins all three Bronze Medals, an across-the-board sweep never accomplished before or since. Robertson then joined the Ice Capades, dazzling audiences year after year with his extraordinary feats on ice. Many experts feel that Robertson's ability as a spinner led to a long eclipse of that aspect of skating in competition: No one could approach his ability in that regard, and skaters emphasized other aspects of skating instead.

ROCA, RENEE *(b. 1963)* *U.S. Ice Dance Champion with Donald Adair (b. 1960) and Gorsha Sur (b. 1967).*

With her first partner, Donald Adair, in 1985, Renee Roca was the U.S. Ice Dance Silver Medalist behind Judy Blumberg and Michael Seibert; and Roca and Adair finished 11th at the World Championships. The following year, with Blumberg and Seibert skating professionally, Roca and Adair became U.S. Champions and moved up to 6th at the World's. But in 1987, the couple were knocked back to the Silver Medal by Suzanne Semanick and Scott Gregory and did not compete at the World's due to an injury to Adair that brought on the couple's retirement.

Then in 1990, the Soviet ice dancer Gorsha Sur defected and came to the United States, where he sought out Renee Roca. She agreed to return to competition as his partner; they became U.S. Gold Medalists in 1993 and finished 11th at the 1993 World Championships. In 1994, Roca and Sur again competed in the Nationals but were forced to withdraw due to an on-ice injury to Roca; they were also prevented from competing at the Olympics that year because Sur was not yet a U.S. citizen.

In 1995, Roca and Sur were again the U.S. champions and moved up to 10th at the World Championships, but in 1996 they lost their U.S. title to the three-time Silver Medalists Elizabeth Punsalan and Jerod Swallow and dropped to 14th place at the 1996 World Championships while Punsalan and Swallow moved up to 7th.

ROCKER *See* SCHOOL FIGURES.

RODNINA, IRINA *(b. 1949) Soviet European, World and Olympic Pairs Champion with Alexsei Ulanov (b. 1948) and Alexandr Zaitsev (b. 1951).*

Born and raised in Moscow, Russia, Irina Rodnina survived tuberculosis as an infant and grew up to win more figure-skating medals than any other individual. Only Sonja Henie won as many World and Olympic Gold Medals, but Irina had more European medals because the competition had not begun until Henie had been skating internationally for several years.

Rodnina attended a children's sports school; her potential was recognized soon after she began to skate at the age of six. Later, she trained at the Moscow Central Musical Culture school. Her first Pairs partner was Alexsei Ulanov, who was a year older. At the start of their career they were overshadowed by two other Soviet Pairs, the legendary Protopopovs, Olympic Gold Medalists in 1964 and 1968 and World Champions from 1965 to 1968, and Tatiana Zhuk and Alexandr Gorelik, who were World Silver or Bronze Medalists four times from 1963 to 1968. In fact, when Rodnina and Ulanov won their first World Gold in 1969, the Protopopovs were still Soviet Champions, although they fell to 3rd in the World that year. Rodnina and Ulanov succeeded them as Soviet Champions in 1970.

Rodnina and Ulanov were World Champions 1969–72. Emphasizing strength and speed and tending toward somewhat bombastic musical selections, they were the antithesis of the classically pure Protopopovs. Their only close competition was another Soviet Pair, Ludmila Smirnova and Andrei Suraikin, who were 2nd to them at the World's from 1970 to 1972 and at the 1972 Olympics in Sapporo, Japan.

A personal drama involving the two Soviet Pairs was played out at these Olympics. Word had gotten out that Rodnina's partner Alexei Ulanov was going to marry Ludmila Smirnova after the Olympics and would henceforth be her partner, with Andrei Suraikin retiring. Rodnina's public displays of tears at the Olympics and the World Championships led to open speculation in the press that she was herself in love with Ulanov and was losing much more than a skating partner.

But Rodnina's career was actually just getting going. She took a new partner, Alexandr Zaitsev, who proved to be even better matched with her in terms of skating style than Ulanov had been. Over the next two years, Rodnina had the pleasure of beating her former partner and his new wife at every turn—as Soviet Champion, at the European's and at the World's. Alexandr Zaitsev worked with weights both on and off the ice to further increase his strength, and the couple were able to perform prodigious lifts. But this was not just a matter of his strength: Olympic weightlifters can bench press hundreds of pounds over their heads from a stationary stance, but no male dancer or ice skater, with his lithe frame, could possibly lift a partner *while moving* without a great deal of help from that partner. This is a matter of technique, and Irina Rodnina had mastered it completely. She was also able to teach Alexandr a great deal about the timing that leads to perfectly symmetrical joint jumps and spins.

Their first World Championship win in 1973, however, occurred under extraordinary circumstances. They had won both the Soviet and European Championships handily, but during their long program at the World Championships at Bratislava, Czechoslovakia, a technical malfunction cut off their music after they had skated only three minutes of their five-minute routine. They simply kept going, skating so well in the silence that members of the audience told a reporter from *Sports Illustrated* afterward that it almost seemed as though they could hear the music. Most experts on the sport believe that the referee should have stopped the proceedings and let them pick up where they had left off when the music problem had been fixed. But the referee said that it was up to the skaters to request such a move. Because Rodnina and Zaitsev were given straight 5.9 scores for technical merit and 5.7s or 5.8s for artistry, the argument was moot: the Gold Medal was theirs, anyway.

After Smirnova and Ulanov retired in 1974, West Germany's Romy Kermer and Rolf Osterreich challenged them for the next two years, taking the Silver Medal at both World Championships and the 1976 Olympics at Innsbruck, Austria. They then retired, and the 1977 World Silver went to another Soviet Pair, Irina Vorobieva and Alexandr Vlasov, but they were not really in the same class and dropped out of World medal contention after that. A more likely future threat was offered by the 1977 World Bronze Medalists, U.S. Champions Tai Babilonia and Randy Gardner.

What made Babilonia and Gardner serious competition was the fact that they were still developing as a Pair even as they had already reached a technical level in some areas that rivaled Rodnina and Zaitsev. Both, for example, had mastered triple throw jumps, in which the woman is launched into the air by her partner to complete three revolutions and land on a clean edge of one foot. Very few other skaters could perform a triple throw jump, and none could do it with breathtaking confidence of these two couples.

Rodnina and Zaitsev married in April 1975, and in 1979 they took the year off so Irina could have a child, Sasha Alexandr. In their absence, Babilonia and Gardner took the World Gold Medal with a performance that, in terms both of exceptionally high marks and expert reaction, suggested that they might well have beaten Rodnina and Zaitsev. The skating world looked forward to a head-to-head competition between them at the 1980 Olympics in Lake Placid, New York. But a groin injury suffered by Randy Gardner got worse instead of better after a period of enforced rest, and he was forced to withdraw minutes before skating the short program. Thus Rodnina garnered her third Gold Medal and her husband his second. They both said that they would have preferred to see Babilonia and Gardner skate to find out which Pair was indeed preeminent.

The couple retired from amateur competition after the 1980 Olympics, although Rodnina went on to coach several Soviet Pairs. Divorced from Zaitsev and remarried to Leonid Minkowvski, she began to teach in the United States in 1990.

ROLES, BARBARA *(b. 1940) U.S. Champion.*

Barbara Roles was the U.S. Bronze Medalist in 1959 behind sisters Carol and Nancy Heiss and was 5th at the World Championships that year. In 1960, she was 2nd to Carol Heiss, while 15-year-old Laurence Owen took the Bronze. Barbara skated splendidly at both the 1960 Olympics and the World Championships, winning the Bronze Medal at both competitions. In 1961, with the retirement of Carol Heiss, a tight contest was expected between Roles and Owen, but Roles was unable to compete. What had seemed a lost opportunity turned out to be a literal life-saver, as the entire U.S. team was killed at Brussels in a plane crash on the way to the World Championships. In 1962, she returned to win the U.S. Ladies' Gold Medal but did not compete in the World Championships.

ROMAN, PAVEL *(b. 1942) Czechoslovakian World Champion Ice Dancer with Eva Romanova (b. 1945), his sister.*

In their hometown of Prague, Czechoslovakia, brother-and-sister team Pavel Roman and Eva Romanova (she used the traditional Czech feminine ending to her last name) won the first of four Ice Dance World Championships in 1962. Extraordinarily well matched even for a brother-sister team, they remained untouchable by any challenger through 1965. They were the only non-British

World Champions in Ice Dance in the nearly two decades from 1952 to 1969, when the Soviets established a run that lasted until Torvill and Dean's triumph in 1981.

ROMANOVA, EVA *See* ROMAN, PAVEL.

ROTCH, EDITH *(1893) First U.S. Silver Medalist.*

Edith Rotch came in 2nd to Theresa Weld at the first U.S. Figure Skating Championships, at New Haven, Connecticut in 1914. The next competition was not held until 1918, and unlike Weld, Rotch did not return to competition.

ROTTER, EMILIE *(b. 1906) Hungarian World Champion Pairs skater with Lazlo Szollas (b. 1910).*

Emilie Rotter and Lazlo Szollas vaulted into prominence in 1931, winning the World Gold Medal over their Hungarian teammates Olga Orgonista and Sandor Szalay. But in 1932, the French husband-and-wife team of Pierre and Andrée Brunet, who had revolutionized Pairs skating beginning in the mid-1920s by adding many lifts, returned from a year's hiatus to defend their 1928 Olympic Gold Medal. They succeeded, and Rotter and Szollas had the Silver Medal snatched from them by Beatrix Loughran and Sherwin Badger of the United States. At the World's that year, the Hungarians managed to come in 2nd to the Brunets, with the U.S. Pair in 3rd.

From 1933 to 1935, however, Rotter and Szollas reigned again as World Champions, twice holding off challenges from Austria's Idi Papez and Karl Zwack and then from the new Austrian Champions, the sister-and-brother team of Ilse and Erich Pausin, in 1935. A year later, their expectation of Olympic Gold was rudely upset by Maxi Herber and Ernst Baier, the sensational German Pair who would also become World Champions that year and defend the title three more times. Worse, the Pausins took the Silver, leaving Rotter and Zollas to claim a second Olympic Bronze. They did not compete in the World Championships and retired in disappointment.

ROUILLARD, NANCY *See* LUDINGTON, RONALD.

RUGH, CARRIE *(b. 1960) U.S. medalist.*

During the four-year championship reign of Linda Fratianne, the U.S. Bronze Medalist was a different woman each year. Carrie Rugh was the third, taking the Bronze in 1979. She placed 11th at the World Championships.

RYAN, DANIEL *See* PETERS, CAROL ANN.

S

SABOVCIK, JOZEF (*b. 1964*) *Czech Olympic Bronze Medalist.*

At the 1984 Olympic Games, Jozef Sabovcik took the Bronze Medal behind Scott Hamilton of the United States and Canada's Brian Orser. Long a resident in America, he was little noticed in ensuing years, until he achieved new prominence in the mid-1990s as a professional. His enormous jumps put him into contention at one professional skating competition after another and earned him many fans on the ice show circuit.

SALCHOW, ULRICH (*1877–1949*) *Swedish winner of the most Men's titles ever.*

Ulrich Salchow took his first World medal at the second such event, held in his home city of Stockholm, Sweden in 1897, winning the Silver Medal behind Gustav Hugel of Austria. In 1899 and 1900, he took two more Silver Medals behind Hugel. His first World Championship title came in 1901, again in Stockholm, but it didn't matter where the competition was held over the next 10 years. Salchow was a winner from 1901 to 1911, except in 1906 when he did not compete and Germany's Gilbert Fuchs took a second Gold Medal 10 years after his first victory in 1896. But Salchow beat Fuchs when both competed in 1901, 1907 and 1908; he also triumphed over other major figures such as Germany's Werner Rittberger and Heinrich Burger, Austria's Max Bohatch and his countryman Per Thoren.

The most remarkable competition in which he was involved was undoubtedly that of 1902. This competition was for men; no ladies' event existed as yet though the by-laws did not specifically bar women. On this basis, the young English skater Madge Syers applied for a place in the competition. In part because her husband Edgar was the most important force in organizing British skating, and because the competition was being held in London, she was allowed to skate. She did so well that some experts believed she should have won instead of getting the Silver Medal. Ulrich Salchow may have been among them because he presented her with his own Gold Medal. A rule was quickly written to exclude women. Women were given their own competition in 1906, which was won by Madge Syers.

Aside from his ten World and nine European victories, Salchow also won the first Olympic Men's figure-skating Gold Medal, in London in 1908, although this was one of his narrowest wins, by three judges to two over his countryman Richard Johansson. For the fun of it, he also competed in the 1920 Olympics, and while he did not win a medal, the Gold went to fellow Swede Gillis Grafstrom, the first of three successive Olympic Championships he won. Ulrich Salchow's name is immortalized by the classic jump he invented (described in its own entry below), but he also had enormous influence on the development of the sport through his position as president of the International Skating Union for the long period between the two World Wars.

SALCHOW (JUMP)

Invented in 1907 at the height of his career by 10-time World Champion Ulrich Salchow of Sweden, this jump is distinctive because it involves a takeoff and a landing on different edges. Moving backward on the inside edge of one foot, the skater takes off, makes one full revolution and then lands on a back outside edge. Because a back inside edge is carrying the skater in a curve in one direction while the motion of the turn in the air is in the opposite direction, the salchow has a visual element of surprise at takeoff. It looks, in a sense, as though a loop jump has been turned inside out.

Although the salchow is performed by both men and women, its history is particularly associated with women competitors at various historic points. The first full-revolution jump performed in competition by a woman, U.S. Champion Theresa Weld unveiled it at the 1920 Olympics in Antwerp, Belgium, where figure skating was included for the second time in what we now call the Summer Olympics. The furthest any woman skater had previously gone in terms of jumping rather than gliding and spinning was the simple half-revolution waltz jump. Theresa Weld hoped that by performing a salchow she would gain points with the judges; instead, she was penalized for her efforts, given only the Bronze Medal and informed afterward that she had made an "unfeminine" exhibition of herself. This may seem absurd in terms of today's standards, but it should be remembered that as recently as 1982, after the U.S.'s Elaine Zayak won the World Championship performing seven triple jumps, a new rule was instituted that limited the number of triples that could be performed by women to five. The rule has since been rescinded, but it illustrates the long-standing conservative view that women shouldn't be *too* athletic.

The salchow also made history at the 1972 World Championships, when Sonya Morgenstern of East Germany completed a triple salchow, the first triple jump ever successfully landed by a woman in competition. Morgenstern, whose school figures were weak, was not a medal contender, but she paved the way for the widespread use of triple jumps by women in the coming years, and, unlike Blanchard a half-century earlier, she was not scolded by the judges.

SALLAY, ANDRAS

See REGOECZY, KRISZTINA.

SAMUEL, CONSTANCE *(b. 1911)*

Canadian World medalist.

In 1932, Sonja Henie took the Gold Medal at both the Olympics and the World Championships, and Austria's Fritzi Burger was the Silver Medalist both times. The Bronze Medal, however, went to two different women: At the Olympics, held at Lake Placid, New York, the Bronze was won by the then five-time U.S. Champion Maribel Vinson; at the World Championships in Montreal, Canada, that country's champion, Constance Samuel, took the Bronze, with Vinson 4th.

The location of major international competitions seldom seems to influence the judges in terms of deciding on the Gold Medalist, but the record suggests that the home ice does have some effect on who wins the Bronze. The judges are not supposed to be swayed by audience reaction, but multitudes of screaming home-country fans may have some effect, possibly simply because they bring out the very best in a competitor for the host country. The 1932 results in the two Ladies' competitions do

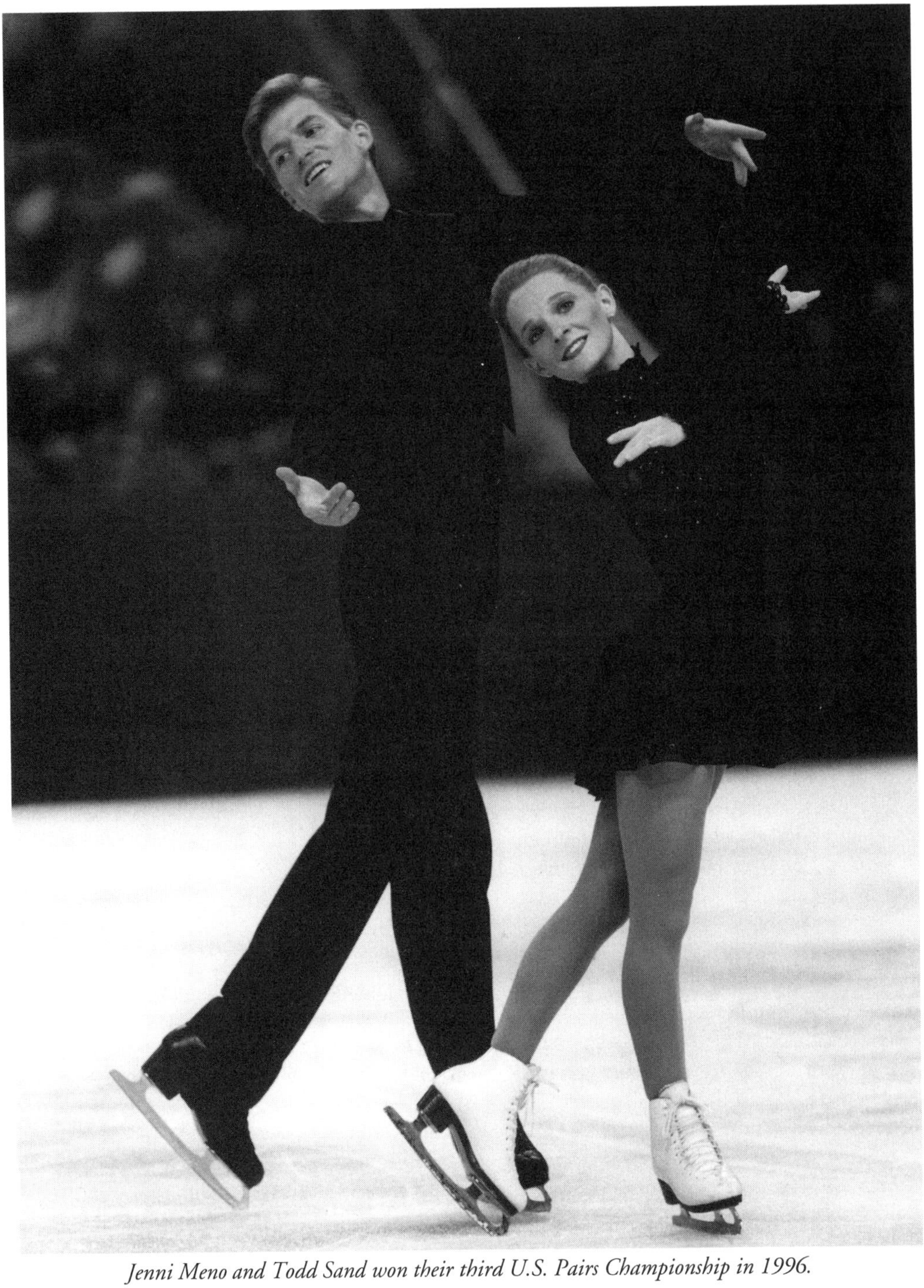

Jenni Meno and Todd Sand won their third U.S. Pairs Championship in 1996.
(Courtesy Paul Harvath)

suggest the existence of a home-ice advantage on some occasions.

SAND, TODD *(b. 1963) U.S. Pairs Champion with Natasha Kuchiki (b. 1977) and Jenni Meno (b. 1970).*

Todd Sand competed in the Men's division and then in Pairs, with good results but no medals, well into his 20s before it all began to gel for him. In 1990, at 26, he and 13-year-old partner Natasha Kuchiki became the U.S. Silver Medalists behind Kristi Yamaguchi and Rudy Galindo and placed 11th at the World Championships. The next year brought great improvement as they won the U.S. Championship and took the World Bronze Medal behind Russia's Natalia Mishkutenok and Artur Dmitriev and Canada's Isabelle Brasseur and Lloyd Eisler. The following year, however, they faltered. Natasha had grown considerably and Sand was having difficulty adjusting to the change. They took only the Bronze at the U.S. Championships, as Carla Urbanski and Rocky Marval won the Gold and Jenni Meno and Scott Wedland took the Silver. At the Olympics, Sand and Kuchiki did the best of the three couples but finished only 6th. They were 8th right behind Urbanski and Marval at the World's.

At the Olympics, Sand and Jenni Meno spent a lot of time together and fell in love. Two months later, Sand was still having problems with Kuchiki and Meno was upset that partner Scott Wendland would not commit to a professional career, as reported subsequently by the *New York Times*. Sand and Meno decided to form a new partnership together. They clicked on the ice as well as off and were the U.S. Silver Medalists behind Urbanski and Marval in 1993 and 5th at World's. They became national champions in 1994. With two former Olympic Champion couples returning for the 1994 Olympics in Lillehammer, Norway, Sand and Meno said beforehand that their goal was to finish 5th—which they did, with a 5th-place finish at the World's as well.

As they prepared for 1995, they announced that they would be married that July, regardless of what happened in competition; they had a glorious season in competition as well. At the U.S. Championships, they not only retained their title but also received six perfect 6.0s from the judges for artistic presentation, more than any other Pair in U.S. skating history, including Tai Babilonia and Randy Gardner. Their coach, John Nicks, who had also coached Babilonia and Gardner, was quoted by Jere Longman of the *New York Times* as saying, "I see an extra closeness between Todd and Jenni. Tai and Randy had closeness, but it was just a special relationship, not romantic. This is a romance. Often during my instructional period with Todd and Jenni, I feel like an intruder."

The lyrical quality of Meno and Sand's skating is of a kind that appeals to European judges, but they are hardly lacking in daring lifts. They are one of the few couples to perform the head-banger, in which the woman is lifted above the man and swung downward headfirst, with her hair almost touching the ice. The combination of such bravura feats and their artistic flair brought Todd Sand and Jenni Meno the 1995 World Bronze in an extremely tough competition.

Todd Sand could be particularly proud. There had been only three World medals won in Pairs competition by U.S. skaters since Kitty and Peter Carruthers took the Bronze in 1982, and two of them belonged to him, with two different partners, the second of whom was soon to become his wife.

Meno and Sand repeated as U.S. Pairs Champions in 1996, winning over Kyoko Ina and Jason Dungjen and the recently formed team of Shelby Lyons and Brian Wells. Despite a fall by Meno on the throw triple salchow, she and Todd received seven 5.9s for artistry. At the World Championships, they were 5th after the short program, but as in 1995, they skated a top-notch long program to take the Bronze Medal once again, behind Russia's Marina Eltsova and Andrei Bushkov and Germany's Mandy Woetzel and Ingo Steuer.

SANDAHL, GOSTA *(b. 1896) Swedish World Champion.*

Swedish and international Men's skating was dominated from the turn of the century until his retirement in 1911 by Ulrich Salchow. Austria's Fritz Kachler won the next two World Championships, but in 1914, Salchow's protégé Gosta Sandahl took the World Gold, pushing Kachler back into 2nd place. It is likely that Sandahl would have had a great career, but World War I intervened.

After the war, figure skating was included in the 1920 Olympic Games, and that competition was won by the new Swedish master, Gilles Grafstrom; he would win two more Olympic Gold Medals and a final Silver Medal over the next 16 years. Grafstrom also won the first postwar World Championship in 1922, but he very often did not compete at the World's, absenting himself in 1923. Gosta Sandahl competed for Sweden in his stead and added a Bronze to his Gold Medal of 10 years earlier as another "old timer," Austria's Fritz Kachler, gained a third Gold Medal to go with his 1912 and 1913 victories.

SANTEE, DAVID *(b. 1955) Multiple U.S. medalist.*

Like Paul Wylie a few years later, David Santee was continually expected to become the U.S. Champion, but he never quite managed it. His first Bronze Medal came in 1973. He was just 18 but had terrific jumps and was immediately pegged as a future champion despite some weakness in school figures. But he did not make the medal stand for the next two years. Then in 1976, he almost gained the Gold Medal, but was edged by Terry Kubicka. Yet at the Olympics he was 6th and Kubicka 7th; at the World's, he was 5th and Kubicka 6th.

The 1977 U.S. Gold Medal went to Charlie Tickner, with Santee dropping back to the Bronze behind Scott Cramer. At the World Championships he beat both of them and very nearly captured the Bronze Medal, coming in 4th behind the unheralded Minoru Sano of Japan. In 1978, he was second in the United States to Tickner, who went on to win the World Championship with Santee dropping to 6th there. Tickner was U.S. Champion again in 1979 with Santee again behind Scott Cramer for his third Bronze Medal. Santee had an even worse year at the World's, falling (literally) to 8th place. In 1980, Santee regained his composure, but it was perhaps his most disappointing year: He was second to Tickner at the U.S. Championships and 4th at both the Olympics and the World Championships; Tickner took the Bronze both times.

Tickner turned professional, and in 1981 Santee seemed to have his best shot at the U.S. Championship since 1976. But Scott Hamilton, who had finished behind him at all three competitions the previous year, won not only the U.S. Gold but also the World Championship. Still, this was a year of triumph for Santee as he took the Silver Medal behind Hamilton at the World's. In 1982, David tried once more, but he took another U.S. Bronze behind Hamilton and Robert Wagenhoffer and then had a disastrous World's that left him in 8th place.

Santee then turned professional, skating with a number of shows and making an especially well-reviewed appearance with John Curry's company. He had won more U.S. Men's medals than anyone but Roger Turner and Hayes Jenkins, but unfortunately none of them was Gold.

SATO, YUKA *(b. 1974) Japanese World Champion.*

From the beginning of the 1990s, Yuka Sato of Japan received high marks for her artistic impression and was renowned for her complex footwork, but she had problems with her triple jumps and was never quite able to snag a medal. Her best showing was at the 1993 World Championships, where she finished 4th. At the 1994 Olympics in Lillehammer,

Norway, she was 5th behind Oksana Baiul, Nancy Kerrigan, Lu Chen, and Surya Bonaly. But the 1994 World Championships in her home country, at Chiba, presented a special opportunity: All three of the Olympic Ladies' medal winners bowed out of the World's, Baiul and Chen because of injuries and Nancy Kerrigan because she had had enough competition limelight after the Tonya Harding affair, which dominated Olympic coverage.

Yuka Sato made the most of her opportunity, winning the short program over France's Surya Bonaly by a narrow margin and then skating a perfect long program; the program showed off her customary artistry but also included six clean triple jumps. With by far her best competition performance ever, she was awarded the World Gold Medal before a delighted home-country audience. She was placed 1st by five of the nine judges, while Bonaly had four 1st place votes and was placed 3rd by three judges. Sato then turned professional.

SAVAGE, JOSEPH *(b. 1907) Multiple U.S. medalist in Pairs and Ice Dancing.*

From 1926 through 1943, Joseph Savage won 22 U.S. medals in Pairs or Ice Dancing with eight different partners. With Edith Secord (b. 1910), he won the Bronze Medal in Pairs in 1929 and 1930. Switching partners, he again won the Pairs Bronze with Gertrude Meredith (b. 1913) in 1932 and 1933. But his primary record was in Ice Dancing. In the period before 1936, during which separate medals were given for each of two dances, usually the waltz and the fourteen step, he won seven Gold Medals, four Silver Medals and two Bronze Medals with five different partners: Rosalie Dunn (see separate entry), with both his Pairs partners Secord and Meredith, with Grace Madden (see separate entry) and with Ladies' Champion Maribel Vinson (see separate entry).

At the first Ice Dance competition conducted according to the modern form, he took the Gold Medal in 1936 with new partner Marjorie Parker. In 1937, the couple took the Silver. In 1938, Savage joined forces with Katherine Durbrow (see separate entry) to take another Silver and did the same with Nettie Prantell (see separate entry) in 1939. Four years later he gained a final Ice Dance Silver Medal after reuniting with former partner Parker, now Mrs. Marjorie Smith. Because World competition in Ice Dancing did not begin until 1952, there is no way to rank him internationally, but in Pairs he did compete in both the 1930 World Championships and the 1932 Olympics, placing 8th with Secord in 1930 and 7th with Meredith in 1932. Without question he was one of the most enthusiastic and indefatigable skaters of his era.

SAWBRIDGE, JANET *(b. 1943) British Ice Dance Champion and World medalist with David Hickinbottom (b. 1942).*

Janet Sawbridge and David Hickinbottom became British Champions in 1964 and took the World Bronze Medal that year behind Pavel Roman and Eva Romanova; this Czechoslovakian brother-and-sister team claimed their third Gold Medal, followed by Silver Medalists Paulette Doan and Kenneth Ormsby of Canada. In 1965, the British couple moved up to take the Silver behind the Czechoslovakian team. They retired as another British team, Diane Towler and Bernard Ford, came to the fore in 1966. Sawbridge later returned with a new partner, Jon Lane (b. 1946), and came in 2nd to Towler and Ford at the British Championships, with the two couples taking Gold and Bronze at the World Championships.

Janet Sawbridge turned to coaching at the end of the 1960s; in 1972 it was her idea to put together teenage skaters Jayne Torvill, who had lost her Pairs partner, and Christopher Dean, who had split with his Ice Dance partner. Sawbridge coached them until 1978 when Torvill and Dean won their first British Championship. Sawbridge was later to voice disapproval of the large money grant given to Torvill and Dean by their home city of Birmingham. The young skaters were hurt by the criticism, but they have always given Sawbridge every credit for seeing their possibilities as partners and for guiding them through the early stages of their development into the most highly acclaimed ice dancers in figure-skating history.

SCHAFER, KARL *(1909–76) Austrian World and Olympic Champion.*

At the age of 17, Karl Schafer won the Austrian Bronze Medal behind World Champion Willy Boeckl and World Silver Medalist Otto Preissecker and then joined them on the medal platform at the 1927 World Championships for an Austrian sweep. In 1928, Schafer failed to take a medal at the Olympics, as Sweden's Gilles Grafstrom competed for the first time in four years to win his second Olympic Gold. Boeckl took the Silver and Belgium's Robert van Zeebroeck captured the Bronze for his only World or Olympic Medal. At the World Championships, which Grafstrom skipped, Schafer was second to Boeckl. Although Boeckl then turned professional, Grafstrom made one of his rare appearances at the 1929 World Championship and took the Gold, leaving Schafer with a second Silver Medal.

In 1930, however, Karl Schafer finally became World Champion, and successfully defended his title six times. Only Ulrich Salchow's 10 World Golds exceed Schafer's record. Over the years, Schafer turned back two challenges by the U.S.'s Roger Turner, one by Canada's Montgomery Wilson, two by Germany's Pairs Champion Ernst Baier, and in 1935 and 1936, the best efforts of successive British Champions Jack Dunn and Graham Sharp. Schafer also won two Olympic Gold Medals, successfully fending off a final appearance by Grafstrom in 1932 and surviving a tough contest with Baier in 1936. He then retired and was succeeded as World Champion by fellow Austrian Felix Kaspar.

SCHANTZ, SALLY *See* URBAN, STANLEY.

SCHNEIDER, PAMELA *(b. 1947) U.S. medalist.*

Pam Schneider was the U.S. Bronze Medalist behind Peggy Fleming and Albertina Noyes in 1966. She placed 12th at the World Championships, where Fleming won the first of her three Gold Medals.

SCHNELLDORFER, MANFRED *(b. 1944) West German World and Olympic Champion.*

Manfred Schnelldorfer is one of the least remembered World and Olympic Champions of the modern era—not because he lacked ability but because he arrived and departed so quickly. In 1963, he took the World Bronze Medal behind Canada's Donald McPherson and France's Alain Calmat. The following year he won the Olympic Gold Medal over Calmat and 14-year-old Scotty Allen of the United States, and then beat Calmat again for the World title, with Czechoslovakia's Karol Divin taking the Bronze. An elegant skater, equally good at school figures and free-skating, Schnellendorfer had nothing left to win and so turned professional for a brief period.

SCHOLZ, LILLY *(b. 1903) Austrian World Pair Champion with Otto Kaiser (b. 1901).*

Young Lilly Scholz and Otto Kaiser were runners-up to Austrian Pairs Champions Herma Jaross-Szabo and Ludwig Wrede in 1925. That year Jaross-Szabo pulled off a feat that has never been duplicated—winning her fourth World Ladies' Championship and taking the World Gold in Pairs at the same time. Scholz and Kaiser showed their own mettle, however, by taking the World Bronze with the Silver going to an innovative husband-and-wife team from France, Pierre and Andrée Brunet. The following year, Scholz and Kaiser moved up to win the World Silver as Jaross-Szabo and Wrede fell back to the Bronze. In 1927, the Brunets did not compete, and the Jaross-Szabo/Wrede team again captured the Gold with Scholz and Kaiser second.

The Brunets returned in 1928 to win both the Olympics and the World Championship, Scholz and Kaiser taking the Silver Medal both times. Wrede with new partner Melitta Brunner (Jaross-Szabo had retired) took both Bronze Medals. With the Brunets again absent, Lilly and Otto then seized the opportunity to win the World Gold in 1929, just ahead of teammates Brunner and Wrede. Having reached the top, they then retired.

SCHOOL FIGURES

Even though they are no longer included in competition, the variations on the figure eight known as school figures remain the basis of figure skating. The very name of the sport derives from the execution of these fundamental tracings on the ice. Figures were the most important aspect of competition from the 1890s through 1972, counting 60 percent of the score at all competitions. Starting in 1973, their place in Senior competition was gradually diminished until they were eliminated altogether at the top competitive level in 1990. The compulsories, as they had been called, were thereafter skated only as separate medal events at some competitions. Even these events will be eliminated in the year 2000.

When a tracing for a school figure is laid down on the ice by a skater, the result looks like a number 8, or, in more complicated figures, like an 8 with an additional circle attached to it: 8. In the performance of school figures, a skater lays down a tracing that must be retraced twice more with no full stop in between. The lines left in the ice in the course of these three tracings should ideally overlap so perfectly that the result looks as though there is only one tracing. This ideal is beyond human achievement, of course, but the closer a skater comes to it, the higher the marks will be. The difficulty of achieving such perfection is indicated by the fact that a score of 4.9 for a school figure would be very high, of championship caliber, whereas on the same basis of 6.0 representing perfection, a 5.9 would be a Gold Medal score in free-skating, with 6.0s sometimes being awarded.

Of the total of 42 different school figures, 28 can be skated in either a clockwise or counterclockwise direction, making a total of 70 school figures to be mastered. There were eight levels of tests that figure skaters used to be required to pass to show their proficiency as they moved from the Juvenile, or beginners, level of competition up through the Novice and Junior ranks to the Senior level, at which national champions are crowned. A skater had to pass the Gold test—the eighth—in order to compete at the Senior level. These tests also included increasingly difficult free-skating elements such as jumps and spins, but the greater focus was on school figures. Now there are required free-skating tests and optional figures tests.

Although school figures are performed slowly—too much speed will cause loss of control—the entire body comes into play in executing them properly. School-figure judges take style into account in determining scores; in fact, good style results in good figures. The technical and the graceful are tightly intertwined in school figures. Erect posture is essential to balance. The head—whether a figure is being performed on a forward edge or a backward edge—needs to be held upright so that the skater can look ahead, or over the shoulder when skating backward, to where the tracing is leading because each lobe or circle of a figure should be about three times the individual skater's height. The free leg is kept slightly bent so that it is high enough above the ice for the toe to be pointed downward. The arms are held just below the waist with the palm of the leading hand facing down toward the ice and the palm of the other hand angled so that the thumb is on top. All of these stylistic elements aid in developing the calm and intense focus that is necessary to good figures.

All figures are begun from a stationary point, the only momentum coming from a push-off using the free leg. Once in motion, the skater must continue around the tracing of the figure eight without stopping, without touching the free leg to the ice until the push-off for the second tracing and then the third, above all leaving only a single line in the ice with a single edge of the skating blade. A double track on the ice, which indicates that the skater has touched both edges to the ice (called a "flat"), is a major error.

There are six fundamental forms of the figure eight:

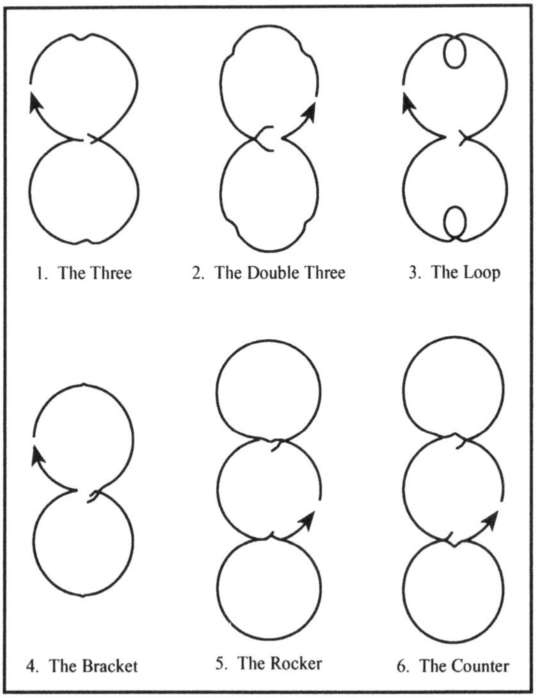

1. *The Three.* This involves making a turn on one foot at the apex of each lobe. The turn is effected with a change of edge that results in a change of direction (from forward to backward, for example). The tracing shows an indentation at the point of change that resembles a figure 3.
2. *The Double Three.* Here, two turns are made on each lobe of a figure eight, each turn (with change of direction and edge), executed at a distance of one third of the radius of the circle.
3. *The Loop.* The skater makes a small, elongated circle within each lobe of the figure eight, using the same edge and with no change of direction.
4. *The Bracket.* The skater changes edges of the same blade at the apex of each circle but without changing direction. The resultant tracing is the opposite of The Three, and resembles the bracket used in typography at that point on the circle.
5. *The Rocker.* This is a figure eight with an extra lobe. Each lobe is laid down in a different direction, but the change in direction is made without changing the skating edge.
6. *The Counter.* Here, a half turn is made, using the same edge but resulting in a change of direction. Again, this is a figure eight with an additional lobe.

Basic figure eights call for a skater to change feet at the central starting point at the figure's center so that one lobe is skated on one foot and the next on the other. Thus the skate with which the first lobe has been laid down is used for the push-off as the other foot traces the second lobe. In more advanced figures, however, the entire figure eight is skated on the same foot. When this kind of figure is called for, it is identified by the word *Paragraph*, as in a *Paragraph Three.*

When the school figures were still a major part of competition, the figures to be skated by all competitors at a given event were chosen by lot at the beginning of that event. That meant that every skater had to have a thorough mastery of every possible variation required at the particular level of competition—at the World Championships, a skater had to be prepared to skate any of the 70 existing variations (although in fact the most basic were not included in the group chosen by lot).

The more advanced figures—the Bracket, the Rocker and the Counter—were invented in the 1880s by Henry E. Vandevell of Great Britain, but it was not until the 1930s that all 70 figures were incorporated in the internationally accepted eight levels of tests. Thus, earlier figure skaters sometimes found themselves required to perform figures they had rarely even practiced when one of these advanced variations was selected by lot at a competition. Because they were *variations*, the skater theoretically had mastered all the elements necessary to skating such a figure, but by including them in the tests the level of performing them increased. T.D. Richardson, an extremely influential British skating judge and official who had been instrumental in this testing development, also invented some new and even more complex figures, but they were never adopted.

The exclusion of school figures from competition has been a boon to those skaters who excel at free-skating and have less ability at the figures. It is likely that Japan's Midori Ito would never have become World Champion if that change in favor of free-skating had not been made. But on the other side of the coin, the great exponent of school figures, Austria's Trixi Schuba, would never have been World and Olympic Champion under the new system. She completely dominated school figures but never won the free-skating.

SCHOYEN, ALEXIA *(b. 1889)*

Norwegian World Pairs medalist with Yngvar Byrn (b. 1881).

Alexia Schoyen and Yngvar Byrn were the Bronze Medalists in Pairs at the 1912 World Championships held in Manchester, England; they placed behind Great Britain's Phyllis and James Johnson and Finland's Ludowicka and Walter Jakobsson. Eleven years later (there were no competitions held between 1915 and 1921), skating on their home turf in Oslo, Norway, they became the 1923 World Silver Medalists, beaten by the Jakobssons. Such long amateur careers in Pairs were not uncommon in an era when there were no lifts performed in the discipline.

SCHUBA, BEATRIX ("TRIXI") *(b. 1950)*

Austrian World and Olympic Champion.

Trixi Schuba is widely regarded as having been the greatest master of school figures in the sport's history. She needed the points accumulated in school figures because her free-skating was "embarrassingly substandard," as British sports journalist and figure skating expert Howard Bass once wrote. In both 1969 and 1970, Schuba was the World Silver Medalist. She became World Champion in 1971 and repeated in 1972, a year when she also won the Olympic Gold Medal. In the 1972 Olympic and World contests, Canada's Karen Magnussen, the Silver Medalist, and the U.S.'s Janet Lynn, Bronze winner, beat Schuba decisively in the free-skating but they were unable to overtake her because of Schuba's near perfect marks in school figures. These then counted for 60 percent of the total score. For several years there had been a debate about whether to reduce the number of school figures skated from six to three and to lower their value to 50 percent of the overall score. The great discrepancy between Schuba's school figures and her free-skating helped tip the balance toward making such a change, which was introduced in 1973. Ultimately, school figures were eliminated altogether from advanced competition, with the short program of required free-skating moves taking their place.

SCHUBACH, DORIS *(b. 1921)*

U.S. Pairs Champion with Walter Noffke (b. 1920).

Doris Schubach and Walter Noffke were a well-matched Pair who became U.S. Champions in 1942 and successfully defended their title in 1943 and 1944. No World Championships were held during those World War II years.

SCHWARTZ, ELIZABETH ("SISSY")

(b. 1935) Austrian World and Olympic Pairs Champion with Kurt Oppelt (b. 1934).

Sissy Schwartz and Kurt Oppelt had a relatively short but perfectly shaped amateur career in Pairs skating. In 1954, they became World Bronze Medalists behind repeat winners Frances Dafoe and Norris Bowden of Canada and France's Silvia and Michel Grandjean. In 1955, they moved up one step to the Silver Medal behind the Canadians. Then, with perfect timing, they reached their peak and defeated Dafoe and Bowden for both the Olympic and World titles in 1956. Having conquered their sport in three short years, they turned professional, performing in both the United States and Europe.

SCHWARTZ, WOLFGANG *(b. 1946)*

Austrian Olympic Champion.

Wolfgang Schwartz was unique in that he won the Olympic Gold Medal without ever being his country's national champion. That champion was Emmerich Danzer, who won the World Gold in 1966 and 1967; Schwartz came in 2nd both times. Danzer won the Austrian title again in 1968, as well as the European Championships, but at the Olympics in Geneva, Switzerland, Danzer faltered badly in school figures, and Schwartz put on the best free-skating performance of his career to win the Gold Medal. Tim Wood of the United States finished 2nd, and France's Patrick Pera was 3rd. Schwartz turned professional on the spot, and Danzer, recovering from the shock of no medal at the Olympics, came back to win his third World Gold and then turned professional himself.

Judy Schwomeyer and James Sladky, America's most successful Ice Dance team.
(Courtesy World Figure Skating Museum)

SCHWOMEYER, JUDY *(b. 1948) U.S.*

Ice Dance Champion with James Sladky (b. 1947).

Judy Schwomeyer and James Sladky are tied with a later couple, Judy Blumberg and Michael Seibert, as winners of the most U.S. Ice Dance Championships: each took five Gold Medals. Schwomeyer and Sladky took the U.S. Bronze in 1967 and captured the national title the following year, defending it successfully through 1972.

They hold the best-ever record in World competition for a U.S. Ice Dance team. At their first World's in 1967, they were 8th but moved up to 4th the next year. From then on they were regulars on the World medal platform. In 1969 they gained the World Bronze behind Ice Dance teams Diane Towler and Bernard Ford of Great Britain, who won their fourth straight World Championship before turning professional, and Ludmila Pakhomova and Aleksandr Gorshkov of the Soviet Union, who would be the winners for the next five years. In 1970, Schwomeyer and Sladky took the Silver behind the Russians and the next two years took the Bronze, with the West German sister-and-brother team of Angelika and Erich Buck winning the Silver. Schwomeyer and Sladky were elected to the U.S. Figure Skating Hall of Fame in 1991.

SCORING SYSTEMS

Because the scoring systems in use at different times since the first World Championships in 1896 have varied, it is problematical to compare great skaters who competed even a decade or two apart. Until the 1970s, however, a solo skater in the Men's or Ladies' divisions who was superb at school figures could always win if he or she was at least near the top in free-skating simply because school figures counted for 60 percent of the score and the free-skating only 40 percent. When Hayes Alan Jenkins and Ronnie Robertson competed against one another for the U.S. and World titles in the early 1950s, the scores reflected what anyone watching could judge for themselves: Ronnie

Robertson was a more proficient free-skater than Jenkins, but Hayes Alan Jenkins always won because he was stronger in school figures than Robertson and because Jenkins was *also* a top notch free-skater. If Robertson had been a little better at figures and Jenkins a little weaker at free-skating, the results would have been reversed.

The conservatives of the figure skating world felt that the system worked just the way it should. Even if school figures were something no audience except the fully initiated wanted to watch, they were the foundation of figure skating. But there were others who took a longer view, especially as television began to play a part in the late 1960s. Audiences flocked to ice shows to see champions free-skate, and if television audiences at home were to be captured, obviously the emphasis needed to be changed so that the free-skating became more important. There was heated debate over this issue, but it was finally decided in favor of emphasizing the free-skating more. A deciding factor was the case of Austrian World and Olympic Champion Beatrix "Trixi" Schuba, called by British skating expert Howard Bass "the most brilliant exponent of figures the world has ever seen" but also "embarrassingly sub-standard" in free-skating. If Janet Lynn had ever skated her best at a World or Olympic competition, she might have beaten Schuba, but Schuba won because her scores in school figures put her so far ahead. At the 1972 Olympics, she was ranked 6th in free-skating and still won the Gold Medal. People watching on television saw only the free-skating and couldn't imagine what was going on. Starting in 1973 the figures and the free-skating counted 50/50; Then the bias was given to free-skating, with a 40/60 ratio. When the short program was introduced, school figures counted 30 percent, the short program 20 percent and the long program 50 percent.

Finally, in 1989, school figures were eliminated altogether, and the short program was given 33.3 percent of the weight and the free-skating 66.7 percent. It was widely predicted that this change would mean that Midori Ito of Japan, who was poor at school figures and a great free-skater, would become World Champion in 1989. So she did. Figure skating had become a different sport.

The Men's, Women's and Pairs competitions all use the same scoring system now: 33.3 percent for the short (technical) program, and 66.7 percent for the long program. The Ice Dance competition is different. Three specific dances selected ahead of time must be performed in the compulsory dance section that counts 20 percent. The set pattern or original dance (the latter is the more descriptive term) must be performed to a certain kind of music —a rhumba one year, a tango the next—and must make use of characteristic steps associated with that dance; otherwise it can be choreographed as the dancers choose. It counts 30 percent. The final free dance gives the competitors the freedom to choose both the music and the choreographic content, and it counts 50 percent.

At national competitions in most countries, there are seven judges for each competition discipline. At the World Championships and the Olympics, there are nine judges. Each section is scored on a basis of 0.0 to 6.0. It is always better to draw a later skating slot because the judges tend to leave room for giving a higher score to someone they haven't seen yet, although it may happen that no one does better than the early 5.8 average already posted. In a close competition, a computer works out the complicated mathematics that are involved; sometimes even the judges aren't certain who won until the computer finishes its analysis. But the judges can be sure of one thing: at least a third of the time they will be second-guessed.

Even with this complicated system, judges can try to skew the results for or against certain skaters. The Soviet and Eastern-bloc judges used to be famous for forming conspiracies, shaving or adding one-tenth of a point here and there. Sometimes they got away with it, but more often they were caught and banned from judging for a given time period. The results, however, stood; that is why skaters these days often say that they are skating for themselves, to do the very best of which they are capable. This may sound like a line of hokum, but actually it is wise psychology: When human nature and a system

Barbara Ann Scott in full ice-show regalia in the late 1940s.
(Courtesy World Figure Skating Museum)

this complex are yoked together, the right skater is not always going to win. As a matter of preserving their sanity, skaters are much better off skating against their own idea of perfection rather than worrying about the judges.

SCOTT, BARBARA ANN *(b. 1929)*

Canadian World and Olympic Champion.

In 1947, as international figure-skating competition resumed following World War II, the first competition was the European Championships, in late January in Davos, Switzerland. For the first time, North American skaters were welcomed at this competition. Press attention focused on three-time U.S. Champion Gretchen Merrill, but in fact, petite blue-eyed, blond, 18-year-old Canadian Champion Barbara Ann Scott had already beaten Merrill in the North American Championships. The European press didn't seem to quite comprehend that North America included the United States, and they were so hazy about life in Canada that Scott was asked several times what it was like to live in an igloo.

In fact, Barbara Ann Scott had been raised in Ottawa, where her father had been a top government military aide. He died in 1941, leaving Barbara Ann and her mother with little money; fortunately, family friends raised the $10,000 necessary to send the new Canadian Champion to Europe. Scott quickly became the center of attention once the competition actually started. A skater with a perfectionist turn of mind, she loved school figures, and practiced them assiduously for a dozen years—it had been estimated that practicing the figures alone, she skated 11 miles a day. Although the figures always gave her an edge, she was equally adept at free-skating, drawing accolades from Ulrich Salchow himself for the ease and liveliness of her program. She won the European Championship and proceeded to the World competition at Stockholm. Once again she did everything perfectly, winning both school figures (then counting 60 percent of the total score) and the free-skating. Great Britain's Daphne Walker was the Silver Medalist, and Gretchen Merrill took the Bronze.

A half holiday for Ottawa schoolchildren was declared so that they could attend the welcome-home parade given the new World Champion, the first ever from North America. Then Scott went back to practicing, refining her skills even further for the upcoming Olympic year. In 1948, she once again bested everyone, becoming Canadian, North American, European, World and Olympic Champion.

Scott was also an immediate success as a professional skater, beginning that fall. She was featured in the stage show at the New York motion-picture palace the Roxy, toured Canada with her own show, skated guest performances with the Ice Capades, starred in a London theatrical ice show based on the musical *Rose Marie*, and had a popular doll modeled after her. She capped her professional career starring in the *Hollywood Ice Revue*, draped in elaborate costumes. She retired in 1955 to marry publicist and businessman Tommy King and has lived in Chicago ever since.

SCOTT, NORMAN *(b. 1893) U.S. Champion.*

The first U.S. Figure Skating Championships, held in 1914, marked the only occasion that Norman Scott competed for a U.S. medal, but he made the most of the circumstances, winning the Gold in both Men's and Pairs. He beat Edward Howland and Nathaniel Niles for the Men's title. All three men also competed in Pairs, and Norman Scott won with partner Jeanne Chevalier (b. 1894), while Niles and Theresa Weld placed 2nd and Howland and Eleanor Crocker 3rd.

SCRATCH SPIN

A scratch spin is one of the few skating moves that is performed on the flat of the blade rather than on an edge of either blade. The rotation is achieved by bringing the free leg and the arms gradually closer and closer to the body, with the arms finally raised above the head at the conclusion of the spin when the speed of rotation is fastest. The greatest generally regarded exponent of the scratch spin is Ronnie Robertson, who was U.S. and World Silver Medalist several times in the first half of the 1950s and at the 1956 Olympics. U.S. Champion in 1993–94 Scott Davis performed the best scratch spins seen in competition in many years.

SEBO, SUSAN *See* BROWN, TIM.

SECORD, EDITH *(b. 1911) Multiple U.S. medalist.*

In 1929, Edith Secord managed to win a Gold, a Silver and a Bronze U.S. medal in three separate disciplines. The Gold Medal came from the waltz and original dance combined, with partner Joseph Savage in the pre-modern Ice Dance competition. The Bronze was won in Pairs also, with Savage. The Silver was taken in the Ladies' competition, where she was runner-up to Maribel Vinson. In 1930, Secord won the same medals in each discipline, plus a Silver Medal with Savage for the original dance; a separate medal was awarded to the winning couple in the Waltz. In 1931, she took a third Silver Medal in the Ladies' division, a Gold in the waltz and a Silver in the original dance with a new partner, Ferrier Martin. Secord's last year of competition was in 1932; teamed again with Savage, she won the Gold in the waltz and the Silver in the original dance. She participated in World competition only once, at the 1930 event held in New York City, where she and Savage placed 8th in Pairs.

SEIBERT, MICHAEL *See* BLUMBERG, JUDY.

SEIBT, HELMUT *(b. 1929) Austrian World and Olympic medalist.*

In 1951, Austrian and European Champion Helmut Seibt was the only European skater to achieve a position among the top five men at the World Championships, winning the Bronze Medal. All the others in the top five were from the United States: Dick Button won his fourth World Gold, James Grogan took the first of four Silver Medals, Hayes Jenkins was 4th and Dudley Richards was 5th. At the Olympic Games of 1952, Seibt was 2nd to Dick Button after the school figures and maintained that position to take the Silver Medal, while Grogan won the Bronze and Jenkins came in 4th. Seibt then retired from amateur skating.

SEIGH, EILEEN *(b. 1928) U.S. medalist.*

Eileen Seigh took the U.S. Bronze Medal in 1947 behind Gretchen Merrill and Janette Ahrens. At that year's World Championships, she finished 4th, just behind Bronze Medalist Merrill and ahead of 6th-place Ahrens. But Seigh was unable to capitalize on her promise, and the 1947 U.S. Bronze proved to be her only medal.

SEMANICK, SUZANNE *(b. 1968) U.S. Ice Dance Champion.*

In 1985, Suzanne Semanick joined forces with Scott Gregory, who had won two Bronze and one Silver U.S. Ice Dance medal the previous three years with Elisa Spitz. The new partnership brought the Bronze in 1985, the Silver in 1986 and the national title in 1987 and 1988. The couple was 5th in the World in 1986 and 1987 and 6th at the 1988 Olympics.

Gregory then retired from competition, but Semanick found a new partner in Ron Kravette (b. 1963), who hadn't begun skating until he was 19, an age generally regarded as far too old to ever get anywhere in the sport. Nevertheless, with Semanick's seasoned guidance, the couple took the U.S. Bronze in 1989–90.

SERVATIUS, KAY *See* KOTHMAN, SULLY.

SEYBOLD, NATALIE AND WAYNE *(b. 1967, 1966) U.S. Pairs medalists.*

Sister-and-brother team Natalie and Wayne Seybold took the U.S. Pairs Silver Medal in 1985 behind Jill Watson and Peter Oppegard, and finished 9th at the World's that year. In 1986, they slipped back to the U.S. Bronze but improved to 8th at the World's. From a family of modest means, they had terrible problems finding the money to keep skating, until their hometown in Indiana put together a fund to help them; virtually the entire population contributed something, even if only the occasional loose pocket change.

In 1988, the Seybolds were again U.S. Bronze Medalists and placed 10th at both the Olympics and the World Championships. They concluded their amateur career in 1989, moving back up to take the U.S. Silver behind Kristi Yamaguchi and Rudy Galindo and were 9th at the World's.

SEYFERT, GABRIELLE *(b. 1947) East German World Champion.*

Gaby Seyfert was Peggy Fleming's main competition, finishing in 2nd place all three years that Fleming was World Champion, 1966–68, and also taking the Silver Medal at the 1968 Olympics, behind Fleming. A more athletic skater with a less delicate physique than Fleming, Seyfert came into her own in 1969, taking the World Gold at Colorado Springs, beating out Beatrix Schuba of Austria that year and again in 1970.

SHADOW JUMPS

Side-by-side jumps are done by Pairs skaters: the partners rotate in the same direction, as opposed to mirror jumps, where they rotate in opposite directions.

SHAKHRAI, SERGEI *See* CHERKASOVA, MARINA.

SHARP, GRAHAM *(b. 1912) British and World Champion.*

Graham Sharp won more medals than any other British male solo skater, including John Curry and Robin Cousins. Eight-time British Champion throughout the 1930s, he won the first of three successive World Silver Medals in 1936–38, the first behind Austria's Karl Schafer and the other two behind Schafer's successor as Austrian and World Champion, Felix Kaspar. Then in 1939 at Budapest, on the eve of World War II, Sharp became World Champion. It would be 37 years before Great Britain would have another Men's World Champion, John Curry.

SHELLEY, KENNETH *(b. 1951) U.S. Men's and Pairs Champion.*

The only U.S. skater in the post–World War II era to hold national championships in two skating disciplines simultaneously, Ken Shelley was a most popular figure, both with audiences and fellow skaters. His first U.S. medal came in Pairs in 1968 when he and partner JoJo Starbuck won the Bronze Medal. The young couple had a first taste of international competition at both the Olympics and the World Championships that year, placing 13th and 11th at the two competitions. They made great strides as a Pair during the next year, taking the U.S. Silver behind Cynthia and Ronald Kauffman, who won their 4th national title. Shelley and Starbuck then took 6th place at the World Championships, a huge advance over the previous year.

In 1970, with the retirement of the Kauffmans, Shelley and Starbuck won the U.S. Gold and moved up to 5th at the World's. At the same time, Ken won the U.S. Men's Bronze and placed 8th in the World. In 1971, the Pair retained their national title and took the Bronze at the World Championships, while Shelley moved up to the U.S. Silver Medal in Men's and again placed 8th in the World. The 1972 U.S. Championships found Shelley on the Gold Medal platform twice as he won the Men's division and retained his Pairs title with Starbuck. The Olympics that year were to prove a relative disappointment, as Starbuck placed 4th in Men's, edged by France's Patrick Pera, who had also won the Bronze at the 1968 Olympics. In Pairs, Shelley and Starbuck just lost the Olympic Bronze to East Germany's Manuela Gross and Uwe Kagelmann, but at the World Championships, the couple won a second Bronze Medal.

The couple turned professional, skating first with the Ice Capades and then with other companies, appearing both together and apart well into the 1990s, winning several professional competitions along the way. Ken Shelley's pizzazz, stamina and outgoing personality were still evident in occasional exhibition appearances as late as the early 1990s. Only two other U.S. skaters, Norman Scott in 1914 and Eugene Turner in 1941, had been Men's and Pairs U.S. Champions in the same year.

SHERMAN, YVONNE *(b. 1927) U.S. Champion in Ladies' and Pairs.*

Like Kristi Yamaguchi more than 40 years later, Yvonne Sherman became U.S. Pairs Champion before taking the Ladies' title. She won the Gold in Pairs in 1947, teamed with Robert Swenning, who had been the U.S. Ice Dance Champion with Kathe Williams in 1945. Sherman and Swenning had not previously won a Pairs medal and had to surpass previous year's Silver Medalists Karol and Peter Kennedy to take the title. Sherman was only 4th in the Ladies' division that year.

In 1948, the Kennedys took the first of their five Gold Medals in Pairs, and Sherman and Swenning dropped back to 2nd place. But Sherman did take the Ladies' Silver that year, as Gretchen Merrill captured her sixth consecutive Gold Medal. At the 1948 Olympics, Sherman and Swenning just missed a medal in Pairs, finishing 4th; the Kennedys placed 6th and Sherman was also 6th in the Olympic Ladies' competition, two places ahead of U.S. Champion Merrill. At that year's World Championships, Sherman was also 6th as the only U.S. woman competing, and she and Swenning were 5th in Pairs, while the Kennedys took 4th.

Giving up Pairs competition, Sherman became U.S. Ladies' Champion in 1949. In doing so, she beat six-time Champion Gretchen Merrill, who publicly predicted the outcome but believed that new champions should have the chance to take the Gold Medal away from older champions; she gave Sherman the opportunity to do just that. A tall artistic skater noted for her beauty, Sherman then took the World Silver Medal behind Czechoslovakia's Alena Vrzanova and just ahead of Great Britain's Jeannette Altwegg. Sherman's 1949 World Silver provided the United States with only its second such medal, Maribel Vinson having managed it in 1928 behind Sonja Henie; it would be another four years before Tenley Albright became the U.S.'s first Gold Medalist. In 1950, Sherman successfully defended her U.S. title against the blazing Sonya Klopfer. Sherman then added a World Bronze behind Vrzanova and Altwegg. She then turned professional for a short time.

SHISHKOVA, EVGENIA *(b. 1972)*

Russian World Pairs medalist with Vadim Naumov (b. 1970).

Evgenia Shishkova and Vadim Naumov became Russian Champions and took the World Bronze in 1993. In 1994, they finsihed 4th at the Olympics and took the Gold at the World's ahead of Isabelle Brasseur and Lloyd Eisler of Canada and Marina Eltsova and Andrei Bushkov of Russia.

With the other two leading Russian pairs, Gordeeva and Grinkov and Mishkutenok and Dmitriev, again pursuing professional careers, Shishkova and Naumov seemed to have a clear path to the World Championship in 1995 but were upset by the Czech Republic's Radka Kovarikova and Rene Novotny and had to be content with another Silver Medal; the U.S.'s Jenni Meno and Todd Sand took the Bronze. In 1996, Shishkova and Naumov were 3rd at the World's after the short program but had trouble in the long program and finished 4th. The Gold Medal went to their Russian compatriots Marina Eltsova and Andrei Bushkov, the Silver to Germany's Mandy Woetzel and Ingo Steuer and the Bronze once again to Meno and Sand; for the second year in a row, these last moved from 5th place after the short program to 3rd after their sterling long program.

SHOOT THE DUCK

One of the first moves young skaters learn when they start taking lessons is this cutely named *trick.* While progressing across the ice on one foot, the skater drops to a sitting position with the free leg extended in front parallel to the ice surface—this is the "rifle" with which to shoot the duck. The maneuver teaches balance and steadiness; it also paves the way for later mastery of the sit spin. This basic trick is almost never seen in competition, but it sometimes shows up in exhibition skating, usually for comic effect.

SIDE-BY-SIDE MOVES

Pair skaters are now required to demonstrate their mastery of numerous side-by-side moves in which both partners separately perform difficult jumps and spins. In the early days of Pairs skating, which was then much more like today's Ice Dance, no more than one or two such maneuvers were used, and they were very simple. The extensive use of side-by-side moves was pioneered by the great French Pair Andrée and Pierre Brunet at the 1924 Olympic Games. Some conservative judges regarded this innovation as a breach of form at the time, but such moves soon became an established element of all Pairs routines, and the difficulty of the jumps and spins increased steadily over the years. Triple side-by-side jumps are now being used by some top Pairs.

Although the spectacular lifts in Pairs skating may look more difficult, top skaters seldom encounter problems with them in competition, even though falls in practice while learning a new lift are common and can result in serious injuries, usually to the woman. Many skaters, however, have lost ground in the medal hunt because of missed side-by-side maneuvers. The jumps or spins performed must not only be properly executed by both partners, but they must be done with precise timing. Jumps should ideally cover the same height and distance—which usually means that the male partner has to rein himself in somewhat—and takeoff and landing should be simultaneous. What quite often happens is that one partner fails to make as many revolutions as the other—or even falls—disrupting the performance and resulting in point deductions. If such a misfire occurs in the short (technical) program, where specific side-by-side maneuvers must be demonstrated by every Pair, a couple can put itself right out of medal contention. Triple side-by-side jumps are not required, but things can go very wrong even with the doubles that are mandated.

Side-by-side spins are seldom missed outright in competition, but the two partners are expected to match each other exactly in the rate of spin and the number of revolutions. When a couple fails to achieve such exactitude, both technical and artistic scores may suffer.

SIKHARULIDZE, ANTON *See* BEREZHNAYA, ELENA.

SIT SPIN

The original classic figure-skating spin was invented by the "father of modern figure skating," U.S.'s Jackson Haines, in the 1860s. The skater begins to spin on one foot while standing erect and then drops to a sitting position with the free leg extended to the front in the basic "shoot-the-duck" position. The skater's torso is bent forward over the free leg with arms crossed at the wrists. The line of the back should be straight, not hunched.

Sweden's Gilles Grafstrom, the only man to win three Olympic Gold Medals in 1920s figure skating, added two major variations on the sit spin: the flying sit spin and the change sit spin. The flying sit spin is jumped into, with the skater assuming the sitting position while still in the air above the ice. The change sit spin calls for the skater to descend into a spin on one foot, rise erect, change feet and descend into a second spin. Although such spins are an expected element of any skater's repertoire, in recent years they have often been performed in a rather perfunctory way, as skaters concentrated on mastering as many triple jumps as possible. But with even 15-year-olds doing triples these days, spins are coming back into fashion as a way of distinguishing oneself from the jumping-jack crowd. The 1993 and 1994 U.S. Men's Champion, Scott Davis, for example, has a flying sit spin in his arsenal that rivals that of Ronnie Robertson's in the 1950s.

SLADKY, JAMES *See* SCHWOMEYER, JUDY.

SLUTSKAYA, IRINA *(b. 1978) Russian World medalist.*

The old Soviet Union's sports authorities had always tended to push its best women skaters into either Pairs or Ice Dancing, and there had never been a Soviet Ladies' World Champion in the history of the sport. Three different Soviet women had won a World Bronze and two World Silvers in the 1980s; by the time Oksana Baiul came along in 1993, the Soviet Union was already breaking up. Baiul was in any case Ukrainian rather than Russian. Thus it had come as something of a shock in 1995 when three Russian women, Olga Markova, Irina Slutskaya and Maria Butyrskaya, had managed to place 2nd, 5th and 7th respectively at the European Championships. None was able to win a World medal, however.

Then, in 1996, Irina Slutskaya made a breakthrough. She first defeated five-time European Champion Surya Bonaly, and went on to take the World Bronze. At 18 she had the jumps of the strongest women skaters of recent years, as well as grace and style. Slutskaya made a sufficiently strong impression in 1996 to be counted among the four or five genuine threats to become Olympic Champion in 1998. While she would be contending with the 1995 and 1996 World Champions, Chen Lu of China and Michelle Kwan of the United States, and 1997 World Champion Tara Lipinski, she appeared to be reaching the peak of her abilities at just the right time.

SMIRNOVA, LUDMILA *(b. 1950) Soviet, World and Olympic Silver Medalist in Pairs.*

For five years in the 1970s, Ludmila Smirnova was the second-best woman Pairs skater in the world. Unfortunately for her, the very best both before and after her own time on the main stage was her countrywoman, Irina Rodnina. Smirnova and her partner, Andrei Suraikin (b. 1946), first won the World Silver in Pairs in 1970; Irina Rodnina and her partner Alexei Ulanov had already beaten Oleg and Ludmila Protopopov for the Soviet and World title the previous year. Smirnova and Suraikin would be Soviet and World Silver Medalists again in 1971 and 1972 and added the Olympic Silver Medal to their trophies in 1972. Each time, Rodnina and Ulanov were the Gold Medalists.

In a dramatic demonstration that winning does not bring everything, a different kind of competition emerged between the two women. Rodnina's partner Alexei Ulanov fell in love with Smirnova, and she with him. With the older Andrei Suraikin wishing to retire, it was agreed that after the 1972 Olympics, Ulanov would skate with Smirnova rather than with Rodnina. Rodnina was in tears after her Gold Medal victories with Ulanov at both the Olympics and the World Championships, and it was widely speculated by skating commentators and by the press that Rodnina was not simply mourning the loss of a partner but had herself been in love with Ulanov.

In terms of competitive results, the change made no difference. Rodnina took as a new partner the younger Alexandr Zaitsev, taught him everything she knew in record time, with him retained both her Soviet and World title in 1973, and went on to win five more World and two additional Olympic Gold Medals. Ludmila Smirnova continued skating for two more years with her new partner and husband, Alexei Ulanov, winning the Soviet and World Silver both years, before turning to coaching.

SMITH, BARBARA (BARBIE)

(b. 1955) U.S. medalist.

In 1977, Barbie Smith was runner-up to U.S. Champion Linda Fratianne, taking the Silver Medal over the experienced Wendy Burge. Smith then placed 4th at the World Championships, also won by Fratianne. A free-skater with real flash, Smith then turned professional.

SMITH, CECIL

(b. 1910) Canadian World medalist.

At the 1930 World Championships in New York City, Canadian Ladies' Champion Cecil Smith became the first skater from her country to win a World Medal, taking the Silver behind Sonja Henie, who won her fourth Gold, and just ahead of the U.S.'s Maribel Vinson.

SONNEKSON, PATTY

See BRINKMAN, CHARLES.

SPECHT, BOBBY

(b. 1924) U.S. Champion and Ice Capades star.

Few skaters have parlayed two medals in national competition into a more successful and durable professional career than Bobby Specht. In 1941, he won the U.S. Bronze Medal in Pairs with partner Margaret Field (b. 1923) behind Pairs Donna Atwood/Eugene Turner and Patricia Vaeth/Jack Might. The following year, concentrating on solo skating, Specht became U.S. Men's Champion. He was immediately signed to a contract by the Ice Capades, then entering its third season. Donna Atwood had also been signed by the Ice Capades, and owner John Harris put the two charismatic young skaters together to form a team that headlined the ice show for nearly two decades. The couple had not only skating ability but glamour, as well as a talent for acting on ice. Year after year, they starred in story ice ballets drawn from classic fairy tales such as Cinderella and such operettas as Sigmund Romberg's *The Student Prince.* The Ice Capades also featured numerous World and Olympic Champions following World War II, but with the exception of Ronnie Robertson, most of these skaters spent only a year or two with the company. World Champions might come and go, but Bobby Specht and Donna Atwood remained at the center of the show to become a skating institution.

SPIRAL

The classic spiral was introduced to skating by former U.S. ballet teacher Jackson Haines, who popularized the beginnings of modern figure skating in Europe, especially in Vienna, Austria in the 1860s and 1870s. A spiral is essentially a long glide across the ice on the outer edge of one skate, with the free leg lifted high behind the skater. The length of the glide and the steadiness with which it is executed demonstrate technical excellence, while the arch of the back and the use of the arms give it artistic style. There are several variations on the move, including a graceful upward bending of the rear leg at the knee. A few women skaters, notably Denise Biellmann, the 1981 World Champion from Switzerland, even reach back and grasp the free leg behind the head. Spirals are performed by both men and women but are a particularly crucial element in women's competition.

SPITZ, ELISA *See* GREGORY, SCOTT.

SPLIT JUMP

Often called a Russian split, this jump is modeled on the Cossack dance element and calls for the legs to be widely extended to either side while the skater is in midair. Performed from the early days of male figure skating, it can be a spectacular audience-pleasing maneuver and is most effective when performed in sequences of two or more in succession. The greater the height achieved and the straighter the leg extension, the more impressive the jump becomes. Despite its long history, the jump has been particularly associated with certain skaters: 1962 World Champion Donald Jackson of Canada was noted for the great height he achieved; more recently, it has been a specialty of Scott Hamilton, who has a remarkable ability to perform one split after another with great elasticity. The jump is also sometimes performed by women, but precisely because their anatomical structure makes the rotation of the hips involved easier to perform, it is less impressive. Also, women can seldom achieve the snap that gives it a sense of difficulty when performed by a male skater.

SPREAD EAGLE

This is one of the first free-skating maneuvers that young skaters learn, giving evidence that they have mastered the use of the outside edges of their skates. The skating feet are turned parallel to the plane of the body and extended outward to the side as the skater leans backward from the skate edges to travel in a semicircle, while the arms are also extended to each side. It is used by both men and women, sometimes leading into or concluding a section of rapid footwork. While it is a fundamental skating move, it is extremely difficult to perform at a level that is likely to make a judge sit up and take notice. No one has perhaps ever performed it to such great effect as Brian Boitano: A crucial element in his Olympic Gold Medal performance, it caused Dick Button to comment that Boitano's elegant and long-held version was "worth as much as any triple jump."

STAG JUMP

A jump in which the skater briefly seems suspended in midair, with one leg thrust backward and the other bent at the knee and lifted in front of the body with the arms held above the head. The greatest exponent of the stag jump was the U.S.'s first Ladies' Olympic Gold Medalist, Tenley Albright: Her straight back gave the jump an extra elegance, and she always turned her head toward the audience and smiled at the precise moment of greatest height.

STARBUCK, JOJO *(b. 1950) U.S. Pairs Champion with* KEN SHELLEY *(b. 1951).*

In 1968, teenage Pair JoJo Starbuck and Ken Shelley garnered the U.S. Bronze Medal behind Cynthia and Ronald Kauffman (taking their third U.S. title) and Sandi Sweitzer and Roy Wagelein. At that year's Olympics and World Championships, Starbuck and Shelley placed 13th and 11th. Improving greatly over the next year, they took the

U.S. Silver behind the Kauffmans and leapt to 6th place at the World Championships in 1969.

With the retirement of the Kauffmans in 1970, Starbuck and Shelley became U.S. Champions and retained their title in 1971 and 1972 with ease. At the World Championships, they were 5th in 1970 and won the Bronze Medal in both 1971 and 1972; Soviet couples Irina Rodnina/Alexei Ulanov and Ludmila Smirnova/Andrei Suraikin were the Gold and Silver Medalists at both competitions. The one great disappointment for Starbuck and Shelley was a 4th-place finish at the 1972 Olympics, where Manuela Gross and Uwe Kagelmann of West Germany edged them for the Bronze.

Their accomplishment as a Pair was made more remarkable by the fact that Ken Shelley was also competing in Men's Singles, taking the U.S. Bronze in 1970, the Silver in 1971 and the Gold in 1972. The couple then turned professional, skating first with the Ice Capades and then with other companies; they appeared both together and apart well into the 1980s. Starbuck made a particular impact skating with two innovative skating groups formed by 1976 Olympic Gold Medalist John Curry, one of which had a sold-out run at New York's Metropolitan Opera House in 1984.

Canada's martial-arts disciple Elvis Stojko first became World Champion in 1994.
(Courtesy Paul Harvath)

STOJKO, ELVIS *(b. 1972) Three-time Canadian World Champion from Canada.*

Named by his mother Irene for Elvis Presley and with an older brother named Attila, after the Hun, Elvis Stojko has never lacked aggressive showmanship on the ice. He gained his first Canadian Championship in 1992 when three-time Canadian and World Champion Kurt Browning was out with an injury. Neither he nor Browning made it to the medal platform at the 1992 Olympics, but Browning was 2nd and Stojko 3rd at that year's World Championships behind Olympic Gold Medalist Viktor Petrenko. In 1993, Stojko was second to Browning at both the Canadian and World Championships; then, on the eve of the 1994 Olympics, Stojko won the Canadian Championship over Browning. At the Olympics, when favorites Browning and the two former Olympic Gold Medalists Brian Boitano and Petrenko self-destructed in the short program, Stojko placed 2nd to Russia's Alexei Urmanov, the previous year's World Bronze Medalist, going into the final free-skate.

He skated brilliantly but was given what some considered shockingly low marks for artistic impression. *Sports Illustrated* described his problem this way: "His arms and legs appear too short for his muscular torso, his head and neck too large. His artistic possibilities, correspondingly, are limited. Stojko's physique was not meant to carve classical lines through the air." Stojko's response to this problem has been to develop a highly charged athletic form with stylistic touches taken from his favorite off-ice sport, karate. But at the Olympics, the judges preferred the classical lines of Urmanov's skating, handing him a Gold Medal he had not expected to have a chance to win until 1998. Stojko was the Silver Medalist, and Philippe Candeloro of France took the Bronze.

The old guard of Browning, Boitano and Petrenko did not compete at the World Championships in 1994, and Urmanov encountered problems in the short program that knocked him out of contention. Although the judges still did not give Stojko the artistic marks he felt he deserved, he won his first World Championship handily. In 1995, Stojko's determination to defend his World Title took precedence over acute pain and doctor's orders not to skate because of a badly injured ankle.

Stojko's main competition proved to be the resurgent U.S. Champion Todd Eldredge, the 1991 World Bronze Medalist who had gone through three years of injuries and heartbreak. After the short program, Eldredge was narrowly in first place, and a strong effort in the Long Program, despite falling on a triple axel that Eldredge then repeated successfully, made it clear that Stojko would have to skate at the top of his form to win. Despite his injury, Stojko flawlessly executed seven triple jumps, including two in combination, and nearly got a clean landing on a quadruple toe loop. It was also a more flowing program than he had skated in the past, raising his artistic marks. Elvis Stojko had his second World Championship, achieved under great duress.

With the 1996 World Championships being held in his home country, at Edmonton, Alberta, it was widely assumed that Stojko would have little trouble winning a third World title, but a home-ice advantage can create special pressures as well as a partisan audience. He allowed those pressures to get to him in the short program, putting him in 7th place and almost out of medal contention after falling on a triple-toe loop-triple axel combination. At this point, Russia's Ilya Kulik was in 1st place with the U.S.'s Eldredge and Rudy Galindo 2nd and 4th respectively, and Russia's Alexei Urmanov in 3rd. Stojko skated much better in long program, finishing 3rd behind Eldredge and Kulik, but Galindo landed eight triple jumps and was close behind Stojko in the long program scores. Because Galindo had placed three slots higher in the short program, he was awarded the Bronze Medal, and Stojko was listed 4th and Urmanov 5th. It was the first time since 1992 that Stojko had failed to win a World medal, but he rectified that situation in 1997, as he regained the World title, with Eldredge a close second.

At the 1998 Olympics in Nagano, Japan, Stojko performed well in the short program, but his long program was lackluster and he had to settle for the Silver behind Ilia Kulik of Russia. After the competition, it was revealed that Stojko was suffering from a groin injury and that he had gone from the medal podium straight to the hospital.

SUMNERS, ROSALYNN *(b. 1965) U.S. and World Champion.*

At the age of 17, without winning a previous senior medal, Rosalynn Sumners became the Ladies' Champion of the United States. She beat Vikki de Vries and the previous year's Gold Medalist, Elaine Zayak, now just 16. At the 1982 World Championships, a rocky short program put a medal out of reach. Zayak took the Gold Medal and East Germany's Katarina Witt took the Silver; Austria's Claudia Kristofics-Binder repeated as Bronze Medalist. Sumners ended up a disappointing 6th.

Sumners repeated as U.S. Champion in 1983, holding off Zayak and Tiffany Chin, but this time she also had a splendid World Championship outing, taking the Gold Medal over Claudia Leistner of West Germany and Elena Vodorezova of the Soviet Union. This performance made her the favorite for the 1984 Olympics; she took the first step by winning the U.S. Championships for the third time in 1984 with Chin in 2nd, and Zayak 3rd. The U.S.

Rosalynn Sumners turned professional after winning Olympic Silver in 1984.
(Courtesy Paul Harvath)

Championships did carry a warning: The judges gave her surprisingly low marks in the technical scoring. Skating commentators suggested that this was a way of telling her to be more daring at the Olympics, but her defenders countered that the problem was that she made her jumps look almost too easy and that her artistic style, regarded as the most feminine among top women skaters since Peggy Fleming, was obscuring her athletic strength.

At the Olympics, Sumners came in first in school figures, ahead of Elena Vodorezova and Katarina Witt, but then Witt won the short program, and Sumners found herself in 2nd going into the final free-skate. Witt skated before her with a showy program of Gershwin; Sumners, skating last, made less effect on the audience with a program that *Newsweek* described as "subtler and slower." She also missed a double axel and turned a triple toe loop into a double. Sumners got the higher artistic marks, including one perfect 6.0, but Witt became the Gold Medalist by one-tenth of a point, with the Soviet Union's Kira Ivanova moving up to a surprise Bronze. With one World Championship Gold and the Olympic Silver in hand, Sumners skipped the 1984 World's and turned professional.

Rosalynn Sumners had an extremely difficult time adapting to professional skating. Only 19 and having led a very protected existence, she put on weight and developed emotional problems that she was later very candid about, saying that she was ultimately glad she had not won the Olympic Gold Medal since she had barely survived the pressures that existed even as a Silver Medalist. But she finally adjusted and went on to a long career, skating with many different show tours and still winning plaudits into the 1990s for her serene and lovely artistic presentations.

SUR, GORSHA *See* ROCA, RENEE.

SURAIKIN, ANDREI *See* SMIRNOVA, LUDMILA.

SUSMAN, ERICA *(b. 1955) U.S. Pairs medalist with Thomas Huff (b. 1953).*

In 1974, Erica Susman and Thomas Huff took the U.S. Bronze in Pairs behind repeat Champion Melissa Militano and her new partner Johnny Johns; the Silver went to Tai Babilonia and Randy Gardner.

SUTTON, HARRIET *(b. 1929) U.S. Pairs medalist with Lyman Wakefield (b. 1927).*

Harriet Sutton and Lyman Wakefield took a single U.S. Bronze Medal in Pairs in 1948, the first year that Karol and Peter Kennedy became U.S. Champions over the previous year's winners, Yvonne Sherman and Robert Swenning. Sutton and Wakefield were unable to repeat as several new Pairs teams emerged over the next few years.

SVEUM, DENNIS *See* FORTUNE, KRISTIN.

SWALLOW, JEROD *(b. 1966) U.S. Ice Dance Champion with Elizabeth Punsalan (b. 1971).*

The first U.S. Ice Dance medal won by Jerod Swallow and Elizabeth Punsalan, a surprise Gold in 1991, marked their very best effort, but they have been on the U.S. medal platform every year since. In 1992 and 1993 they were the Bronze Medalists and, following their marriage in September 1993, took the Gold again in 1994 and then Silver in 1995. At the World Championships in 1994, they were 12th. They represented the United States at the Olympics in 1994 because Gorsha Sur was not yet a U.S. citizen and thus was ineligible. Skating under great pressure after the murder of Elizabeth's father just before the Olympics, they finished 15th.

In 1995, Punsalan and Swallow were again the U.S. Silver Medalists behind Roca and Sur but did not participate in the World Championships, since only one slot was open. Finally, in 1996, they topped Roca and Sur to win the U.S. Gold Medal. The improvement they showed held firm at the World's, where they placed 7th, the best showing that either of the rival U.S. couples had made; Roca and Sur were 14th at this event.

SWEIDING, FRANK *See* HAMULA, GAIL.

SWEITZER, SANDI *See* WAGELEIN, ROY.

SWENNING, RICHARD *See* TYSON, AGNES.

SWENNING, ROBERT *(b. 1925) U.S. Ice Dance and Pairs Champion with different partners.*

In 1945, Robert Swenning teamed with Kathe Williams to win the U.S. Gold Medal in Ice Dancing. Two years later, he and Yvonne Sherman, who would subsequently become U.S. Ladies' Champion, skated to the Gold Medal in Pairs. In 1948, Swenning and Sherman could only manage the Pairs Silver as they were beaten by the sister-and-brother team of Karol and Peter Kennedy, taking the first of their five U.S. Gold Medals. But Swenning and Sherman were ahead of the Kennedys at the Olympics, taking 4th place, and were right behind them in 5th at the World's. Swenning then retired and Sherman concentrated in solo competition.

SYERS, EDGAR *(b. 1863) British skating pioneer and World medalist.*

Edgar Syers was one of the prime movers behind the development of figure skating as a competitive sport in Great Britain. The first British Men's Champion, he founded the British Figure Skating Club in 1896 and was one of the international group who inaugurated the World Championships that same year. He soon happily took a back seat to his young wife, Madge, who beat him more than once in competitions before the Ladies' divisions were established. In 1899, Edgar Syers was the World Bronze Medalist at Davos, Switzerland behind Austria's Gustav Hugel and Sweden's Ulrich Salchow, who was appearing in the first of 12 World Championships, 10 of which he won.

Edgar Syers supported his wife's application to compete in the Men's competition at the 1902 World Championships, in which she was 2nd to Salchow, an event that led to the establishment of the Ladies' division in 1906. The Syerses were the Bronze Medalists in Pairs at the first Olympics in 1908, at which she also took the Ladies' Gold.

SYERS, MADGE *(1881–1917) British, World and Olympic Champion; pioneer of Women's figure skating.*

The first World Figure Skating Championship, then called the International Skating Union Championship, was held in St. Petersburg, Russia in 1896. During the next several years, the site alternated between Stockholm, Sweden; London, England; and Davos, Switzerland. When it was held for the second time in London in 1902, the ISU received an application to compete from Madge Syers. She was well known because her husband, Edgar Syers, 18 years her senior, had founded the British Figure Skating Club in 1896. This organization broke with the stodgy Victorian style still prevalent in Great Britain and instead espoused the International Style developed in Vienna in the 1870s by U.S. teacher Jackson Haines. Largely to accommodate her husband and because there was no specific rule against women competing, the directors of the ISU allowed her to become the first woman to compete in a World Championship.

They were unprepared, however, for the result: She came in second to Sweden's Ulrich Salchow, who had won the year before in Stockholm and who would go on to dominate Men's skating for the remainder of the decade. There were many who thought that Madge Syers ought to have won, and Salchow himself was so impressed that he gallantly presented her with his own Gold Medal. The more conservative members of the ISU were distressed. They quickly moved to amend the rules and barred women from the competition on the grounds that their long skirts made it impossible to see their feet well enough to judge them accurately.

Madge Syers would have none of that nonsense and promptly began to wear her skirts at midcalf when skating, establishing a new fashion trend. In 1903, a Championship of Great Britain was started, open to both men and women, and Madge Syers was the first winner. Her husband came in 2nd, an outcome he wholly endorsed. Madge Syers won again in 1904, further increasing the pressure to create a Women's World Championship division. It was first contested in 1906, and Madge Syers won easily, repeating as champion in 1907.

In 1908, the Olympic Games were held in London, Summer Games that were devoted to track and field, but a showplace indoor skating rink had recently been opened in London, and as the host country, Great Britain decided to hold competitions in Men's, Women's and Pairs Figure Skating. As expected, Madge Syers won the Gold Medal and for good measure captured the Bronze Medal in Pairs, skating with her husband. She then retired from competitive skating, but her example of excellence and fluid style were to stand as the hallmark of Women's skating until Sonja Henie appeared on the international scene in 1926.

SZABO, CHRISTA VON *(b. 1894) Austrian and World medalist in Pairs with Leo Horwitz (b. 1892).*

Christa von Szabo and Leo Horwitz won the World Bronze Medal in Pairs in both 1913 and 1914, but the Austrian couple were only second best in their own country. Austrian Champions Helene Engelmann and Karl Mejstrik were the World Gold Medalists in 1913, topping Ludowika and Walter Jakobsson of Finland; these two couples reversed positions in 1914. World competition was then halted until 1922 by World War I, forestalling any chance for von Szabo and Horwitz to attain the top place.

SZALAY, SANDOR *See* ORGANISTA, OLGA.

SZEWCZENKO, TANJA *(b. 1973) German World medalist.*

Blond ever-smiling Tanja Szewczenko of Germany was often in the top half-dozen skaters at World and Olympic competition in the 1990s, but she managed to break through to the medal platform only at the 1994 World Championships, where she took the Bronze behind Yuka Sato of Japan and Surya Bonaly of France. All three Olympic Ladies' medalists, Oksana Baiul, Nancy Kerrigan and Chen Lu, were absent from this competition.

T

TANGO

There are two tangos included in the list of ice dances from which the group of three compulsory dances are chosen for each year's competition season. The Argentine tango is one of the oldest of all compulsories, having been originated in 1938 by Reginald Wilkie and Daphne Wallis in London. It is one of the most difficult of compulsory dances, requiring both speed and very deep edges. It is also one of the most rewarding dances for audiences to watch because it requires great style.

The much-later tango romantico of 1974 was the first Russian creation to be accepted as a required dance. Invented by Ludmila Pakhomova and Aleksandr Gorshkov, who had just won their fifth World Championship, in collaboration with their coach Elena Tschaikowskaja, it also requires deep edges but is not as difficult as the Argentine tango.

There is also a tango element intermixed with waltz and foxtrot steps in another dance, the paso doble, also invented in 1938 by Wilkie and Wallis. Tango music may also be chosen in some years for the original set pattern that is performed between the compulsories and the final free-dance, although here the competitors may choose their own tango music and invent their own steps to it. If a tango is selected by the international committee for the original set pattern, then the compulsories will not include either the Argentine tango or the tango romantico.

TAYLOR, MEGAN *(b. 1920) British and World Champion.*

In 1934, British Champion Megan Taylor took the World Silver Medal behind Sonja Henie at Oslo, Norway. Aside from Henie, Taylor's greatest competition was at home in the person of Cecilia Colledge, whom many experts regard as the greatest exponent of school figures in skating history and who was also a splendid free-skater. In 1935, Colledge was the one to take the British Championship and the World Silver behind Henie. Colledge was also the Olympic Silver Medalist in 1936, but Megan Taylor was the World Silver Medalist; both competitions were won by Henie in her final appearances as an amateur.

Colledge succeeded Henie as World Champion in 1937, with Taylor 2nd, but the next year the results were reversed, as Taylor finally took her own World Gold Medal. Colledge then turned professional, and Taylor ended her career with another British title and a second World Championship Gold Medal. From start to finish, Megan Taylor was coached by her father, who also was the coach of 1939 Men's World Champion Graham Sharp. It is a rare enough accomplishment for a coach to have two World Champion skaters simultaneously, but Phil Taylor also had a professional career as a stunt skater on stilts.

TEST LEVELS *See* SCHOOL FIGURES.

THOMAS, DEBI *(b. 1968) U.S. and World Champion.*

Flashing into the spotlight at 17, Debi Thomas became U.S. Silver Medalist in 1985, nearly upsetting Champion Tiffany Chin, and went on to take 5th place that year at her first World Championships. A powerful skater whose jumps were higher than those of any woman before her, Thomas clearly had the makings of a champion. But at first the attention was as much focused on the fact that she was African-American as it was on her skating. Like all winter sports, figure skating had seen very few black competitors. Bobby Beauchamp had made his mark at the Junior level, including a 2nd-place finish at the World Junior Championships in 1979, but he then turned professional without competing at the Senior level. Debi Thomas was thus cheered for breaking down what had seemed a color barrier; the fact that she was an A student was also noted.

With power and grace, Debi Thomas became U.S. and World Champion in 1986.
(Courtesy Jeanne Martin, photo by Jerry Wachter)

But Thomas quickly saw to it that the main focus became her skating, winning the U.S. Championship in 1986 and taking the World title away from East Germany's two-time winner Katarina Witt at Geneva, Switzerland that year. Witt could not match Thomas' technical prowess and had to depend on her artistic ability, although Thomas did have a definite flair for musical interpretation. The next year, however, Thomas, now in her second year of college and with a heavy pre-med schedule, lost her U.S. title to Jill Trenary. Then Witt took back the World crown, although Thomas did win the Silver Medal as Trenary, faltering badly, ending in 7th place. U.S. Bronze Medalist Caryn Kadavy took the World Bronze.

The 1988 Olympics would bring the much-hyped confrontation between the two Brians, Boitano of the United States and Orser of Canada. However, much media attention was also focused on the upcoming battle between Witt and Thomas, especially when it turned out that both skaters had chosen to skate their long programs to selections from the opera *Carmen*. Although *Carmen* was a perennial favorite among women skaters and both women seemed suited to the music, if in somewhat different ways, the pre-Olympic speculation was that the situation favored Witt because of her artistic abilities.

Thomas started off the 1988 competitive year superbly, with a brilliant clear-cut victory over Trenary at the U.S. Championships. If Thomas skated like that at the Olympics, the prognosticators were now saying, then Witt was in trouble. And Thomas did skate her short program with her usual flawless authority, but her long program was never fully on track after she missed her opening triple lutz/double axel combination, the most difficult combination performed by any woman in the world and a move she had seemingly perfected. Thomas did not even win the Silver Medal behind Witt; that went to Canadian Champion Elizabeth Manley, who blazed around the Calgary rink before a cheering home-country throng.

Thomas seemed disappointed with her Bronze Medal, but not as much as might have seemed appropriate. She had, in fact, appeared distracted throughout the competition. The reason eventually became clear, when it was revealed that she had secretly married a fellow student just before the Olympics. At the World's, Debi again finished 3rd behind Witt and Manley. She then turned professional and gave some brilliant performances, winning the World Professional title with her old flair. She also continued right along with her college education. Although she did not go as far as Rosalyn Sumners once had and say that she was glad not to have won the Olympic Gold Medal because of the pressures that victory brought with it, Thomas seemed perfectly content with what she had accomplished with her skating and was chiefly interested in her future as a physician—which she had always maintained was her priority in life.

THOMAS, IRMA *See* OLD SMOOTHIES.

THOREN, PER *(b. 1889) Swedish World and Olympic medalist.*

Overshadowed by his compatriot Ulrich Salchow, Per Thoren was nevertheless a highly regarded skater during the first decade of this century. He was the World Bronze Medalist behind Salchow and Max Bohatsch of Austria in 1905 when the competition was held in Stockholm, Sweden. Unlike Salchow, Thoren often did not make the journey to the World competition when it was held in foreign countries, but he did go to London in 1908, when figure skating was for the first time included as an Olympic sport in what were otherwise Summer Games. There he was part of a Swedish sweep, with Salchow winning the Gold, Richard Johansson the Silver and Thoren the Bronze. The following year, the World's were again held in Stockholm, and Thoren won the Silver Medal behind Salchow, who won his 7th Gold Medal.

THRAPP, SHERI *See* DUISCH, LARRY.

THREE TURN

One of the fundamental elements of school figures, the three turn is also used widely in free-skating. The skater forms a half circle while gliding forward on, say, a right outside edge and then turns the body to make another half circle going backward on a right inside edge. As the turn is made, the body is essentially lifted over the skate from one edge to the other, with a swivel of the hips assisting the change. When a three turn occurs during the forming of a school figure, the skater is moving slowly enough so that the shift of the body from one edge to the other can be clearly seen. In free-skating, however, the move often occurs at great speed, and the forming of the half-circles is truncated both before and after the change of direction. Thus what the viewer sees is simply a skater moving forward on one foot and then going backward. But what has occurred is in fact a three turn. Three turns often are used in creating footwork, or they lead into the preparation for a jump or spin.

TICKNER, CHARLES *(b. 1956) U.S. and World Champion.*

Charlie Tickner won the U.S. Bronze Medal in both 1974 and 1975, with Gordie McKellen and Terry Kubicka taking Gold and Silver each time. He missed the 1976 Olympic year because of an injury that seemed to threaten his skating future, but he fully recovered to seize the U.S. Championship in 1977, beating Scott Cramer and David Santee. He was 5th in the World that year, Santee was 4th. But Tickner held off challenges by Santee in 1978,

Four-time U.S. Champion Charles Tickner also captured World Gold in 1978.
(Courtesy Michael Rosenberg)

Cramer in 1979 and Santee again in 1980 to win three more U.S. Gold Medals.

With solid school figures and an elegant free-skating style that was reminiscent of another tall skater, Hayes Alan Jenkins, who was a four-time national champion, Charlie Tickner became Champion of the World in 1978, outskating the 1974 winner, East Germany's Jan Hoffmann, and the British Champion Robin Cousins. In 1979, however, Tickner faltered in his jumping, and the three World medalists were Vladimir Kovalev of the Soviet Union, Cousins and Hoffmann, with Tickner a disappointed 4th.

The 1980 Olympics looked to be wide open in the Men's division, with any of these four men capable of capturing the Gold; David Santee was considered a possible winner as well. Kovalev fell completely apart, however. Cousins finally realized his potential to take the Gold as he bested Hoffmann by one-tenth of a point. Tickner skated strongly to take the Bronze Medal, with Santee 4th and Scott Hamilton a surprising 5th.

At the 1980 World Championships, Tickner completed his amateur career with another Bronze Medal, while Hoffmann and Cousins reversed positions from the Olympics. With four U.S. Gold Medals, a World Gold and an Olympic and World Bronze to his credit, Tickner turned professional for a short period.

TIEDMANN, RAYMOND

See GERKEN, DEBBIE.

TOE LOOP

A variation on the loop jump using the toe pick of the skate to assist at takeoff. See LOOP JUMP; TOE PICK.

TOE PICK

At the very front of the skate blade are a half-dozen saw teeth, called a toe pick. This is used to assist in the takeoff of some jumps, such as the toe loop (see above) and to help in both starting and stopping a spin. There is a special blade for school figures (one of the additional expenses at the higher levels of the sport) that has the toe pick placed higher on the tip of the skate to prevent it from catching the ice and marring a figure tracing.

TORVILL, JAYNE

(b. 1957) Briton joined with Christopher Dean (b. 1958) to form most acclaimed Ice Dance team ever.

The daughter of a bicycle manufacturing machinist in Nottingham, England, Jayne Torvill first went to the city ice rink as part of a school group, but unlike most of her classmates, she quickly became serious about figure skating and was training hard by the time she was 10. At 12, she had become British Junior Pairs Champion with partner Michael Hutchinson. Two years later, they became senior champions but then lost the title in 1972. Hutchinson went off to London and took a new partner. Torvill tried skating solo for the next three years but was becoming discouraged about her prospects. Then, in 1975, she was brought together with Christopher Dean by the new figure-skating coach at the Nottingham rink, former British Ice Dance Champion Janet Sawbridge, who had just turned professional.

Torvill and Dean knew of one another—his former Ice Dance partner, Sandra Elson, with whom he had recently had an acrimonious split, was a friend of Torvill's. But despite the fact that they had both grown up in Nottingham, they were virtual strangers and both very shy. Both had full time jobs, she as an office clerk and he training as a police cadet. They were able to skate only on weekends at first. It also took a while for them to get used to one another, although Torvill was quick to pick up the Ice Dance routines that were already second-nature to Dean. He had won the British Junior Ice Dance Championship with Sandra Elson in 1971.

Within two years, the new partners managed to place 3rd in the British Championships, giving them a place on the national team at the 1978 European and World Championships, where they placed 9th and 11th. At that year's British Championships, which were held after the international competitions, they took the British title for the first of seven times and, in a sign of things to come, scored their first perfect 6.0 for artistry.

They also were taken on by a new coach, Betty Callaway, who already was the coach for the Hungarian Ice Dance team of Krisztina Regoeczy and Andras Sallay, the 1978 World Bronze Medalists. The Hungarians became good friends with Torvill and Dean and advised them on many of the arcane details of international Ice Dance competition, which was known for the extraordinary nit-picking by its judges. During the next two years, Torvill and Dean steadily increased their standing. They were 6th in the European's in 1979 and 4th in 1980; 8th and then 4th at World's; and 5th at the 1980 Olympics. Their Hungarian friends took the Olympic Silver and World Gold in 1980 and retired; Torvill and Dean would replace them at the top in 1981.

But to reach that goal they would have to be free to spend more time training. Dean, now a constable, decided reluctantly to resign, and Torvill followed suit. She said later, "I wasn't sure he would do it because I knew it would be a big decision for him. At the same time I was pleased because it meant that I could leave, too. By now, office work had become a drudgery to me." The Sports Aid Foundation gave them a grant of 8,000 pounds for that winter, but they would eventually need much more and applied to the City of Nottingham for help. To their astonishment, they were given a grant of 42,000 pounds to carry them through the 1984 Olympics, almost the exact amount an accountant had said they would need. They were able to return the Sports Aid check, but the City grant was not without controversy, with critics saying the money could be put to more important use.

They immediately justified the grant, however, by winning the European Championship and, a month later, the World Championship. Great Britain had dominated ice dancing in the 1950s and 1960s and was the original home of the sport, but there had not been a British World Champion team in a dozen years. Torvill and Dean were national heroes—with all the press conferences and pressures to keep winning that such stature entailed.

Win they did, repeating as European and World Champions in 1982 and 1983. It was now that they began to show the qualities they would set them apart from all ice dancers who had gone before. The Ice Dance competition is divided into three parts, the compulsory dances, the original set pattern and the free-dance. The International Skating Union had chosen the blues as the kind of music to which the original set pattern had to be skated in 1982. For their dance, Torvill and Dean decided upon a Larry Adler harmonica version of George Gershwin's "Summertime" from his opera *Porgy and Bess.* The result was a number that the British Team Leader Joan Wallis described as so emotional that "there were strong men standing round me with tears running down their faces" at the European Championships in Lyons, France. Torvill and Dean received three perfect 6.0s from the nine judges for artistic presentation of this routine. Their free-dance, skated to a medley from the Broadway musical *Mack and Mabel* then brought three perfect 6.0s for technical composition, and eight out of nine 6.0s for artistic presentation, a total of 11 for the free-dance, and 14 for the whole competition, both records in figure skating in an international competition.

They then moved on to the 1982 World's at Copenhagen, Denmark. Here they became so deeply involved in the sad, soulful music of "Summertime" that Torvill found it difficult to accept the enormous applause: "I had to consciously think to myself, 'It's the end. Smile.'" They received six 6.0s for their effort, including one for technical composition, a score rarely given in the original set pattern. The *Mack and Mabel* free-dance was not quite as fine as it had been at Lyons, they both agreed. Because there were four top couples to skate after them, they did not receive any 6.0s in the technical marks but did have five out of seven among the artistic marks. They easily retained their World title.

How could they possibly top what they had achieved in 1982? The answer came from Dean. He gave up his ticket to the Bolshoi Ballet when they were in Moscow later in the year for an exhibition and sneaked off to see the Moscow Circus instead. Back in England, the couple managed to contact Michael Crawford, who was starring in the British production of the Broadway musical *Barnum.* A great fan of theirs, he saw to it that a special arrangement of the show's score was developed for them. The circus would be their theme, but it took months to develop a routine that met their standards.

Disaster struck while they were practicing: Torvill fell on her side during a difficult lift and injured herself so badly that she could not even move her arm into proper position. They had to withdraw from the European Championships, which would bring even greater pressure at the World Championships. She was still wearing a shoulder strap at the World Championships in Helsinki, but it was sufficiently disguised so that neither the press nor the judges noticed. In their original set pattern—the first rock 'n' roll number ever called for by the International Skating Union—they performed to music from Andrew Lloyd Webber's *Song and Dance,* in which he had given a rock 'n' roll beat to a theme by Paganinni. They received one technical 6.0 and six perfect scores for artistry. The *Barnum* free-dance was everything they could have hoped for, drawing straight 5.9s technically and straight 6.0s artistically. They had topped their previous year's triumph. Their biographer John Henessy described the reaction: "Usually, Jayne is not given to a show of histrionics. Now she gave vent to an enormous shriek and a fiery light appeared in her eyes, betokening turbulent passions below that cool exterior."

Once again, Torvill and Dean found themselves in the heady but difficult position of having to top a performance that had received the highest marks in the history of their sport. This time the direction they would take was her idea, and it was a daring one: They would skate their free-dance to Ravel's *Bolero.* Although the bolero is an ancient Spanish dance, Ravel's driving interpretation of it, with its insistent beat and ever-increasing tempo, was unlike anything Ice Dancers had ever skated to. The unwritten rule was that the free-dance should show off as many different kinds of dance steps as possible. How could that be done to a piece of music as tightly focused as *Bolero*?

Dean had always been the chief choreographic creator for the duo, but Torvill's contributions were also vital to the finished product. She had a special knack, according to him, for finding ways to make a move work better in terms of nuts-and-bolts technique, and with *Bolero,* their collaboration meshed more completely than ever before. They swept through the British and European Championships with their usual complement of perfect 6.0s, although at European's, a couple of the Eastern-bloc judges felt they had gone too far this time and marked them down technically.

But at the Sarajevo Olympics of 1984, they could do no wrong. They were placed 1st by every judge in all three required dances and given three

The incomparable Jayne Torvill and Christopher Dean in 1995.
(Courtesy Michelle Harvath)

6.0s for the Westminster Waltz—the first time in Ice Dancing history that a perfect score had been awarded in the compulsories. They were unanimously first in the original set pattern as well. Then came their final free-dance, the hottest ticket at the entire Olympics. Their intense, sensual and sexy performance to *Bolero* brought a roaring standing ovation, three 6.0s in technical scores and row of nine 6.0s for artistry, a first in Olympic figure-skating history in any of the four disciplines. Words like *magnificent, sublime,* and *unequaled* were commonplace in press reports of the occasion. They went on to repeat their triumph at the World Championships in Ottawa, Canada, concluding their amateur career with 6.0s totaling 136 since their first in 1978, an accomplishment no other skaters had even begun to approach.

The professional careers of Torvill and Dean began with an international tour in 1984–85, a 60-city U.S. tour in 1986, not to mention capturing two complete rows of perfect marks, for both technical and artistic achievement, and the $120,000 first prize at the 1985 World Professional Competition. They won many more professional competitions, made several television specials, starred with the Ice Capades for two years in shows built around them and in 1988 organized a tour featuring themselves and a group of Russian All-Stars.

They continued to make many special appearances even as Dean worked intensively, choreographing competitive ice dances for the Canadian-born French Champions, sister-and-brother team Paul and Isabelle Duchesnay, who were World Champions in 1991 and Olympic Silver Medalists in 1992. In 1993, Torvill and Dean decided to apply for reinstatement as amateurs to compete in the 1994 Olympics. The oldest of the dozen skaters who were reinstated, she at 36 and he at 35 made it clear that they were not taking this step just for nostalgia's sake: they wanted another Gold Medal.

They won the British Championships easily but began to see the difficulties they faced at the European's. After building up a lead in the compulsories and the original set pattern, they came in 2nd to Russia's Oksana Gritschuk and Evgeny Platov in the free-dance and barely won the Gold Medal. The free-dance was supposed to be their greatest strength, and they made changes in its choreography to the Gershwin tune "Let's Face the Music and Dance" before the Olympics began at Lillehammer, Norway two weeks later.

At the Olympics they found themselves in 3rd place after the compulsories, but came back to win the original set pattern with a rhumba that was as sophisticated and perfectly executed as in their championship years. They were tied for first place with Gritschuk and Platov entering the free-dance. They also skated perfectly in the free-dance, which Dean had deliberately made more conservative to reflect a recent tightening of the rules. To their shock, the judges placed them 3rd in that event and they ended up with only the Bronze Medal.

Of the seemingly endless controversial judging decisions at Lillehammer, none drew more fire than this one. The chief dance critic of the *New York Times,* who had long found their performances as worthy of review as any of the world's major dance companies, concluded a long discussion of why they should have won the Gold Medal in the following words: "Typically, they left everyone else behind. While other couples were emoting all over the ice in the free dance, Torvill and Dean opted for pure dance. There was a tinge of courtship . . . but basically it was a display of intricate steps and daring partnering. . .

Plotless choreography was once alien to Torvill and Dean, but this time they told no stories; they just faced the music and skated. Better than anyone else."

TOWLER, DIANE *(b. 1948) British, European and World Ice Dance Champion with Bernard Ford (b. 1948).*

Diane Towler and her partner Bernard Ford swept to the top of the Ice Dancing World in 1966. They became British Champions, and with the retirement of Czech couple Eva Romanova and Pavel

Roman took the European and World titles as well. Even in a head-to-head contest with the Czechs, Towler and Ford might have won because they brought a new approach to Ice Dancing that made it a far more dynamic and exciting discipline than it had been before. The British had been the most important force in Ice Dancing from the start, and it was thoroughly appropriate that a British couple should be the ones to take it in another new direction.

Towler and Ford had an ability to skate with exceptionally deep edges, maintaining their balance at an angle that almost appeared dangerous at times. Their skill created new fans for a discipline that had emphasized sheer beauty to the point of blandness. At the same time, Towler and Ford achieved a level of synchronization that was extraordinary and skated with a smoothness that quelled any thought on the judges' part that they were too daring.

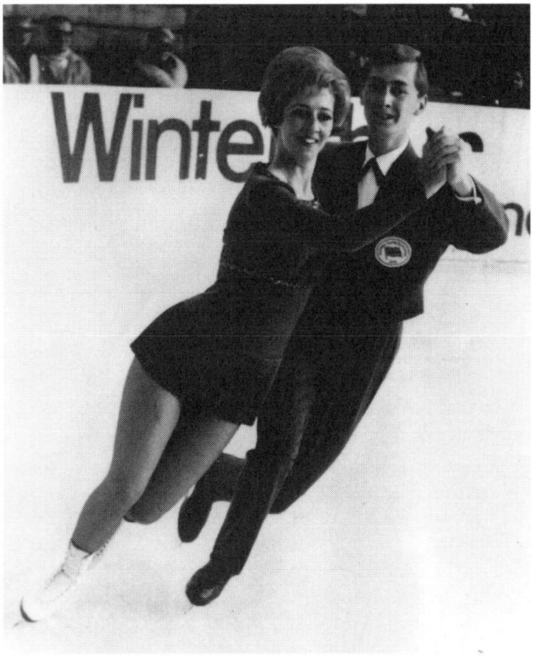

Four-time World Ice Dance Champions, Diane Towler and Bernard Ford of Great Britain.
(Courtesy World Figure Skating Museum)

They also used livelier music, especially in the long program, than had been customary, scoring a particular success with the exotic music from *Zorba the Greek.* In the area of costuming, they made use of the bright colors and shirt-and-vest combinations of the mod fashion designers of London's Carnaby Street. At the same time, their matching outfits were always superbly cut.

Towler and Ford held the British, European and World titles from 1966 through 1969 and changed their discipline in ways that would lead to Ice Dancing finally becoming a Winter Olympics sport in 1976. Both went on to become major coaches in England.

TOWNSHEND, RAYNHAM *(b. 1895)*
U.S. medalist.

At the very first U.S. Championships, at New Haven, Connecticut in 1914, Raynham Townshend took the Ladies' Bronze Medal, behind Theresa Weld and Edith Rotch. Due to the First World War, the next competition was not held until 1918, and neither Rotch nor Townshend competed.

TOZZER, JOAN *(b. 1921) U.S. Ladies' and Pairs Champion.*

Joan Tozzer had not previously won a medal in Ladies' competition when she became U.S. Champion in 1938, but she had won the Bronze Medal in Pairs the previous year with partner Bernard Fox. She and Fox also became U.S. Pairs Champions in 1938; Tozzer duplicated the achievement of just-retired Maribel Vinson, who had held both titles the previous three years. Tozzer went on to retain her Ladies' Championship as well as the Pairs Championship in 1939 and 1940.

She did not compete at the World Championships in either division, but the fact that she beat Hedy Stenuf for the U.S. Ladies' Gold in 1940 suggests that Tozzer might well have been World Champion because Stenuf had been 2nd at the World Championships in 1939 and 3rd in 1938.

1990 World Champion Jill Trenary in 1996.
(Courtesy Paul Harvath)

TRAPP, SHERI *See* DUISCH, LARRY.

TRENARY, JILL *(b. 1969) U.S. and World Champion.*

Jill Trenary zoomed to the top of U.S. skating in 1987 when she won the U.S. Ladies' Gold Medal over 1986 U.S. and World Champion Debi Thomas, who had a below-par competition. At the World's, however, Thomas was the Silver Medalist and Trenary's disastrous short program left her 7th. In 1988, Trenary was runner-up to Thomas in the United States, 4th at the Olympics and 5th at the World's.

In 1989, Trenary held off a challenge by Kristi Yamaguchi to again become U.S. Champion, and she won the World Bronze behind Japan's Midori Ito and West Germany's Claudia Leistner. The following year, she beat Yamaguchi again for the U.S. Championship and, with a superb performance, bested an unsteady Midori Ito for the World Championship. But a knee injury eventually required a major operation, leaving her unable to compete in 1991. Her plans to come back for the 1992 Olympic year were derailed by a slow and difficult recovery. By the time she was skating full out again, she had decided to turn professional.

TUCKER, PHEBE *(b. 1923) U.S. medalist.*

In a period marked by tough competition below the top two places, Phebe Tucker took the U.S. Bronze Medal in 1942 behind Jane Vaughn and Gretchen Merrill, both of whom repeated as Gold and Silver Medalists.

TUCKERMAN, JOHN *(b. 1925) U.S. medalist.*

There had been no U.S. Men's competition held in 1944–45 because of World War II. When competition resumed in 1946, John Tuckerman won the Bronze Medal, but the Gold was captured by Dick Button, just 16, who took the first of seven national championships. With John Lettengarver and James Grogan coming up quickly as well, Tuckerman retired from amateur skating.

TURNER, EUGENE *(b. 1920) U.S. Champion.*

The younger brother of seven-time U.S. Champion Roger Turner, Eugene garnered his first senior Men's medal in 1939, taking the Bronze Medal behind five-time Champion Robin Lee and Silver Medalist Ollie Haupt, Jr. In 1940, Eugene Turner jumped over Haupt to become U.S. Champion. He repeated as Gold Medalist in 1941 and added to his laurels that year by also becoming U.S. Pairs Champion with partner Donna Atwood; she then turned professional to become the star of the Ice Capades. Turner did not compete after 1941 but went on to become a major judge and skating official. He was elected to the U.S. Figure Skating Hall of Fame in 1983.

TURNER, ROGER *(b. 1910) U.S. Champion.*

Roger Turner won the U.S. Silver Medal in 1927 behind Nathaniel Niles. In 1928, with Niles' retirement from Men's competition, Turner moved up to become U.S. Champion, winning over Fredrick Goodridge. He beat Goodridge again in 1929 and then held off challenges by J. Lester Madden for four years in a row, 1930–33. He defeated Robin Lee for his seventh and final title in 1934.

Roger Turner competed in the World Championships four times during his seven-year reign as U.S. Champion. He was 5th in 1928, then Silver Medalist behind Austria's Karl Schafer in 1930 and 1931, and 5th again in 1932. He had bad luck in the Olympics, finishing 10th in 1928 and 6th in 1932. After he stopped competing in the Men's division, he decided to try his hand at Pairs and won the U.S. Silver Medal with Polly Blodgett in 1936.

TWIST LIFT *See* HAND-TO-HAND LOOP LIFT.

TYSON, AGNES *(b. ?) U.S. Pairs medalist with Richard Swenning (b. ?).*

Agnes Tyson and Richard Swenning were the U.S. Bronze Medalists in Pairs in 1955 behind Carole Ormaca and Robin Greiner, who were taking their third national title, and Lucille Ash and Sully Kothman. They did not compete at the World's because there were only two spots open on the team.

U

UHL, HELEN *(b. 1929) U.S. medalist.*

Helen Uhl was the 1948 U.S. Ladies' Bronze Medalist behind Gretchen Merrill (this, her sixth straight title) and Yvonne C. Sherman. Uhl did not compete at the Olympics or World Championships.

ULANOV, ALEXSEI *See* RODNINA, IRINA.

UNDERHILL, BARBARA *(b. 1962)*

Canadian World Pairs Champion with Paul Martini (b. 1960).

Following the Irina Rodnina era that concluded in 1980 with her third Olympic Gold Medal in Pairs (her second with Aleksandr Zaitsev) and the concurrent retirement from amateur skating of Tai Babilonia and Randy Gardner, there was no dominant Pair for several years. This is not to suggest that there was any lack of world-class competitors; rather there were a half-dozen teams that were equally exciting and very evenly matched. Among those who made a strong mark in this period were the four-time Canadian Champions, Barbara Underhill and Paul Martini.

In 1983, Underhill and Martini took the World Bronze, just edging the U.S. sister-and-brother team of Kitty and Peter Carruthers, who had won the Bronze the previous year. Ahead of Martini and Underhill in 1983 were Silver Medalists Sabine Baess and Tassilo Thierbach of East Germany, who had been champions the year before, and Soviet Champions and World Gold Medalists Elena Valova and Oleg Vasiliev. Although none of these couples was a favorite for the 1984 Olympic Games, there was some feeling that both Underhill and Martini and the Carrutherses were just hitting their peak. But at Sarajevo, Yugoslavia, Underhill and Martini had a serious bobble in the short program that virtually knocked them out of Olympic medal contention. Valova and Vasiliev finally took the Gold Medal, with the Silver going to a superb performance by the Carrutherses, and the Bronze grabbed by a second Soviet couple, Larissa Selezneva and Oleg Makarov; the East Germans were shut out along with the Canadians.

That year's World Championships in Ottawa, Canada proved a very different story. Underhill and Martini, skating the best of their career in their home country, captured the Gold over Olympic Champions Valova and Vasiliev, while East Germany's Baess and Thierbach took the Bronze (the Carrutherses had already signed a professional contract and did not compete). Underhill and Martini then turned professional, and their daring, athletic style was a major draw with various ice shows for the next several years.

Canadians Barbara Underhill and Paul Martini won World Pairs in 1984.
(Courtesy Michael Rosenberg)

UNITED STATES FIGURE SKATING ASSOCIATION

This organization was founded in 1921 to govern and promote the sport of figure skating in the United States. Previous U.S. Figure Skating Championships, which were first held in 1914, were mounted under the auspices of the International Skating Union of America, which oversaw both speed and figure skating. The new U.S. Figure Skating Association (USFSA) also became affiliated with the International Skating Union, which by that time had entirely separate committees for the governance of speed and figure skating.

At the time of its founding, the U.S. Figure Skating Association had seven member clubs around the country. There are now more than 450, with 100,000 members. The USFSA oversees the tests that skaters must pass (formerly in school figures, now in free-skating) as they move up in the competition ranks. It sanctions all competitions at the regional, sectional and national levels, as well as ice shows and carnivals put on by member clubs.

Dynamic U.S. Pairs Champions of the early 1990s, Calla Urbanski and Rocky Marval.

(Courtesy Michael Rosenberg)

UPGREN, ROBERT

See AHRENS, JANETTE.

URBAN, STANLEY AND SUSAN

(b. 1942, 1945) U.S. Ice Dancers.

Stanley Urban teamed with Sally Schantz (b. 1943) in 1963 to win the U.S. Gold Medal in Ice Dancing. The couple placed 7th at that year's World Championships. Sally Schantz then retired from amateur skating, but Urban returned in 1965 with his younger sister Susan to take the Bronze Medal. They won it again in 1966. At the World Championships the couple finished 7th in 1966 and 11th in 1967.

URBANSKI, CALLA

(b. 1964) U.S. Pairs Champion with Rocky Marval (b. 1969).

Dubbed "the waitress and the truck driver" by the press, Calla Urbanski and Rocky Marval were as colorful a team of Pairs skaters as any in U.S. skating history. She did indeed wait tables in Maryland to help pay skating expenses, and he owned a small trucking firm in New Jersey.

Calla Urbanski had been skating for many years when she linked up with Rocky Marval, who did not take up figure skating until he was in his 20s. On the ice they immediately clicked and took the

U.S. Silver Medal behind Todd Sand and Natasha Kuchiki in 1991, and then placed 9th at their first World Championship. In 1992, Urbanski and Marval became U.S. Champions with an exciting routine and went on to place 10th at the Olympics, where they had problems that reflected their short time skating together. At the World's they improved to 7th place. Repeating as U.S. Champions in 1993, they finished 8th at the World's, three places behind U.S. Silver Medalists Sand and his new partner Jenni Meno.

Urbanski and Marval had always had a tempestuous relationship; they were often observed fighting during practice sessions. Urbanski openly blamed Marval for their poor showing at the 1993 World Championships. They split up as a result and took new partners but they failed to get to the medal podium with their new partners in 1994. A subsequent reunion ensued on the professional level.

URMANOV, ALEXEI *(b. 1974) Russian Olympic Champion.*

Following the disintegration of the Soviet Union, in 1993 Alexei Urmanov became the first Russian, as opposed to Soviet, Champion since before World War I. He then showed his mettle at the World Championships in Prague, capital of the new Czech Republic, by taking the Bronze Medal behind Kurt Browning and Elvis Stojko, both of Canada. With the reinstatement as amateurs of former Olympic Champions Brian Boitano and Viktor Petrenko for the 1994 Olympics, he was not expected to gain a medal at Lillehammer, Norway and said himself that he was looking toward the 1998 Olympics. In addition, he was recovering from a broken foot.

But the Olympics at Lillehammer were full of surprises. Boitano, Petrenko and current World Champion Browning all met inexplicable disaster in the short program; Urmanov found himself winning, to his considerable astonishment. Stojko was 2nd after the short program, with Philippe Candeloro of France 3rd. Stojko was thought to have the most difficult long program, but he left out a combination jump and reduced a triple axel to a single. He also, as in the past, was marked down artistically by several judges who clearly did not approve of his style, with its tinge of the martial arts. Urmanov took advantage of the situation, skating with more artistry than he had in the past and landing eight triple jumps. By a narrow margin, he became the Olympic Gold Medalist with Stojko taking the Silver and Candeloro the Bronze. As at every other skating competition at the Lillehammer Olympics, the judging was immediately second-guessed, with many commentators feeling that Stojko should have won.

Stojko did win the World Championships a month later, with Urmanov finishing only 4th. In 1995, the result was exactly the same. Urmanov was philosophical about it, saying that he was about where he had expected to be en route to the 1998 Olympics. But all the Russian skaters were faced with problems. Many training facilities had been shut down because of lack of funds, and the stipends for athletes had been cut as well. It was crucial to tour in order to earn the fees necessary for training, but the tours themselves cut into training time. Still, Urmanov persevered and started off well at the 1996 World Championships, placing 3rd in the short program. In the long, he was 5th and ended up in that position for the second year in a row; worse, his younger countryman Ilya Kulik took the Silver Medal behind Todd Eldredge. It was beginning to look as though Urmanov's Olympic Gold Medal, while not exactly a fluke, would remain his high-water mark in the sport.

USING THE ICE

This terms refers to how well a skater's program is choreographed to distribute the jumps, spins and other elements throughout the available rink area. Ideally, for example, if a skater is performing a half-dozen triple jumps, at least one should occur at each of the four corners of the ice. This not only gives the overall program a spatial balance but also permits the judges to view a skater's jumping technique from various angles. In addition, it allows spectators in various parts of the arena to see some maneuvers in close proximity.

Advanced skaters are also well aware of the effect proper placement of jumps can have on television presentation of a program. It was no accident that Nancy Kerrigan, for instance, would perform her long, graceful spirals so that her smiling uplifted face was coming straight at the television camera for part of the move. On the other hand, the blatant mugging at television cameras that U.S. Champion Christopher Bowman sometimes indulged in was not regarded as nearly as "cool" as he appeared to think.

In regard to mugging, a number of skaters over the years have been accused of mugging directly at the judges in a way that is often disparaged but sometimes seems to work. Some female skaters, in particular, have been accused of "waggling their fannies" at the judges. There is a fine line here: Skaters will try to perform two or three of their strongest elements directly in front of the judges, and skaters with a particular weakness may try to disguise it by performing that element as far across the rink from the judging stand as possible.

It is not uncommon, even among top skaters, to see a skater approach so close to the boards at the sides of the rink, especially after landing a jump, as to give viewers the willies. Once in a while, a skater will even have to abort a jump or turn an intended triple into a double in order to keep from crashing into the boards. Crashing does occur occasionally, and in one famous instance at the World Championships, Japan's Midori Ito jumped right off the ice, fortunately at a juncture where the boards were down to give a television camera a clear view. The incident cost her dearly in her scores, however, because no such problem should arise.

Rinks do come in different sizes, of course, and especially in exhibition skating, the performers may have to tailor their routines to a more confining space. But almost all major championships are held on Olympic-size rinks; coming too close to the boards, therefore, is clearly the skater's fault.

USOVA, MAIA *(b. 1969) Soviet/Russian World Ice Dance Champion with husband Aleksandr Zhulin (b. 1970)*

With the retirement from amateur competition of four-time World Champions Natalia Bestemianova and Andrei Bukin after their Olympic victory in 1988, Maia Usova and Aleksandr Zhulin won their first World Medal, the Silver, behind compatriots Marina Klimova and Sergei Ponomarenko in 1989. The Canadian brother-and-sister team of Isabelle and Paul Duchesnay, skating for France, won the Bronze Medal that year. In 1990, Klimova and Ponomarenko were again World Champions, but the increasingly exciting Duchesnays moved past Usova and Zhulin to take the Silver, and the latter were left with the Bronze. Usova and Zhulin repeated as Bronze Medalists in 1991, with the Duchesnays taking the Gold—using choreography by 1984 Gold Medalist Christopher Dean —with Klimova and Ponomarenko in second place.

At the 1992 Olympics at Albertville, France, the judges awarded the Gold Medal to Klimova and Ponomarenko, to the outrage of the largely French audience, as the Duchesnays' free dance proved a little too daring for the judges this time. Usova and Zhulin were once again the Bronze Medalists. The Duchesnays, however, were so furious at being denied Olympic Gold that they did not participate in the World Championships. Klimova and Ponomarenko gained their third World Championships; Usova and Zhulin moved up to Silver; and a new Russian couple, Oksana Grischuk and Evgeny Platov, took the Bronze.

Usova and Zhulin's relationship, often characterised by the press as "stormy," was marked by public outbursts at practice sessions, but this did not prevent them from winning the Gold at the 1993 World Championships in Prague. As expected, Grischuk and Platov took the Silver.

The 1994 Winter Olympics would provide not only a new face-off between these two Russian couples, but would bring back into amateur competition the revered 1984 Gold Medalists from

Great Britain, Jayne Torvill and Christopher Dean, who had been enjoying enormous success as professionals for a decade. There were many controversies about the decisions of the figure skating judges at the Lillehammer, Norway, Olympics, but none caused a greater ruckus than that in Ice Dancing. At the start of the free dance competition, Usova and Zhulin were tied with Torvill and Dean, but Grischuck and Platov were extremely close behind, with any one of the three couples a potential winner, depending on the free dance outcome. In a result that Ice Dance enthusiasts will probably debate for years, the Gold Medal went to Grischuk and Platov, the Silver to Usova and Zhulin and the Bronze to Torvill and Dean. Usova and Zhulin skipped the World Championships, turned professional and subsequently divorced, which seemed to lead to a better relationship off the ice and in performance as they proved extremely successful and popular with audiences and professional judges.

V

VANDERVELL, HENRY E. *(b. 1840?, d.?) Pioneer of British figure skating.*

Figure skating was growing in popularity across Europe in the 1870s, but the honor of establishing the first national figure-skating committee was claimed by Great Britain. A National Skating Association, embracing all aspects of skating, was formed in Cambridge in 1879. The first figure-skating committee was inaugurated in early 1880. Its chairman was Henry E. Vandervell, who went on to invent the first three classic school-figure tracings—the bracket, the counter and the rocker (see SCHOOL FIGURES). It was his idea to establish a series of tests to confirm the advancement of figure skaters to various levels of skill as evidenced by mastery of increasingly difficult variations on the basic figures.

After further development, this system was adopted internationally and served as the basis for competitive categories, eventually including Juvenile, Novice, Junior and Senior. The skill with which these figures were executed also became the basis for judging skaters in the school-figure portion of competition.

VAN ZEEBROECK, ROBERT *(b. 1907) Belgian Olympic medalist.*

In 1928, Gillis Grafstrom of Sweden returned to international competition for the first time since 1924 to win his third consecutive Olympic Gold Medal. The Silver was won by three-time World Champion Willy Boeckl in a repeat of the 1924 outcome. But the Bronze Medalist was a surprise: Robert van Zeebroeck beat several more established skaters. It proved to be his only international medal, however.

VAUGHN, ARTHUR JR. *(b. 1921) U.S. Champion.*

Arthur Vaughn Jr.was the U.S. Silver Medalist behind Eugene Turner in 1941, the Bronze Medalist in 1942, and U.S. Champion in 1943. There were no international competitions held during this World War II period.

VAUGHN, JANE *(b. 1920) U.S. Champion.*

The older sister of Arthur Vaughn Jr., Jane Vaughn took the U.S. Bronze Medal in 1940 and then succeeded Joan Tozzer as national champion in 1941. In 1942, she topped Gretchen Merrill for the second year in a row and then retired; Merrill went on to win six successive Championships.

VERLICH, MICHAEL *See* MILEY, JEANNE.

VINSON, MARIBEL *See* OWEN, MARIBEL VINSON.

VISCONTI, GARY *(b. 1947) U.S. Champion.*

A major U.S. figure-skating rivalry was begun in 1965, when Gary Visconti beat defending U.S. Men's Champion Scotty Allen for the Gold Medal. At the World Championships, however, where Allen had been competing since 1962 and finishing 8th, 5th and 4th, it was Allen who took the 1965 Silver Medal, while Visconti, being seen by international judges for the first time, came in 6th. In 1966, Allen reclaimed the U.S. title, with Visconti taking the Silver, but at the World's, Visconti took the Bronze and Allen finished 4th. Visconti turned the tables again in 1967, beating Allen for the U.S. Gold and again took the World Bronze; Allen once more came in 4th. In the Olympic year of 1968, the U.S. Championship was taken for the first of three consecutive times by Tim Wood, who had been the Bronze Medalist the previous year and in 1965. Visconti was the U.S. Silver Medalist and finished 5th at the Olympics where Wood took the Silver. Those standings were exactly repeated at the 1968 World's.

Gary Visconti continued as an amateur for one more year, but he could only manage the U.S. Bronze behind both Wood and John Misha Petkevich, and he was 4th at the World Championships where Wood took the Gold Medal. Despite this diminished ending to his amateur career, Visconti had five U.S. and two World medals to his credit, a fine record during a very competitive period in U.S. Men's skating.

VLASOV, ALEXANDR *See* VOROBIEVA, IRINA.

VOLKOV, SERGEI *(b. 1955) Soviet World Champion.*

Skating during a period of remarkable strength among Soviet male skaters, Sergei Volkov was initially in the shadow of Sergei Chetverukhin and then was overtaken by Vladimir Kovalev. He was at the top of his form in 1974 and 1975. In 1974, he was the World Silver Medalist behind Jan Hoffmann of East Germany, and in 1975 he won the World Championship by beating Kovalev and John Curry of Great Britain. He was then eclipsed by Kovalev and became a coach.

VON HORVATH, OPIKA *(b. 1892) Hungarian World Champion.*

In 1911, at Vienna, Austria, Opika von Horvath was the Silver Medalist at the World Championships behind her countrywoman Lily Kronberger, who won her fourth World Championship. Von Horvath became Hungarian Champion in 1912 and succeeded Kronberger as World Champion, beating Great Britain's Dorothy Greenough and Phyllis Johnson. She repeated as World Champion in 1913 and 1914, holding off challenges first by Johnson and then by Austria's Angela Hanka. World War I then interrupted the World Championships, which did not resume for seven years.

VOROBIEVA, IRINA *(b. 1956) Soviet World Pairs medalist with Aleksandr Vlasov (b. 1955).*

Irina Vorobieva and Aleksandr Vlasov were one of several Pairs who had the misfortune to skate in the same period as Irina Rodnina and her two partners. Vorobieva and Vlasov won the World Bronze Medal in 1976 behind Rodnina and Alexandr Zaitsev and East Germany's Romy Kermer and Rolf Osterreich. In 1977 they moved up to take the World Silver behind their compatriots Rodnina and Zaitsev.

VRZANOVA, ALENA *(b. 1928) Czechoslovakian World Champion.*

Alena Vrzanova succeeded Barbara Ann Scott of Canada as World Champion in 1949, holding off tough competition from the U.S.'s Silver Medalist Yvonne Sherman and Great Britain's Jeannette Altwegg. After barely winning the Gold again in 1950 over Altwegg, Vrzanova retired.

W

WACHSMAN, GILLIAN *(b. 1965) U.S. Pairs Champion with Todd Waggoner (b. 1964).*

A strong Pair, Gillian Wachsman and Todd Waggoner were in close contention with Pairs Jill Watson/Peter Oppegard and Natalie and Wayne Seybold for several years. In 1985, Watson and Oppegard won the U.S. Gold; the Seybolds were 2nd and Wachsman and Waggoner 3rd. Wachsman and Waggoner were the 1986 Champions over Watson and Oppegard, but the latter took the Gold in 1987 and 1988; Wachsman and Waggoner were Silver Medalists both years. At the World's, Wachsman and Waggoner finished 7th in both 1986 and 1987 and 4th in 1988. They placed 5th at the 1988 Olympics. They then turned professional for a few years.

WAGELEIN, ROY *(b. 1946) U.S. Pairs medalist with Susan Berens (b. 1945) and Sandi Sweitzer (b. 1948).*

Roy Wagelein won the U.S. Silver Medal in Pairs behind Cynthia and Ronald Kauffman in both 1966 and 1967. When Susan Berens had to give up figure skating because of an injury, Wagelein found a new partner in Sandi Sweitzer. It is a difficult for a new team to mesh quickly, but Wagelein and Sweitzer were able to maintain the Silver Medal position in 1968. Wagelein and Berens were 11th and then 7th at the World Championships in 1966 and 1967, and then he and Sweitzer were 7th at the 1968 Olympics and 8th at that year's World's.

WAGENHOFFER, ROBERT *(b. 1960) U.S. Men's medalist and Pairs medalist with Vicki Heasley (b. 1959).*

Robert Wagenhoffer won his first U.S. medal in 1979, taking the Silver in Pairs with Vicki Heasley. The couple were 6th at the World Championships. Robert then concentrated on solo skating, and in 1981 he became the U.S. Bronze Medalist and was 10th at the World Championships. In 1982 he was the Silver Medalist behind repeat champion Scott Hamilton and came in 6th at the World's as Hamilton took his second World title.

WAGGONER, TODD *See* WACHSMAN, GILLIAN.

WAGNER, BARBARA *(b. 1937) Canadian, World and Olympic Pairs Champion with Robert Paul (b. 1936).*

For a decade, beginning in 1953, Canada dominated Pairs skating, producing three different couples who became World Champions for a total of seven times. The second of these couples, following Frances Dafoe and Norris Bowden, was Barbara

Wagner and Robert Paul. They became Canadian Champions in 1957 and also won the first of four successive World Championships, defeating Marika Kilius and Franz Ningel of West Germany; the World Bronze went to Maria and Otto Jelnick, who had defected from Czechoslovakia and settled in Canada.

Wagner and Paul, who possessed both great athletic ability and elegance on the ice won the World Gold over the Czechoslovakian couple, Vera Suchankova and Zdenek Dolezal, in 1958; topped Marika Kilius and her new partner Hans Jurgen Baumler in 1959; and edged their teammates, the Jelinicks, in 1960. They also won the Olympic Gold Medal in 1960 over Kilius and Baumler. They then turned professional to join the Ice Capades.

WAHLMAN, PETROS *(b. 1898) U.S. medalist.*

In 1920, as U.S. competition resumed following World War I, Petros Wahlman won the U.S. Bronze Medal behind Sherwin Badger and Nathaniel Niles.

WAKEFIELD, LYMAN *See* SUTTON, HARRIET.

WALKER, DAPHNE *(b. 1920) British World medalist and ice show star.*

Runner-up for the British Ladies' title in 1939 to Megan Taylor, Daphne Walker took the World Bronze Medal that year as Taylor won her second World Gold Medal. Walker might well have become World Champion herself, but the cancellation of World competition for the next seven years because of World War II put what might have been a great amateur career in limbo. Remarkably, she was able to win the World Silver in 1947 behind Barbara Ann Scott of Canada. But it was clear that, already in her late 20s, Walker would be unable to beat Scott, so she turned professional, starring in the stage ice show *Stars on Ice* at the London Stoll Theatre.

WALSH, JENNIE *(b. 1948) U.S. medalist.*

During Peggy Fleming's five-year reign as U.S. Champion, the Ladies' Bronze Medalist was a different young woman each year. Jennie Walsh took that medal in 1967, with three-time Silver Medalist Albertina Noyes ahead of her. Walsh was 8th at the World Championships, but she was not able to repeat as U.S. Bronze winner the next year; Janet Lynn took her place.

WALTER, HANNAH *(b. 1938) Austrian World medalist.*

Hannah Walter took the World Bronze Medal in 1958 behind the U.S.'s Carol Heiss and Austrian Champion, Walter's teammate Ingrid Wendl. Walter became Austrian Champion in 1959 and finished 2nd to Heiss at the World's, but she was unable to win an international medal in 1960. The Netherlands' Sjoukje Dijkstra and Barbara Roles of the United States took Silver and Bronze behind Heiss at both the Olympics and the World Championships.

WALTHER, CHARLOTTE *(b. 1920) U.S. medalist.*

Charlotte Walther was the U.S. Bronze Medalist twice, in 1939 behind Joan Tozzer and Audrey Peppe, who were repeating as Gold and Silver Medalists, and again in 1941 behind Jane Vaughn and Gretchen Merrill.

WALTZ

This fundamental dance has always been central to Ice Dancing. Before the modern Ice Dancing competition format was inaugurated in 1936, the waltz was one of the two dances, along with the fourteen step, for which separate medals were given at the U.S. Championships beginning in 1914. Two of the famous waltzes used in the Ice Dancing compulsories are the Westminster waltz, created by Eric Van der Weyden and Eva Keats in London in 1938, and the Ravensburg waltz, invented in 1973 by Angela and Erich Buck, the three-time World Silver Medalists from West Germany.

WALTZ JUMP

This is the first jump learned by beginning skaters. It involves only a single half-revolution in the air. The takeoff and landing are on different feet.

WARING, LOIS

(b. 1930) Five-time U.S. Ice Dance Champion with both Walter Bainbridge (b. 1926) and Michael McGean (b. 1929).

Lois Waring became the U.S. Silver Medalist in Ice Dance in 1946 with partner Walter Bainbridge behind Anne Davies and Carleton Hoffner. Waring and Bainbridge took the Gold the following year and defended it successfully in 1948 and 1949. Walter Bainbridge then retired from competition and Waring teamed up with Michael McGean to retain her title in 1950. The couple did not compete in 1951 but returned to take the national title one last time in 1952. They did not compete at the first World Championship competition for Ice Dancing in 1952, however, at which Carol Peters and Daniel Ryan, the 1952 U.S. Silver Medalists, took the Bronze Medal.

WATERBURY, CARMEL

See BODEL, EDWARD.

WATSON, JILL

(b. 1964) U.S. Pairs Bronze Medalist with Burt Lancon (b. 1963) and Gold Medalist with Peter Oppegard (b. 1961).

Jill Watson won the U.S. Bronze in Pairs in 1983 with Burt Lancon (who had been the Silver Medalist

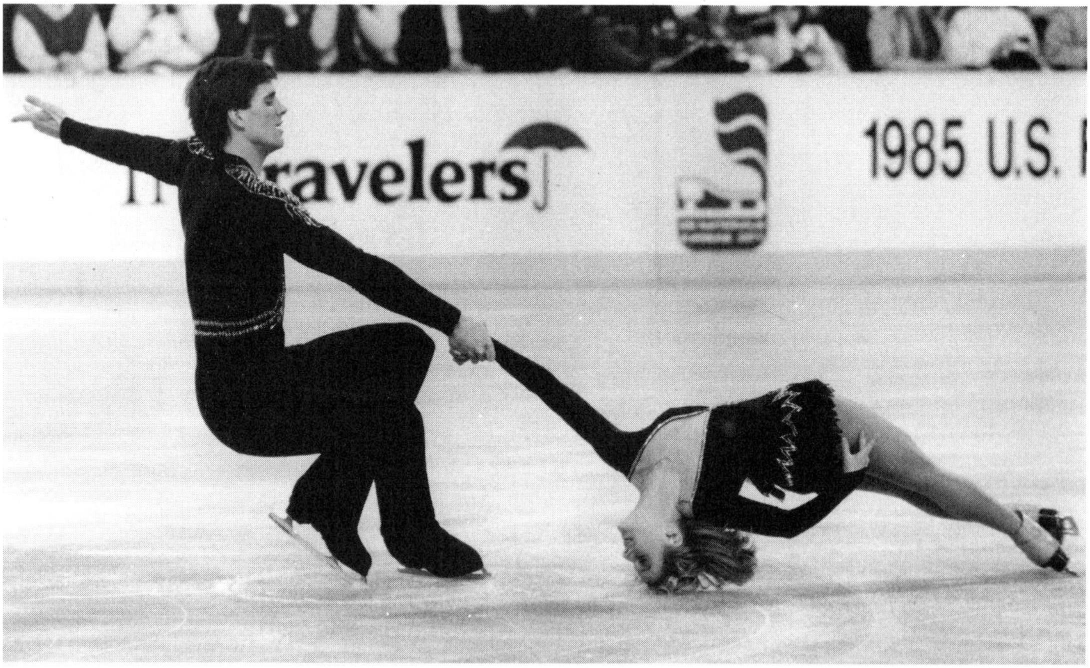

Three-time U.S. Pairs Champions Jill Watson and Peter Oppegard perform a death spiral.
(Courtesy Paul Harvath)

the previous year with Maria DiDomenico) behind Pairs Kitty/Peter Carruthers and Lea Ann Miller/William Fauver. Exactly the same outcome prevailed the following year. Watson and Lancon were 11th at the 1983 World Championships, but only two places were open on the World team in 1984. She and Lancon were on the Olympic team for 1984, however, and placed 6th. Lancon then retired from amateur skating.

With a new partner, Peter Oppegard, Watson found a better match, and the couple became U.S. Champions in 1985, beating Pairs Natalie and Wayne Seybold and Gillian Wachsman/Todd Waggoner. Watson and Oppegard then placed 4th at the 1985 World Championships, just losing the Bronze to Canada's Katherine Matousek and Lloyd Eisler. Watson and Oppegard's 1986 program did not show them at their best, and they lost the U.S. title to Wachsman and Waggoner and dropped to 6th place at the World's.

Watson and Oppegard were back in form in 1987, regaining the U.S. Championship from Wachsman and Waggoner and taking the World Bronze behind two World Champion Soviet Pairs, Ekaterina Gordeeva/Sergei Grinkov and Elena Valova/Oleg Vasiliev. Retaining their U.S. title in 1988, they also won the Olympic Bronze behind the same two Soviet Couples. A disappointing World's that year found them in 6th place, but they turned professional with three U.S. Gold Medals, a U.S. Silver Medal and a World and Olympic Bronze to their credit.

WATSON, MARY J. *(b. 1938) U.S. Pairs medalist with John Jarmon (b. 1937).*

From 1957 to 1960, Nancy and Ron Ludington reigned as U.S. Pairs Champions, but the field behind them was highly competitive; only Maribel Owen and Dudley Richards took medals in consecutive years. The 1957 Silver Medalists were Mary J. Watson and John Jarmon, who then placed 9th at the World's.

WATTS, GLYN *See* GREEN, HILARY.

WEIGEL, ESTELLE *(b. 1915) U.S. medalist.*

Estelle Weigel won one U.S. medal, taking the Bronze in 1934. Her older sister Louise captured the Silver, and Suzanne Davis won the Gold.

WEIGEL, KENT *See* GENOVESI, JUDI.

WEIGEL, LOUISE *(b. 1913) U.S. medalist.*

Louise Weigel won the U.S. Ladies' Bronze in 1932 and came in 14th at that year's Olympics. She repeated as Bronze Medalist in 1933 and then moved up to Silver in 1934 behind Suzanne Davis and ahead of her sister Estelle, the Bronze Medalist. In 1935, as Maribel Vinson took her 7th Gold Medal after a one-year absence, Louise was pushed back to 3rd place with Suzanne Davis taking the Silver. Louise was runner-up to Vinson in 1936 but dropped to 21st place at the Olympics and retired.

WELCH, CAROLYN *See* BRINKMAN, CHARLES.

WELD, THERESA *See* BLANCHARD, THERESA WELD.

WELLS, SHEILA *See* GREINER, ROBIN.

WENDL, INGRID *(b. 1937) Austrian World medalist.*

Ingrid Wendl was a major contender at the highest level of women's figure skating in the mid-1950s, but she was never able to top Tenley Albright or Carol Heiss of the United States. She won both the World and Olympic Bronze in 1956 with Albright 1st at the Olympics and 2nd at the World's and

Heiss 2nd at the Olympics and 1st at the World's. With Albright's retirement, it seemed that Wendl was poised to move up a notch, but she was foiled by her own Austrian rival Hanna Eigel, who had won the World Bronze in 1955 and took the Silver in 1957 behind Heiss with Wendl again the Bronze Medalist. In 1958 Wendl did win the World Silver behind Heiss with Hanna Eigel Walter taking the Bronze under her married name. Wendl then retired from amateur skating.

WESTERFELD, STEPHANIE

(1942–1961) U.S. medalist.

In 1961, Stephanie Westerfeld won the U.S. Silver Medal behind Laurence Owen, making her mark as an important member of the new generation of U.S. skaters. But she was killed that year along with the rest of the U.S. team in a plane crash at Brussels on the way to the World Championships.

WESTWOOD, JEAN *(b. 1932) British World Champion Ice Dancer with Laurence Demmy (b. 1931).*

When Ice Dancing was first included in the World Championships in 1952, the leaders in this form of figure skating who were largely responsible for its development over the previous quarter century were British, although U.S. skaters were also strong in the sport. Jean Westwood and Laurence Demmy were the first of several great British Ice Dance couples to dominate the sport in the course of the next two decades.

Westwood and Demmy won the first four World Gold Medals in Ice Dancing from 1952 to 1955. Three other British couples were the Silver Medalists in that period, with the United States taking the Bronze except in 1955, when the British swept the competition. Models for a generation of British ice dancers, Westwood and Demmy both continued to have a great influence on the form after their competitive years were over. Westwood became an important coach in Canada and the United States, and Demmy eventually became the head of the Ice Dance Committee of the International Skating Union, which was responsible for setting the rules and choosing the dances required for each year's competition.

Britain's Jean Westwood and Laurence Demmy, first World Ice Dance Champions.
(Courtesy World Figure Skating Museum)

WILKES, DEBBI *(b. 1943) Canadian World and Olympic Bronze Medalist in Pairs with Guy Revell (1942–81).*

The Pairs events at the Olympics and World Championships in 1964 were among the most exciting and closely contested in the history of the sport. At the Olympics, Ludmila Belousova and Oleg Protopopov won the first of two Olympic Gold Medals, with reigning World Champions

Marika Kilius and Hans Jurgen Baumler of West Germany taking the Silver. The fight for the Bronze was also very tight, with Debbi Wilkes and Guy Revell edging Vivian and Ronald Joseph of the United States. Further drama ensued when it was discovered that the West Germans had signed a show contract prior to the Games. They were stripped of their Silver, which was then awarded to Wilkes and Revell, and the Americans gained the Bronze. At the World Championships, the Germans prevailed over the Russians, and once again Wilkes and Revell topped the Josephs. Wilkes and Revell then retired from amateur skating, having won two Bronze medals that, given the competition, shone almost as brightly as gold.

WILLIAMS, BASIL *See* JOHNSON, PHYLLIS.

WILLIAMS, SCOTT *(b. 1966) U.S. medalist.*

Scott Williams became the U.S. Bronze Medalist in 1985 behind Brian Boitano and Mark Cockerell. In 1986, he moved up a place, taking the Silver behind Boitano and was 9th at the World's. He was edged by Christopher Bowman for the Silver in 1987 but was able to go to the World's because his own finish the previous year had put three male U.S. skaters in the top ten; this time he finished 10th.

WILSON, MONTGOMERY *(1909–64) Canadian World medalist.*

The first Canadian to win a World or Olympic medal in the Men's division was Montgomery Wilson. At the 1932 Olympics in Lake Placid, New York he won the Bronze Medal behind Austria's Karl Schafer and Sweden's Gillis Grafstrom, who had taken the Gold Medal at the three previous Olympics. At the 1932 World Championships, held at Montreal, Canada, Grafstrom—as had often been the case in his career—did not compete. Wilson won the Silver Medal behind Schafer, edging Ernst Baier of Germany.

WILSON, TRACY *(b. 1965) Canadian World and Olympic Bronze Medalist in Ice Dancing with Robert McCall (1964–91).*

From 1986 to 1988, Tracy Wilson and Robert McCall took the World Bronze Medal in Ice Dancing behind the two top Soviet couples, Natalia Bestemianova and Andrei Bukin and Marina Klimova and Sergei Ponomarenko. This order of finish also prevailed at the 1988 Winter Olympics in Calgary, Canada, where the home-country crowd went wild over Wilson and McCall's lively ragtime performance in the free dance.

WINTER OLYMPICS

The first Winter Olympic Games were held at Chamonix, France in 1924. The winner of the Gold Medal for Men's Figure Skating was Gillis Grafstrom of Sweden. One of the most important male skater of his era, he would win again four years later at St. Moritz, Switzerland. Of even more interest is the fact that at the first official Winter Olympics, Grafstrom was the defending Olympic Champion, having already won the title in Antwerp, Belgium in 1920 at what we now call the Summer Olympics.

Today, too many newspaper and television sports reporters tend to disparage figure skating by questioning whether it is really a sport at all. But it was figure skating, more than any other winter sport, that led the way toward the creation of a separate Winter Olympics.

Figure skating had made its Olympic debut amid the regular track and field events at the 1908 Olympic Games in London, England. A huge indoor skating rink had been built in London in 1906, and the British were anxious to show it off. Using their leverage as host country, the British persuaded the International Olympic Committee to approve figure-skating events for Men, Women and Pairs. Figure skating had still not become particularly popular in the United States (the first national competition was not held until 1914), but most European countries had avid devotees of the sport. Because the track and field events were expected to be dominated by the United States, Europeans were hardly averse to adding three winter sports at which they excelled.

At the London Olympics, Sweden's Ulrich Salchow won the Men's Gold Medal, Great Britain's Madge Syers triumphed in the Women's competition, and Germany's Heinrich Burger and Anna Hubler were Pairs Champions. The next Olympic Games were held in Stockholm in 1912, but because of the long Swedish winters, no indoor rink was built in that country. Without one, figure skating could not be held in midsummer's warm weather.

The Olympics were bypassed in 1916 because of World War I, but when Antwerp hosted the 1920 Games, an existing indoor rink was once again available, and figure skating was brought back as an out-of-season Olympic sport. Figure skating was certainly popular in northern European countries, but speed skating, cross-country skiing and ice hockey were even more so. The practitioners of these sports and their fans wanted the same level of competition and reward that already existed for figure skating. Thus the Winter Olympics were organized, although the now-glamorous alpine-skiing events were not contested until 1948.

The Winter Olympic Games have been held at the following sites:

1924: Chamonix, France
1928: St. Moritz, Switzerland
1932: Lake Placid, United States
1936: Garmisch-Partenkirchen, Germany
1940: None held
1944: None held
1948: St. Moritz, Switzerland
1952: Oslo, Norway
1956: Cortina d'Ampezzo, Italy
1960: Squaw Valley, United States
1964: Innsbruck, Austria
1968: Grenoble, France
1972: Sapporo, Japan
1976: Innsbruck, Austria
1980: Lake Placid, United States
1984: Sarajevo, Yugoslavia
1988: Calgary, Canada
1992: Albertville, France
1994: Lillehammer, Norway
1998: Nagano, Japan

WITT, KATARINA *(b. 1965) East German, World and Olympic Champion.*

Born in Karl-Marx-Stadt, East Germany (which reverted to its original name of Chemnitz following the collapse of East Germany), Katarina Witt began skating at the age of five. Quickly spotted as having special talent, she was enrolled in intensive training that lasted from 7 A.M. to 8 P.M., including school classes with other skaters. At age nine, she was placed in the hands of East Germany's premier skating coach, Jutta Muller. Although not a political person, Witt continues to this day to give full credit to the communist state athletic training program that nurtured her talent, a stance that has caused some controversy but that she has refused to soften.

Witt was doing a triple salchow at age 11, and three years later she placed 10th at her first World competition. The following year, 1981, just three months past her 15th birthday, she was 5th in both the European and World Championships, vaulting past others several years her senior. That same year she succeeded 1980 World and Olympic Gold Medalist Anett Poetzch, who would become her sister-in-law, as East German Champion. In 1982, Witt continued her rapid climb to the top, taking 2nd at both the European and World Championships. At the World's she was bested by the equally young U.S. jumping sensation Elaine Zayak.

Witt suffered a setback in 1983, managing only a 4th place finish at the World's, despite taking the European Championship for the first time. Elaine Zayak did not compete at the World's that year

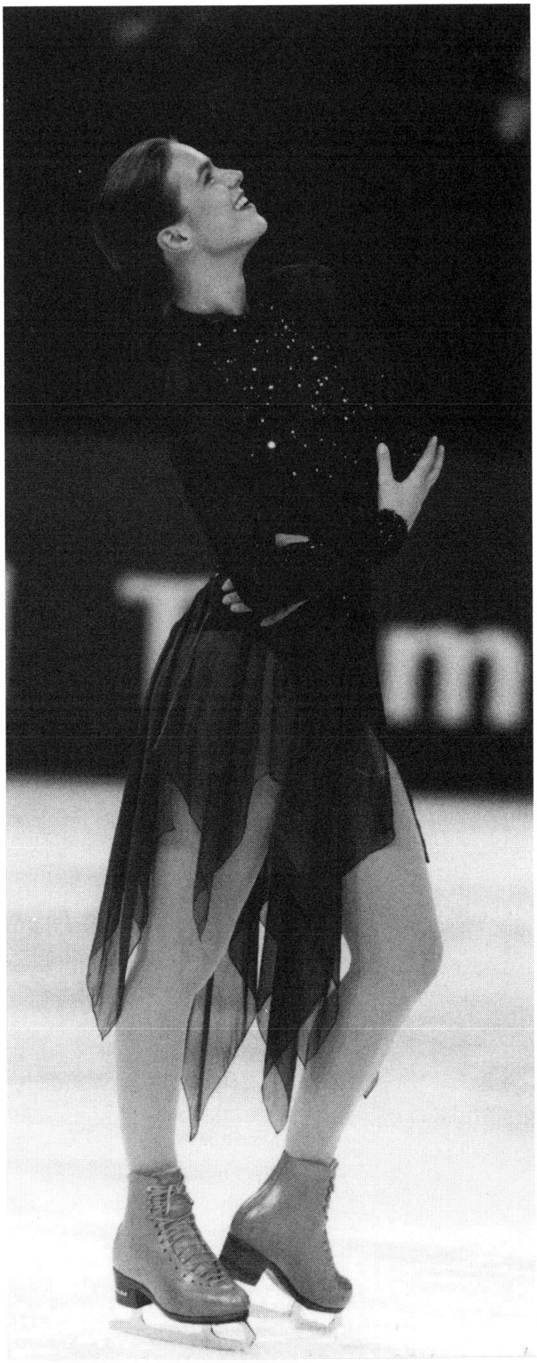

Two-time Olympic Champion Katarina Witt in 1995.
(Courtesy Michelle Harvath)

because of an injury, but her fellow U.S. skater Rosalynn Sumners took the Gold. That set up a difficult test for Witt at the 1984 Olympics in Sarajevo, Yugoslavia. On paper it looked as though one of the two U.S. World Champions, Zayak or Sumners, would be able to win, but few skaters have ever been as hardworking as Katarina Witt, and she put in grueling hours of training in the intervening year. The work paid off as she narrowly won the Olympic Gold over Rosalynn Sumners, with Zayak having a rocky outing that left her a distant 6th. At the World's, with Sumners not competing, Witt also became World Champion, over Anna Kondrashova of the Soviet Union, while Zayak took the Bronze.

Witt was still only 19. The East German authorities wouldn't allow her to take advantage of U.S. ice-show offers, but she has always maintained that she didn't want to turn professional at that point anyway. She had her sights set on another Olympic Gold Medal four years down the road. In 1985, she repeated as both European and World Champion, winning the latter easily over the Soviet Union's Kira Ivanova (who had been the Olympic Bronze Medalist the previous year) and U.S. champion, Tiffany Chin.

But 1986 brought a prime example of the difference a year can make in figure skating. The U.S.'s Debi Thomas, who had been 2nd in the United States but only 5th in the world the previous year, powered her way to the top of women's figure skating, becoming both U.S. and World Champion. Witt skated extremely well but could not beat Thomas' electrifying performance. Suddenly, Witt's dream of a second Olympic Gold seemed in jeopardy.

Thomas proved to be slightly off stride in 1987. First, she lost her U.S. title to Jill Trenary; at the World's, she skated well but not up to the standard she had set the previous year. In a very close contest, Witt regained her World title with Thomas 2nd. It was not so much a matter of Witt improving as of Thomas failing to skate up to expectations. Either one, it appeared, could take the Gold Medal at the upcoming Olympics in Calgary, Canada.

By happenstance, both Witt and Thomas decided to skate to selections from *Carmen* for their long program in 1988. It was widely predicted that this coincidence would put Thomas at a slight disadvantage. Thomas was the stronger athlete—her triple jumps attained extraordinary height, and she performed more difficult jump combinations than Witt. But while Thomas certainly had presence on the ice and a definite musical flair, Witt was the kind of polished and graceful artistic skater the judges tended to favor. Because the artistic marks are used as the tiebreaker in competition, Witt appeared to have a small edge in the free-skating. At the U.S. Championships in 1988, Thomas skated very strongly, reclaiming the national title from Jill Trenary. Witt, meanwhile, was taking her national title for the 8th time and winning her 6th European Championship.

The press buildup for the showdown between "the two Carmens," as they were dubbed, didn't quite match that for the two Brians, Boitano and Orser, in the men's division, but it was intense enough to cause both skaters to admit to being bothered by it. What neither the press nor practically anyone else knew was that Thomas had been secretly married just after the national competitions. This event, together with the pressures of her pre-med college courses, was subsequently seen as causing the lack of focus that seemed to affect her skating. In her long program at the Olympics, she missed her trademark triple-lutz combination and never fully recovered. Although her program was technically more difficult than Witt's, the judges clearly favored Witt's interpretation of *Carmen.*

Witt later admitted that her performance had involved a degree of what she called "posturing," but she also noted that it worked. She had her second Olympic Gold Medal. In the end, the skater who came closest to beating her was the surprising Canadian Champion, Elizabeth Manley, who had had a very up-and-down career but who skated superbly before a partisan audience in Calgary. She took the Silver Medal and Thomas ended up with the Bronze. A month later in Budapest, Hungary, the order of finish was the same at the World Championships.

Witt was the first woman skater to win two Olympic Gold Medals since Sonja Henie, who won three medals more than a half-century earlier. It was difficult for Witt to capitalize on her triumph because of the reluctance of the East German government to allow her to skate in the West. It took her six months of negotiation to get permission to appear in a television special starring Boitano that was taped in the autumn of 1988 and shown on ABC. Additional months of pleading were necessary to appear in the 1989 made-for-television film *Carmen on Ice*, in which she portrayed Carmen, Boitano Don José and Brian Orser the bullfighter Escamillo, for which all three won Emmy Awards in the classical music/dance category. While they were filming in Seville, Spain, the East German communist government was ousted. That made it possible for Witt to appear regularly in the West. In 1990 and 1991, she toured the United States and Canada in sophisticated ice shows developed by Boitano that focused on skating rather than production numbers and featured many international skating stars. Subsequently, she made numerous other appearances and skated in several professional competitions, which she usually won but was sometimes bested by her rival Debi Thomas.

Along with Boitano, Viktor Petrenko, ice dancers Torvill and Dean and several other skaters, Witt applied for readmission to the amateur ranks in order to attend one more Olympics in 1994. This was a calculated risk, but she said that she did not really entertain the idea of winning another Gold Medal, as many of the others did. She said that she wanted to enjoy being part of another Olympic festival in a less-pressured situation. In the end, handicapped by flubs in her short program, she gained only 5th place. But her long program, skated to the haunting Pete Seeger anthem "Where Have All the Flowers Gone?" in tribute to war-torn Sarajevo, Yugoslavia, where she had won her first Olympic Gold Medal in

1984, moved many people to tears. Although her goal was different this time, again Katarina Witt achieved what she wanted.

WOETZEL, MANDY *(b. 1973) World Pairs medalist with Ingo Steuer (b. 1972), from Germany.*

Mandy Woetzel and Ingo Steuer have had an up-and-down amateur career. They were the Silver Medalists at the 1993 World Championships behind Isabelle Brasseur and Lloyd Eisler and won the European Championships in 1995, but they missed out on several other medal opportunities. In 1996, Woetzel and Steuer won the short program at the World Championships but were topped by Russia's Marina Eltsova and Andrei Bushkov in the long program. Once again they had to be content with a Silver Medal, while the U.S.'s Jenni Meno and Todd Sand took a second successive Bronze. But the following year Woetzel and Steuer prevailed and won World Gold. In 1998 at the Olympics in Nagano, Japan, the pair took the Bronze behind Russians Kazakova and Dmitriev and Berezhnaya and Sikharulidze.

WOMEN'S COMPETITION

When the first World Championship for figure skating was held in 1896 in St. Petersburg, Russia, no thought was given to women. There was not even a Pairs competition, which would be first contested in 1908; and it would not be until 1952 that Ice Dancing was made a competitive event at the international level. In 1896, however, women were in fact skating regularly, wearing long skirts and fancy hats as they were escorted over frozen ponds by top-hatted gentlemen. But the idea of women competing against one another for an award was not socially acceptable.

The first six World Championships were for men only. But in 1902, a lone woman skater, Madge Syers of Great Britain, decided to change that. She was the young wife of Edgar Syers, who had founded the British Figure Skating Club in 1898. Her application to compete in the 1902 Championships was met with considerable astonishment by the International Skating Union officers, but she had three factors in her favor. In legalistic terms, there was no by-law forbidding the participation of women—the idea had seemed so outlandish that no one had thought to outlaw it. Second, her husband supported her bid to compete, even though she would in fact be competing against him as well as men from numerous European countries. And since the competition was to be held in London, as it had also been in 1898, Edgar Syers was one of the chief hosts of the event, and it didn't seem proper to go against his wishes. Besides, it was deemed unlikely that Madge Syers would even do all that well.

Madge Syers, however, was a brilliant skater, and the judges, all male, found themselves forced to award her the Silver Medal behind Ulrich Salchow of Sweden, who had also won the Gold Medal the year before in Stockholm. There were those who thought Madge Syers should in fact have been awarded the Gold Medal. Apparently Ulrich Salchow, who would go on to win eight more World Gold Medals and one Olympic Gold, agreed with that view, since he took off his own Gold Medal and presented it to this remarkable young woman.

The ISU promptly wrote a law banning women from the World Championships, on the grounds that their long skirts made it too difficult for the judges to see their feet. Syers countered that nonsense by wearing shorter skirts when skating. The following year, Great Britain held the first Championships event open to both men and women, and Madge Syers won it, narrowly defeating her own husband, who was delighted with the outcome. The International Skating Union realized that it was embarrassing itself and created a Ladies' Competition to begin in 1906. Madge Syers won that year and the next, beating Jenny Herz of Austria and Lily Kronberger of Hungary both times.

In 1908, the Olympic Games were to be held in London. In addition to the scheduled track-and-field events that we now call the Summer Olympics, it was decided to hold a figure skating competition for Men, Ladies and Pairs at an artificial rink that had recently been built in London. Madge Syers won the Ladies' Olympic Gold Medal, beating Elsa Rendschmidt of Germany and a fellow British woman, Dorothy Greenough-Smith. Having changed the face of figure skating, she then retired from competition.

In the ensuing few years before World War I, male competitors began adding more jumps to their programs, particularly the jump invented by Ulrich Salchow and named after him, still a staple of figure skating, although now performed as a triple by both men and women. But in these pre-war years, women were still expected to be decorous and feminine. It wasn't until the 1920 Olympics in Antwerp, Belgium (where another case of an artificial rink made figure skating a possible event in the Summer Olympics), that a woman dared to perform a full-revolution jump. A salchow was successfully landed by the U.S. Champion, Theresa Weld, but instead of gaining her points with the judges, it brought a reprimand for "unfeminine" behavior and probably cost her the Gold Medal; she was awarded only the Bronze.

But from that landmark Olympic competition onward, other women began performing jumps. A more athletic form of Ladies' skating became the rule, although feminine grace and charm still counted for a good deal in women's skating, and the judges rewarded it with higher artistic marks. In the first half of the 1920s, Austria's Herma Jaross-Szabo, who won both the Ladies' and Pairs Gold Medals at the 1925 World Championships, carried women's skating forward. She was then succeeded by the legendary Sonja Henie of Norway, who became World Champion in 1926. Henie won ten World Championships and three Olympic Gold Medals. Her movie career, which began in 1926, did much to move women's skating into the lielight and give the Ladies' Competition the glamorous reputation among the public that it still holds today.

Beginning with the Olympic victory of Tenley Albright in 1956, American women have been a major force in international figure skating competitions: Carol Heiss, Peggy Fleming, Dorothy Hamill and Kristi Yamaguchi have won Olympic Gold Medals and 13 World Championships; Linda Fratianne, Elaine Zayak, Rosalynn Sumners, Debi Thomas, Jill Trenary, Michelle Kwan and Tara Lipinski all have become World Champions. There have only been four World Championships since 1949 that have not counted an American woman among the medalists, and three of those were in the years immediately following the Brussels plane crash of 1961 in which the entire U.S. World team was killed. Canadian and European women have always challenged the Americans strongly, however, with Sjoukje Dijkstra of the Netherlands in the 1960s and Katarina Witt of East Germany in the 1980s making the most indelible impressions. Today's women figure skaters can match the men almost triple jump for triple jump, while retaining a grace and glamour that puts the Ladies' competitions among the premiere sporting events on television in terms of popularity.

WOOD, TIM *(b. 1947) U.S. and World Champion.*

A tall, elegant skater, Tim Wood won the U.S. Bronze in 1965 and 1967, both times behind Gary Visconti and Scott Allen. At his first World Championships, in 1967, he was 9th. In 1968, he improved immensely, winning the U.S. Gold Medal and then taking the Silver Medal at both the Olympics and the World Championships; he was behind Wolfgang Schwarz of Austria at the Olympics and behind Emmerich Danzer, also of Austria, at the World's. No previous U.S. Men's competitor had ever made such a large leap up in the World standings in a single year. In 1969, he confirmed his great ability, repeating as U.S. Champion and also becoming Champion of the World. In 1970 he repeated both victories and then turned professional for a short time.

WREDE, LUDWIG *(b. 1905) Austrian World Champion Pairs skater with Herma Jaross-Szabo.*

In 1925, Ludwig Wrede teamed with Herma Jaross-Szabo (who won her third Ladies' Gold Medal that year) to win the Gold Medal in Pairs. The following year, the couple took the Bronze behind the French husband-and-wife team Andrée and Pierre Brunet and another Austrian couple, Lilly Scholz and Otto Kaiser. In 1927, when the Brunets did not compete, Wrede and Jaross-Szabo took the Gold again over their Austrian rivals. Jaross-Szabo then retired from amateur skating, but Ludwig Wrede found a new partner in Melitta Brunner. They took the 1928 World Bronze behind the Brunets and Scholz/Kaiser. The same placements prevailed at the 1928 Olympics. In 1929, Wrede and Brunner were World Silver Medalists behind Schloz and Kaiser (the Brunets again absent) and took a final Silver in 1930 behind the Brunets.

WRIGHT, BERT *See* MCKENZIE, SHARON.

WYLIE, PAUL *(b. 1969) U.S. and Olympic Silver Medalist.*

Figure-skating history is full of hard-luck stories about almost-champions. Paul Wylie had an extremely difficult amateur career that concluded with one of skating's foremost happy endings. His first U.S. medal came in 1988, when he took the Silver behind Brian Boitano and ahead of Christopher Bowman. He was 10th at that year's Olympics and 9th at the World Championships. Expected to succeed Boitano as U.S. Champion, he had a dreadful 1989 competition and did not win a medal. In 1990 he came back to win the Silver Medal behind young Todd Eldredge; he would very likely have become champion if he had not missed jumps in his long program. Problems continued at the World Championships, where he finished 10th.

He was by now regarded by many as the finest male skater in the world—in practice. He also shone at skating exhibitions, but in competition something always went wrong in either the short or the long program, and 1991 saw him place 3rd at the U.S. Championships and 11th at the World's. He had come to be regarded as one of those skaters so afflicted by nerves that he simply could not skate cleanly in competition despite his superb practices. In 1992, he just barely took the U.S. Silver Medal behind Christopher Bowman.

Paul Wylie in 1991, a year away from Olympic glory.
(Courtesy Paul Harvath)

At the Olympics he placed 3rd after skating a brilliant short program, putting him right behind Viktor Petrenko of Ukraine. Most people expected him to fall apart, as usual, in the long program;

however, Scott Hamilton, who was doing television commentary, believed that Wylie had finally put it together. Wylie *had* put it together, skating a long program that many reporters felt was superior to Petrenko's, one that deserved the Gold Medal. Wylie was perfectly happy with his Silver and kept his word about not skating at the World's, allowing U.S. Bronze Medalist Mark Mitchell to take his place.

Wylie's subsequent professional career has involved one great success after another, including winning the 1994 Professional Championship. He toured extensively and participated in several television specials, including a 1995 CBS professional competition, *Skates X2*, which brought him perfect 6.0s from all the judges. This performance, skated to Carl Orff's *Carmina Burana*, brought the audience screaming to its feet and was called "absolutely perfect skating" by commentator Scott Hamilton.

WYNNE, SUSAN *(b. 1965) U.S. Ice Dance Champion.*

A native of Syracuse, New York, Susan Wynne won four U.S. Ice Dancing medals with her first partner, Joseph Druar (b. 1964). The couple were Bronze Medalists in 1987, moved up to take the Silver in 1988 and were U.S. Champions in 1989–90. Smooth and well matched, the couple steadily improved their international standing from 1987 to 1990, with World Championship placings of 12th, 9th, 5th and 4th. They also placed 11th at the 1988 Olympics.

When Joseph Druar retired from amateur skating in 1990, Wynne joined him on the sidelines, but she was drawn back into the sport in 1993 when she joined forces with Russ Witherby (b. 1962). He had been U.S. Champion the previous year with April Sargent. After skating together for only six months, the new partners drew on their long experience to place 2nd at the U.S. Championships in 1993. They managed only 15th at the 1993 World Championships, a surprisingly low finish. In 1994, they were the U.S. Silver Medalists, thus missing out on the Olympic and World Championships, where only one entry was open to U.S. ice dancers because of their weak showing in international competition in previous years.

Y

YAMAGUCHI, KRISTI *(b. 1972) U.S., World and Olympic Champion.*

Kristi Yamaguchi came to the attention of the figure-skating world in 1989 when she took the U.S. Ladies' Silver Medal behind Jill Trenary, as well as the Pairs Gold Medal with partner Rudy Galindo. The last U.S. woman to gain simultaneous medals in the two categories was Yvonne Sherman in 1948 when she was Pairs Champion with Robert Swenning and Ladies' Silver Medalist. A 6th-place finish in the Ladies' division at the 1989 World Championships and a 5th-place position with Galindo in Pairs put the world on notice that this 17-year-old was a skater to be reckoned with.

In 1990, Yamaguchi and Galindo repeated as U.S. Pairs Champions and she was again second to Trenary. At the World's, Yamaguchi and Galindo were again 5th, but she moved up to 4th in the Ladies' division, a showing that made her decide to give up Pairs and concentrate on solo skating. Skating experts felt widely that it was virtually impossible to become World Champion in either discipline while skating in both. No one had managed to win two medals of any kind while skating in two disciplines since Herma Jaross-Szabo in the 1920s, and in those days Pairs skating involved none of the difficult lifts associated with the sport today.

Concentrating on solo skating did not immediately bring Yamaguchi the national championship, however. Even with Trenary out of competition because of an injury, in 1991 Yamaguchi had to settle again for 2nd place because Tonya Harding skated what was probably the finest program of her checkered career. At the World Championships, however, things turned out differently. Harding faltered slightly and Yamaguchi became World Champion in a U.S. sweep, Harding taking the Silver and Nancy Kerrigan the Bronze. The 1992 Olympic year promised an extremely tight competition in the Ladies' division. Japan's Midori Ito, who had won the Gold in 1989 but then struggled with injuries, was back in top form. Ito and Harding alone among women skaters were able to complete a triple axel, which gave them an advantage. Kerrigan, European Champion Surya Bonaly and China's Chen Lu were all in the running for medals.

But the short program at the Olympics, which has derailed so many favorites in competition in recent years, brought problems for both Ito and Harding. Ito decided to do a triple-lutz combination instead of the more difficult triple-axel combination, but fell anyway; Harding took an even bigger fall attempting her triple-axel combination. When the smoke cleared, Yamaguchi was in 1st place, Kerrigan in 2nd, Bonaly in 3rd with Ito in 4th and Harding in 6th going into the long program. Yamaguchi had her problems here, falling once, but all the others fell too, and with the highest artistic marks, Kristi Yamaguchi became Olympic Gold Medalist, something she had not really hoped to achieve until 1994. Ito did land one of two attempts at a triple axel and took the Silver with Kerrigan getting the Bronze. At the World

Championships in 1992, Yamaguchi skated flawlessly and won easily; Kerrigan took the Silver and Chen Lu the Bronze. Ito, Harding and Bonaly had bad falls.

Kristi Yamaguchi turned professional. Although only 20, she had no difficulty handling the rigors of ice-show touring and showed herself to be the most consistent of the top female skaters—even after Oksana Baiul and Kerrigan turned pro in 1994—skating with great assurance and delighting audiences everywhere.

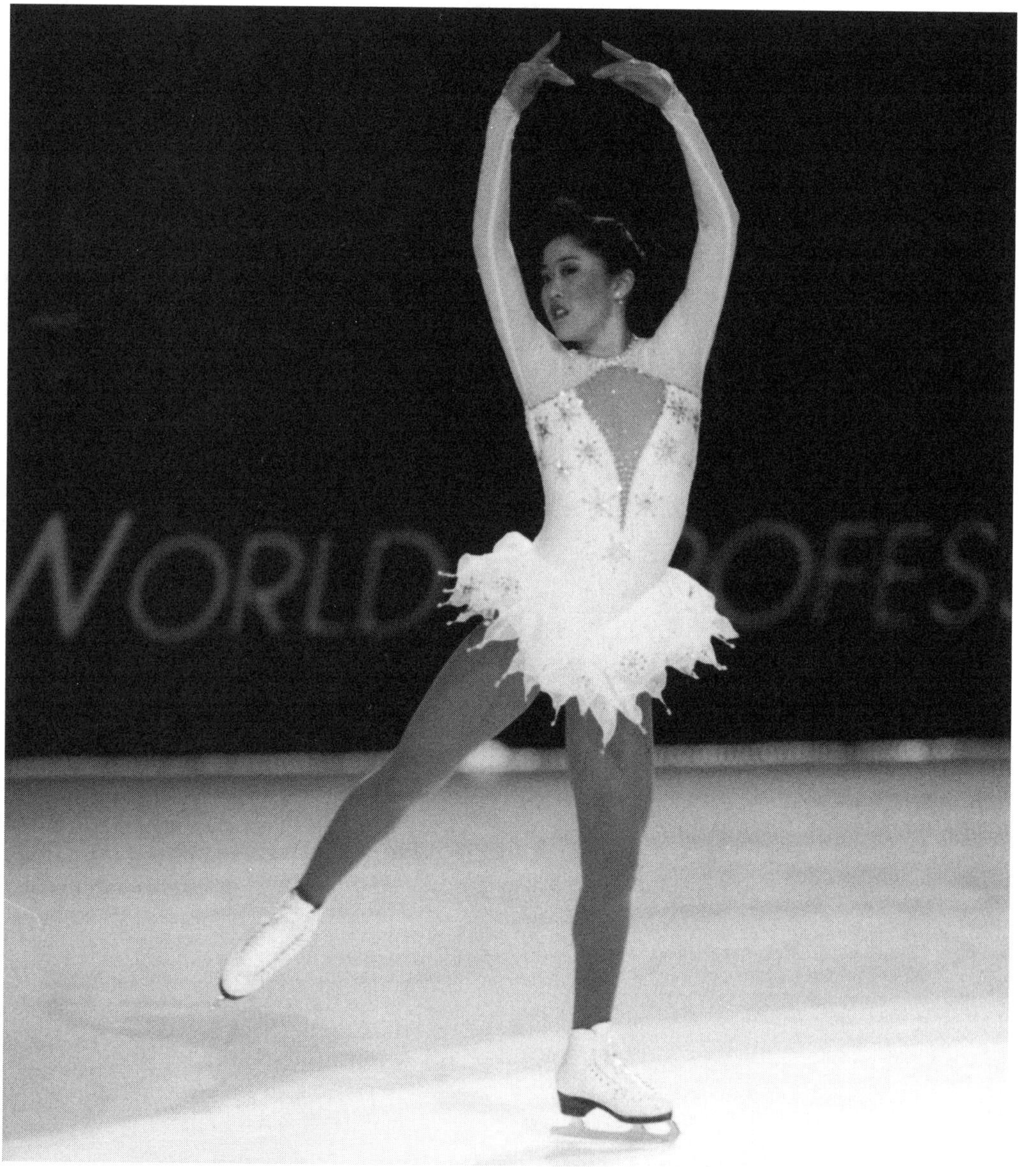

Olympic Champion Kristi Yamaguchi combined athletic and balletic grace.
(Courtesy Paul Harvath)

Z

ZAITSEV, ALEKSANDR *See* RODNINA, IRINA.

ZAMBONI, JOAN *(b. 1937) U.S. Ice Dance Champion.*

As the second partner of Roland Junso, Joan Zamboni won the U.S. Silver Medal in Ice Dancing in 1955 behind Carmel and Edward Bodel. Zamboni and Junso defeated the Bodels for the national title the following year, but in an extremely close contest, Zamboni and Junso slipped back to the Bronze in 1957 behind Sharon McKenzie/Bert Wright and Andrée Anderson/Donald Jacoby. They were 5th, 4th and 4th at the World Championships in 1955, 1956 and 1957.

ZAMBONI

George Zamboni owned a construction company and was the proud father of figure-skater Joan Zamboni (see above). His daughter often complained about the condition of the ice she had to skate on and how long it took for the infrequent resurfacing of the ice (this was carried out by men with giant squeegies). Zamboni decided to do something about the problem, and using principles derived from construction machines of various kinds, he put together a prototype machine that traveled around a rink on large rubber wheels shaving off a thin layer of ice while a cloth roller at the back lays down a film of hot water to form fresh ice. The Zamboni, named after him, quickly became an essential piece of equipment for every ice show and arena. Anyone who has attended an ice show, a figure-skating competition or a hockey game in the past 40 years has seen a Zamboni in action.

ZAYAK, ELAINE *(b. 1965) U.S. and World Champion.*

Perhaps the most notable child prodigy in figure skating since Sonja Henie, Elaine Zayak became U.S. and World Junior Champion at the age of 13. Moving into the senior ranks, she was 4th in 1980 but replaced the injured Sandy Lenz at the World's and placed 11th. In 1981, she became the U.S. Ladies' Champion and was the Silver Medalist at the World's behind Denise Biellmann of Switzerland. Falling to 3rd place at the Nationals in 1982 behind Rosalynn Sumners and Vikki de Vries, she took the World Championships by storm, winning the Gold Medal over Katarina Witt with a program that included seven triple jumps.

Zayak's rise to the top of the skating world was remarkable not only because of her age but also because she was missing two toes on her right foot as a result of a childhood accident with a lawn mower. It was to help her learn to deal with her disability that doctors recommended she take up figure skating in the first place. But after winning the World Championship at 16, her career hit some rough spots.

Elaine Zayak always bubbled with joy whatever medal she won.
(Courtesy Michael Rosenberg)

In 1983, she was again beaten by Rosalynn Sumners for the national title and was forced to withdraw from the World Championships because of an injury. In 1984 she was 3rd at the Nationals behind Sumners and Tiffany Chin. There was also a roadblock to success in international skating: The year before, the World Championship committee instituted what became known as "the Zayak rule," limiting women skaters to five triple jumps, thus effectively removing two weapons from her athletic arsenal. At the Olympics she had a difficult outing and was 6th, but she came back to win the Bronze Medal at the World Championships, behind Katarina Witt and Anna Kondrashova of the Soviet Union. (Olympic Silver Medalist Rosalyn Sumners did not compete.)

Zayak then turned professional, skating with a number of ice-show tours. She applied for reinstatement as an amateur for 1994, and although she finished only 4th at the U.S. Championships, she was accorded a standing ovation for her pluck in returning to competition as an "old lady" of 28.

ZAGORODNIUK, VIACHESLAV

(b. 1974) Ukrainian World medalist.

Viacheslav Zagorodniuk was one of several skaters around the world who had reason to be bitter about the decision to allow professional skaters to apply for reinstatement as amateurs for the 1994 Olympics. His fellow Ukrainian Viktor Petrenko, who had won the Olympic Gold Medal in 1992 skating under the banner of an improvised group of former Soviet states, was one of those to gain reinstatement. He beat Zagorodniuk for the Ukrainian Championship, and because the country was allowed only one representative, Zagorodniuk was out in the cold. But Petrenko failed to win a medal at the Olympics, and as Ukrainian representative to the World Championships a month later, Zagorodniuk won the Bronze Medal behind Canada's Elvis Stojko and France's Philippe Candeloro, beating Russian Olympic Champion Alexei Urmanov in the process. Zagorodniuk was not able to win a 1995 World medal, however; Stojko repeated as champion, a revitalized Todd Eldredge of the United States took the Silver and Candeloro held on for the Bronze.

ZHUK, TATIANA *(b. 1942) Soviet World and Olympic Pairs medalist with Aleksandr Gorelik (b. 1941).*

Tatiana Zhuk and Aleksandr Gorelik were among the foremost Pairs teams in the world for six years in the 1960s, but they had the bad luck to skate at the same time as their fellow Soviet team Oleg and Ludmila Protopopov. In 1963, Zhuk and Gorelik were runners-up for the Soviet title behind the Protopopovs and took their first World medal, a Bronze, behind Gold Medalists Marika Kilius and Hans Jurgen Baumler and the Protopopovs. They did not win a medal at either the Olympics or World Championships in 1964, but they were back as World Bronze Medalists in 1965 behind the Protopopovs and Vivian and Ronald Joseph of the United States. In 1966 they won the Silver Medal behind the Protopopovs, edging Cynthia and Ronald Kauffman of the United States. Out of competition in 1967, they had their best year in 1968, winning the Silver Medal behind the Protopopovs at both the Olympics and the World Championships. They then retired, as Irina Rodnina and her first partner, Alexei Ulanov, flashed onto the scene to displace even the Protopopovs.

ZHULIN, ALEKSANDR *See* USOVA, MAIA.

ZWACK, KARL *See* PAPEZ, IDI.

APPENDIX I

United States Championships Medalists
1914–1996

UNITED STATES FIGURE SKATING CHAMPIONSHIPS

MEN'S SINGLES

Date	*Venue*	*Gold*	*Silver*	*Bronze*
1914	New Haven, CT	Norman M. Scott	Edward Howland	Nathaniel Niles
1915–1917		No Competition Held		
1918	New York, NY	Nathaniel Niles	Karl Engel	Edward Howland
1919		No Competition Held		
1920	New York, NY	Sherwin Badger	Nathaniel Niles	Petros Wahlman
1921	Philadelphia, PA	Sherwin Badger	Nathaniel Niles	Edward Howland
1922	Boston, MA	Sherwin Badger	Nathaniel Niles	———
1923	New Haven, CT	Sherwin Badger	Chris Christenson	Julius Nelson
1924	Philadelphia, PA	Sherwin Badger	Nathaniel Niles	Chris Christenson
1925	New York, NY	Nathaniel Niles	George Braakman	Carl Engel
1926	Boston, MA	Chris Christenson	Nathaniel Niles	Ferrier Martin
1927	New York, NY	Nathaniel Niles	Roger Turner	George Braakman
1928	New Haven, CT	Roger Turner	Fredrick Goodridge	Dr. Walter Langer
1929	New York, NY	Roger Turner	Fredrick Goodridge	J. Lester Madden
1930	Providence, RI	Roger Turner	J. Lester Madden	George Hill
1931	Boston, MA	Roger Turner	J. Lester Madden	George Hill
1932	New York, NY	Roger Turner	J. Lester Madden	George Borden
1933	New Haven, CT	Roger Turner	J. Lester Madden	Robin Lee
1934	Philadelphia, PA	Roger Turner	Robin Lee	George Hill
1935	New Haven, CT	Robin Lee	Roger Turner	J. Lester Madden
1936	New York, NY	Robin Lee	Erle Reiter	George Hill
1937	Chicago, IL	Robin Lee	Erle Reiter	William Nagle
1938	Philadelphia, PA	Robin Lee	Erle Reiter	Ollie Haupt Jr.
1939	St. Paul, MN	Robin Lee	Ollie Haupt Jr.	Eugene Turner

Date	*Venue*	*Gold*	*Silver*	*Bronze*
1940	Cleveland, OH	Eugene Turner	Ollie Haupt Jr.	Skippy Baxter
1941	Boston, MA	Eugene Turner	Arthur Vaughn Jr.	William Nagle
1942	Chicago, IL	Bobby Specht	William Grimditch	Arthur Vaughn Jr.
1943	New York, NY	Arthur Vaughn Jr.	Arthur Preusch	William Nagle
1944–1945		No Competition Held		
1946	Chicago, IL	Richard Button	James Lochead	John Tuckerman
1947	Berkeley, CA	Richard Button	John Lettengarver	James Grogan
1948	Colorado Springs, CO	Richard Button	James Grogan	John Lettengarver
1949	Colorado Springs, CO	Richard Button	James Grogan	Hayes Jenkins
1950	Washington, DC	Richard Button	Hayes Jenkins	Richard Dwyer
1951	Seattle, WA	Richard Button	James Grogan	Hayes Jenkins
1952	Colorado Springs, CO	Richard Button	James Grogan	Hayes Jenkins
1953	Hershey, PA	Hayes Jenkins	Ronald Robertson	Dudley Richards
1954	Los Angeles, CA	Hayes Jenkins	David Jenkins	Ronald Robertson
1955	Colorado Springs, CO	Hayes Jenkins	David Jenkins	Hugh Graham
1956	Philadelphia, PA	Hayes Jenkins	Ronald Robertson	David Jenkins
1957	Berkeley, CA	David Jenkins	Tim Brown	Tom Moore
1958	Minneapolis, MN	David Jenkins	Tim Brown	Tom Moore
1959	Rochester, NY	David Jenkins	Tim Brown	Robert Brewer
1960	Seattle, WA	David Jenkins	Tim Brown	Robert Brewer
1961	Colorado Springs, CO	Bradley Lord	Gregory Kelley	Tim Brown
1962	Boston, MA	Monty Hoyt	Scott Allen	David Edwards
1963	Long Beach, CA	Thomas Litz	Scott Allen	Monty Hoyt
1964	Cleveland, OH	Scott Allen	Thomas Litz	Monty Hoyt
1965	Lake Placid, NY	Gary Visconti	Scott Allen	Tim Wood
1966	Berkeley, CA	Scott Allen	Gary Visconti	Billy Chapel
1967	Omaha, NE	Gary Visconti	Scott Allen	Tim Wood
1968	Philadelphia, PA	Tim Wood	Gary Visconti	J. Misha Petkevich
1969	Seattle, WA	Tim Wood	J. Misha Petkevich	Gary Visconti
1970	Tulsa, OK	Tim Wood	J. Misha Petkevich	Kenneth Shelley
1971	Buffalo, NY	J. Misha Petkevich	Kenneth Shelley	Gordon McKellen
1972	Long Beach, CA	Kenneth Shelley	J. Misha Petkevich	Gordon McKellen
1973	Minneapolis, MN	Gordon McKellen	Robert Bradshaw	David Santee
1974	Providence, RI	Gordon McKellen	Terry Kubicka	Charles Tickner
1975	Oakland, CA	Gordon McKellen	Terry Kubicka	Charles Tickner
1976	Colorado Springs, CO	Terry Kubicka	David Santee	Scott Cramer
1977	Hartford, CT	Charles Tickner	Scott Cramer	David Santee
1978	Portland, OR	Charles Tickner	David Santee	Scott Hamilton
1979	Cincinnati, OH	Charles Tickner	Scott Cramer	David Santee
1980	Atlanta, GA	Charles Tickner	David Santee	Scott Hamilton

Date	*Venue*	*Gold*	*Silver*	*Bronze*
1981	San Diego, CA	Scott Hamilton	David Santee	Robert Wagenhoffer
1982	Indianapolis, IN	Scott Hamilton	Robert Wagenhoffer	David Santee
1983	Pittsburgh, PA	Scott Hamilton	Brian Boitano	Mark Cockerell
1984	Salt Lake City, UT	Scott Hamilton	Brian Boitano	Mark Cockerell
1985	Kansas City, MO	Brian Boitano	Mark Cockerell	Scott Williams
1986	Long Island, NY	Brian Boitano	Scott Williams	Daniel Doran
1987	Tacoma, WA	Brian Boitano	Christopher Bowman	Scott Williams
1988	Denver, CO	Brian Boitano	Paul Wylie	Christopher Bowman
1989	Baltimore, MD	Christopher Bowman	Daniel Doran	Paul Wylie
1990	Salt Lake City, UT	Todd Eldredge	Paul Wylie	Mark Mitchell
1991	Minneapolis, MN	Todd Eldredge	Christopher Bowman	Paul Wylie
1992	Orlando, FL	Christopher Bowman	Paul Wylie	Mark Mitchell
1993	Phoenix, AZ	Scott Davis	Mark Mitchell	Michael Chack
1994	Detroit, MI	Scott Davis	Brian Boitano	Aren Neilsen
1995	Providence, RI	Todd Eldredge	Scott Davis	Aren Neilsen
1996	San Jose, CA	Rudy Galindo	Todd Eldredge	Dan Hollander
1997	Nashville, TN	Todd Eldredge	Michael Weiss	Dan Hollander

UNITED STATES FIGURE SKATING CHAMPIONSHIPS

LADIES' SINGLES

Date	*Venue*	*Gold*	*Silver*	*Bronze*
1914	New Haven, CT	Theresa Weld	Edith Rotch	Raynham Townshend
1915–1917		No Competition Held		
1918	New York, NY	Rosemary Beresford	Theresa Weld	———
1919	No Competition Held			
1920	New York, NY	Theresa Weld	Martha Brown	Lilian Cramer
1921	Philadelphia, PA	Theresa W. Blanchard	Lilian Cramer	———
1922	Boston, MA	Theresa W. Blanchard	Beatrix Loughran	———
1923	New Haven, CT	Theresa W. Blanchard	Beatrix Loughran	Lilian Cramer
1924	Philadelphia, PA	Theresa W. Blanchard	Rosalie Knapp	———
1925	New York, NY	Beatrix Loughran	Theresa W. Blanchard	Rosalie Kapp
1926	Boston, MA	Beatrix Loughran	Theresa W. Blanchard	Maribel Vinson
1927	New York, NY	Beatrix Loughran	Maribel Vinson	Theresa W. Blanchard
1928	New Haven, CT	Maribel Vinson	Suzanne Davis	———
1929	New York, NY	Maribel Vinson	Edith Secord	Suzanne Davis
1930	Providence, RI	Maribel Vinson	Edith Secord	Suzanne Davis

Date	*Venue*	*Gold*	*Silver*	*Bronze*
1931	Boston, MA	Maribel Vinson	Edith Secord	Hulda Berger
1932	New York, NY	Maribel Vinson	Margaret Bennett	Louise Weigel
1933	New Haven, CT	Maribel Vinson	Suzanne Davis	Louise Weigel
1934	Philadelphia, PA	Suzanne Davis	Louise Weigel	Estelle Weigel
1935	New Haven, CT	Maribel Vinson	Suzanne Davis	Louise Weigel
1936	New York, NY	Maribel Vinson	Louise Weigel	Audrey Peppe
1937	Chicago, IL	Maribel Vinson	Polly Blodgett	Katherine Durbrow
1938	Philadelphia, PA	Joan Tozzer	Audrey Peppe	Polly Blodgett
1939	St. Paul, MN	Joan Tozzer	Audrey Peppe	Charlotte Walther
1940	Cleveland, OH	Joan Tozzer	Hedy Stenuf	Jane Vaughn
1941	Boston, MA	Jane Vaughn	Gretchen Merrill	Charlotte Walther
1942	Chicago, IL	Jane Vaughn Sullivan	Gretchen Merrill	Phebe Tucker
1943	New York, NY	Gretchen Merrill	Dorothy Goos	Janette Ahrens
1944	Minneapolis, MN	Gretchen Merrill	Dorothy Goos	Ramona Allen
1945	New York, NY	Gretchen Merrill	Janette Ahrens	Madelon Olson
1946	Chicago, IL	Gretchen Merrill	Janette Ahrens	Madelon Olson
1947	Berkeley, CA	Gretchen Merrill	Janette Ahrens	Eileen Seigh
1948	Colorado Springs, CO	Gretchen Merrill	Yvonne C. Sherman	Helen Uhl
1949	Colorado Springs, CO	Yvonne C. Sherman	Gretchen Merrill	Virginia Baxter
1950	Washington, DC	Yvonne C. Sherman	Sonya Klopfer	Virginia Baxter
1951	Seattle, WA	Sonya Klopfer	Tenley Albright	Virginia Baxter
1952	Colorado Springs, CO	Tenley Albright	Frances Dorsey	Helen Geekie
1953	Hershey, PA	Tenley Albright	Carol Heiss	Margaret Graham
1954	Los Angeles, CA	Tenley Albright	Carol Heiss	Frances Dorsey
1955	Colorado Springs, CO	Tenley Albright	Carol Heiss	Catherine Machado
1956	Philadelphia, PA	Tenley Albright	Carol Heiss	Catherine Machado
1957	Berkeley, CA	Carol Heiss	Joan Shenke	Claralynn Lewis
1958	Minneapolis, MN	Carol Heiss	Carol Wanek	Lynn Finnegan
1959	Rochester, NY	Carol Heiss	Nancy Heiss	Barbara Roles
1960	Seattle, WA	Carol Heiss	Barbara Roles	Laurence Owen
1961	Colorado Springs, CO	Laurence Owen	Stephanie Westerfeld	Rhode Michelson
1962	Boston, MA	Barbara Roles	Lorraine Hanlon	Victoria Fisher
1963	Long Beach, CA	Lorraine Hanlon	Christine Haigler	Karen Howland
1964	Cleveland, OH	Peggy Fleming	Albertina Noyes	Christine Haigler
1965	Lake Placid, NY	Peggy Fleming	Christine Haigler	Albertina Noyes
1966	Berkeley, CA	Peggy Fleming	Albertina Noyes	Pamela Schneider
1967	Omaha, NE	Peggy Fleming	Albertina Noyes	Jennie Walsh
1968	Philadelphia, PA	Peggy Fleming	Albertina Noyes	Janet Lynn
1969	Seattle, WA	Janet Lynn	Julie Holmes	Albertina Noyes
1970	Tulsa, OK	Janet Lynn	Julie Holmes	Dawn Glab

Date	*Venue*	*Gold*	*Silver*	*Bronze*
1971	Buffalo, NY	Janet Lynn	Julie Holmes	Suna Murray
1972	Long Beach, CA	Janet Lynn	Julie Holmes	Suna Murray
1973	Minneapolis, MN	Janet Lynn	Dorothy Hamill	Juli McKinstry
1974	Providence, RI	Dorothy Hamill	Juli McKinstry	Kath Malmberg
1975	Oakland, CA	Dorothy Hamill	Wendy Burge	Kath Malmberg
1976	Colorado Springs, CO	Dorothy Hamill	Linda Fratianne	Wendy Burge
1977	Hartford, CT	Linda Fratianne	Barbie Smith	Wendy Burge
1978	Portland, OR	Linda Fratianne	Lisa-Marie Allen	Priscilla Hill
1979	Cincinatti, OH	Linda Fratianne	Lisa-Marie Allen	Carrie Rugh
1980	Atlanta, GA	Linda Fratianne	Lisa-Marie Allen	Sandy Lenz
1981	San Diego, CA	Elaine Zayak	Priscilla Hill	Lisa-Marie Allen
1982	Indianapolis, IN	Rosalynn Sumners	Vikki de Vries	Elaine Zayak
1983	Pittsburgh, PA	Rosalynn Sumners	Elaine Zayak	Tiffany Chin
1984	Salt Lake City, UT	Rosalynn Sumners	Tiffany Chin	Elaine Zayak
1985	Kansas City, MO	Tiffany Chin	Debi Thomas	Caryn Kadavy
1986	Hicksville, NY	Debi Thomas	Caryn Kadavy	Tiffany Chin
1987	Tacoma, WA	Jill Trenary	Debi Thomas	Caryn Kadavy
1988	Denver, CO	Debi Thomas	Jill Trenary	Caryn Kadavy
1989	Baltimore, MD	Jill Trenary	Kristi Yamaguchi	Tonya Harding
1990	Salt Lake City, UT	Jill Trenary	Kristi Yamaguchi	Holly Cook
1991	Minneapolis, MN	Tonya Harding	Kristi Yamaguchi	Nancy Kerrigan
1992	Orlando, FL	Kristi Yamaguchi	Nancy Kerrigan	Tonya Harding
1993	Phoenix, AR	Nancy Kerrigan	Lisa Ervin	Tonia Kwiatkowski
1994	Detroit, MI	Tonya Harding*	Michelle Kwan	Nicole Bobek
1995	Providence, RI	Nicole Bobek	Michelle Kwan	Tonia Kwiatkowski
1996	San Jose, CA	Michelle Kwan	Tonia Kwiatkowski	Tara Lipinski
1997	Nashville, TN	Tara Lipinski	Michelle Kwan	Nicole Bobek

* Harding was subsequently stripped of the title by the USFSA after she admitted in a plea bargain to withholding information about the attack on Nancy Kerrigan at the U.S. Championships. The 1994 title was then left vacant.

UNITED STATES FIGURE SKATING CHAMPIONSHIPS

PAIRS

Date	*Venue*	*Gold*	*Silver*	*Bronze*
1914	New Haven, CT	Jeanne Chevalier Norman M. Scott	Theresa Weld Nathaniel Niles	Eleanor Crocker Edward Howland
1915–1917		No Competition Held		
1918	New York, NY	Theresa Weld Nathaniel Niles	Clara Frothingham Sherwin Badger	———
1919		No Competition Held		
1920	New York, NY	Theresa Weld Nathaniel Niles	Edith Rotch Sherwin Badger	———
1921	Philadelphia, PA	Theresa Weld Blanchard Nathaniel Niles	Mrs. Edward Howland Mr. Edward Howland	Channing Frothingham Charles Rotch
1922	Boston, MA	Theresa W. Blanchard Nathaniel Niles	Mrs. Edward Howland Mr. Edward Howland	Edith Rotch Francis Munroe
1923	New Haven, CT	Theresa W. Blanchard Nathaniel Niles	———	———
1924	Philadelphia, PA	Theresa W. Blanchard Nathaniel Niles	Grace Munstock Joel Liberman	———
1925	New York, NY	Theresa W. Blanchard Nathaniel Niles	Ada Bauman George Braakman	Grace Munstock Joel Liberman
1926	Boston, MA	Theresa W. Blanchard Nathaniel Niles	Sydney Goode James Greene	Grace Munstock Joel Liberman
1927	New York, NY	Theresa W. Blanchard Nathaniel Niles	Beatrix Loughran Raymond Harvey	Ada Bauman George Braakman
1928	New Haven, CT	Maribel Vinson Thornton Coolidge	Theresa W. Blanchard Nathaniel Niles	Ada Bauman George Braakman
1929	New York, NY	Maribel Vinson Thornton Coolidge	Theresa W. Blanchard Nathaniel Niles	Edith Secord Joseph Savage
1930	Providence, RI	Beatrix Loughran Sherwin Badger	Maribel Vinson George Hill	Edith Secord Joseph Savage
1931	Boston, MA	Beatrix Loughran Sherwin Badger	Maribel Vinson George Hill	Grace Madden J. Lester Madden
1932	New York, NY	Beatrix Loughran Sherwin Badger	Maribel Vinson George Hill	Gertrude Meridith Joseph Savage
1933	New Haven, CT	Maribel Vinson George Hill	Grace Madden J. Lester Madden	Gertrude Meridith Joseph Savage
1934	Philadelphia, PA	Grace Madden J. Lester Madden	Eva Schwerdt William Bruns	———
1935	New Haven, CT	Maribel Vinson George Hill	Grace Madden J. Lester Madden	Eva Schwerdt William Bruns
1936	New York, NY	Maribel Vinson George Hill	Polly Blodgett Roger Turner	Marjorie Parker Howard Meredith

Date	Venue	Gold	Silver	Bronze
1937	Chicago, IL	Maribel Vinson George Hill	Grace Madden J. Lester Madden	Joan Tozzer Bernard Fox
1938	Philadelphia, PA	Joan Tozzer Bernard Fox	Grace Madden J. Lester Madden	Ardelle Sanderson Roland Janson
1939	St. Paul, MN	Joan Tozzer Bernard Fox	Annah M. Hall William Hall	Eva S. Bruns William Bruns
1940	Cleveland, OH	Joan Tozzer Bernard Fox	Hedy Stenuf Skippy Baxter	Eva S. Bruns William Bruns
1941	Boston, MA	Donna Atwood Eugene Turner	Patricia Vaeth Jack Might	Joan Mitchell Bobby Specht
1942	Chicago, IL	Doris Schubach Walter Noffke	Janette Ahrens Robert Uppgren	Margaret Field Jack Might
1943	New York, NY	Doris Schubach Walter Noffke	Janette Ahrens Robert Uppgren	Dorothy Goos Edward LeMaire
1944	Minneapolis, MN	Doris Schubach Walter Noffke	Janette Ahrens Arthur Preusch	Marcella May James Lochead
1945	New York, NY	Donna J. Pospisil Jean Pierre Brunet	Ann McGean Michael McGean	Marcella M. Willis James Lochead
1946	Chicago, IL	Donna J. Pospisil Jean Pierre Brunet	Karol Kennedy Peter Kennedy	Patty Sonnekson Charles Brinkman
1947	Berkeley, CA	Yvonne Sherman Robert Swenning	Karol Kennedy Peter Kennedy	Carolyn Welch Charles Brinkman
1948	Colorado Springs, CO	Karol Kennedy Peter Kennedy	Yvonne Sherman Robert Swenning	Harriet Sutton Lyman Wakefield
1949	Colorado Springs, CO	Karol Kennedy Peter Kennedy	Irene Maguire Walter Muehlbronner	Anne Davies Carleton Hoffner
1950	Washington, DC	Karol Kennedy Peter Kennedy	Irene Maguire Walter Muehlbronner	Anne Davies Carleton Hoffner
1951	Seattle, WA	Karol Kennedy Peter Kennedy	Janet Gerhauser John Nightingale	Anne Holt Austin Holt
1952	Colorado Springs, CO	Karol Kennedy Peter Kennedy	Janet Gerhauser John Nightingale	———
1953	Hershey, PA	Carole Ormaca Robin Greiner	Margaret A. Graham Hugh C. Graham	Kay Servatius Sully Kothman
1954	Los Angeles, CA	Carole Ormaca Robin Greiner	Margaret A. Graham Hugh C. Graham	Lucille Ash Sully Kothman
1955	Colorado Springs, CO	Carole Ormaca Robin Greiner	Lucille Ash Sully Kothman	Agnes Tyson Robert Swenning
1956	Philadelphia, PA	Carole Ormaca Robin Greiner	Lucille Ash Sully Kothman	Maribel Owen Charles Foster
1957	Berkeley, CA	Nancy Rouillard Ronald Ludington	Mary J. Watson John Jarmon	Anita Tefkin James Barlow
1958	Minneapolis, MN	Nancy R. Ludington Ronald Ludington	Sheila Wells Robin Greiner	Maribel Owen Dudley Richards

Date	*Venue*	*Gold*	*Silver*	*Bronze*
1959	Rochester, NY	Nancy Ludington Ronald Ludington	Gayle Freed Karl Freed	Maribel Owen Dudley Richards
1960	Seattle, WA	Nancy Ludington Ronald Ludington	Maribel Owen Dudley Richards	Ila Ray Hadley Ray Hadley, Jr.
1961	Colorado Springs, CO	Maribel Owen Dudley Richards	Ila Ray Hadley Ray Hadley, Jr.	Laurie Hickox William Hickox
1962	Boston, MA	Dorothyann Nelson Pieter Kollen	Judianne Fotheringill Jerry Fotheringill	Vivian Joseph Ronald Joseph
1963	Long Beach, CA	Judianne Fotheringill Jerry Fotheringill	Vivian Joseph Ronald Joseph	Patti Gustafson Pieter Kollen
1964	Cleveland, OH	Judianne Fotheringill Jerry Fotheringill	Vivian Joseph Ronald Joseph	Cynthia Kauffmann Ronald Kauffman
1965	Lake Placid, NY	Vivian Joseph Ronald Joseph	Cynthia Kauffman Ronald Kauffman	Joanne Heckart Gary Clark
1966	Berkeley, CA	Cynthia Kauffman Ronald Kauffman	Susan Berens Roy Wagelein	Page Paulsen Larry Duisch
1967	Omaha, NE	Cynthia Kauffman Ronald Kauffman	Susan Berens Roy Wagelein	Betty Lewis Richard Gilbert
1968	Philadelphia, PA	Cynthia Kauffman Ronald Kauffman	Sandi Sweitzer Roy Wagelein	JoJo Starbuck Kenneth Shelley
1969	Seattle, WA	Cynthia Kauffman Ronald Kauffman	JoJo Starbuck Kenneth Shelley	Melissa Militano Mark Militano
1970	Tulsa, OK	JoJo Starbuck Kenneth Shelley	Melissa Militano Mark Militano	Sheri Thrapp Larry Duisch
1971	Buffalo, NY	JoJo Starbuck Kenneth Shelley	Melissa Militano Mark Militano	Barbara Brown Doug Berndt
1972	Long Beach, CA	JoJo Starbuck Kenneth Shelley	Melissa Militano Mark Militano	Barbara Brown Doug Berndt
1973	Minneapolis, MN	Melissa Militano Mark Militano	Gale Fuhrman Joel Fuhrman	Emily Benenson Johnny Johns
1974	Providence, R.I	Melissa Militano Johnny Johns	Tai Babilonia Randy Gardner	Erica Susman Thomas Huff
1975	Oakland, CA	Melissa Militano Johnny Johns	Tai Babilonia Randy Gardner	Emily Benenson Jack Courtney
1976	Colorado Springs, CO	Tai Babilonia Randy Gardner	Alice Cook William Fauver	Emily Benenson Jack Courtney
1977	Hartford, CT	Tai Babilonia Randy Gardner	Gail Hamula Frank Sweiding	Sheryl Franks Michael Botticelli
1978	Portland, OR	Tai Babilonia Randy Gardner	Gail Hamula Frank Sweiding	Sheryl Franks Michael Botticelli
1979	Cincinnati, OH	Tai Babilonia Randy Gardner	Vicki Heasley Robert Wagenhoffer	Sheryl Franks Michael Botticelli
1980	Atlanta, GA	Tai Babilonia Randy Gardner	Caitlin Carruthers Peter Carruthers	Sheryl Franks Michael Botticelli

Date	*Venue*	*Gold*	*Silver*	*Bronze*
1981	San Diego, CA	Caitlin Carruthers Peter Carruthers	Lea Ann Miller William Fauver	Beth Flora Keb Flora
1982	Indianapolis, IN	Caitlin Carruthers Peter Carruthers	Maria DiDomenico Burt Lancon	Lea Ann Miller William Fauver
1983	Pittsburgh, PA	Caitlin Carruthers Peter Carruthers	Lea Ann Miller William Fauver	Jill Watson Burt Lancon
1984	Salt Lake City, UT	Caitlin Carruthers Peter Carruthers	Lea Ann Miller William Fauver	Jill Watson Burt Lancon
1985	Kansas City, MO	Jill Watson Peter Oppegard	Natalie Seybold Wayne Seybold	Gillian Wachsman Todd Waggoner
1986	Hicksville, NY	Gillian Wachsman Todd Waggoner	Jill Watson Peter Oppegard	Natalie Seybold Wayne Seybold
1987	Tacoma, WA	Jill Watson Peter Oppegard	Gillian Wachsman Todd Waggoner	Katy Keeley Joseph Mero
1988	Denver, CO	Jill Watson Peter Oppegard	Gillian Wachsman Todd Waggoner	Natalie Seybold Wayne Seybold
1989	Baltimore, MD	Kristi Yamaguchi Rudy Galindo	Natalie Seybold Wayne Seybold	Katy Keeley Joseph Mero
1990	Salt Lake City, UT	Kristi Yamaguchi Rudy Galindo	Natasha Kuchiki Todd Sand	Sharon Carz Doug Williams
1991	Minneapolis, MN	Natasha Kuchiki Todd Sand	Calla Urbanski Rocky Marval	Jenni Meno Scott Wendland
1992	Orlando, FL	Calla Urbanski Rocky Marval	Jenni Meno Scott Wendland	Natasha Kuchiki Todd Sand
1993	Phoenix, AZ	Calla Urbanski Rocky Marval	Jenni Meno Todd Sand	Karen Courtland R. Todd Reynolds
1994	Denver, CO	Jenni Meno Todd Sand	Kyoko Ina Jason Dungjen	Karen Courland R. Todd Reynolds
1995	Providence, RI	Jenni Meno Todd Sand	Kyoko Ina Jason Dungjen	Stephanie Stiegler Lance Travis
1996	San Jose, CA	Jenni Meno Todd Sand	Kyoko Ina Jason Dungjen	Shelby Lyons Brian Wells
1997	Nashville, TN	Kyoko Ina Jason Dungjen	Jenni Meno Todd Sand	Stephanie Stiegler John Zimmerman

UNITED STATES FIGURE SKATING CHAMPIONSHIPS

ICE DANCING

Medals for Ice Dancing were awarded in the first two decades of national competition in the United States, but for individual dances, such as the waltz and the fourteen step, with different sets of winners for each dance. A new format, yielding a national championship Ice Dance couple, was begun in 1936.

Date	*Venue*	*Gold*	*Silver*	*Bronze*
1936	Boston, MA	Marjorie Parker Joseph Savage	Nettie Prantell Harold Hartshorne	Clara Frothingham Ashton Parmeter
1937	Chicago, IL	Nettie Prantell Harold Hartshorne	Marjorie Parker Joseph Savage	Ardelle Kloss Roland Jansea
1938	Philadelphia, PA	Nettie Prantell Harold Hartshorne	Katherine Durbrow Joseph Savage	Louise W. Atwell Otto Dallmayr
1939	St. Paul, MN	Sandy MacDonald Harold Hartshorne	Nettie Prantell Joseph Savage	Marjorie Parker George Boltres
1940	Cleveland, OH	Sandy MacDonald Harold Hartshorne	Nettie Prantell George Boltres	Vernafay Thysell Paul Harrington
1941	Boston, MA	Sandy MacDonald Harold Hartshorne	Elizabeth Kennedy Eugene Turner	Edith Whetstone A.L. Richards
1942	Chicago, IL	Edith Whetstone A.L. Richards	Sandy MacDonald Harold Hartshorne	Ramona Allen Herman Torrano
1943	New York, NY	Marcella May James Lochead	Marjorie P. Smith Joseph Savage	Nettie Prantell Harold Hartshorne
1944	Minneapolis, MN	Marcella May James Lochead	Kathe Mehl Harold Hartshorne	Mary Andersen Jack Andersen
1945	New York, NY	Kathe M. Williams Robert Swenning	Marcella M. Willis James Lochead	Anne Davies Carleton Hoffner
1946	Chicago, IL	Anne Davies Carleton Hoffner	Lois Waring Walter Bainbridge	Carmel Waterbury Edward Bodel
1947	Berkeley, CA	Lois Waring Walter Bainbridge	Anne Davies Carleton Hoffner	Marcella Willis Frank Davenport
1948	Colorado Springs, CO	Lois Waring Walter Bainbridge	Anne Davies Carleton Hoffner	Irene Maguire Frank Davenport
1949	Colorado Springs, CO	Lois Waring Walter Bainbridge	Irene Maguire Walter Muehlbronner	Carmel Bodel Edward Bodel
1950	Washington, DC	Lois Waring Michael McGean	Irene Maquire Walter Muehlbronner	Anne Davies Carleton Hoffner
1951	Seattle, WA	Carmel Bodel Edward Bodel	Virginia Hoyns Donald Jacoby	Carol Ann Peters Daniel Ryan
1952	Colorado Springs, CO	Lois Waring Michael McGean	Carol Ann Peters Daniel Ryan	Carmel Bodel Edward Bodel
1953	Hershey, PA	Carol Ann Peters Daniel Ryan	Virginia Hoyns Donald Jacoby	Carmel Bodel Edward Bodel

Date	Venue	Gold	Silver	Bronze
1954	Los Angeles, CA	Carmel Bodel Edward Bodel	Phyllis Forney Martin Forney	Patsy Reidel Roland Junso
1955	Colorado Springs, CO	Carmel Bodel Edward Bodel	Joan Zamboni Roland Junso	Phyllis Forney Martin Forney
1956	Philadelphia, PA	Joan Zamboni Roland Junso	Carmel Bodel Edward Bodel	Sydney Arnold Franklin Nelson
1957	Berkeley, CA	Sharon McKenzie Bert Wright	Andrée Anderson Donald Jacoby	Joan Zamboni Roland Junso
1958	Minneapolis, MN	Andrée Anderson Donald Jacoby	Claire O'Neil John Bejshak	Susan Sebo Tim Brown
1959	Rochester, NY	Andrée A. Jacoby Donald Jacoby	Margie Ackles Charles Phillips	Judy Ann Lamar Ronald Ludington
1960	Seattle, WA	Margie Ackles Charles Phillips	Marily Meeker Larry Pierce	Yvonne Littlefield Roger Campbell
1961	Colorado Springs, CO	Dianne Sherbloom Larry Pierce	Donna Lee Carter Roger Campbell	Patricia Dineen Robert Dineen
1962	Boston, MA	Yvonne Littlefield Peter Betts	Dorothyann Nelson Pieter Kollen	Lorna Dyer John Carrell
1963	Long Beach, CA	Sally Schantz Stanley Urban	Yvonne Littlefield Peter Betts	Lorna Dyer John Carrell
1964	Cleveland, OH	Darleen Streich Charles Fetter	Carole MacSween Robert Munz	Lorna Dyer John Carrell
1965	Lake Placid, NY	Kristin Fortune Dennis Sveum	Lorna Dyer John Carrell	Susan Urban Stanley Urban
1966	Berkeley, CA	Kristin Fortune Dennis Sveum	Lorna Dyer John Carrell	Susan Urban Stanley Urban
1967	Omaha, NE	Lorna Dyer John Carrell	Alma Davenport Roger Berry	Judy Schwomeyer James Sladky
1968	Philadelphia, PA	Judy Schwomeyer James Sladky	Vicki Camper Eugene Heffron	Debbie Gerken Raymond Tiedemann
1969	Seattle, WA	Judy Schwomeyer James Sladky	Joan Bitterman Brad Hislop	Debbie Gerken Raymond Tiedemann
1970	Tulsa, OK	Judy Schwomeyer James Sladky	Anne Miller Harvey Miller	Debbie Ganson Brad Hislop
1971	Buffalo, NY	Judy Schwomeyer James Sladky	Anne Miller Harvey Miller	Mary Campbell Johnny Johns
1972	Long Beach, CA	Judy Schwomeyer James Sladky	Anne Miller Harvey Miller	Mary Campbell Johnny Johns
1973	Minneapolis, MN	Mary Campbell Johnny Johns	Anne Miller Harvey Miller	Jane Pankey Richard Horne
1974	Providence, RI	Colleen O'Connor Jim Millns	Anne Miller Harvey Miller	Michelle Ford Glenn Patterson
1975	Oakland, CA	Colleen O'Connor Jim Millns	Judi Genovesi Kent Weigle	Michelle Ford Glenn Patterson

Date	*Venue*	*Gold*	*Silver*	*Bronze*
1976	Colorado Springs, CO	Colleen O'Connor Jim Millns	Judy Genovesi Kent Weigle	Susan Kelley Andrew Stroukoff
1977	Hartford, CT	Judy Genovesi Kent Weigle	Susan Kelley Andrew Stroukoff	Michelle Ford Glenn Patterson
1978	Portland, OR	Stacey Smith John Sumners	Carol Fox Richard Dalley	Susan Kelley Andrew Stroukoff
1979	Cincinnati, OH	Stacey Smith John Sumners	Carol Fox Richard Dalley	Judy Blumberg Michael Seibert
1980	Atlanta, GA	Stacey Smith John Sumners	Judy Blumberg Michael Seibert	Carol Fox Richard Dalley
1981	San Diego, CA	Judy Blumberg Michael Seibert	Carol Fox Richard Dalley	Kim Krohn Barry Hagan
1982	Indianapolis, IN	Judy Blumberg Michael Seibert	Carol Fox Richard Dalley	Elisa Spitz Scott Gregory
1983	Pittsburgh, PA	Judy Blumberg Michael Seibert	Elisa Spitz Scott Gregory	Carol Fox Richard Dalley
1984	Salt Lake City, UT	Judy Blumberg Michael Seibert	Carol Fox Richard Dalley	Elisa Spitz Scott Gregory
1985	Kansas City, MO	Judy Blumberg Michael Seibert	Renee Roca Donald Adair	Suzanne Semanick Scott Gregory
1986	Hicksville, NY	Renee Roca Donald Adair	Suzanne Semanick Scott Gregory	Lois Luciani Russ Witherby
1987	Tacoma, WA	Suzanne Semanick Scott Gregory	Renee Roca Donald Adair	Susan Wynne Joseph Druar
1988	Denver, CO	Susanne Semanick Scott Gregory	Susan Wynne Joseph Druar	April Sargent Russ Witherby
1989	Baltimore, MD	Susan Wynne Scott Gregory	April Sargent Russ Witherby	Susanne Semanick Ron Kravette
1990	Salt Lake City, UT	Susan Wynne Scott Gregory	April Sargent Russ Witherby	Susanne Semanick Ron Kravette
1991	Minneapolis, MN	Elizabeth Punsalan Jerod Swallow	April Sargent Ross Witherby	Jeanne Miley Michael Verlich
1992	Orlando, FL	April Sargent Russ Witherby	Rachel Mayer Peter Breen	Elizabeth Punsalan Jerod Swallow
1993	Phoenix, AZ	Renee Roca Gorsha Sur	Susan Wynne Russ Witherby	Elizabeth Punsalan Jerod Swallow
1994	Denver, CO	Elizabeth Punsalan Jerod Swallow	Susan Wynne Russ Witherby	Amy Webster Ron Kravette
1995	Providence, RI	Renee Roca Gorsha Sur	Elizabeth Punsalan Jerod Swallow	Amy Webster Russ Witherby
1996	San Jose, CA	Elizabeth Punsalan Jerod Swallow	Renee Roca Gorsha Sur	Eve Chalom Mathew Gates
1997	Nashville, TN	Elizabeth Punsalan Jerod Swallow	Eve Chalom Mathew Gates	Kate Robinson Peter Breen

APPENDIX II

World Championships Medalists
1896–1996

WORLD CHAMPIONSHIPS

MEN'S SINGLES

Date	*Venue*	*Gold*	*Silver*	*Bronze*
1896	St. Petersburg, RUS	Gilbert Fuchs (GER)	Gustav Hugel (AUT)	Georg Sanders (RUS)
1897	Stockholm, SWE	Gustav Hugel (AUT)	Ulrich Salchow (SWE)	Johan Lefstad (NOR)
1898	London, GBR	Henning Grenander (SWE)	Gustav Hugel (AUT)	Gilbert Fuchs (GER)
1889	Davos, SUI	Gustav Hugel (AUT)	Ulrich Salchow (SWE)	Edgar Syers (GBR)
1900	Davos, SUI	Gustav Hugel (AUT)	Ulrich Salchow (SWE)	———
1901	Stockholm, SWE	Ulrich Salchow (SWE)	Gilbert Fuchs (GER)	———
1902	London, GBR	Ulrich Salchow (SWE)	Madge Syers* (GBR)	Martin Gordan (GER)
1903	St. Petersburg, RUS	Ulrich Salchow (SWE)	Nicolai Panin (RUS)	Max Bohatsch (AUT)
1904	Berlin, GER	Ulrich Salchow (SWE)	Heinrich Berger (GER)	Martin Gordan (GER)
1905	Stockholm, SWE	Ulrich Salchow (SWE)	Max Bohatsch (AUT)	Per Thoren (SWE)
1906	Munich, GER	Gilbert Fuchs (GER)	Heinrich Berger (GER)	Bror Meyer (SWE)
1907	Vienna, AUT	Ulrich Salchow (SWE)	Max Bohatsch (AUT)	Gilbert Fuchs (GER)
1908	Troppau, CZE	Ulrich Salchow (SWE)	Gilbert Fuchs (GER)	Heinrich Berger (GER)
1909	Stockholm, SWE	Ulrich Salchow (SWE)	Per Thoren (SWE)	Ernest Herz (AUT)
1910	Davos, SUI	Ulrich Salchow (SWE)	Werner Rittberger (GER)	Andor Szende (HUN)
1911	Berlin, GER	Ulrich Salchow (SWE)	Werner Rittberger (GER)	Fritz Kachler (AUT)
1912	Manchester, GBR	Fritz Kachler (AUT)	Werner Rittberger (GER)	Andor Szende (HUN)
1913	Vienna, AUT	Fritz Kachler (AUT)	Willy Boeckl (AUT)	Andor Szende (HUN)
1914	Helsinki, FIN	Gosta Sandahl (SWE)	Fritz Kachler (AUT)	Willy Boeckl (AUT)
1915–1921		No Championship Held		
1922	Stockholm, SWE	Gillis Grafstrom (SWE)	Fritz Kachler (AUT)	Willy Boeckl (AUT)

* Because there was no Ladies' Championship, Madge Syers applied to skate in the Men's division and was granted permission. Women were then disallowed entry, but a separate division for them was established in 1906.

Date	*Venue*	*Gold*	*Silver*	*Bronze*
1923	Vienna, AUT	Fritz Kachler (AUT)	Willy Boeckl (AUT)	Gosta Sandahl (SWE)
1924	Manchester, GBR	Gillis Grafstrom (SWE)	Willy Boeckl (AUT)	Ernst Oppacher (AUT)
1925	Vienna, AUT	Willy Boeckl (AUT)	Fritz Kachler (AUT)	Otto Preissecker (AUT)
1926	Berlin, GER	Willy Boeckl (AUT)	Otto Preissecker (AUT)	John Page (GBR)
1927	Davos, SUI	Willy Boeckl (AUT)	Otto Preissecker (AUT)	Karl Schafer (AUT)
1928	Berlin, GER	Willy Boeckl (AUT)	Karl Schafer (AUT)	Hugo Distler (AUT)
1929	London, GBR	Gillis Grafstrom (SWE)	Kark Schafer (AUT)	Ludvig Wrede (AUT)
1930	New York, USA	Karl Schafer (AUT)	Roger Turner (USA)	Georg Gautschi (SUI)
1931	Berlin, GER	Karl Schafer (AUT)	Roger Turner (USA)	Ernst Baier (GER)
1932	Montreal, CAN	Karl Schafer (AUT)	Montgomery Wilson (CAN)	Ernst Baier (GER)
1933	Zurich, SUI	Karl Schafer (AUT)	Ernst Baier (GER)	Markus Nikkanen (FIN)
1934	Stockholm, SWE	Karl Schafer (AUT)	Ernst Baier (GER)	Erich Erdos (AUT)
1935	Budapest, HUN	Karl Schafer (AUT)	Jack Dunn (GBR)	Denes Pataky (HUN)
1936	Paris, FRA	Karl Schafer (AUT)	Graham Sharp (GBR)	Felix Kaspar (AUT)
1937	Vienna, AUT	Felix Kaspar (AUT)	Graham Sharp (GBR)	Elemer Tertak (HUN)
1938	Berlin, GER	Felix Kaspar (AUT)	Graham Sharp (GBR)	Herbert Alward (AUT)
1939	Budapest, HUN	Graham Sharp (GBR)	Freddie Tomlins (GBR)	Horst Faber (GER)
1940–1946		No Championship Held		
1947	Stockholm, SWE	Hans Gerschwiler (SUI)	Richard Button (USA)	Arthur Apfel (GBR)
1948	Davos, SUI	Richard Button (USA)	Hans Gerswiler (SUI)	Ede Kiraly (HUN)
1949	Paris, FRA	Richard Button (USA)	Ede Kiraly (HUN)	Edi Rada (AUT)
1950	London, GBR	Richard Button (USA)	Ede Kiraly (HUN)	Hayes Jenkins (USA)
1951	Milan, ITA	Richard Button (USA)	James Grogan (USA)	Helmut Seibt (AUT)
1952	Paris, FRA	Richard Button (USA)	James Grogan (USA)	Hayes Jenkins (USA)
1953	Davos, SUI	Hayes Jenkins (USA)	James Grogan (USA)	Carlo Fassi (ITA)
1954	Oslo, NOR	Hayes Jenkins (USA)	James Grogan (USA)	Alain Giletti (FRA)
1955	Vienna, AUT	Hayes Jenkins (USA)	Ronald Robertson (USA)	David Jenkins (USA)
1956	Garmisch, FRG	Hayes Jenkins (USA)	Ronald Robertson (USA)	David Jenkins (USA)
1957	Colorado Springs, USA	David Jenkins (USA)	Tim Brown (USA)	Charles Snelling (CAN)
1958	Paris, FRA	David Jenkins (USA)	Tim Brown (USA)	Alain Giletti (FRA)
1959	Colorado Springs, USA	David Jenkins (USA)	Donald Jackson (CAN)	Tim Brown (USA)
1960	Vancouver, CAN	Alain Giletti (FRA)	Donald Jackson (CAN)	Alain Calmat (FRA)
1961		No Championship Held		
1962	Prague, CZE	Donald Jackson (CAN)	Karol Divin (CZE)	Alain Calmat (FRA)
1963	Cortina, ITA	Donald McPherson (CAN)	Alain Calmat (FRA)	Manfred Schnelldorfer (FRG)
1964	Dortmund, FRG	Manfred Schnelldorfer (FRG)	Alain Calmat (FRA)	Karol Divin (CZE)
1965	Colorado Springs, USA	Alain Calmat (FRA)	Scott Allen (USA)	Donald Knight (CAN)
1966	Davos, SUI	Emmerich Danzer (AUT)	Wolfgang Schwartz (AUT)	Gary Visconti (USA)
1967	Vienna, AUT	Emmerich Danzer (AUT)	Wolfgang Schwartz (AUT)	Gary Visconti (USA)
1968	Geneva, SUI	Emmerich Danzer (AUT)	Tim Wood (USA)	Patrick Pera (FRA)

Date	*Venue*	*Gold*	*Silver*	*Bronze*
1969	Colorado Springs, USA	Tim Wood (USA)	Ondrej Nepela (CZE)	Patrick Pera (FRA)
1970	Ljubljana, YUG	Tim Wood (USA)	Ondrej Nepela (CZE)	Gunter Zoller (GDR)
1971	Lyon, FRA	Ondrej Nepela (CZE)	Patrick Pera (FRA)	Sergei Chetverukhin (USSR)
1972	Calgary, CAN	Ondrej Nepela (CZE)	Sergei Chetverukhin (USSR)	Vladimir Kovalev (USSR)
1973	Bratislava, CZE	Ondrej Nepela (CZE)	Sergei Chetverukhin (USSR)	Jan Hoffmann (GDR)
1974	Munich, FRG	Jan Hoffmann (GDR)	Sergei Volkov (USSR)	Toller Cranston (CAN)
1975	Colorado Springs, USA	Sergei Volkov (USSR)	Vladimir Kovalev (USSR)	John Curry (GBR)
1976	Gothenberg, SWE	John Curry (GBR)	Vladimir Kovalev (USSR)	Jan Hoffmann (GDR)
1977	Tokyo, JPN	Vladimir Kovalev (USSR)	Jan Hoffmann (GDR)	Minoru Sano (JPN)
1978	Ottawa, CAN	Charles Tickner (USA)	Jan Hoffmann (GDR)	Robin Cousins (GBR)
1979	Vienna, AUT	Vladimir Kovalev (USSR)	Robin Cousins (GBR)	Jan Hoffmann (GDR)
1980	Dortmund, FRG	Jan Hoffmann (GDR)	Robin Cousins (GBR)	Charles Tickner (USA)
1981	Hartford, USA	Scott Hamilton (USA)	David Santee (USA)	Igor Bobrin (USSR)
1982	Copenhagen, DEN	Scott Hamilton (USA)	Norbert Schramm (FRG)	Brian Pockar (CAN)
1983	Helsinki, FIN	Scott Hamilton (USA)	Norbert Schramm (FRG)	Brian Orser (CAN)
1984	Ottawa, CAN	Scott Hamilton (USA)	Brian Orser (CAN)	Alexandr Fadeev (USSR)
1985	Tokyo, JPN	Alexandr Fadeev (USSR)	Brian Orser (CAN)	Brian Boitano (USA)
1986	Geneva, SUI	Brian Boitano (USA)	Brian Orser (CAN)	Alexandr Fadeev (USSR)
1987	Cincinnati, USA	Brian Orser (CAN)	Brian Boitano (USA)	Alexandr Fadeev (USSR)
1988	Budapest, HUN	Brian Boitano (USA)	Brian Orser (CAN)	Viktor Petrenko (USSR)
1989	Paris, FRA	Kurt Browning (CAN)	Christopher Bowman (USA)	Grzegorz Filipowski (POL)
1990	Halifax, CAN	Kurt Browning (CAN)	Viktor Petrenko (USSR)	Christopher Bowman (USA)
1991	Munich, GER	Kurt Browning (CAN)	Viktor Petrenko (USSR)	Todd Eldredge (USA)
1992	Oakland, USA	Viktor Petrenko (CIS)	Kurt Browning (CAN)	Elvis Stojko (CAN)
1993	Prague, CZE R.	Kurt Browning (CAN)	Elvis Stojko (CAN)	Alexei Urmanov (RUS)
1994	Ciba, JPN	Elvis Stojko (CAN)	Philippe Candeloro (FRA)	V. Zagorodniuk (UKR)
1995	Birmingham, GB	Elvis Stojko (CAN)	Todd Eldredge (USA)	Philippe Candeloro (FRA)
1996	Edmonton, CAN	Todd Eldredge (USA)	Ilya Kulik (RUS)	Rudy Galindo (USA)
1997	Lausanne, SUI	Elvis Stojko (CAN)	Todd Eldredge (USA)	Alexei Yagudin (RUS)

WORLD CHAMPIONSHIPS

LADIES' SINGLES

Date	*Venue*	*Gold*	*Silver*	*Bronze*
1906	Davos, SUI	Madge Syers (GBR)	Jenny Herz (AUT)	Lily Kronberger (HUN)
1907	Vienna, AUT	Madge Syers (GBR)	Jenny Herz (AUT)	Lily Kronberger (HUN)
1908	Troppau, CZE	Lily Kronberger (HUN)	Elsa Rendschmidt (GER)	———
1909	Budapest, HUN	Lily Kronberger (HUN)	———	———
1910	Berlin, GER	Lily Kronberger (HUN)	Elsa Rendschmidt (GER)	———
1911	Vienna, AUT	Lily Kronberger (HUN)	Opika von Horvath (HUN)	Ludowika Eilers (GER)
1912	Davos, SUI	Opika von Horvath (HUN)	Dorothy Greenhough (GBR)	Phyllis Johnson (GBR)
1913	Stockholm, SWE	Opika von Horvath (HUN)	Phyllis Johnson (GBR)	Svea Boren (SWE)
1914	St. Moritz, SUI	Opika von Horvath (HUN)	Angela Hanka (AUT)	Phyllis Johnson (GBR)
1915–1921		No Competition Held		
1922	Stockholm, SWE	Herma Plank-Szabo (AUT)	Svea Noren (SWE)	Margot Moe (NOR)
1923	Vienna, AUT	Herma Plank-Szabo (AUT)	Gisela Reichmann (AUT)	Svea Noren (SWE)
1924	Oslo, NOR	Herma Jaross-Szabo (AUT)	Ellen Brockhofft (GER)	Beatrix Loughran (USA)
1925	Davos, SUI	Herma Jaross-Szabo (AUT)	Ellen Brockhofft (GER)	Elizabeth Bockel (GER)
1926	Stockholm, SWE	Herma Jaross-Szabo (AUT)	Sonja Henie (NOR)	Kathleen Shaw (GBR)
1927	Oslo, NOR	Sonja Henie (NOR)	Herma Jaross-Szabo (AUT)	Karen Simensen (NOR)
1928	London, GBR	Sonja Henie (NOR)	Maribel Vinson (USA)	Fritzi Burger (AUT)
1929	Budapest, HUN	Sonja Henie (NOR)	Fritzi Burger (AUT)	Melitta Bonner (AUT)
1930	New York, USA	Sonja Henie (NOR)	Cecil Smith (CAN)	Maribel Vinson (USA)
1931	Berlin, GER	Sonja Henie (NOR)	Hilde Holovsky (AUT)	Fritzi Burger (AUT)
1932	Montreal, CAN	Sonja Henie (NOR)	Fritzi Burger (AUT)	Constance Samuels (CAN)
1933	Stockholm, SWE	Sonja Henie (NOR)	Vivi-Anne Hulten (SWE)	Hilde Holovsky (AUT)
1934	Oslo, NOR	Sonja Henie (NOR)	Megan Taylor (GBR)	Liselotte Landbeck (AUT)
1935	Vienna, AUT	Sonja Henie (NOR)	Cecilia Colledge (GBR)	Vivi-Anne Hulten (SWE)
1936	Paris, FRA	Sonja Henie (NOR)	Megan Taylor (GBR)	Vivi-Anne Hulten (SWE)
1937	London, GBR	Cecilia Colledge (GBR)	Megan Taylor (GBR)	Vivi-Anne Hulten (SWE)
1938	Stockholm, SWE	Megan Taylor (GBR)	Cecilia Colledge (GBR)	Hedy Stenuf (USA)
1939	Prague, CZE	Megan Taylor (GBR)	Hedy Stenuf (USA)	Daphne Walker (GBR)
1940–1946		No Competition Held		
1947	Stockholm, SWE	Barbara Ann Scott (CAN)	Daphne Walker (GBR)	Gretchen Merrill (USA)
1948	Davos, SUI	Barbara Ann Scott (CAN)	Eva Pawlik (AUT)	Jirina Nekolova (CZE)
1949	Paris, FRA	Alena Vrzanova (CZE)	Yvonne Sherman (USA)	Jeannette Altwegg (GBR)
1950	London, GBR	Alena Vrzanova (CZE)	Jeannette Altwegg (GBR)	Yvonne Sherman (USA)
1951	Milan, ITA	Jeannette Altwegg (GBR)	Jacqueline du Bief (FRA)	Sonya Klopfer (USA)
1952	Paris, FRA	Jacqueline du Bief (FRA)	Sonya Klopfer (USA)	Virginia Baxter (USA)
1953	Davos, SUI	Tenley Albright (USA)	Gundi Busch (FRG)	Valda Osborn (GBR)

Date	*Venue*	*Gold*	*Silver*	*Bronze*
1954	Oslo, Norway	Gundi Busch (FRG)	Tenley Albright (USA)	Erica Bathelor (GBR)
1955	Vienna, AUT	Tenley Albright (USA)	Carol Heiss (USA)	Hanna Engel (AUT)
1956	Garmisch, FRG	Carol Heiss (USA)	Tenley Albright (USA)	Ingrid Wendll (AUT)
1957	Colorado Springs, USA	Carol Heiss (USA)	Hanna Eigel (AUT)	Ingrid Wendl (AUT)
1958	Paris, FRA	Carol Heiss (USA)	Ingrid Wendl (AUT)	Hanna Walter (AUT)
1959	Colorado Springs, USA	Carol Heiss (USA)	Hanna Walter (AUT)	Sjoukje Dijkstra (NED)
1960	Vancouver, CAN	Carol Heiss (USA)	Sjoukje Dijkstra (NET)	Barbara Roles (USA)
1961	No Championship Held			
1962	Prague, CZE	Sjoukje Dijkstra (NED)	Wendy Griner (CAN)	Regine Heitzer (AUT)
1963	Cortina, ITA	Sjoukje Dijkstra (NED)	Regine Heitzer (AUT)	Nicole Hassler (FRA)
1964	Dortmund, FRG	Sjoukje Dijkstra (NED)	Regine Heitzer (AUT)	Petra Burke (CAN)
1965	Colorado Springs, USA	Petra Burke (CAN)	Regine Heitzer (AUT)	Peggy Fleming (USA)
1966	Davos, SUI	Peggy Fleming (USA)	Gabriele Seyfert (FRA)	Petra Burke (CAN)
1967	Vienna, AUT	Peggy Fleming (USA)	Gabriele Seyfert (GDR)	Hana Maskova (CZE)
1968	Geneva, SUI	Peggy Fleming (USA)	Gabriele Seyfert (GDR)	Hana Moskova (CZE)
1969	Colorado Springs, USA	Gabriele Seyfert (GDR)	Beatrix Schuba (AUT)	Zsuzsa Almassy (HUN)
1970	Ljubljana, YUG	Gabrielle Seyfert (GDR)	Beatrix Schuba (AUT)	Julie Holmes (USA)
1971	Lyon, FRA	Beatrix Schuba (AUT)	Julie Holmes (USA)	Karen Magnussen (CAN)
1972	Calgary, CAN	Beatrix Schuba (AUT)	Karen Magnussen (CAN)	Janet Lynn (USA)
1973	Bratislava, CZE	Karen Magnussen (CAN)	Janet Lynn (USA)	Christine Errath (GDR)
1974	Munich, FRG	Christine Errath (GDR)	Dorothy Hamill (USA)	Dianne de Leeuw (NED)
1975	Colorado Springs, USA	Dianne de Leeuw (NED)	Dorothy Hamill (USA)	Christine Errath (GDR)
1976	Gotheberg, SWE	Dorothy Hamill (USA)	Christine Errath (GDR)	Dianne de Leeuw (NED)
1977	Tokyo, JPN	Linda Fratianne (USA)	Anett Poetzsch (GDR)	Dagmar Lurz (FRG)
1978	Ottawa, CAN	Anett Poetzsch (GDR)	Linda Fratianne (USA)	Susanne Driano (ITA)
1979	Vienna, AUT	Linda Fratianne (USA)	Anett Poetzsch (GDR)	Emi Watanabe (JPN)
1980	Dortmund, FRG	Anett Poetzsch (GDR)	Dagmar Lurz (FRG)	Linda Fratianne (USA)
1981	Hartford, USA	Denise Biellmann (SUI)	Elaine Zayak (USA)	Claudia Kristofics-Binder (AUT)
1982	Copenhagen, DEN	Elaine Zayak (USA)	Katarina Witt (GDR)	Claudia Kristofics-Binder (AUT)
1983	Helsinki, FIN	Rosalynn Sumners (USA)	Claudia Leistner (FRG)	Elena Vodorezova (USSR)
1984	Ottawa, CAN	Katarina Witt (GDR)	Anna Kondrashova (USSR)	Elaine Zayak (USA)
1985	Tokyo, JPN	Katarina Witt (GDR)	Kira Ivanova (USSR)	Tiffany Chin (USA)
1986	Geneva, SUI	Debi Thomas (USA)	Katarina Witt (GDR)	Tiffany Chin (USA
1987	Cincinnati, USA	Katarina Witt (GDR)	Debi Thomas (USA)	Caryn Kadavy (USA)
1988	Budapest, HUN	Katarina Witt (GDR)	Elisabeth Manley (CAN)	Debi Thomas (USA)
1989	Paris, FRA	Midori Ito (JPN)	Claudia Leistner (FRG)	Jill Trenary (USA)
1990	Halifax, CAN	Jill Trenary (USA)	Midori Ito (JPN)	Holly Cook (USA)
1991	Munich, GER	Kristi Yamaguchi (USA)	Tonya Harding (USA)	Nancy Kerrigan (USA)
1992	Oakland, USA	Kristi Yamaguchi (USA)	Nancy Kerrigan (USA)	Chen Lu (CHN)
1993	Prague, CZE R.	Oksana Baiul (UKR)	Surya Bonaly (FRA)	Chen Lu (CHN)

Date	*Venue*	*Gold*	*Silver*	*Bronze*
1994	Chiba, JPN	Yuka Sato (JPN)	Surya Bonaly (FRA)	Tanja Szewczenko (GER)
1995	Birmingham, GB	Chen Lu (CHN)	Surya Bonaly (FRA)	Nicole Bobek (USA)
1996	Edmonton, CAN	Michelle Kwan (USA)	Chen Lu (CHN)	Irina Slutskaya (RUS)
1997	Lausanne, SUI	Tara Lipinski (USA)	Michelle Kwan (USA)	Vanessa Gusmeroli (FRA)

WORLD CHAMPIONSHIPS

PAIRS

Date	*Venue*	*Gold*	*Silver*	*Bronze*
1908	St. Petersburg, RUS	Anna Hubler Heinrich Burger (GER)	Phyllis Johnson James Johnson (GBR)	A. Fischer L. Popova (RUS)
1909	Stockholm, SWE	Phyllis Johnson James Johnson (GBR)	Valborg Lindahl Nils Rosenius (SWE)	Gertrud Strom Richard Johanson (SWE)
1910	Berlin, GER	Anna Hubler Heinrich Burger (GER)	Ludowika Eilers Walter Jakobsson (FIN)	Phyllis Johnson James Johnson (GBR)
1911	Vienna, AUT	Ludowicka Eilers Walter Jakobsson (FIN)	———	———
1912	Manchester, GBR	Phyllis Johnson James Johnson (GBR)	Ludowika Jakobsson Walter Jakobsson (FIN)	Alexia Schoyen Yngvar Byrn (NOR)
1913	Stockholm, SWE	Helene Engelmann Karl Mejstrik (AUT)	Ludowika Jakobsson Walter Jakobsson (FIN)	Christa von Szabo Leo Horwitz (AUT)
1914	St. Moritz, SUI	Ludowika Jakobsson Walter Jakobsson (FIN)	Helene Engelmann Karl Mejstrik (AUT)	Christa von Szabo Leo Horwitz (AUT)
1915–1921		No Championship Held		
1922	Davos, SUI	Helene Engelmann Alfred Berger (AUT)	Ludowika Jakobsson Walter Jakobsson (FIN)	Margaret Metzner Paul Metzner (GER)
1923	Oslo, NOR	Ludowika Jakobsson Walter Jakobsson (FIN)	Alexia Bryn Yngvar Byrn (NOR)	Elna Henrikson Kaj af Ekstrom (SWE)
1924	Manchester, GBR	Helene Engelmann Alfred Berger (AUT)	Ethel Muckelt John Page (GBR)	Elna Hernikson Kaj af Ekstrom (SWE)

Date	*Venue*	*Gold*	*Silver*	*Bronze*
1925	Vienna, AUT	Herma Jaross-Szabo Ludwig Wrede (AUT)	Andrée Brunet Pierre Brunet (FRA)	Lilly Scholz Otto Kaiser (AUT)
1926	Berlin, GER	Andrée Brunet Pierre Brunet (FRA)	Lilly Scholz Otto Kaiser (AUT)	Herma Jaross-Szabo Ludwig Wrede (AUT)
1927	Vienna, AUT	Herma Jaross-Szabo Ludwig Wrede (AUT)	Lilly Schloz Otto Kaiser (AUT)	Else Hoppe Oscar Hoppe (CZE)
1928	London, GBR	Andrée Brunet Pierre Brunet (FRA)	Lilly Schloz Otto Kaiser (AUT)	Melitta Brunner Ludwig Wrede (AUT)
1929	Budapest, HUN	Lilly Schloz Otto Kaiser (AUT)	Melitta Bruner Ludwig Wrede (AUT)	Olga Orgonista Sandor Szalay (HUN)
1930	New York, USA	Andrée Brunet Pierre Brunet (FRA)	Melitta Bruner Ludwig Wrede (AUT)	Beatrix Loughran Sherwin Badger (USA)
1931	Berlin, GER	Emilie Rotter Laszlo Szollas (HUN)	Olga Orgonista Sandor Szalay (HUN)	Idi Papez Karl Zwack (AUT)
1932	Montreal, CAN	Andrée Brunet Pierre Brunet (FRA)	Emilie Rotter Laszlo Szollas (HUN)	Beatrix Loughran Sherwin Badger (USA)
1933	Stockholm, SWE	Emilie Rotter Laszlo Szollas (HUN)	Idi Papez Karl Zwack (AUT)	Randi Bakke Christen Christensen (NOR)
1934	Helsinki, FIN	Emilie Rotter Laszlo Szollas (HUN)	Idi Papez Karl Zwack (AUT)	Maxi Herber Ernst Baier (GER)
1935	Budapest, HUN	Emilie Rotter Laszlo Szollas (HUN)	Ilse Pausin Erich Pausin (AUT)	Lucy Gallo Rezso Dillinger (HUN)
1936	Paris, FRA	Maxi Herber Ernst Baier (GER)	Ilse Pausin Erich Pausin (AUT)	Violet Cliff Leslie Cliff (GBR)
1937	London, GBR	Maxi Herber Ernst Baier (GER)	Ilse Pausin Erich Pausin (AUT)	Violet Cliff Leslie Cliff (GBR)
1938	Berlin, GER	Maxi Herber Ernst Baier (GER)	Ilse Pausin Erich Pausin (AUT)	Inge Koch Gunther Noack (GER)
1939	Budapest, HUN	Maxi Herber Ernst Baier (GER)	Ilse Pausin Erich Pausin (AUT)	Inge Koch Gunther Noack (GER)
1940–1946		No Competition Held		

Date	*Venue*	*Gold*	*Silver*	*Bronze*
1947	Stockholm, SWE	Micheline Lannoy Pierre Baugniet (BEL)	Karol Kennedy Peter Kennedy (USA)	Suzanne Diskeuve Edmond Verbustel (BEL)
1948	Davos, SUI	Micheline Lannoy Pierre Baugniet (BEL)	Andrea Kekesy Ede Kiraly (HUN)	Suzanne Morrow Walter Diestelmeyer (CAN)
1949	Paris, FRA	Andrea Kekesy Ede Kiraly (HUN)	Karol Kennedy Peter Kennedy (USA)	Anne Davies Carleton Hoffner (USA)
1950	London, GBR	Karol Kennedy Peter Kennedy (USA)	Jennifer Nicks John Nicks (GBR)	Marianne Nagy Laszlo Nagy (HUN)
1951	Milan, ITA	Ria Falk Paul Falk (FRG)	Karol Kennedy Peter Kennedy (USA)	Jennifer Nicks John Nicks (GBR)
1952	Paris, FRA	Ria Falk Paul Falk (FRG)	Karol Kennedy Peter Kennedy (USA)	Jennifer Nicks John Nicks (GBR)
1953	Davos, SUI	Jennifer Nicks John Nicks (GBR)	Francis Dafoe Norris Bowden (CAN)	Marianne Nagy Laszlo Nagy (HUN)
1954	Oslo, NOR	Francis Dafoe Norris Bowden (CAN)	Silvia Grandjean Michel Grandjean (SUI)	Elisabeth Schwarz Kurt Oppelt (AUT)
1955	Vienna, AUT	Francis Dafoe Norris Bowden (CAN)	Elisabeth Schwarz Kurt Oppelt (AUT)	Marianne Nagy Laszlo Nagy (HUN)
1956	Garmisch, FRG	Elisabeth Schwarz Kurt Oppelt (AUT)	Francis Dafoe Norris Bowden (CAN)	Marika Kilius Franz Ningel (FRG)
1957	Colorado Springs, USA	Barbara Wagner Robert Paul (CAN)	Marika Kilius Franz Ningel (FRG)	Maria Jelineck Otto Jelineck (CAN)
1958	Paris, FRA	Barbara Wagner Robert Paul (CAN)	Vera Suchankova Zdenek Dolezal (CZE)	Maria Jelineck Otto Jelineck (CAN)
1959	Colorado Springs, USA	Barbara Wagner Robert Paul (CAN)	Marika Kilius Hans Baumler (FRG)	Nancy Ludington Ronald Ludington (USA)
1960	Vancouver, CAN	Barbara Wagner Robert Paul (CAN)	Maria Jelineck Otto Jelineck (CAN)	Marika Kilius Hans Baumler (FRG)
1961		No Championship Held		
1962	Prague, CZE	Maria Jelineck Otto Jelineck (CAN)	Ludmila Belousova Oleg Protopopov (USSR)	Margaret Gobl Franz Ningel (FRG)

Date	Venue	Gold	Silver	Bronze
1963	Cortina, ITA	Marika Kilius Hans Baumler (FRG)	Ludmila Belousova Oleg Protopopov (USSR)	Tatiana Zhuk Alexandr Gavrilov (USSR)
1964	Dortmund, FRG	Marika Kilius Hans Baumler (FRG)	Ludmila Belousova Oleg Protopopov (USSR)	Debbi Wilkes Guy Revell (CAN)
1965	Colorado Springs, USA	Ludmila Belousova Oleg Protopopov (USSR)	Vivan Joseph Ronald Joseph (USA)	Tatiana Zhuk Alexandr Gorelik (USSR)
1966	Davos, SUI	Ludmila Belousova Oleg Protopopov (USSR)	Tatiana Zhuk Alexandr Gorelik (USSR)	Cynthia Kauffman Ronald Kauffman (USA)
1967	Vienna, AUT	Ludmila Belousova Oleg Protopopov (USSR)	Margot Glockshuber Wolfgang Danne (FRG)	Cynthia Kauffman Ronald Kauffman (USA)
1968	Geneva, SUI	Ludmila Belousova Oleg Protopopov (USSR)	Tatiana Zhuk Alexandr Gorelik (USSR)	Cynthia Kauffman Ronald Kauffman (USA)
1969	Colorado Springs, USA	Irina Rodnina Alexsei Ulanov (USSR)	Tamara Moskvina Alexsei Mishin (USSR)	Ludmila Belousova Oleg Protopopov (USSR)
1970	Ljubjlana, YUG	Irina Rodnina Alexsei Ulanov (USSR)	Ludmila Smirnova Andrei Suraikin (USSR)	Heidemarie Steiner Heinz Walther (GDR)
1971	Lyons, FRA	Irina Rodnina Alexsei Ulanov (USSR)	Ludmila Smirnova Andrei Suraikin (USSR)	JoJo Starbuck Kenneth Shelley (USA)
1972	Calgary, CAN	Irina Rodnina Alexsei Ulanov (USSR)	Ludmila Smirnova Andrei Suraikin (USSR)	JoJo Starbuck Kenneth Shelley (USA)
1973	Bratislava, CZE	Irina Rodnina Alexandr Zaitsev (USSR)	Ludmila Smirnova Alexei Ulanov (USSR)	Manuela Gross Uwe Kagelmann (FRG)
1974	Munich, FRG	Irina Rodnina Alexandr Zaitsev (USSR)	Ludmila Smirnova Alexsei Ulanov (USSR)	Romy Kermer Rolf Osterreich (GDR)
1975	Colorado Springs, USA	Irina Rodnina Alexandr Zaitsev (USSR)	Romy Kermer Rolf Osterreich (GDR)	Manuela Gross Uwe Kagelmann (FRG)
1976	Gothenberg, SWE	Irina Rodnina Alexandr Zaitsev (USSR)	Romy Kermer Rolf Osterreich (GDR)	Irina Vorobieva Alexandr Vlasov (USSR)
1977	Tokyo, JPN	Irina Rodnina Alexandr Zaitsev (USSR)	Irina Vorobieva Alexandr Vlasov (USSR)	Tai Babilonia Randy Gardner (USA)

Date	*Venue*	*Gold*	*Silver*	*Bronze*
1978	Ottawa, CAN	Irina Rodnina Alexandr Zaitsev (USSR)	Manuela Mager Uwe Bewersdorff (GDR)	Tai Babilonia Randy Gardner (USA)
1979	Vienna, AUT	Tai Babilonia Randy Gardner (USA)	Marina Cherkosova Sergei Shakhrai (USSR)	Sabine Baess Tassilo Thierbach (GDR)
1980	Dortmund, FRG	Marina Cherkosova Sergei Shakhrai (USSR)	Manuela Mager Uwe Bewersdorf (GDR)	Marina Pestova Stanislav Leonovich (USSR)
1981	Hartford, USA	Irina Vorobieva Igor Lisovsky (USSR)	Sabine Baess Tassilo Thierbach (GDR)	Christina Riegel Andreas Nischwitz (FRG)
1982	Copenhagen, DEN	Sabine Baess Tassilo Thierbach (GDR)	Marina Pestova Stanislav Leonovich (USSR)	Caitlin Carruthers Peter Carruthers (USA)
1983	Helsinki, FIN	Elena Valova Oleg Vasiliev (USSR)	Sabine Baess Tassilo Thierbach (GDR)	Barbara Underhill Paul Martini (CAN)
1984	Ottawa, CAN	Barbara Underhill Paul Martini (CAN)	Elena Valova Oleg Vasiliev (USSR)	Sabine Baess Tassilo Thierbach (GDR)
1985	Tokyo, JPN	Elena Valova Oleg Vasiliev (USSR)	Larisa Selezneva Oleg Makarov (USSR)	Katerina Matousek Lloyd Eisler (CAN)
1986	Geneva, SUI	Ekaterina Gordeeva Sergei Grinkov (USSR)	Elena Valova Oleg Vasiliev (USSR)	Cynthia Coull Mark Rowsom (CAN)
1987	Cincinnati, USA	Ekaterina Gordeeva Sergei Grinkov (USSR)	Elena Valova Oleg Vasiliev (USSR)	Jill Watson Peter Oppegard (USA)
1988	Budapest, HUN	Elena Valova Oleg Vasiliev (USSR)	Ekaterina Gordeeva Sergei Grinkov (USSR)	Larisa Selezneva Oleg Makarov (USSR)
1989	Paris, FRA	Ekaterina Gordeeva Sergei Grinkov (USSR)	Cindy Landry Lyndon Johnson (CAN)	Elena Bechke Dennis Petrov (USSR)
1990	Halifax, CAN	Ekaterina Gordeeva Sergei Grinkov (USSR)	Isabelle Brasseur Lloyd Eisler (CAN)	Natalia Mishkutenok Artur Dmitriev (USSR)
1991	Munich, GER	Natalia Mishkutenok Artur Dmitriev (USSR)	Isabelle Brasseur Lloyd Eisler (CAN)	Natasha Kuchiki Todd Sand (USA)
1992	Oakland, USA	Natalia Mishkutenok Artur Dmitriev (CIS)	Radka Kovarikova Rene Novotny (CIS)	Isabelle Brasseur Lloyd Eisler (CAN)

Date Venue	Gold	Silver	Bronze
1993 Prague, CZE R.	Isabelle Brasseur Lloyd Eisler (CAN)	Mandy Woetzel Ingo Steuer (GER)	Evgenia Shishkova Vadim Naumov (RUS)
1994 Ciba, JPN	Evgenia Shishkova Vadim Naumov (RUS)	Isabelle Brasser Lloyd Eisler (CAN)	Marina Eltsova Andrei Bushkov (RUS)
1995 Birmingham, GB	Radka Kovarikova Rene Novotny (CZE. R.)	Evgenia Shishkova Vadim Naumov (RUS)	Jenni Meno Todd Sand (USA)
1996 Edmonton, CAN	Marina Eltsova Andrei Bushkov (RUS)	Mandy Woetzel Ingo Steuer (GER)	Jenni Meno Todd Sand (USA)
1997 Lausanne, SUI	Mandy Woetzel Ingo Steuer (GER)	Marina Eltsova Andrei Bushkov (RUS)	Oksana Kazakova Artur Dmitriev (RUS)

WORLD CHAMPIONSHIPS

ICE DANCING

Date Venue	Gold	Silver	Btonze
1952 Paris, FRA	Jean Westwood Laurence Demmy (GBR)	Joan Dewhurst John Slater (GBR)	Carol Peters Daniel Ryan (USA)
1953 Davos, SUI	Jean Westwood Laurence Demmy (GBR)	Joan Dewhurst John Slater (GBR)	Carol Peters Daniel Ryan (USA)
1954 Oslo, NOR	Jean Westwood Laurence Demmy (GBR)	Nesta Davies Paul Thomas (GBR)	Carmel Bodel Edward Bodel (USA)
1955 Vienna, AUT	Jean Westwood Laurence Demmy (GBR)	Pamela Weight Paul Thomas (GBR)	Barbara Radford Raymond Lockwood (GBR)
1956 Garmisch, FRG	Pamela Weight Paul Thomas (GBR)	June Markham Courtney Jones (GBR)	Barbara Thompson Gerard Rigby (GBR)
1957 Colorado Springs, USA	June Markham Courtney Jones (GBR)	Geraldine Fenton William McLachlan (CAN)	Sharon McKenzie Bert Wright (USA)
1958 Paris, FRA	June Markham Courtney Jones (GBR)	Geraldine Fenton William McLachlan (CAN)	Andrée Anderson Donald Jacoby (USA)

Date	*Venue*	*Gold*	*Silver*	*Bronze*
1959	Colorado Springs, USA	Doreen Denny Courtney Jones (GBR)	Andrée Anderson Donald Jacoby (USA)	Geraldine Fenton William McLachlan (CAN)
1960	Vancouver, CAN	Doreen Denny Courtney Jones (GBR)	Virginia Thompson William McLachlan (CAN)	Christine Guhel Jean Paul Guhel (FRA)
1961		No Competition Held		
1962	Prague, CZE	Eva Romanova Pavel Roman (CZE)	Christine Guhel Jean Paul Guhel (FRA)	Virginia Thompson William McLachlan (CAN)
1963	Cortina, ITA	Eva Romanova Pavel Roman (CZE)	Linda Shearman Michael Phillips (GBR)	Paulette Doan Kenneth Ormsby (CAN)
1964	Dortmund, FRG	Eva Romanova Pavel Roman (CZE)	Paulette Doan Kenneth Ormsby (CAN)	Janet Sawbridge David Hickinbottom (GBR)
1965	Colorado Springs, USA	Eva Romanova Pavel Roman (CZE)	Janet Sawbridge David Hickinbottom (GBR)	Lorna Dyer John Carrell (USA)
1966	Davos, SUI	Diane Towler Bernard Ford (GBR)	Kristin Fortune Dennis Sveum (USA)	Lorna Dyer John Carrell (USA)
1967	Vienna, AUT	Diane Towler Bernard Ford (GBR)	Lorna Dyer John Carrell (USA)	Yvonne Suddick Malcolm Cannon (GBR)
1968	Geneva, SUI	Diane Towler Bernard Ford (GBR)	Yvonne Suddick Malcolm Cannon (GBR)	Janet Sawbridge Jon Lane (GBR)
1969	Colorado Springs, USA	Diane Towler Bernard Ford (GBR)	Ludmila Pakhomova Aleksandr Gorshkov (USSR)	Judy Schwomeyer James Sladky (USA)
1970	Ljubljana, YUG	Ludmila Pakhomova Aleksandr Gorshkov (USSR)	Judy Schwomeyer James Sladky (USA)	Angelika Buck Erich Buck (FRG)
1971	Lyon, FRA	Ludmila Pakhomova Aleksandr Gorshkov (USSR)	Angelika Buck Erich Buck (FRG)	Judy Schwomeyer James Sladky (USA)
1972	Calgary, CAN	Ludmila Pakhomova Aleksandr Gorshkov (USSR)	Angelika Buck Erich Buck (FRG)	Judy Schwomeyer James Sladky (USA)
1973	Bratislava, CZE	Ludmila Pakhomova Aleksandr Gorshkov (USSR)	Angelika Buck Erich Buck (FRG)	Hilary Green Glyn Watts (GBR)
1974	Munich, FRG	Ludmila Pakhomova Aleksandr Gorshkov (USSR)	Hilary Green Glyn Watts (GBR)	Natalia Linichuk Gennadi Karponosov (USSR)

Date	*Venue*	*Gold*	*Silver*	*Bronze*
1975	Colorado Springs, USA	Irina Moiseeva Andrei Minenkov (USSR)	Colleen O'Connor Jim Millns (USA)	Hilary Green Glyn Watts (GBR)
1976	Gothenberg, SWE	Ludmila Pakhomova Aleksandr Gorshkov (USSR)	Irina Moiseeva Andrei Minenkov (USSR)	Colleen O'Connor Jim Millns (USA)
1977	Tokyo, JPN	Irina Moiseeva Andrei Minenkov (USSR)	Janet Thompson Warren Maxwell (GBR)	Natalia Linichuk Gennadi Karponosov (USSR)
1978	Ottawa, CAN	Natalia Linichuk Gennadi Karponosov (USSR)	Irina Moiseeva Andrei Minenkov (USSR)	Kristina Regoczy Andras Sallay (HUN)
1979	Vienna, AUT	Natalia Linichuk Gennadi Karponosov (USSR)	Krisztina Regoeczy Andras Sallay (HUN)	Irina Moiseeva Andrei Minenkov (USSR)
1980	Dortmund, FRG	Krisztina Regoeczy Andras Sallay (HUN)	Natalia Linichuk Gennadi Karponosov (USSR)	Irina Moiseeva Andrei Minenkov (USSR)
1981	Hartford, USA	Jayne Torvill Christopher Dean (GBR)	Irina Moiseeva Andrei Minenkov (USSR)	Natalia Bestemianova Andrei Bukin (USSR)
1982	Copenhagen, DEN	Jayne Torvill Christopher Dean (GBR)	Natalia Bestemianova Andrei Bukin (USSR)	Irina Moiseeva Andrei Minenkov (USSR)
1983	Helsinki, FIN	Jayne Torvill Christopher Dean (GBR)	Natalia Bestemianova Andrei Bukin (USSR)	Judy Blumberg Michael Seibert (USA)
1984	Ottawa, CAN	Jayne Torvill Christopher Dean (GBR)	Natalia Bestemianova Andrei Bukin (USSR)	Judy Blumberg Michael Seibert (USA)
1985	Tokyo, JPN	Natalia Bestemianova Andrei Bukin (USSR)	Marina Klimova Sergei Ponomarenko (USSR)	Judy Blumberg Michael Seibert (USA)
1986	Geneva, SUI	Natalia Bestemianova Andrei Bukin (USSR)	Marina Klimova Sergei Ponomarenko (USSR)	Tracy Wilson Robert McCall (CAN)
1987	Cincinnati, USA	Natalia Bestemianova Andrei Bukin (USSR)	Marina Klimova Sergei Ponomarenko (USSR)	Tracy Wilson Robert McCall (CAN)
1988	Budapest, HUN	Natalia Bestemianova Andrei Bukin (USSR)	Marina Klimova Sergei Ponomarenko (USSR)	Tracy Wilson Robert McCall (CAN)
1989	Paris, FRA	Marina Klimova Sergei Ponomarenko (USSR)	Maia Usova Alexander Zhulin (USSR)	Isabelle Duchesnay Paul Duchesnay (FRA)

Date	*Venue*	*Gold*	*Silver*	*Bronze*
1990	Halifax, CAN	Marina Klimova Sergei Ponomarenko (USSR)	Isabelle Duchesnay Paul Duchesnay (FRA)	Maia Usova Aleksandr Zhulin (USSR)
1991	Munich, GER	Isabelle Duchesnay Paul Duchesnay (FRA)	Marina Klimova Sergei Ponomarenko (USSR)	Maia Usova Aleksandr Zhulin (USSR)
1992	Oakland, USA	Marina Klimova Sergei Ponomarenko (CIS)	Maia Usova Aleksandr Zhulin (CIS)	Oksana Grischuk Evgeny Platov (CIS)
1993	Prague, CZE R.	Maia Usova Aleksandr Zhulin (RUS)	Oksana Grischuck Evgeny Platov (RUS)	Anjelika Krylova Vladimir Fedorov (RUS)
1994	Chiba, JPN	Oksana Grischuk Evgeny Platov (RUS)	Sophie Moniotte Pascal Lavanchy (FRA)	Susanna Rahkamo Petri Kokko (FIN)
1995	Birmingham, GB	Oksana Grischuk Evgeny Platov (RUS)	Susanna Rahkamo Petri Kokko (FIN)	Sophie Moniotte Pascal Lavanchy (FRA)
1996	Edmonton, CAN	Oksana Grischuk Evgeny Platov (RUS)	Anjelika Krylova Oleg Ovsiannikov (RUS)	Shae-Lynn Bourne Victor Kraatz (CAN)
1997	Lausanne, SUI	Oksana Grischuk Evgeny Platov (RUS)	Anjelika Krylova Oleg Ovsiannikov (RUS)	Shae-Lynn Bourne Victor Kraatz (CAN)

APPENDIX III

Winter Olympic Games Medalists
1908–1994

OLYMPIC WINTER GAMES

MEN'S SINGLES

Date	*Venue*	*Gold*	*Silver*	*Bronze*
1908	London, GBR*	Ulrich Salchow (SWE)	Richard Johansson (SWE)	Per Thoren (SWE)
1920	Antwerp, BEL*	Gillis Grafstrom (SWE)	Andreas Krogh (NOR)	Martin Stixrud (NOR)
1924	Chamonix, FRA	Gillis Grafstrom (SWE)	Willy Boeckl (AUT)	Georg Gautschi (SUI)
1928	St. Moritz, SUI	Gillis Grafstrom (SWE)	Willy Boeckl (AUT)	Robert van Zeebroeck (BEL)
1932	Lake Placid, USA	Karl Schafer (AUT)	Gillis Grafstrom (SWE)	Montgomery Wilson (CAN)
1936	Garmisch, GER	Karl Schafer (AUT)	Ernst Baier (GER)	Felix Kaspar (AUT)
1940, 1944		No Olympic Games Held		
1948	St. Moritz, SUI	Richard Button (USA)	Hans Gerschwiler (SUI)	Edi Rada (AUT)
1952	Oslo, NOR	Richard Button (USA)	Helmut Seibt (AUT)	James Grogan (USA)
1956	Cortina, ITA	Hayes Jenkins (USA)	Ronald Robertson (USA)	David Jenkins (USA)
1960	Squaw Valley, USA	David Jenkins (USA)	Karol Divin (CZE)	Donald Jackson (CAN)
1964	Innsbruck, AUT	Manfred Schnelldorfer (FRG)	Alain Calmat (FRA)	Scott Allen (USA)
1968	Grenoble, FRA	Wolfgang Schwartz (AUT)	Tim Wood (USA)	Patrick Pera (FRA)
1972	Sapporo, JPN	Ondrej Nepela (CZE)	Sergei Chetverukhin (USSR)	Patrick Pera (FRA)
1976	Innsbruck, AUT	John Curry (GBR)	Vladimir Kovalev (USSR)	Toller Cranston (CAN)
1980	Lake Placid, USA	Robin Cousins (GBR)	Jan Hoffmann (GDR)	Charles Tickner (USA)
1984	Sarajevo, YUG	Scott Hamilton (USA)	Brian Orser (CAN)	Jozef Sabvcik (CZE)
1988	Calgary, CAN	Brian Boitano (USA)	Brian Orser (CAN)	Viktor Petrenko (USSR)
1992	Albertville, FRA	Viktor Petrenko (CIS)	Paul Wylie (USA)	Petr Barna (CZE)
1994	Lillehammer, NOR	Aleksei Urmanov (RUS)	Elvis Stojko (CAN)	Philippe Candeloro (FRA)
1998	Nagano, JPN	Ilya Kulik (RUS)	Elvis Stojko (CAN)	Philippe Candeloro (FRA)

* Figure skating was included in what are now called the Summer Olympic Games in 1908 and 1920. The first full-fledged Winter Olympics was instituted in 1924.

OLYMPIC WINTER GAMES

LADIES' SINGLES

Date	*Venue*	*Gold*	*Silver*	*Bronze*
1908	London, GBR*	Madge Syers (BGR)	Elsa Rendschmidt (GER)	Dorothy Greenough (GBR)
1920	Antwerp, BEL*	Magda Julin-Mauroy (SWE)	Svea Noren (SWE)	Theresa Weld (USA)
1924	Chamonix, FRA	Herma Plank-Szabo (AUT)	Beatrix Loughran (USA)	Ethel Muckelt (GBR)
1928	St. Moritz, SUI	Sonja Henie (NOR)	Fritzi Burger (AUT)	Beatrix Loughran (USA)
1932	Lake Placid, USA	Sonja Henie (NOR)	Fritzi Burger (AUT)	Maribel Vinson (USA)
1936	Garmisch, GER	Sonja Henie (NOR)	Cecilia Colledge (GBR)	Vivi-Anne Hulten (SWE)
1940, 1944		No Olympic Games Held		
1948	St. Moritz, SUI	Barbara Ann Scott (CAN)	Eva Pawlik (AUT)	Jeannette Altwegg (GBR)
1952	Oslo, NOR	Jeannette Altwegg (GBR)	Tenley Albright (USA)	Jacqueline du Bief (FRA)
1956	Cortina, ITA	Tenley Albright (USA)	Carol Heiss (USA)	Ingrid Wendl (AUT)
1960	Squaw Valley, USA	Carol Heiss (USA)	Sjoukje Dijkstra (NED)	Barbara Roles (USA)
1964	Innsbruck, AUT	Sjoukje Dijkstra (NED)	Regine Heitzer (AUT)	Petra Burke (CAN)
1968	Grenoble, FRA	Peggy Fleming (USA)	Gabriele Seyfert (GDR)	Hana Maskova (CZE)
1972	Sapporo, JPN	Beatrix Schuba (AUT)	Karen Magnussen (CAN)	Janet Lynn (USA)
1976	Innsbruck, AUT	Dorothy Hamill (USA)	Dianne de Leeuw (NED)	Christine Errath (GDR)
1980	Lake Placid, USA	Anett Poetzsch (GDR)	Linda Fratianne (USA)	Dagmar Lurz (FRG)
1984	Sarajevo, YUG	Katarina Witt (GDR)	Rosalynn Sumners (USA)	Kira Ivanova (USSR)
1988	Calgary, CAN	Katarina Witt (GDR)	Elizabeth Manley (CAN)	Debi Thomas (USA)
1992	Albertville, FRA	Kristi Yamaguchi (USA)	Midori Ito (JPN)	Nancy Kerrigan (USA)
1994	Lillehammer, NOR	Oksana Baiul (UKR)	Nancy Kerrigan (USA)	Chen Lu (CHN)
1998	Nagano, JPN	Tara Lipinski (USA)	Michelle Kwan (USA)	Chen Lu (CHN)

* Figure skating was included in what are now called the Summer Olympic Games in 1908 and 1920. The first full-fledged Winter Olympics was instituted in 1924.

OLYMPIC WINTER GAMES

PAIRS

Date	*Venue*	*Gold*	*Silver*	*Bronze*
1908	London, GBR*	Anna Hubler Heinrich Burger (GER)	Phyllis Johnson James Johnson (GBR)	Madge Syers Edgar Syers (GBR)
1920	Antwerp, BEL*	Ludowika Jakobsson Walter Jakobsson (FIN)	Alexia Bryn Yngvar Bryn (NOR)	Phillis Johnson James Johnson (GBR)
1924	Chamonix, FRA	Helene Engelmann Alfred Berger (AUT)	Ludowika Jakobsson Walter Jakobsson (FIN)	Andrée Brunet Pierre Brunet (FRA)
1928	St. Moritz, SUI	Andrée Brunet Pierre Brunet (FRA)	Lilly Schloz Otto Kaiser (AUT)	Melitta Brunner Ludwig Wrede (AUT)
1932	Lake Placid, USA	Andrée Brunet Pierre Brunet (FRA)	Beatrix Loughran Sherwin Badger (USA)	Emilie Rotter Laszlo Szollas (AUT)
1936	Garmisch, GER	Maxie Herber Ernst Baier (GER)	Ilse Pausin Erich Pausin (AUT)	Emilie Rotter Laszlo Stollas (HUN)
1940, 1944		No Olympic Games Held		
1948	St. Moritz, SUI	Micheline Lannoy Pierre Baugniet (BEL)	Andrea Kekesy Ede Kiraly (HUN)	Suzanne Morrow Wallace Distelmeyer (CAN)
1952	Oslo, NOR	Ria Falk Paul Falk (FRG)	Karol Kennedy Peter Kennedy (USA)	Marianne Nagy Laszlo Nagy (HUN)
1956	Cortina, ITA	Elizabeth Schwartz Kurt Oppelt (AUT)	Frances Dafoe Norris Bowden (CAN)	Marianne Nagy Laszlo Nagy (HUN)
1960	Squaw Valley, USA	Barbara Wagner Robert Paul (CAN)	Marika Kilius Hans Baumler (FRG)	Nancy Luddington Ronald Luddington (USA)
1964	Innsbruck, AUT	Ludmila Belousova Oleg Protopopov (USSR)	Debbi Wilkes Guy Revell (CAN)	Vivian Joseph Ronald Joseph (USA)
1968	Grenoble, FRA	Ludmila Protopopov Oleg Protopopov (USSR)	Tatiana Zhuk Alexandr Gorelik (USSR)	Margot Glockshuber Wolfgang Danne (FRG)

* Figure skating was included in what are now called the Summer Olympic Games in 1908 and 1920. The first full-fledged Winter Olympics was instituted in 1924.

Date	*Venue*	*Gold*	*Silver*	*Bronze*
1972	Sapporo, JPN	Irina Rodnina Alexsei Ulanov (USSR)	Ludmila Smirnova Andrei Suraikin (USSR)	Manuela Gross Uwe Kagelmann (GDR)
1976	Innsbruck, AUT	Irina Rodnina Aleksandr Zaitsev (USSR)	Romy Kermer Rolf Osterreich (GDR)	Manuela Gross Uwe Kagelmann (GDR)
1980	Lake Placid, USA	Irina Rodnina Aleksandr Zaitsev (USSR)	Marina Cherkosova Sergei Shakhrai (USSR)	Manuela Mager Uwe Bewersdorff (GDR)
1984	Sarajevo, YUG	Elena Valova Oleg Vasiliev (USSR)	Caitlin Carruthers Peter Carruthers (USA)	Larissa Selezneva Oleg Makarov (USSR)
1988	Calgary, CAN	Ekaterina Gordeeva Sergei Grinkov (USSR)	Elena Valova Oleg Vasiliev (USSR)	Jill Watson Peter Oppegard (USA)
1992	Albertville, FRA	Natalia Mishkutenok Artur Dmitriev (CIS)	Elena Bechke Denis Petrov (CIS)	Isabelle Brasseur Lloyd Eisler (CAN)
1994	Lillehammer, NOR	Ekaterina Gordeeva Sergei Grinkov (RUS)	Natalia Mishkutenok Artur Dmitriev (RUS)	Isabelle Brasseur Lloyd Eisler (CAN)
1998	Nagano, JPN	Oksana Kazakova Artur Dmitriev (RUS)	Elena Berezhnaya Anton Sikharulidze (RUS)	Mandy Woetzel Ingo Steuer (GER)

OLYMPIC WINTER GAMES

ICE DANCING

Ice Dancing did not become an official sport of the Winter Olympics until 1976.

Date	*Venue*	*Gold*	*Silver*	*Bronze*
1976	Innsbruck, AUT	Ludmilla Pakhomova Aleksandr Gorshkov (USSR)	Irina Moiseeva Andrei Minenkov (USSR)	Colleen O'Connor Jim Millns (USA)
1980	Lake Placid, USA	Natalia Linichuk Gennadi Karponosov (USSR)	Kristina Regoczy Andras Sallay (HUN)	Irina Moiseeva Andrei Minenkov (USSR)
1984	Sarajevo, YUG	Jayne Torvill Christopher Dean (GBR)	Natalia Bestemianova Andrei Bukin (USSR)	Marina Klimova Sergei Ponomarenko (USSR)
1988	Calgary, CAN	Natalia Bestemianova Andrei Bukin (USSR)	Marina Klimova Sergei Ponomarenko (USSR)	Tracy Wilson Robert McCall (CAN)
1992	Albertville, FRA	Marina Klimova Sergei Ponomarenko (USSR)	Isabelle Duchesnay Paul Duchesnay (FRA)	Maia Usova Alexander Zhulin (USSR)
1994	Lillehammer, NOR	Oksana Grischuk Evgeny Platov (RUS)	Maia Usova Aleksandr Zhulin (RUS)	Jayne Torvill Christopher Dean (GBR)
1998	Nagano, JPN	Oksana Grischuk Evgeny Platov (RUS)	Angelika Krylova Oleg Ovsiannikov (RUS)	Marina Anissina Gwendel Peizerat (FRA)

ABBREVIATIONS OF COUNTRIES

World Championships and Olympic Winter Games

AUS	Australia
AUT	Austria
BEL	Belgium
CAN	Canada
CHN	China
CIS	Commonwealth of Independent States (used in 1992 only, following the breakup of the Soviet Union; indicates former Soviet constituents, including Russia and Ukraine)
CZE	Czechoslovakia
CZE R.	Czech Republic (following breakup of Soviet Union in 1991)
FIN	Finland
FRA	France
FRG	Federal Republic of Germany (West Germany)
GBR	Great Britain
GDR	German Democratic Republic (East Germany)
GER	Germany (prior to World War II and after reunification in 1990)
HUN	Hungary
ITA	Italy
JPN	Japan
NED	Netherlands
NOR	Norway
POL	Poland
RUS	Russia (prior to 1920 and after breakup of Soviet Union in 1991)
SUI	Switzerland
SWE	Sweden
UKR	Ukraine
USA	United States of America
USSR	Union of Soviet Socialist Republics (1922–1991)
YUG	Yugoslavia

Index

Page numbers in **boldface** refer to main entries. Page numbers in *italics* refer to photographs.